VIRTUAL
GOVERNMENT

VIRTUAL
GOVERNMENT

CIA Mind Control
Operations in America

Alex Constantine

FERAL HOUSE

Virtual Government © 1997 Alex Constantine

ISBN 0-922915-28-8

Feral House
2532 Lincoln Blvd. Suite 359
Venice, CA 90291

Design by Linda Hayashi

First edition 1997

10 9 8 7 6 5 4 3 2

For Gloria Brighton

Virtual Acknowledgements

Nicole Angiler, Dave Bader, Val Bankston, Douglas Barr, Joseph Bosco, Walter Bowart, the late Mae Brussell, Ann Chin, Marilyn Colman, Mike Coyle, "Curio," Melissa Darpino, Dick Farley, the editors of *Filth*, Vicky Flores-Guerra, Cynthia Ford, "Fortfan," Patrick Fourmey & Al Marcelliene of *Prevailing Winds*, Donald Freed, Harlan Girard, Catherine Gould, Charles Higham, D.K., Paul Krassner, Ed Light, Ben Lindsay, M., Jackie MacGauley, Dave Manning, Betty Martini, Virginia McCullough, Claudia Mullens, Sandy Munro, Adam Parfrey, Claire Reeves, Lynn Moss-Sharman, Claudia Mullens, Tony Van Rentergheim, Paul Ruiz, Thomas Savona, Steve Smith, Kathleen Sullivan, Wes Thomas, the editors and staff of *Survivorship*, Beth Vargo.

PREAMBLE

On the Road to the Fourth Reich

The Geopolitical Framework of Virtual Government

The Dragon of Order Castle

In February, 1945 the U.S. Army's Ninth Division, still smarting after a brief exchange of bullets with a band of Nazi die-hards near Vogelsburg, trudged along a fire-gap cut into the spine of a mountain. Saw-toothed pine breached the fog swirling in the valleys on either side and sloped to a sprawling lake far below. The soldiers rounded a bluff and the fog scattered at the sudden rise of immense brownstone towers and flying buttresses.

The Americans entered the castle and explored its cavernous corridors, passed splashing marble fountains, moribund gargoyles and murals of the Teutonic Knights.

The interlocking fortresses sprawled over hundreds of acres.

The castles of Vogelsburgen were training grounds of the Hitler SS elite— "the elite of the elite," per William Shirer. The "Order Castles" (there were four) represented the pinnacle of the Aryan romance. Vogelsburgen lent the SS a sense of mystery and power. Only the highest-scoring students of the academies were accepted. Graduates acquired discipline, knowledge, elitist myopia and blind obedience to authority.

Following the German defeat at Stalingrad in 1943, the Order Castles were transformed into bustling wombs of future political leaders, scientists, spies, military officers and industrialists. Students of the *Ordensburgen* were given new identities and dispatched to countries around the globe to settle in as "sleepers."

Racial hatred was applied on a mass scale, parading as ideology. Like Hitler, to whom the students of the Order Castles swore allegiance, they were inculcated in, as Pope Pius XII described it, "the cult of violence, the idolatry of race and blood, the overthrow of human liberty and dignity." The castles were modeled after the fortresses of the Teutonic Knights, and students were trained to rule over "inferior" men with conspiratorial terror. The school operated in much the same way as a criminal organization. A charter retrieved from the castle of *Vogelsburg* by the Ninth Division explained that students were expected to be "dedicated to the Order for life and death. These men must know that there is no road back for them. He who fails, or would betray the part of his leaders, will be destroyed by this Order. Every National Socialist leader must know that he is climbing a steep grade." Confidence of success was inspired by "an absolute belief in ... Adolph Hitler."

In 1944, more than 2,000 Order graduates were trained at Vogelsburgen in the event of an Allied victory. The purpose of the castle, its ominous implications, may have been clear to the Americans. Or, after the horrors of World War

II, it is possible they overlooked the ominous implications.

A wind, a low, growl, rumbled up through the castle, growing louder and subsiding like the lugubrious moan of a waking dragon.

"Un-American Activities"

Those were days when, as we have since found out, Project Paperclip brought such Nazi scientists as Arthur Rudolph and Otto von Bolschwing into the American aerospace industry; when our Central Intelligence Agency was formed by the wholesale grafting of Hitler's Eastern Front intelligence corps onto the remnants of the Office of Secret Services; when friends became enemies and enemies, friends.

Nowadays, when the world takes industrial might for granted as the only order all must march to, one can do no more than pray that the truth will continue to pick its slow way through the blood and smog.

—Peter Carey, *San Jose Mercury-News,* July 18, 1986

In 1933, the year of the Long Knives, Representative Hamilton Fish's life was derailed by a reading of *Communism in Germany,* issued by a Nazi propaganda house. Inspired by this tract, Fish joined forces with George Sylvester Viereck, ranking Nazi agent in the United States. Ever the public servant, Fish graciously conferred upon Viereck free reign of the Congressman's suite in the House Office Building.

A few years later, hours of thunderous Congressional oratory followed the arrest of George Hill, Fish's office clerk, on charges of spying for Himmler's SS.

Well before the Martin Dies Committee convened, Congressman Fish conducted the very first inquisitional federal "investigation of Communism," otherwise known as the House Un-American Activities Committee (HUAC). Between the pair of right-wing hot-seats, Dies and HUAC, came the McCormack-Dickstein Committee, formed in 1934 to investigate the dissemination of Nazi propaganda in the United States. This panel discovered that there was, in progress, a "fascist plot to seize the government." Shortly thereafter, the McCormack-Dickstein Committee was dissolved and its successor turned a deaf ear to any mention of fascist agitation on domestic soil.

But confirmation that Nazis were quietly rallying for the next phase of the war came with the publication of *Treason's Peace,* by Howard Armbruster, in

1947. Ambruster: "A few weeks after the surrender, Democratic Senator Harley M. Kilgore returned from an early postwar trip to occupied Germany with the announcement that he had uncovered proof of the plot to revive I.G. Farben and other German war industries, and that German industrial leaders were already preparing for the next world war."

Domestic fascists conspired with their European counterparts to transform the American political and military bureaucracies into a low-intensity battle-ground.

In *The Yahoos* (Marzani and Munsell, 1964), a study of Aryan Nations-type groups in America, author Mike Newberry detailed the *bona fidés* of ranking HUAC "investigators," among them:

EDWARD SULLIVAN: HUAC's first "chief investigator," a career criminal with a record of nine arrests [ranging from sodomy to larceny]. Co-editor of a Nazi hate sheet with James "Kike Killer" True. Addressed German-American Bund rallies prior to his concern with "Un-Americanism" and was director of an openly fascistic Ukrainian group.

DR. J.B. MATTHEWS: HUAC's "second chief investigator." Predicted in his autobiography that America's answer to Communism would be fascism or "something so closely akin to it that the difference will not greatly matter." His autobiography was published by John Cecil, a veteran anti-Semite, and his writings were reprinted by *Contra-Komintern*, the official house organ of the Nazi Foreign Office. He was a close advisor to Robert Welch of the John Birch Society.

DR. FRED SCHWARTZ: One of HUAC's most revered "experts." Chairman of the Christian Anti-Communist Crusade.

FULTON LEWIS, III: Rabidly "Christian" leader of Young Americans for Freedom, a front for Nazis entering the country from Munich. Earned his spurs on the HUAC staff. He wrote for the anti-Semitic *American Mercury*, edited by Harold Lord Varney, formerly a propagandist for the Italian Fascisti.

The National Record Is the Official Organ of the American Nationalists' Committee, the Nationalists' Confederation and the Nationalist Party

Sec. 502 P. L. & R.
U. S. Postage Paid
Washington 5, D. C.

NATIONAL RECORD

Vol. 3, No. 1   WASHINGTON, D. C., APRIL, 1945   Price 10 Cents

IS IT TO BE GOODBYE AMERICA?

Let America Live Her Own Life | **Communists in the Army** | **Are You Assisting In the Liquidation**

The *National Record* was festering homegrown Nazi propaganda of a patriotic strain, published in the 1940s by Senator Robert Rice Reynolds. Prior to WWII, the Senator travelled to Germany and returned chanting his praises for Hitler. He called for the formation of a Nationalist Party back home, and wrote in the *Congressional Record:* "The dictators are doing what is best for their people. I say it is high time we found out how they are doing it."

Dance of the Antipodes

We Germans should be realistic. We lost two wars to the Jews.
Why should we lose another?
    —Nazi Propagandist, Werner Naumann to British intelligence agents, July 1953

"Let us show them who is the natural elite!
Who is the world's greatest killer? White man!"
    —Dan Burros, national secretary, American National Party

In September 1944, Sims Carter, then assistant chief of the economic warfare section of the Justice Department, testified before the Kilgore Committee that despite military defeat, the industrial cartels of German had renewed activity from bases in Argentina. "All the machinery," he said, "is ready for safeguarding German supremacy in the steadily expanding South American market." Much of that economy had been *incorporated* by I.G. Farben and other financial backers of Hitler years before the war began.

In the 1930s, as German factories tooled for the onslaught, Nazi entrepreneurs quietly constructed manufacturing bases, railroads and chemical and steel plants throughout South America. The munitions industry was all but cartelized by Farben and Krupp, providing business fronts for the Nazi fifth column. The insinuation of Nazism into Caribbean politics was directed by Alfred Becker and Arnold Margerie, officers of Farben La Quimica Bayer in Caracas. Down in Argentina, Axel Wenner-Gren, the Swedish millionaire, inventor of the modern refrigerator and a crony of Herman Goering, Hitler's propaganda minister, established subsidiaries and gracefully snatched up key industrial plants.

After the war, Nazis quietly assumed new posts *en masse* within the German government, and the Adenauer administration adopted an anti-Nazi facade in public while elevating war criminals to bureaucratic seats of power. By 1951, 134 former members of the National Socialist Party held senior positions in the West German Foreign Office. One of them was Dr. Franz Massfeller, a specialist on racial blood purges. Massfeller once advised his superiors in the Hitler regime to kill all *half*-Jews after the full-blooded victims were completely decimated. In the 50s, Dr. Massfeller was employed as a counselor in the Bonn Ministry of Justice.

In Germany, as in the United States, a virtual government was conceived with the trappings of democratic rule by the engineers of the Holocaust.

Attorney Hans Globke, author of the legal rationale underlying the Third Reich's racial laws, was entrusted with the directorship of President Adenauer's Federal Press and Chancellory Bureau.

Werner Naumann, formerly an officer of the SS and Goebbels' propaganda machine, was the founder of the German Reich Party, secretly abetted by the Adenauer government in Bonn. Herr Naumann's role in the postwar Reich was the placing of Nazis in business and industry.

On May 10, 1996, the Reuters news service released a story that trotted up to the door of the resuscitated Reich, nearly entering for a look-see ...

NEW YORK (Reuter)—Realizing they were losing the war in 1944, Nazi leaders met top German industrialists to plan a secret postwar international network to restore them to power, according to a newly declassified U.S. intelligence document.

The document, which appears to confirm a meeting historians have long argued about, says an SS general and a representative of the German armaments ministry told such companies as Krupp and Roehling that they must be prepared to finance the Nazi party after the war when it went underground. They were also told "existing financial reserves in foreign countries must be placed at the disposal of the party so that a strong German empire can be created after the defeat."

The three-page document, released by the National Archives, was sent from

Supreme Headquarters of the Allied Expeditionary Force to the U.S. secretary of state in November 1944. It described a secret meeting at the *Maison Rouge* (the Red House Hotel) in Strasbourg, occupied France, on August 10, 1944.

Jeffrey Bale, a Columbia University expert on clandestine Nazi networks, said historians have debated whether such a meeting could have taken place, because it came a month after the attempt on Adolph Hitler's life, which had led to a crackdown on discussions of a possible German military defeat.

Bale said the meeting was mentioned in Nazi hunter Simon Wiesenthal's 1967 book *The Murderers Among Us,* and again in a 1978 book by French Communist Victor Alexandrov, *The SS Mafia.*

"As soon as the [Nazi] party becomes strong enough to re-establish its control over Germany, the industrialists will be paid for their efforts and cooperation by concessions and orders," the intelligence document said. The meeting was presided over by a "Dr. Scheid," described as an SS *Obergruppenfuhrer* [general] and a director of Hermsdorff & Schonburg Company.

Attending were representatives of seven German companies including Krupp, Roehling, Messerschmidt, and Volkswagenwerk and officials of the ministries of armaments and the navy. The industrialists were from companies with extensive interests in France and Scheid is quoted as saying the battle of France was lost and "from now on ... German industry must realize that the war cannot be won and it must take steps in preparation for a postwar commercial campaign."

The Real McCloy

In October, 1929, Martin Heidegger, [the existentialist and constructivist] warned an official in the German Ministry of Education against Verjudung (growing Judaisation) as a threat to "our German spiritual life.".... Heidegger was to Sartre what Hegel was to Marx.
> —D. CAUTE, 1995, Spectator 21 x Reviewing Elzbieta Ettinger,
> *Hannah Arendt/Martin Heidegger,* Yale University Press

Meanwhile, backstage at the war crimes show trials, Rockefeller counsel John J. McCloy, the high commissioner of Germany (later a high commissioner of the JFK murder investigation) courted Nazi officials on behalf of the U.S. government. Defendant Gustav Krupp once controlled 138 private concentration camps utilizing slave labor—yet the German industrialist was permitted to hold board meetings with executives of the Krupp business empire while still a prisoner at Nuremberg. McCloy freed Krupp and kindly returned the munition-builder's property. The CIA banker also assembled a panel chaired by David Peck, leading justice of the New York Supreme Court, to "review" the sentences of Germans wanted for recruitment by the Allies. Otto Skorzeny, Krupp's representative in Argentina, Hitler's very own Commando, was among the first German spies surreptitiously placed on the American Cold War intelligence dole.

On January 19, 1953, the *New York Times* took notice: "Nazism is not dead in Germany." Given time and opportunity, "a form of Nazism could again rise to power. Materially speaking, Nazism was smashed into a pulp by 1945," but the "vigorous roots remained."

A national priority was made of economic recovery in the Fatherland. A memo from the German Press Department of B'nai B'rith to officials of the Jewish organization on July 1, 1953, detailed a meeting of the former Waffen SS in Verden, once a Nazi garrison town: "The reason this little alumni club exists is, one might say, plausible, even sentimental—to care for those in their ranks who survived and to locate lost comrades. The reunion, their first since the war, brought five thousand men to Verden. Mufti-clad, they marched through cramped, flag-bedecked streets to the rally with all their famous and former military precision."

Among their contacts in the United States, the Nazi "elite" could rely on the generous assistance of a patron, Pedro Del Valle, who went on to become a vice president of ITT. In 1954, Del Valle, a retired Marine Corps lieutenant general, was soundly defeated in his bid for the Republican gubernatorial nomination. His campaign was spiced with public endorsements of a foaming, anti-Semitic booklet, *Know Your Enemy*. In 1974, Del Valle and ITT consultant John McCone, formerly a CIA director, threw in to overthrow Allendé in Chile's 1970 coup. ITT funneled some $350,000 into the elections, and when the brutal dictatorship of Pinochet was installed, conspired with other politically "conservative" companies to pirate the country's natural resources.

As a hedge against the fall of the Third Reich, German industrialists made provisions in 1944 for protecting their loot from confiscation by the U.S and England. On the instruction of Martin Bormann, the surviving SS, now ODESSA, established hundreds of corporations abroad, donated handsomely to far-right political candidates and cleared the path for the reconstruction of the Reich on foreign soil. All of this was accomplished by channeling the loot through a labyrinth of secret bank accounts. The funds were transferred to non-belligerent nations and under Bormann's direction financed some 750 new companies to oversee the Nazi Party's revival.

Over 100 of those companies were based in the United States.

Funds materialized in the accounts of Germany's agents around the world. They were instructed to invest in selected businesses and propaganda fronts in the U.S. and elsewhere, channel legal aid to indicted Nazis, purchase out-of-the-way estates for Nazi leaders in foreign countries, and so on. These funds also supported the "ratlines," ports-of-call situated every 40 miles along the German border for Nazis fleeing the Allied noose.

In December 1946, a memorandum from Laurence Frank, the US Consul in Austria, was sent to the State Department noting that Goering and Goebbels had moved funds to Geneva in diplomatic bags to avoid detection. "It is reported that Reichsmarshall Goering lately used this method to transfer personal funds," wrote Frank. "Goering sent more than $20 million of his personal fortune to Argentina." He shipped some of this fortune via submarine in the summer of 1943. Goebbels secreted $1.3 million in a safety deposit box in Buenos Aires.

The *Times of London* reported on December 6, 1996 that the Nazis "secretly sent more than $1 billion to Argentina in the last month of the war and scoured the world for sanctuaries for their plundered wealth. It was reported that Eva Perón may have conspired with the Nazis to set up secret accounts on behalf of her husband to hide hundreds of millions of dollars obtained from looted Nazi gold, cash and art treasures."

Reactionary opinion in the United States was fomented by American Nazis. For America, a spin-off of the America First Committee, was formed in 1954, steered by leading WWII isolationists. One of the organization's steatorian spokesmen was Colonel Robert McCormick, publisher of the *Chicago Tribune*. The Chairman of For America was Clarence Manion, formerly dean of law at Notre Dame University. Manion once sat on Eisenhower's Commission on Inter-Governmental Affairs. Robert Wood, then CEO of Sears, Roebuck, was a ramrod leader of the bund.

The stated aim of For America was support of political candidates sympathetic to the Nazi cause. Three Congressmen made up the recruiting arm of the organization: Burton K. Wheeler, Hamilton Fish and Howard Buffett. Fish, the Republican Party leader, had as his greatest ambition the start of a third party based on principles of National Socialism. The others were already in disrepute for involvement in pro-Nazi, "non-interventionist" groups during the war.

"What will it take to disband this group?" asked the *Atlanta Journal* of this reincarnation of America First, "*World War III?*"

General Wedemeyer's Ultraconservative, Lonely-Hearts Club Bund & Dr. Becher's Beltway Brotherhood

The war came marching home. The German military machine had been pounded to scrap in Europe and Japan, but the propaganda that fueled it resurfaced in San Antonio, Texas ... and the proletariat, including veterans, greased the gears. The 1961 "Let's Look at America" seminar, sponsored by the Fourth Army and the San Antonio Chamber of Commerce Jaycees, drew a crowd of 3,500 strong. Retired General Alfred Wedemeyer, a supporter of the John Birch Society, railed at President Kennedy's "appeasement" of the Soviet Union. Cleon Skousen, formerly an FBI agent and a scion of the Christian Anti-Communist Crusade, demanded the end of all diplomatic relations with the Eastern Bloc. Dr. Gerhart Niemeyer, a writer for the *National Review,* spoke at the rally, and so did Senator Strom Thurmond and Donald Jackson of HUAC.

The "seminar" spurned direct orders from the Pentagon—a "violation of Army policy," Army Secretary Elvis Stahat cautioned. Unmoved by orders, Colonel William Blythe of the Fourth Army's G-2 Division shot back: "We are not interested in *politics*! The Army intends to stand up and be counted!"

General Wedemeyer flew from the San Antonio session to Dallas, where he met with oil baron H.L. Hunt, a financial sponsor of Joseph McCarthy (Borger, *Texas News Herald,* September 25, 1961).

A small battalion of military personalities threw in with a host of fascist front organizations, figureheads for the domestic war, among them:

Generals Nathan Twining, Admiral Radford, J.B. Medaris and Rear Admiral Chester Ward: Military-Industrial Institute.

Admiral Arleigh Burke: Featured speaker of the Christian Anti-Communist Crusade.

General Charles Willoughby and General Peyton Campbell: Christian Anti-Communist Crusade.

General Stratemeyer: Liberty Lobby and the Christian Crusade.

General Bonner Fellers: Endorsed the Birch Society and Americans for Constitutional Action.

Admiral Strauss and General Wedemeyer: National Advisory Board of Young Americans for Freedom.

And a blue-ribbon coalition of military officers who joined forces with Ultracons and Aryan Nationals alike. While ranking officials raised the rabble against Soviet "expansionism," the Nazis sought influence in D.C. One of the most influential Nazi spies in the U.S. was Dr. Walter Becher, an anti-Communist "refugee leader" from Germany. Becher joined the National Socialist Party in December, 1931, and took the job of editor of *Die Zeit*, a Nazi propaganda sheet, in 1937. He was a brownshirt for a spell, and a recruit of the National Socialist Student Bund. Dr. Becher editorialized for the purge of all Jews from state-owned radio in Prague. During the war, he worked in the Goebbels Propaganda Ministry and for the *Wehrmacht* as a correspondent. Shortly after the fall of the German military, he founded a newspaper and agitated for a restoration of National Socialism.

Herr Becher had his advocates in Washington, a powerful collection of dupes and political operatives. In 1957, Congressman Usher Burdick inserted one of Dr. Becher's propaganda pieces in the *Congressional Record;* in August 1959, seven more appeared in the pages of the same journal. When Becher traveled to the States, conferences were arranged for him by the State Department. His political views were trumpeted by the Mutual Broadcasting Network and scores of newspapers.

Dr. Becher's early contacts in Washington were Joe McCarthy, William Jenner in the Senate and a handful of Congressmen in the House. T.H. Tetens, in *The New Germany and the Old Nazis*, was awed by the Nazi's camaraderie with Beltway politicians, and tracked Becher's movements through the District of Columbia: "During the early fifties, when he first came to Washington, he began to build for himself a formidable political machine. His scheme was very simple. If he could obtain the support of leading politicians in the United States, his prestige and stature would grow enormously at home.... With the help of the McCarthy faction in the United States, he could establish a nationwide reputation as the foremost leader of the anti-Communist crusade."

Among the senators who sent personal letters of support to Dr. Becher in Munich in the 1950s, count: Prescott Bush, Albert Gore, Pat McNamara, William Knowland, Strom Thurmond, Thomas Dodd, Robert Byrd, William Langer and Stuart Symington. House Speaker John McCormack also tendered a letter of support to the Nazi propagandist.

Ultraconservatives place much emphasis on character, a quality all too often absent within their own ranks. A glaring example is Willis Carto, publisher of *Spotlight*, a populist newspaper that backed Patrick Buchanon for president in the 1996 election. Carto was the protégé of Francis Parker Yockey, a radical right-winger indicted for sedition during WWII. Yockey's indictment included charges of supporting the Nazi Party.

Carto's organization was one of five "Liberty Lobbies" founded in 1957 at the first major world anti-Communist conference in Mexico City. The faction known today as the Liberty Lobby was run by a steering committee of American fascist leaders and Nazi spies, including:

Major Gen. Charles A. Willoughby: Born Adolph Tscheppe Weidenbach, born in Heidelberg, Germany in 1892. Nazi agent in the Army Supreme Command and intelligence chief under MacArthur in Korea. "Security Director" of the Shickshinny Knights of Malta.

Willis A. Carto: Treasurer and founder.

Major General Edwin Walker: US Army, John Birch Society.

Lt. Col. Philip Corso (ret): US Army Intelligence under Willoughby-Weidenbach.

Robert Morris: American Security Council (ASC), Young Americans for Freedom, Birch Society.

Senator Strom Thurmond (D-S.C.): Since, a "defector to the Republican Party," a senator his mid-90s.

Otto Otepka: Director, security evaluations, State Dept.

Senator James O. Eastland (D-Miss.): The director of internal security in the U.S. Senate.

A maze of bridges was erected by the Liberty Lobby to Germany's Nazi Party. Edwin Walker was the coeval of Gerhard Frey, publisher of the neo-Nazi *Deutsche National-Zeitung und Soldaten-Zeitung*. A bosom ally of Major General Willoughby-Weidenbach. Theodor Oberlander, the German commander of the Ukraine Nightingales during the war, wrote for the German newspaper. He settled in Canada after the war. Dick Russell, in *The Man Who Knew Too Much*, drew connections between the Munich-based Reinhard Gehlen apparat under Allen Dulles and sundry WACL "lobbies" under Charles Willoughby-Weidenbach: "German veterans were included, notably Fritz Kramer [another German agent, a crony of American economist Peter Drucker and an intelligence asset from Nazi Germany. Kramer haunted the Plans Division of the DoD during the Vietnam War]—a former Abwehr officer who once headed up a private vigilanté cadré that ferreted out German leftists at the behest of private industry. Its U.S. sister organization was the ASC." The American Security Council a private, Washington-based security force, was established in 1955 by former FBI agents, and compiled an index of over one million alleged "subversives" for the corporations. Willoughby-Weidenbach, a close friend of Fritz Kramer, went on to sit on the ASC board.

Kennedy assassination researcher William McLoughlin, in an unpublished essay on Willoughby-Weidenbach, notes that MacArthur's Nordic intelligence chief engaged in a lifetime of acts "with the direct intention of facilitating either the success of the Third Reich or the rise of the Fourth. The most frightening thing to consider is that he almost succeeded in his intentions on several different occasions.

"It is my contention that Charles [Adolph] Willoughby will eventually be remembered as one of the most prolific mass murderers in the history of mankind, behind only Joseph Stalin and Adolph Hitler."

McLoughlin cites "the surprise attack on Pearl Harbor on December 7, 1941 and the ensuing bombing of the U.S. Far Eastern Command in the Philippines. Both of these events fell under the aegis of MacArthur and his sidekick Willoughby [Weidenbach] as head of intelligence for the Far Eastern Command. Even after he was told of [the] Pearl Harbor attack, Willoughby [Weidenbach] declined to suggest a search of the Pacific rim for the Japanese carriers supporting the surprise attack and instead opted for leaving the U.S. Army's entire air strike capability sitting on the tarmac in the Philippines in closely clustered groups, which made them easy targets for the Japanese Zeroes ten hours later."

The presence of ranking military officers at extreme right-wing political rallies did not pass unnoticed. In *The Warfare State* (1962), Fred J. Cook detailed the doomed attempt of Senator Fulbright to rein in the "Prussianized" officers:

Senator J. William Fulbright, the intellectual and independent Arkansas Democrat who is chairman of the Senate Foreign Relations Committee, sent Secretary McNamara a memorandum protesting against the activities of the military in indoctrinating the public at a nationwide series of Radical Right forums. Fulbright made the vital point that the military, whose proper role is the execution of it, were attempting to determine public policy by lending the prestige of their rank and uniforms to some of the most rabidly extremist groups in the nation....

He had struck at the juncture, at the military link of the military-industrial complex, and the roars of outrage that were emitted from the jungles of the Radical Right filled the halls of Congress and reverberated across the nation. The bellowing was led by Senator J. Strom Thurmond, a Major General in the Army Reserves and a Dixiecrat from South Carolina whose mind rebelled at the racial heresies of the twentieth century. Thurmond denounced the Fulbright memorandum and thundered that a "dastardly" attempt was being made to "muzzle" the military and keep them from fighting the Communist enemies of America.

Joined by other far-out conservatives, Thurmond kept a daily oratorical barrage rolling in the Senate....

Here, visually demonstrated in action, was the military-industrial combine of which Eisenhower had spoken as a potential menace to the nation. The revolt of the Military Brass against the rule of a civilian Secretary, the collaboration of the military and big business in whipping up war-like passions among the people limned an overall issue of greatest magnitude.... At conflict, in essence, were traditional American principles and the kind of Prussianized military-industrial concept that produced Hitler.

The Economics of Virtual Government

Confiscated Jewish assets were poured into the Nazi rebirth and turned up in the oddest places. On September 20, 1996, a half century after the fact, the Associated Press at long last noticed: "Tons of gold looted by Nazis during World War II—some of it possibly taken from the fillings in Holocaust victims' teeth—are stored in the Federal Reserve Bank of New York and the Bank of England in London. Recently declassified federal documents show that six tons of gold looted by Nazis are stored in the two banks, the World Jewish Congress [WJC] said. The group's president has written to the two countries asking that the gold be returned to Holocaust survivors."

Elan Steinberg, speaking for the WJC, based his allegations on declassified State Department documents that confirm two tons of Nazi gold had turned up in New York vaults (worth about $28 million) and four tons ($56 million) in London.

One of the concealed links in the gold transfers was the Wallenberg family. The Wallenbergs ran Sweden's largest commercial bank during the war and assisted the Nazis in the movement of gold and jewels stolen from the Jews. In *The Art of Cloaking*, Dutch authors Gerard Aalders and Cees Wiebes describe the Wallenberg family as front men cozy with Hitler and Co., a covert arm of the regime that disguised foreign subsidiaries of German corporations. Jakob Wallenberg's Stockholm *Enskilda* was the largest privately-owned bank in Sweden. The authors suggest that the family's links to Hitler may explain why the famed Raoul Wallenberg—an agent of a "semi-clandestine U.S. agency," according to a Reuters report on October 1, 1993—was seized by Soviet troops in 1945. Aarons and Loftus came to the conclusion "the Soviets captured Raoul and tortured him for several weeks before they realized they had the wrong Wallenberg."

In March, 1996, Senator Alphonse D'Amato tinted the whitewash with gold: "From the 1930's until the onset of the Holocaust, European Jews and others deposited funds and other assets in Swiss banks for safekeeping. In doing so, they were trying to avoid what some inevitably saw as the writing on the wall, namely the coming Nazi onslaught. Others did so simply for business reasons. At the end of the war, however, a great many Swiss banks denied holding these assets."

Throughout the intervening years, Allied governments requested cooperation in finding the assets. Several organizations made a determined effort to persuade the Swiss to examine their records and find the missing assets. For the Swiss, though, the matter was simple: they did all they possibly could to evade an audit to conceal evidence of collusion with the Nazis. The Swiss cowered behind the 1934 Bank Secrecy Act, originally implemented to protect the identity of Jewish clients, to withhold the assets from survivors and rightful heirs of Holocaust victims.

Edward Stettinius, U.S. secretary of state, speaking at an inter-American conference in 1945, warned that the Nazis would attempt "to escape the consequences of their crimes. We must be constantly on the alert for the flight into this hemisphere of Nazi funds and Nazi underground leaders who will seek to find a refuge here for an ultimate comeback."

Among those to slip through the Allied dragnet in occupied Germany, scrabble across the ratlines set up by American intelligence and the secret orders of the Vatican and settle in South America were Klaus Barbie (Bolivia), Heinrich Mueller (Argentina), Joseph Mengele (Paraguay), Walter Rauff (Chile), and Freidrich Schwend (Peru). Financial and political ties in South America, the collusion of American and Latin officials and military intelligence, subverted any attempt to block the resurgence. The heart of the Nazi Party, the General German Staff, remained nearly intact.

In *A Combine of Aggression,* German emigré Karl Otten described the underground leadership's ability "to perpetuate itself, and to render itself immortal, through its innermost core, the brains of a bellicose nation's brains ... in anonymity, [residing in] unknown places, secluded from the world, controlling politics no less than operations in the field."

The Nazis were created by the world oligarchy for war and wore Gnostic vestments. German terrorist units had names like "The Death's Heads" and were known to commit ritualistic murder. "The roots of the Nazi Party were buried in hidden places," declared Hitler's friend Hermann Rauschning. The German military is not to be confused with the Nazi covert operators; the former fought on the battlefield, the other undercover.

After the military was flattened, the Nazis gracefully pushed on with the war.

In August, 1945 the U.S. argued for, and succeeded in disbanding, the UN War Crimes Commission in favor of the Nuremberg Tribunal. The one-man think tank who planned Nuremberg was Henry Stimson, former secretary of state under Herbert Hoover. Stimson, a vocal atom bomb proponent, suggested it be dropped on Japan and every wheel and cog in the Uranium Wing of virtual government went into motion to accommodate him.

At Nuremberg, he fell back on a strategy that would become standard in all pupeteered Congressional hearings—*narrowing the scope of the investigation.*

"With judgment at Nuremberg," wrote Stimson in *Foreign Relations* (January 1947), "we at last reach to the core of international strife." Articulate, smooth, disingenuous words.

Stimson's tribunal reached to "the core of the strife," but the "penalty" for participation in Nazi genocide was set by agents of virtual government. The directors of I.G. Farben, the economic and industrial sponsor of the Nazi party, and Krupp, *the* principal supplier of munitions, were tried for making war in violation of the Briand-Kellogg Treaty ... and were led through a revolving door—seems it couldn't be "proven beyond a doubt" that their intent was "aggressive," as stipulated by the treaty. Upon their release, the directors of Krupp and Farben immediately went on to exchange Nazi gold for Swiss notes on the sly. They stashed reserves away for the cold phase of the war.

All I.G. Farben facilities were left standing by American bombers on strict order from Washington. To smooth the path to corporate growth, General Patton stepped in and—in violation of the Potsdam Agreement, which specifically called for the dismantling of Farben—reorganized the company and promoted many of its former mid-level executives.

For every Nazi convicted at Nuremberg, four were released. With "Judgment at Nuremberg" constricted by such reasoning, it was hardly surprising that the first trial ended with the conviction of a dozen Nazis from a pool of 22. For the next trial the definitions of intent and authority were constrained even further, and 49 of the 52 leading German officers and industrialists were freed.

Dr. Robert Kempner, who might be described as an early "conspiracy theorist," wrote that with few exceptions, "the other SS leaders convicted at Nuremberg on charges of murder have been prematurely pardoned and freed, as a result of strong pressure by certain, partly still anonymous hinter-manner [sponsors]." In June, 1949, jurisdiction over the war criminals was handed off to High Commissioner John McCloy, the hard-core "anti-Nazi." His attitude underwent a drastic change in closed sessions, however. McCloy's secret Clemency Board reduced the sentences of all but the most intractable SS. Nearly a third were released for "good behavior" at the behest of the General German Staff. Others were granted amnesty by the thousands.

A year later, Jim Martin, a Defense Department investigator, traveled to Germany to track down Gerhard Westrick, the CEO of ITT in Germany and

MENE, MENE, TEKEL, UPSHARON

THE JEW IS OUR SOCIAL PERIL
GET RID OF ROOSEVELT
AND HIS JEWS
ELIMINATE JEWS FROM PUBLIC OFFICE
SMASH JEW-DOMINATION OF
W.P.A. and S.R.A.
AND ALL STATE AND COUNTY CHARITY RELIEF

A handbill distributed by the American White Council of California.

16

already a mover in the formation of the Fourth Reich. Westrick had fled the Berlin bombing and took refuge in a castle to the south. By post he appealed for help from his Army cronies, who smuggled him to Paris to apprise Colonel Alex Sanders of the condition of ITT's German holdings. Westrick received a token prison sentence and was released.

Hermann Abs, one of Hitler's principal financial backers, was employed as a consultant in the British zone for Deutsche Bank.

As an agent for the OSS in eastern Europe, Frank Wisner had compiled a list of SS men. In Pullach, a Bavarian village, Wisner and Dulles contacted Reinhard Gehlen, formerly the head of Hitler's eastern military intelligence corps. Gehlen was decked out in American uniform and flown to Fort Hunt, Virginia, where he was interrogated, processed and returned to Germany in July, 1946 to recruit SS and White Russian operatives for the Cold War. Gehlen, rapidly promoted to the rank of U.S. intelligence official, took up residence in Martin Bormann's mansion, or the "White House" to enlistees.

The emerging order was a reorganization of the old. Anyone who caught on was ignored, or if the whistle was blown, tarred by government officials as Communists, including Dexter White and Lauchlin Currie of the Treasury Department. White and Currie were investigating financial dealings with Germany throughout the course of the war by Standard Oil, Chase and National City Banks, the Morgan family, ITT, Ford and GM, among others. The careers of both investigators were buried by the McCarthy hearings and they were conveniently silenced.

Telford Taylor, the chief counsel at Nuremberg, saw the proceedings for what they were. He was beside himself that the most powerful Nazis had been acquitted on legal technicalities. "Murder, maiming, enslavement, ravage and plunder are a familiar litany," he wrote in 1970. The unique ingredient, especially in Eastern Europe, he argued, "was the enormous scope of the atrocities and the systematic planning and meticulous execution of these hideous enterprises."

One of those strategists was General Adolf Ernst Heusinger, inspector general of the West German Bundeswehr, former Wehrmacht General and chief of operations and planning of Hitler's land forces, responsible for ordering the wholesale atrocities in Poland and Russia. At Nuremberg, Heusinger testified that he was but a humble courier and denied any connection with the Nazi Party. Not only was he released—he turned around and talked American officials into letting his colleagues in the General Staff off as well. Among those freed as a result of his intercessions were several SS officers responsible for shooting unarmed American pilots downed over Germany. Killing American prisoners, it seems, was a standing order of "courier" Heusinger.

After Nuremberg, the Nazi joined the Gehlen spy organization, now split into the early CIA and the security arm of the Bonn government. Heusinger and Gehlen immediately set out to assemble a new German General Staff and an underground army that drew heavily upon the European criminal element. In the early 1950s, Heusinger was named West German Chancellor Konrad Adenauer's security adviser, and accepted his kind invitation to rebuild the German army.

"The new look of the next German army will be strictly non-Prussian," announced the *New York Times,* "middle class.... Its brains and boss will be Adolf Heusinger ... a very *American* type." In 1963, Heusinger was appointed chairman of the Permanent Military Committee of NATO.

Nuremberg was an inside job, instigated by Stimson, George Kennen, Allen Dulles and Dean Acheson at the State Department. Dulles was a vocal apologist for Hitler's Germany until Pearl Harbor, and as a lawyer at Sullivan & Cromwell planted Farben subsidiaries in the United States. Dean Acheson was an unabashed "Pan-German." The *San Francisco Chronicle* for August 4, 1963 captured his bilateral enthusiasm before a group at Yale and Smith college students: "I believe the single most important country in Europe is Germany, and we should treat her like a 51st state. We should consult her on every move we make."

The Cold War German-American alliance was the source of the Adenauer regime's "economic miracle." In *The Paperclip Conspiracy,* Tom Bower details the machinations behind Germany's miraculous recovery:

> The truth is sinister. In Washington a number of officials expected the resurgence of German industry, but only Samuel Klaus and a few sympathizers had wanted to prevent it, and they had failed for a series of reasons. Within Germany, the early schemes of the American military government to destroy the masonic industrial cartels had been curbed as a result of unrelenting political, commercial and diplomatic pressure from Congress, New York bankers and the British government....
>
> The publicly-stated policy of the U.S. to remove Nazis and their supporters "from the civil service, the judiciary, the educational system, the professions and the police" lamentably failed. Germany was not denazified.

The National Security Act of 1947 gave rise to dual governments, the existing system and a covert military regime. Among the authors of this virtual constitution was Paul Nitze, an employee of the the Nazi-entangled Dillon, Read investment firm and a political protégé of James Forrestal. Nitze's affinity with the Nazi cause fell under the scrutiny of the FBI in 1940.

The investigation was ordered up by Alfred Berle, then assistant secretary of defense, and Nelson Rockefeller, coordinator of inter-American affairs, who appears in fact to have been scouting for new talent—Paul Nitze resigned from Dillon, Read a few months later to take the job of financial manager of Nelson Rockefeller's office.

Nitze's doting respect for the Hitler regime was acknowledged by all he knew. One "reliable, confidential informant," who furnished "valuable information" to Hoover's FBI, said of Nitze that his political thoughts were "leaning more and more" toward Nazism, that he had "expressed feelings of admiration for totalitarianism and considerable contempt for the processes of democracy."

Transcontinental Ultraconservative Cold War cross-breeding was at play in the formation of a new U.S. intelligence group formed in May, 1948, the Office for Policy coordination (OPC), the nascent bureaucracy of America's Cold War army. The OPC and its liaisons in the intelligence sector operated with unrestrained freedom, according to NSC directive.

The early Cold War turned on the decisions of Kennon's staff. Another intelligence branch, the fledgling CIA, was an appendage of the OPC early on, but fear of exposure led the State Department to conceal the latter inside the former, away from the prying eyes of Congress and the public.

Roscoe Hillenkoetter, an early CIA director, wasn't at all pleased with this arrangement, or with this mysterious sub-agency with its WASP agents, but followed orders to look the other way while the OPC escorted Nazi war criminals to the States. Immigration irregularities were ironed out by the so-called International Rescue Committee, a CIA enterprise headed by a young intelligence agent named William Casey.

The OPC was established to take any assignment the CIA didn't have the stomach to accept. It soon became the operating arm of the Agency, acting on information gathered by CIA operatives, often at cross-purposes.

On Acheson's recommendation, a wealthy Wall Street attorney, Frank Wisner, formerly an OSS operative, accepted the position of director. If the OPC charter opened the Cold War floodgate, Wisner held the throttle. His orders to terrorize the Soviets was limited only by "plausible deniability" on the part of his superiors. Wisner was granted license to employ economic warfare, propaganda and wide-open terrorism to assist underground resistance groups.

Wisner's political power base included John McCloy, Averell Harriman (like Stimson and Kennan, a Yale Bones man), and Secretary of Defense James Forrestal. The Agency was initially supplied with 302 agents and a budget of $4.7 million. By 1952, the OPC employed 4,000 people and inhaled $84-million in federal revenues.

But Wisner's Nazi-hunting operation had a hidden source of funding to place emigrés in the U.S. as well.

Many of the mysterious emigrés found employment with the newly-established "research institutes." Operating funds were donated by the Committee for Liberation from Bolshevism, or Radio Liberty. The Committee was an OPC front founded by George Kennan well before the CIA was chartered. Funds gushed through "private" fund-raising organizations, including the "Crusade for Freedom," chaired by General Lucius Clay, who retired from his post as the American governor of the American Zone in 1949. Dwight Eisenhower and Ronald Reagan, among others, solicited public contributions. But more than 90 percent of its income was drawn from the unvouchered accounts of the CIA, not public donations. The State Department laundered the cash through private charities. The Rockefeller and Carnegie Funds were the fattest sugar daddies. And the Ford Foundation's Russian Research Committee performed a little public relations number applauding its own contributions to the flagrantly seditious Crusade for Freedom.

The Pentagon embraced the Nazis' refreshing ideas for waging covert warfare and devising horrific new weapons. It would be 40 years after the dust settled on the detritus of Berlin that the United States government acknowledged that domestic intelligence services frequently employed Nazi and Eastern European Quisling refugees as "informants," and even conspired to scuttle their prosecution for war crimes. In *Unholy Trinity,* a history of the Vatican's collusion with Old Guard fascists and the Soviet intelligence apparat, authors Aaron and Loftus observe: "It seems certain the Ratlines are *still* alive and well in America. The Nazis ... have found a new home: the World Anti-Communist League [WACL], formerly headed by retired US General John Singlaub. This is the same organization suspected by the US Congress of complicity in running guns [and drugs] for Contragate."

At the Chemical Warfare Service, founded in 1944 with $2.5 million in its bankroll, anthrax and botulism, two strains of biochemical poisons the military has had no qualms about using on Third World populations, became a mainstay of the American arsenal. George W. Merck, the pharmaceutical kingpin and an adviser to Secretary of War Henry Stimson, was the founder of the Biochemical Warfare Division, drawing on scientists from ivied American universities. The show was run in the early 1950s by Lawrence Laird Layton, a Nazi agent who resettled in the U.S. after WWII. His family made up the inner-circle of the People's Temple, the CIA's mind control and medical experimentation center in Guyana.

Thirty years after the CIA was founded, some of its most appalling abuses of public trust seeped out. There were demands for a Congressional inquiry, in effect circumvented by President Gerald Ford, who issued an executive order establishing a presidential commission to "investigate" the Agency. Nelson Rockefeller, then vice president, chaired it. Knowledgeable observers compared the appointment to setting the fox to guard the hen-house, given Rockefeller's links to the intelligence community and his vast working knowledge of covert activities. A second investigation concluded that the Rockefeller panel had been convened to undermine further investigations of abuses by the intelligence groups.

The godparents of the organized insanity about to be unleashed across the fresh green breast of the New World were "Wild Bill" Donovan and Allen Dulles from the inner-circle of a reorganized American "intelligence" network. Donovan was a bundle of raging contradictions. In public he despised fascism but was a staunch elitist himself. He rose Gatsby-like from poor Irish stock and grew to be an outwardly warm if professionally ruthless lawyer of influence on Wall Street. The firm is currently located at Rockefeller Plaza: Donovan, Leisure, Newton and Irvine. It was whispered in Washington that Wild Bill was the crony of wretched European aristocrats.

The Round Table of the Fourth Reich

As one OpEd town crier moaned: "If the Bilderberger group is not a conspiracy of some sort, it is conducted in such a way as to give a remarkably good imitation." The commentary was the complaint of G. Gordon Tether, a writer for England's *Financial Times*. He was subsequently ordered not to write about the organization again. Within a year, Tether was sacked.

Prince Bernhard was the first chairman of the Bilderberger Round Table, but the founder of the conference was Dr. Joseph Retinger, a compulsive financial and political schemer. Retinger was also the founder of the European League of Economic Cooperation and other groups formed to promote European solidarity.

Retinger, born in Poland in 1888, studied psychology in Munich and received his Ph.D in literature at the Sorbonne. In 1911 he settled in England and made contacts in government circles through London's Polish Bureau. Before long, Retinger made the acquaintance of Prime Minister Asquith—but lost that contact when the social climber publicly declared Lady Asquith to be a lesbian.

During the First World War, Retinger lived in Paris until, for unknown reasons, he was roughly expelled. From France he moved on to Cuba and Mexico, where he founded a nationalistic secret society, and ran intelligence missions for the Mexican government under diplomatic cover. On a trip to Italy in the 20s to warm relations between the Mexican government and the Vatican, Retinger found allies in Rome.

During World War II, Retinger was back in England, in league with General Sikorski and the Polish exile movement. Following the death of Sikorski in 1943, Retinger boarded the SOE under the direction of Sir Colin Gubbins, code-named "M," a Scottish Highlander and seething anti-Communist. Gubbins was born in 1896 in Yokahama, the son of a short-tempered British linguist. He graduated from Woolwich and fought in a field artillery unit throughout the First World War. When Hitler picked off Norway, Gubbins led the Independent Companies, the direct forerunner of the commandos. Gubbins was selected to organize "stay-behind parties," secret death squads formed to prey on any German troops that might step foot on British soil. Under Gubbins, Retinger trained as a paratrooper.

He resumed his obsession with a unified Europe with a fervor after the war, accompanied Winston Churchill on his 1949 tour of the United States. Their fund-raising gave birth to the American Committee for a United Europe (ACUE), chaired by William Donovan, former director of the OSS. His second was Allen Dulles, former head of the OSS office in Berne, Switzerland, who provided the group with covert funding. At the top of the agenda of the ACUE (and a slew of CIA clones) was the remilitarization of Germany and Western Europe. An open call for "unification" was delivered at a 1948 Hague conference in which Churchill and Germany's Konrad Adenauer (still busily rebuilding the German government, drawing heavily on Nazi elements) dominated the proceedings. A year later, Retinger's Council of Europe, partially supported by the CIA with a bankroll filtered through the ACUE, was formed in Strasbourg.

The anti-Communist message soon took on the trappings of a political crusade. In 1947, muckraker George Seldes lamented the drift toward unification driven by CIA opinion-shapers with king-making arrogance in their blood, among them Henry Luce at *Life:*

> Historians will discover that the first clarion call for a holy crusade of the Western Democracies for the Third World War was sounded while Second was still in progress, and that it appeared in the pages of a Luce publication.

The author was William C. Bullitt, onetime ambassador to Moscow, and one-

time ambassador to France. The date was September 4, 1944. The editorial introduction called Mr. Bullitt "a special *Life* correspondent" who had gone to Italy
where "he was granted interviews with well-informed and authoritative person-
ages, among them Pope Pius XII." There was more than an inference that Bullitt
was quoting the Pope as favoring what was euphemistically called a holy crusade.

The proposal to divide the world into a Western and an Eastern bloc, and to
fight it out for control, was later taken up by Winston Churchill, whose writings
were purchased by *Life* and the *New York Times,* and eventually by leaders
throughout the world. Mr. Luce may therefore point with journalistic pride to
the fact that one of his publications was the first to propose World War III.

From the anti-Communist annexes of the Vatican came Intermarium, a
Catholic organization on comfortable terms with the Nazi eugenics movement
under Alfred Rosenberg. In Germany, the Abwehr, Hitler's intelligence arm,
drew on Intermarium for information on the movements of East European emigrés and sent members abroad to influence foreign political and corporate leaders. With the assistance of Pope Pius XII, the Vatican offshoot established ratlines for Nazi collaborators from the eastern bloc, the single largest fascist escape
route to the United States and Canada.

Such groups became the army in the holy war against the USSR, and the call
to arms was signaled by the corporate press and several umbrella intelligence
operations, many of them founded by Retinger. These included the Council of
Europe, chaired by Paul Rijkins, the chairman of Unilever. It was Rijkins who
introduced Prince Bernhard of the Netherlands to Dr. Retinger.

Bernhard, soon to become the Bilderberg figurehead, was the son of an early
recruit to Himmler's SS. World War II historian John Keenan notes: "It was a
measure of Himmler's obsession with heredity that he particularly welcomed as
recruits representative of the German aristocracy." Among the early aristocrats
to join the SS were Prince von Waldek, Prince von Mecklenburg, Prince Lippe-
Biesterfeld (Bernhard's father), Prince Hohenzollern-Sigmaringen and the arch-
bishops of Brunswick and Freiburg. Later, with the foundation of the Order
Castles as enclaves of the SS, Himmler molded the upper echelon of the organization into a pagan order of chivalry.

Bernhard was recruited by Retinger, the godfather of right-wing groups
around the world. As Bernard tells it, his ascension to chairman of the
Bilderbergers was an alruistic act. "Retinger came to me," he recalled later, "and
told me about his worries concerning the rising tide of anti-Americanism in
Europe."

Pietro Quarino, an Italian recruited to the Bilderbergers by Retinger, found the doctor to be a born schemer. "A Pole once remarked to me, many years ago, 'every Pole has conspiracy in his blood.' First came very vague hints concerning desirable aims. Then, as I gradually caught on, a few details, then he revealed further details, then a few names ..."

The first meeting of the Bliderbergers took place around a ping-pong table on September 25, 1952. The membership roster included Retinger's old boss at the SOE, Sir Gubbins, and Antoine Pinay, the prime minister of France. The first resolution voted upon was a plan to draw the United States into the group's geo-political activities. Retinger and the Prince traveled to Washington to meet with Allen Dulles, whose exploits on behalf of the Nazis are well documented, and Walter Bedell Smith, director of central intelligence and former chief of staff to Eisenhower during WWII—and one of the key officers to rubber-stamp the residency papers of genocidal Ukranian Nazi emigré Mykola Lebed for "national security" reasons. The American Bilderberger Committee had David Rockefeller, Dean Rusk, Henry Heinz II and Joseph Johnson of the Carnegie Endowment for Intenational Peace.

The first full-blown conference took place in May, 1954 at the Hotel de Bilderberg in Oosterbeck, Holland with the CIA and the Dutch government graciously picking up the tab. Topics of discussion included "the attitude toward European integration and the European defense community." The press was barred from the proceedings. The world outside remained blissfully unaware of the telling resolution made and recorded in the "strictly confidential" minutes of the first meeting:

"Insufficient attention has so far been paid to long term planning, and to evolving an international order which would look beyond the present-day crisis. When the time is ripe our concepts should be extended to the whole world."

The attendance list at Bilderberger conclaves read like a *Who's Who* of bloodless American Nazi collaborators. Arthur Dean, a partner with John Foster Dulles at the Sullivan & Cromwell law firm since 1929, was named co-chairman. Dean invited a group of German bankers and industrialists to the meetings. J.F. Dulles was chairman of the Rockefeller Foundation (with $854 million in assets) and the Carnegie Endowment. Allen Dulles liaisoned with Gerhard Westrick, the ITT-Nazi financial operative, until 1944, and was a director of the Schroeder Trust Company, a wing of the international banking empire of Baron Kurt von Schroeder of the German General Staff. The bank run by Henry and his brother Bruno was credited by *Time* as an "economic booster of the Rome-

Berlin axis." And Schroeder, Rockefeller and Co., Investment Bankers was the financial nexus of the Nazi fifth column on the East Coast during the war. John J. McCloy from the law firm of Milbank, Tweed and Chase Manhattan Bank was a regular at the conferences.

On the steering committee sat Robert Murphy, chairman of Corning Glass and Eisenhower's Foreign Intelligence Advisory Board, and William Baker, a Rockefeller Institute trustee. Robert Lovett, a former secretary of defense, also attended. Lovett was a business partner of Averell Harriman in Brown Brothers, Harriman and Co., the firm that employed George Bush's father and grandfather.

Noting the involvement of the same corporate conspirators in the running of the leading American universities, Congressman John Rarick was moved in September 15, 1971 to lament: "The university as a strategic institution within American society provides both the technical manpower and the ideological justification of ... state capitalism. Since the legal and political power of the university system clearly rests in the hands of the ruling class, it follows that as an institution the university's primary function is to *serve the interest of wealth and power rather than free inquiry.*"

The influence of Joseph Retinger on the organization continued until his death in 1960. The first American secretary general was Joseph Johnson, the Carnegie Foundation scion, succeeded in 1974 by William Bundy, another Bonesman from Yale (described by David Halberstam as "a shadowy figure on the outside center of power"). In 1979, Bundy's chair was passed to Paul Finney, an editor of *Fortune.* Henry Kissinger was appointed to the steering committee years before he was asked to serve in the Nixon administration.

In the 1980s, participants included:

George Ball: Former undersecretary of state and an author of the National Security Act of 1947, the *carte blanche* charter of the CIA.

Paul Volcker: Federal Reserve.

Giovanni Agnelli: The Italian fascist, president of Fiat.

David Kearns: Chairman of Xerox.

Arnold Horelick: Director of the Rand/UCLA Center for the Study of Soviet International Behavior.

Jack Bennett: A senior VP at Exxon.

David Daustresme: A partner at Lazard Frere.

Charles Mathias: U.S. senator.

Robert Reid: Chairman of Shell UK, Ltd.

Robert Jecker: Executive board president of Credit Suisse.

... and a midnight colonade of "conservative" government leaders.

And what are they up to? Ultraconservative Phyllis Schlafly once called the "Bergers" "a little clique of powerful men who meet secretly and plan world events that appear to just happen."

Joy

William Donovan

We have nothing with the outcast and the unfit: let them die in their misery. For they feel not. Compassion is the vice of kings: stamp down on the wretched and the weak: this is the law of the strong: this is our law and the joy of the world.

—Aleister Crowley, *Book of the Law*

All of this empire-building took its toll on the sanity of two of the most powerful aspiring bureaucrat-soldiers in the intelligence netherworld, William Donovan and James Jesus Angleton. After the war, Donovan was stricken with severe "brain atrophy" and unceasing, violent hallucinations. Donovan, his mind wheeling with paranoid aberrations, once saw a swarm of Soviet troops marching across Washington's 59th Street Bridge. The visions hounded him until his death in 1959, appearing for all the world to be caused by massive drug overdoses, suspicious given his close association with Allen Dulles, Albert Hoffmann of Sandoz, Aldous Huxley and other Knights of the Holy Order of LSD.

Both sides of the Second World War had undertaken a quest for the ideal truth drug. OSS Director Donovan assembled a team of psychologists and drug researchers to create chemicals capable of altering and controlling behavior. This coalition included Drs. Winifred Overhulser, Harry J. Anslinger, Edward Strecker and George White. At the same time, in Germany, Nazi doctors at Dachau pursued the same ends by experimenting on Jews, Slavs and other genetic "inferiors."

Forrestal was generally high-strung, but on the day of his resignation as secretary of war, he was found *frozen* in place at his desk. An aide whisked him to his home in Georgetown. Forrestal, like Donovan, claimed that "Communists and Jews" were conspiring against him, and was obsessed with a coming invasion of Communist hordes. He attempted suicide and was admitted to Bethesda

Naval Hospital. Jacob Heilbrun, a Georgetown University scholar of postwar European history, wrote in the October 5, 1992 issue of the *New Republic* that George Kennan exercised a decisive influence on Forrestal: "Writing to Forrestal in October 1947, he proposed the creation of what he called a 'guerilla warfare corps' trained by the American military, which could 'fight fire with fire.' Forrestal agreed, but he felt that such an effort should be established under the auspices of the CIA. On December 13, 1947, the NSC approved a program of covert propaganda under CIA direction. More than likely he approved the recruitment of Ukranian Nazi collaborators for 'Operation Nightingale.' The guerillas were trained in the United States and sent to certain deaths in the Ukraine."

Forrestal was in the midst of transcribing Winthrop Mackworth Praed's translation of *Ajax*, whereupon he stood up, strolled to a kitchen storeroom, looped his pajama cord around his neck, secured it to a sill and leapt out the window. The cord broke.

James Forrestal, secretary of defense, the man who designed the postwar Navy, went out in the classic Sophoclean manner: "worn by the waste of time—comfortless, nameless, *hopeless* save in the dark prospect of the yawning grave."

If the minds of Donovan and Forrestal were broken by drug overdosing, a likely medium would have been a critical dose of BZ, a chemical sibling of LSD and an offshoot of Albert Hoffmann's labors for Sandoz, a subsidiary of Warburg and Farben. The CIA's Arnold Rothman, known as "Mr. Death" inside the Agency, discussed his leery flirtation with the potent hallucinogen in his capacity as a gadgeteer, as he explained in the January, 1977 issue of *Playboy:*

Playboy: Were you ever asked to work with drugs?

Mr Death: Only twice that I remember. My contact brought me a half gram of LSD, sealed in 27 different bottles inside of each other.... This was in the 50s and I had no idea what LSD was.... That specific job gave me the very distinct, creepy feeling that it was under the counter even for [the CIA]. I had a whole box of Neo-Synephrine spray bottles that I loaded.

Playboy: What dosages were you using.

Mr. Death: Enormous dosage. Probably wipe you out forever.

Playboy: You mentioned two instances. What was the other drug you worked with?

Mr. Death: The other was called BZ, and I wouldn't ever want to get dosed with that. It was something like LSD, but the dosage was much lower and you had to work with it in a glove box, because it was administered by breathing. I saw some very frightening films of soldiers who had been given BZ. The guys were reduced to catatonics. They would just sit there, drooling, with no control over their bodily functions unless they were given commands, like "get up," or "put your helmet on."

There was a panting interest in the human brain in some intelligence circles. *Maclean's* reported on March 13, 1991 that mind control experimentation is still a "touchy" subject, that the silence of the government on this lost chapter of military history persists: "The Mulroney government appointed a one-lawyer commission to look into the pleas of nine broken victims" of the CIA's ranking Black Psychiatrist, Dr. E. Ewen Cameron.

And who should be entrusted with this most sensitive political investigation? "A defeated Conservative MP, George Cooper of Halifax, who, loyal to the regime that held the answer to his future, concluded that the government bears no 'legal or moral responsibilities' for the experiments. Odd. Deep within the report is buried evidence that Ottawa in fact funded Cameron and his experiments with five times the financing contributed by the CIA. Cooper did meekly suggest a $100,000 payment to each survivor, not because the government was guilty of wrongdoing, but as an expression of 'a collective sense of accountability for events that took place in good faith with ill effect.'"

An FOIA document bearing the signature of the Sidney Gottlieb of the CIA's Chemical Division charts a few early forays into hypnotic mind control:

11 May 1953

MEMORANDUM FOR THE RECORD

SUBJECT: Visit to Project [deleted]

1. On this day the writer spent the day observing experiments with Mr. [deleted] on project [deleted] and in planning next year's work on the project (Mr. [deleted] has already submitted his proposal to the [deleted]).

2. The general picture of the present status of the project is one of a carefully planned series of five major experiments. Most of the year has been spent in screening and standardizing a large group of subjects (approximately 100) and the months between now and September 1 should yield much data, so that these five experiments should be completed by September 1. The five experiments are: (N stands for the total number of subjects involved in the experiment.)

Experiment 1—N-18 Hypnotically induced anxieties to be completed by September 1.

Experiment 2—N-24 Hypnotically increasing the ability to learn and recall complex written matter.

Experiment 3—N-30 Polygraph response under hypnosis....

Experiment 4—N-24 Hypnotically increasing ability to observe and recall a complex arrangement of physical objects.

Experiment 5—N-100 Relationship of personality to susceptibility to hypnosis....

The chemical companies had long engaged in secret political subterfuge. "The DuPont's fascistic behavior" Charles Higham wrote in *Trading with the Enemy*, "was evident in 1936, when Irenee du Pont used General Motors money to finance the notorious Black Legion." The DuPonts' Legionnaires, sporting black robes garnished with the skull and crossbones, killed labor organizers, bombed union halls and plotted to rid the earth of Jews and Communists. They enlisted Klansmen, ex-convicts, rapists, psychopaths, murderers and thugs. This coalition of ne'er-do-wells were the muscle of the notorious Wolverine Republican League of Detroit.

Journalist John Roy Carlson infiltrated the Legion in the 1930s, and received a baptism in organized violence: "Vigilantés pledged an oath of secrecy. Its multiple units bore such names as Black Guards, Bullet Club, Silent Legion, Modern Patriots. Its regiments were divided into squads for special duty: death squads, arson squads, flogging squads." Each squad received special "patriotic" assignments. Charles Poole, a Black factory worker, was beaten to death by the Legion, which boasted 100,000 strong. During the Poole trial it emerged that the Legion had beaten and mutilated 50 Blacks, Jews and "Communist-influenced" union organizers.

After WWII, the American military machine locked onto the Bolsheviks as the ranking dire threat to freedom and democracy and raised the roof over "Soviet expansionism." The fact that Winston Churchill had signed an agreement with Stalin recognizing Soviet domain over Rumania and Bulgaria in exchange for British control of Greece was scarcely mentioned. Poland was an open question—Britain maintained bases there and a schism of loyalties had emerged in the Polish government. Negotiations collapsed. Russia moved prematurely, ruthlessly, to assure that neighboring governments were politically compatible, providing a buffer from the West. Kennen and Acheson scapegoated Communist aggression and the secret war was underway.

In *Thy Will Be Done*, a Rockefeller biography that rakes up entire strata of muck where business and politics meet in Latin America, Gerard Colby tracked the CIA's initial steps into mind control as a strategic weapon: "Nelson Rockefeller merged the Federal Security Agency and its $4.6 million operating budget," Colby writes ...

and the operating units of three federal corporations, into a single, new cabinet-level department, Health, Education & Welfare.... HEW became involved in intelligence matters ... and became the first conduit for the CIA's mind control experiments. Project Artichoke and consequently MK-ULTRA ... was given cover by both HEW and its sub-agency, the National Institute of Mental Health (NIMH). Nelson needed little introduction to MK-ULTRA. The CIA's use of HEW for mind control experiments had been initiated during his tenure as under-secretary. The Rockefeller Foundation was also no stranger to this type of research.

Adolph Berle, a key New Dealer, agreed to sit on the board of the Society for the Investigation of Human Ecology, a foundation established at Cornell University by Nelson Rockefeller and Allen Dulles to conceal the funding of more illicit CIA mind control experimentation.

"I am frightened of this one," Berle wrote in his journal. "If scientists knew what they had laid out for themselves—men will become manageable ants." Colby:

The CIA received a startling proposal to "provide for Agency-sponsored research involving covert biological and chemical warfare." During Nelson's chairmanship of the Special Group, the CIA also searched for the means to pro-gram assassins. The CIA had discovered that a man "could be surreptitiously drugged through the medium of an alcoholic cocktail at a social party ... and the subject induced to perform the attempted assassination" of an official in the gov-ernment in which he was "well-established socially and politically." The CIA offi-cer in charge of the operation was Sheffield Edwards. Edwards later worked with Edward Lansdale in Operation Mongoose, the assassination attempt against Cuba's Fidel Castro.

Mind control experimentation took place behind the private fences of uni-versity campuses across the country, secretly transacted by the CIA's Sidney Gottlieb, director of the chemical section of the CIA's Technical Services Division. Gottlieb hailed from an old boy intelligence cell that had at its nucle-us Nelson Rockefeller's former CIA sidekick in Brazil, J.C. King of the

Directorate of Plans, late of the United Fruit Company's overthrow of Guatemala, then presiding over all clandestine activities in the western hemisphere.

Two pivotal figures in the early cold war cemented forces shortly after the fall of Berlin: Fritz Kramer, schooled in Nazi Germany, and young Henry Kissinger. It was Kramer who convinced Kissinger to study at Harvard and introduced the *basso-vocé* intellectual to Nelson Rockefeller. Kramer became a key strategist at the Pentagon. His son Sven studied under Kissinger and joined the National Security Council under Ronald Reagan.

John Foster Dulles was named Secretary of State after the war. According to CIA historian John Ranelagh, Dulles didn't condescend to to mingle with other federal officials, preferring to work *secretly,* "depending upon his close personal relationships with America's governing elite."

In 1945, Nicolae Malaxa, the key financier and arms supplier to the Iron Guard (an SS advance unit in Austria), signed a confidential contract with Grady McClaussen of the OSS, agreeing to a generous payoff in exchange for entry into the U.S. And so, in September, 1946, Malaxa disembarked with a trade mission for New York. Upon his arrival, Malaxa headed for the Chase National Bank and withdrew several million dollars waiting for him in a firm

---

"CHE GUEVERA ONCE TOLD *I.F. Stone in an interview that the U.S. embassy in Mexico had bought up and junked all the copies it could lay its hands on of the Spanish translation of* Hidden History. *In the United States, on its original appearance in 1952, the book met with an almost complete press blackout and boycott. Though its analysis was extremely damaging to the State Department line on the war, no effort was made to answer it. It achieved better treatment when it appeared in England, as did the translations in Spanish, Italian and Japanese. Two chapters were published in Jean Paul Sartre's Les Temps Modernes. In the U.S., the book has almost entirely disappeared, even from public libraries."*

◆ ◆ ◆

An introductory note to *The Hidden History of the Korean War,* by I.F. Stone, published in 1952. Stone's detailed chronology of the confrontation's early stages found General Douglas MacArthur's intelligence chief, Charles (Adolph) Willoughby (Weidenbach), a Nazi spy, to be a manipulator of events in Korea and reports from the front to draw the United States into a "police action" that strongly resembled a war.

account. For political pull, Malaxa enlisted the aid of Dulles and a young senator from California, Richard Nixon. In May, Malaxa set up a dummy corporation, Western Tube, and proposed to build the plant in Nixon's hometown, Whittier, California. The company's address happened to be the same as Nixon's law firm. Herman Perry, who convinced Nixon to run for the Senate, was now "vice president" of the corporation. The application was approved.

Malaxa was soon flying off to meet with Argentina's Juan Peron, Otto Skorzeny and other principals in the reconstruction of the Reich. Nixon and Malaxa remained bosom allies.

But the U.S. had its own Iron Guard, an underground fascist terrorist cell fronted by the Midtown Sporting Club in New York City, bankrolled by the Morgan family, several Wall Street investment firms and the German General Staff.

"The penalty for betraying our secrets is death," was the warning John Roy Carlson received upon infiltrating the group, echoing the charter found at Vogelsburg Castle. "We have men watching every one of you, men without mercy. Men who don't give a damn. They are the guardians of the Iron Guard. You are the soldiers of Christ.... We are the trained body of Christian citizens who must give aid and defense to all Christian groups."

After swearing never to divulge information regarding the secrets of the Iron Guard, he was permitted to attend a "ritual war" ceremony: "A half dozen straight-backed chairs, several armchairs and a small round table with an open Bible laying on it composed the furniture. Across the pages of the Bible lay a bayonet. Several rifles leaned against the wall. I sat down facing the emblem of the Iron Guard, a large black circle and an inner circle of white. Within the circles was a red arm holding in its fist a flash of lightning."

Hermann Schmitt, the leader of the Guard, stood in the circle and blurted, "We *are* FASCISTS, American *fascists!* Democracy is a tool to do away with Christianity. The time is ripe for something entirely new—*fascism!*"

The lunacy, seeded by the oligarchy, was spreading. A U.S. War Department release to the armed services in 1945 schooled soldiers on the malignancy of fascism:

Fascism is government by the few and for the few. The objective is seizure and control of the economic, political, social and cultural life of the state. The democratic way of life intervenes with their methods and desire for conducting business, living with their fellow men and having the final say in matters concerning others....
They maintain themselves in power by use of force combined with propaganda based on primitive ideas ... by skillful manipulation of fear and hate and by false promise of security.

There are, declared the War Department, "Three Ways to Spot U.S. Fascists":

Fascists deny the need for international cooperation. These ideas contradict the fascist theory of the "master race." The brotherhood of man implies that all people have rights. International cooperation runs counter to the fascist program of war and world domination.

Many fascists make the spurious claim that the world has but two choices ... fascism or Communism, and they label as "Communist" everyone who refuses to support them.

In France, few conformed to the fascist mold like Francois Genoud, a Nazi collaborator who joined the National Socialist Party at 21 and rose to prominence in Switzerland. His National Front for Switzerland was funded by the Oltramaire family, owners of the Lobard-Oldier Bank of Geneva, the secret pocket of OSS Station Chief Allen Dulles and his German contacts.

Many of the most powerful Nazis, of course, settled in the U.S.

Edward Fleckenstein, a Weehawken, New Jersey lawyer, published an open letter in Germany to Dr. Konrad Adenauer, offering "observations regarding U.S.-German affairs." The letter circulated widely in Germany. The American government, Fleckenstein said, was "corrupt at every level ... a quasi-dictatorship ruled by the hidden tyranny of money and satanic special interest groups. Well-meaning bourgeois are still in the majority here but they get nowhere [as] the U.S. administration is dominated by a secret, invisible government." This "secret government and its conspirators," Fleckenstein wrote, "put Eisenhower in office."

Sources

Charles R. Allen, Jr., *Heusinger of the Fourth Reich* (1963); Scott Anderson and Jon Lee Anderson, *Inside the League* (1986); Herbert Aptheker, *Dare We Be Free?* (1961); Tom Bower, *The Paperclip Conspiracy: The Hunt for the Nazi Scientists* (1987); John Roy Carlson, *Undercover: My Four Years in the Nazi Underworld of America* (1943); Fred J. Cook, *The Warfare State* (1962); Transcripts of Senator D'Amato's hearings on Swiss handling of Jewish assets, 1996; Ladislas Farago, *Aftermath* (1974); M.R.D. Foot, "Subtle Maker of War" (re: Joseph Retinger), *London Telegraph,* July 31, 1993; Arnold Foster & Benjamin R. Epstein, *Cross-Currents* (1956); Charles Higham, *American Swastika* (1985); Glen Infield, *Secrets of the SS* (1981); John Loftus, *The Belarus Secret* (1982), and with Mark

Aarons, *Unholy Trinity: The Vatican, the Nazis, and Soviet Intelligence* (1991) and *The Secret War Against the Jews* (1994); Ferdinand Lundberg, *The Rockefeller Syndrome,* (1975); William Manchester, *American Ceasar: Douglas MacArthur 1880–1964* (1978); William Morris McLoughlin, "General Charles Adolph Willoughby, Looking for 'Hate' in all the 'Right' Places," undated monograph, *Prevailing Winds Research,* Santa Barbara, CA; Mike Newberry, *The Yahoos* (1964); E.A. Piller, *Time Bomb* (1945); Dick Russell, *The Man Who Knew Too Much* (1992); Michael Sayers & Albert E. Kahn, *Sabotage! The Secret War Against America* (1942) and *The Plot Against the Peace* (1947); Anthony Sampson, *The Arms Bazaar: From Lebanon to Lockheed* (1977); Christopher Simpson, *Blowback: America's Recruitment of Nazis and its Effect on the Cold War* (1988); Telford Taylor (chief counsel at the Nuremberg trials), *Nuremberg and Vietnam: an American Tragedy* (1970); T.H. Tetens, *The New Germany and the Old Nazis* (1961); Lucian K. Truscott, IV, "Even in Arcadia" *Vague,* London, England, no. 18: Spring 1989; others cited in the text.

"And Now, A Few Words From our Sponsor"

THE CIA

The Birth of Operation MOCKINGBIRD, the Takeover of the Corporate Press & the Programming of Public Opinion

"My lips have been kind of buttoned for almost twenty years ..."
—Walter Cronkite

Little has been written about the CIA's hidden relationship with the media. John Ranelagh's *The Agency*—an officially-sanctioned, Bible-length history—mentions few occasions of meddling. One of them was exposed at the oversight level in 1973 when Vernon Walters, then acting director, asked William Colby to draw up a list of "skeletons" in the CIA's burial ground of a history to submit at a closed Congressional hearing...

The list was single-spaced. It was 693 pages long.

Among the confessed abuses of power was a Project Mockingbird: "During the period from March 12, 1963 to June 15, 1963, the Office of Security installed telephone taps on two prominent Washington-based newsmen suspected of disclosing classified information obtained from a variety of governmental and congressional sources."[1]

A routine wiretap. Not a particularly damning disclosure. But this Mockingbird is not to be confused with the wholesale political and cultural pollution of the media known to the ink-stained wretches who study the CIA's international underground as Operation MOCKINGBIRD.

In the early gusts of the Cold War, the American intelligence services competed with Communist activists to influence European labor unions. With or without the cooperation of local embassies, Frank Wisner, an undercover State Department official assigned to the Foreign Service, hired students abroad to enter the Cold War as agents of his Office of Policy Coordination. Philip Graham, an alumnus of the Army Intelligence School in Harrisburg, Pennsylvania, publisher of the *Washington Post*, signed on to direct the propaganda program.[2]

The following decade, Wisner and Graham would both resign their CIA commissions by committing "suicide."

In the early 1950s, former *Village Voice* reporter Deborah Davis wrote in her biography of Katharine Graham, "Wisner had implemented his plan and 'owned' respected members of the *New York Times, Newsweek,* CBS and other communications vehicles, plus stringers, four to six hundred in all, according to a former CIA analyst."[3] The partnership was overseen by Allen Dulles, the ultimate insider, a virtual government templar for German and American corporations who wanted their point of views represented in the media. Early MOCKINGBIRD swelled to influence some 25 newspapers and wire agencies by 1955, consenting, in the most frigid period of the Cold War, to act as founts of right-wing propaganda.[4] Many of these were already operated by men with highly reactionary views, among them William Paley (CBS), C.D. Jackson (*Fortune*), Henry Luce (*Time*) and Arthur Hays Sulzberger (*N.Y. Times*).

Curious activists nosing into the dense mysteries of MOCKINGBIRD have been shocked to find, in heavily-redacted FOIA documents, agents boasting of their pride at having placed "important assets" inside every major news outlet in the country.[5] It was not until 1982 that the Agency openly admitted for the first time that journalists on the CIA dole have acted as case officers to agents in the field.[6]

I. MOCKINGBIRDGATE

So the muckrakers were suppressed, the newspapers were reduced, brought into safe hands, writers were controlled, books privately censored, publishing houses bought into and influenced, peace societies and philanthropic and educational foundations linked up with financial houses and the universities by interlocking directorates, our university teachers kept looking forward to pensions, young recalcitrants dismissed or set in their places ...

—Porter Sargent, "What Makes Lives"

The seeding of public opinion, often explained (when the straining dams of secrecy leak) as a necessary reaction to Communism, has since served to conceal the criminalization of the intelligence agencies. The CIA's early forays into mind control experimentation on unconsenting subjects, for example, were justified by an ersatz cover story that POWs of the Korean War had been "brainwashed" by their captors. In fact, the Army investigation was unable to document a single case of "brainwashing" among the prisoners released by the North Koreans. The word was coined by Edward Hunter, a veteran OSS propagandist recruited by Dulles, the Nazi-collaborating oligarch who, in fact, conceived of MOCK-INGBIRD as a mass mind control operation.

The Korean War itself was urged along by propaganda oozing from the front pages of the country's leading newspapers. A detailed study of the disinformation assault, I.F. Stone's *Hidden History of the Korean War*, first appeared in 1952. The book sold well overseas, but in the States, as explained in a note from the publisher in later editions, it "met with an almost complete press blackout and boycott. The book has almost entirely *disappeared*, even from public libraries, and it rarely turns up in the second-hand book market.".

The muckracking era was yesterday's coffee grounds—corporate franchising of the print media saw to it. "When it began," lamented George Seldes in *1000 Americans,* a survey of American corporate power published in 1947, muckraking journalism had advocates in "all people who had the general welfare at heart, but as the probes went deeper and further, and seemed to spare none of the hidden powers, the politicians as well as other spokesmen for money, business and profiteering turned savagely upon the really free press and *destroyed it*.... Trash may indeed be the opium of the people, but it was not the real aim of the magazines to stupefy the public, merely to suppress the facts, merely to pullify, to create a wasteland."

A Niagara of pro-American propaganda sponsored by the U.S. Information Agency (USIA), a CIA symbiont, shaped domestic and foreign political sensibilities beginning in the early 1950s. In this period, a niagara of books with USIA funding were disseminated by Praeger, Inc., the Franklin Press and other publishing houses bearing, of course, no indication of their actual origin.

By the mid-Reagan era, the USIA would spend nearly a billion dollars per anum to export propagandizing magazines, books (an average of three million a year) and exhibitions. The Agency sponsored ten magazines and commercial bulletins in twenty languages, including *Topic* (South Africa) and a radio teletype network that disseminated propaganda to 159 outlets overseas. Some 200 films acquired from private domestic studios were distributed, and a television program entitled *Worldnet.*[7]

The CIA came to dominate the Monopoly board of the corporate press, and drew a card from the stack marked with that monocled millionaire in the top hat (bearing a curious resemblance to Allen Dulles) calling for a strategy of psychological warfare, the art of calculated deceit, often with catastrophic results.

Cord Meyer, Jr., the ranking Mockingbird in Europe, then a *Newsweek* correspondent, swung widely throughout Europe inciting student and union protests. "This localized psychological warfare is ultimately, of course, warfare against the Russians," Davis emphasized, "who are presumed to be the source of every leftist political sentiment in Italy, France, the entire theater of Meyer's operations. In Eastern Europe his aim [was] to foment rebellion."

In 1956, "the CIA learns that the Soviets will indeed kill 60,000 MOCKINGBIRD-roused Hungarians with armored tanks."[8] Nevertheless, Radio Free Europe urged the people of Hungary to resist the Kremlin, the conclusion of an investigative committee of the UN: Many Hungarians "had the feeling that Radio Free Europe promised help." They believed military aid from the West would arrive to back an uprising. On November 5, a year later, a dry, unsteady voice crackled through the static of a Hungarian radio station:

> Attention: Radio Free Europe, hello. Attention. This is Roka speaking. The radio of revolutionary youth.... Continual bombing. Help. help. help ... Radio Free Europe ... forward our request. Forward our news. Help ...

And on November 6, another broadcast:

> We appeal to the conscience of the world. Why cannot you hear the call for help of our murdered women and children? Have you received our transmission?
> Attention! Attention! Munich! Munich! Take immediate action. In the Dunapentele area we urgently need medicine, bandages, arms, food and ammunition.

The final transmission, 24 hours later:

> Must we appeal once again? We have wounded ... who have given their blood for the sacred cause of liberty, but we have no bandages ... no medicine. The last piece of bread has been eaten.
> Those who have died for liberty ... accuse you who are able to help and who have not helped. We have read an appeal to the UN and every honest man. Radio Free Europe, Munich! Radio Free Europe, Munich ...[9]

Operation MOCKINGBIRD was an immense financial undertaking. Funds flowed from the CIA largely through the Congress for Cultural Freedom (CCF), founded by Tom Braden, a "liberal" who would make his mark as a syndicated columnist and co-host of CNN's *Crossfire* opposite Ultracon Pat Buchanon. The CCF was founded in June, 1950 by prominent academics assembled in Berlin's U.S. zone at the Titania Palace Theater. The CCF, directed by Denis de Rougemont, was formed to "defend freedom and democracy against the new tyranny sweeping the world." About 20 periodicals were financed by the front, including *Encounter* in the UK, *The New Leader, Africa Report* and *El Mundo Nuevo* in Latin America.[10]

The hidden source of CCF's income—and the influence the CIA had been exercising over the intellectual life of Europe—erupted in a wave of scandal that filled a page of the England's *Observer* in 1967. The *Sunday Times* also drew down on "CIA Culture," exposing a "Literary Bay of Pigs." *Encounter*, the epicenter of the scandal, was presided over by Melvin Lasky, a former Army captain. Lasky negotiated with the CIA for funding from the start, and he edited the journal for 32 years.

Most literati embroiled in the scandal denied any role in it, including co-editors Stephen Spender and Frank Kermode, who immediately resigned in a huff. Editor Lasky claimed to have "learned" of the true source of funding in 1963. However, Tom Braden, in disclosures that appeared in *The Saturday Evening Post,* acknowledged that he'd constructed the "front" program for the Central Intelligence Agency, and had appointed one agent to preside over the CCF and another to edit *Encounter.*[11]

Lasky shaped the reputations of some of the UK's most respected anti-Communist "scholars," including Hugh Trevor-Roper, a military intelligence officer, and George Urban, previously director of Radio Free America and later adviser to Margaret Thatcher on German affairs. From the Lasky crowd emerged historian and poet Robert Conquest, whose *The Great Terror,* an account of the Stalin purge, is widely considered a minor classic (gratis the CIA).[12]

The Nation reported a major stink over the subsidies to *Encounter,* noting: "The journal, with a circulation of 42,000, put a number of journals not funded by the CIA out of business." Lasky was unruffled, even though the British press found an "agonizing debate" raging in academia "around the question of what a free thinker should do when he finds out that his free thought has been subsidized by a ruthlessly aggressive intelligence agency as part of the international cold war."[13]

In 1965 the CCF was renamed Forum World Features and purchased by Kern House Enterprises—a CIA front directed by Mockingbird John Hay Whitney, publisher of the *International Herald Tribune* and formerly ambassador to England.[14]

Without a rumble, even a quiver, the cold war propaganda machine rolled into the book publishing business. Deals were struck with a host of writers, commercial publishers and distributors. The CIA, in collaboration with the USIA, financed the publication of well over a thousand books of anti-Soviet propaganda by 1967.

The CIA publication list included *The Communist Front* and *Political Warfare* by James D. Atkinson, *In Pursuit of World Order* by Richard N. Gardner and *The Dynamics of Soviet Society* by Walt Rostow. Langley also financed the worldwide distribution of an animated version of George Orwell's *Animal Farm.*[15]

The book business still pumps out radically "conservative" propaganda for mass consumption. In an unpublished proposal for a book on the life of Joe Coors, Delaware writer S.T. Shields reports that the brewer determined the economic policy of Ronald Reagan in his first run for the presidency. To hammer out the details of Reagan's economic plank, Coors, who maintained close ties to the intelligence sector, "recruited his friend and financial mentor, University of Chicago economist Milton Friedman, well-known but controversial. Friedman's 1976 Nobel Prize for economics had offended many prior laureates who protested in a letter to the Swedish academy that following the overthrow and assassination of Chilean president Salvador Allendé, Friedman had been invited by the Pinochet-headed junta to help the new regime formulate a conservative economic policy."

With backing from MOCKINGBIRD's Richard Scaife, publisher of the *Pittsburgh Tribune-Review* and a leading financier of Accuracy in Media (AIM, a military-industrial propaganda mill), Joe Coors paid a conservative Erie, Pennsylvania television station, WQLN, to make a ten-part series, *Free to Choose,* starring Friedman and his "monetarist" theories. Widely aired on public television in 1980 and anywhere else its sponsors could find audiences, the series was an effective propaganda tool, convincing millions of Americans that the Reagan economic policies could work. Issued as a book, *Free to Choose* was a non-fiction bestseller.

The building of corporate media empires by the CIA occurred throughout the western hemisphere. In the early 1950s, the CIA gave $7 million to press baron Axel Springer toward the formation of an immense media conglomerate. The Berlin mogul's holdings came to include a daily newspaper with 11 million readers, *Bild Zeitung,* an arch-conservative tabloid spiced with sex and violence, several popular magazines and the Ullstein publishing house. Rudolph Augstein, a competitor, publisher of *Der Spiegel,* laments: "No single man in Germany, before or after Hitler, with the possible exception of Bismarck or the two emperors, has had so much power as Springer."

When the CIA came along, Herr Springer was well known for his liberal views. As he gained power, however, the MOCKINGBIRD publisher espoused increasingly conservative political opinions. Within 20 years his dailies were snatched up by about 35% of the German readership and his Sunday papers exceeded 80% of the market. His star was still rising when he launched an aggressive editorial campaign against German liberals. In the Spring of 1968, students marched against his media monopoly in Hamburg, Berlin and Munich and stormed the editorial offices.

One CIA official told reporter Murray Waas that some at the Agency felt they'd played the role of Dr. Frankenstein: "We had in the long run helped create something that served neither American interests nor West German ones."[16]

By the time MOCKINGBIRD's ties to Springer were exposed, outlays for global propaganda climbed to a full third of the CIA's covert operations budget. Some 3,000 salaried and contract CIA employees were engaged in propaganda efforts. The cost of disinforming the world cost American taxpayers an estimated $265 million a year by 1978, a budget larger than the combined expenditures of Reuters, UPI and the AP news syndicates. In 1977, the *New York Times* ran a front-page story detailing a worldwide propaganda effort, with direct CIA ownership of some 50 newspapers in the U.S. and elsewhere.[17] In 1977, the Copely News Service admitted that it worked closely with the Company—to be sure, 23 employees at Copley alone were full-time employees of the Agency.[18]

And the corporate media was no potted plant in the Agency's secret garden of political subterfuge. One CIA dispatch, dated April 1, 1967, declassified nine years later under FOIA, advised planted "assets" in the media on "Countering Criticism of the Warren Report." Features and book reviews "are particularly appropriate for this purpose," the CIA dispatch observed. Strategies to "answer and refute" critics of the government's investigation of the JFK murder included accusations that they were "financially interested," "hasty and inaccurate in their research," "infatuated with their own theories," and "wedded to theories adopted before the evidence was in," The CIA's mouthpieces in the press were directed to emphasize: "No significant new evidence has emerged," "there is no agreement among the critics," or the ever-popular, "Conspiracy on the large scale often suggested would be impossible to conceal."

Most consumers of "CIA culture" were—and are—widely unaware of the scale the Mockingbirds have granted themselves in the coloring of public opinion. There is no way to gauge the political and cultural damage done by censorship and politically-contrived reporting. But the brute finances of CIA propaganda are another story. Sean Gervasi, a visiting professor of economics at the University of Paris, audited the CIA books in 1978. "Some $270 million, or 60 percent of the sum, is allocatable to covert action support. One-third of the $270 million, or $90 million, could be considered the indirect cost of covert propaganda."

2. Old Boys in the Sauerkraut & Pizza Divisions

But some sensed there was something very, well, odd about the folksy editors over at *Reader's Digest.* For one thing, the magazine appealed to a political fringe group. Throughout the war, the Nazi party made reference to articles in the

Digest because they proved to be stirring propaganda. The *Digest* was often cited in a magazine distributed to American POWs. *Stars & Stripes* reported that Germany's 805th Tank Destroyer Battalion went so far as to blast canisters stuffed full of *Digest* reprints from 105mm cannons at American troops.[19]

On December 2, 1996, *Newsday* staffer Dan Cryer described the crafting of an American end-table fixture and identified the Promethean Rockefeller who dismembered the dream of founder DeWitt Wallace:

> Wallace fashioned the *Digest* into an American original, a mighty instrument for global education and uplift. Meanwhile, his wife, Lila Acheson Wallace, not only stood by her man but periodically stepped inside the organization to wield a stiletto against her "enemies." Alas, the ambitions of the Wallaces were "sabotaged and destroyed." Their magazine was cheapened, their formerly pampered employees fired, and their six billion dollar empire "overrun by salesmen and profiteers." The orchestrator of this outrage was Laurance Rockefeller, a wolf wearing sheep's clothing, who had been brought in by the Wallaces to protect their legacy.

Dr. Goebbels was an avid reader, as he admitted in a January, 1942 journal entry: "*The Reader's Digest* ... has published a sensational article that asserts that the United States in the last analysis is unable to undertake anything against the armed force of the Axis. America's war was a hopeless undertaking and could only result in bleeding the nation white. At last *one voice* in the wilderness."[20]

Stateside, the *Digest* was publicly pullified when a 1944 release from the Field News Syndicate reported that the Air Force distributed the strange little magazine around the word, opened foreign *Digest* editorial offices, even supplied the magazine's paper.

In the Eisenhower decade, a brood of MOCKINGBIRD propagandists contributed regularly to the *Digest,* including Allen Dulles, Carl Rowan, James Burnham, Brian Crozier, Stewart Alsop—a great-nephew of Teddy Roosevelt (who once explained in correspondence to the magazine's readers that in Africa, "female posteriors have the same symbolic significance as bosoms in this country") and Claire Sterling.[21]

"World War III has *begun,*" Henry's Luce's *Life* declared in March, 1947. "It is in the opening skirmish stage already." The issue featured an excerpt of a book by the CIA's James Burnham, who called for the creation of no less than an "American Empire": "*world-dominating* in political power, set up at least in part through coercion (probably including war, but certainly the threat of war) and in which one group of people ... would hold more than its equal share of power."

The same vision was captured a shade more bluntly by Baroness Ella van Heemstra, the mother of Audrey Hepburn, according to Alexander Walker in *Audrey—Her Real Story.* The Baroness opined in a newspaper published by the English Fascist Party that "a new world" should be built on fascist principles.

The presiding power broker at Langley, Allen Dulles, was the source of much of the news gathered in the formative years of the Cold War. His key political operative was Thomas E. Dewey. Allen Dulles and the mob's Meyer Lansky contributed handsomely to Dewey's political campaigns, including his 1948 presidential bid, and his firebrand reactionary protégé, Richard Nixon.[22]

Cap Cities/ABC rose like Mothra from this Republican social cocoon. Dewey's neighbor, newsman Lowell Thomas, purchased a stake to launch the company's direct forerunner, the notorious Resorts International, said to be the corporate front for Meyer Lansky's branch of the Mafia crime family. Another of the original investors was one James Crosby, who donated $100,000 to Nixon's 1968 presidential campaign. In 1965, James Crosby's Mary Carter Paint Company purchased the Paradise Island resort across the bay from Nassau, and opened a casino through Wallace Groves, founder of the Grand Bahama Port Authority and an "advisor and possible officer" of the CIA, according to an internal "Covert Security Approval" memorandum dated December 30, 1965.[23] The casino was registered in the name of Groves's wife.[24] Crosby hired Ed Cellini, the brother of Dino Cellini, one of Lansky's closest business associates, to manage the casino.[25] In 1968, the company chiseled into casino interests in Atlantic City. Police in New Jersey attempted, without success, to block the issuance of a gambling license to the company, basing their opposition on its Mafia ties.

In 1954, this same circle of investors, all Catholics, founded Cap Cities. The company's chief counsel was OSS veteran William Casey, who clung to his shares by concealing them in a blind trust even after he was appointed CIA director by Ronald Reagan in 1981.[26]

"Black Radio" was the phrase CIA critic David Wise coined in *The Invisible Government* to describe the CIA's intertwining interests in the emergence of the transistor radio with the entrepreneurs who took to the airwaves. "Daily, East and West beam hundreds of propaganda broadcasts at each other in an unrelenting babble of competition for the minds of their listeners. The low-price transistor has given the hidden war a new importance."[27] By 1958, the UPI could report: "A second mysterious Arab radio station went on the air yesterday calling itself the 'Voice of Justice' and claiming to be broadcasting from Syria.

Earlier, the 'Voice of Iraq' went on the air with attacks against the Iraqi revolutionary government. The 'Voice of Justice' called Kruschev the 'Hangman of Hungary.'"[28]

On the domestic front, a lasting relationship was struck between the CIA and William Paley, a wartime colonel and the founder of CBS. A staunch believer in "all forms of propaganda" to foster loyalty to the military, Paley hired CIA agents to work undercover at the behest of his close friend Allen Dulles. Paley's designated liaison in dealings with the CIA was Sig Mickelson, president of CBS News from 1954 to 1961.[29] Mickelson was also the reigning official at Radio Free Europe and Radio Liberty in the 1970s.

The domestic counterpart to these bulwarks of conservative propaganda was the Crusade for Freedom, a lavishly-funded public relations effort employing media celebrities to weave a spell of Cold War hysteria. Another was the so-called National Committee for a Free Europe, directed by MOCKINGBIRD'S Allen Dulles, "Wild Bill" Donovan, Henry Luce, C.D. Jackson and *Reader's Digest* editor Eugene Lyons. Both organizations martinized CIA funds to finance the emigration of European Nazis to the U.S. Ultimately, some 90% of the Crusade's funding came from Langley, passing briefly through the accounts of RCA among other major corporations, and such well-heeled charitable fronts as the Carnegie Fund and Ford Foundation.[30]

The ratings for the most popular political radio personalities of 1950 were a barometer of the political climate[31]:

COMMENTATOR	ESTIMATED AUDIENCE	SALARY
Walter Winchell	25 Million	$650,000
Drew Pearson	15 Million	$400,000
Fulton Lewis, Jr.	10 Million	$350,000
Westbrook Pegler	45 Million	$90,000

Of the four, Walter Winchell was the closest to political moderation. Pearson wrote scathing exposés of McCarthy's backstair dealings. But two of the most popular pulpit bullies in America, Nazi agents Fulton Lewis and Westbrook Pegler, pandered to McCarthy, voluntarily slanted news stories for him and ignored unfavorable press reports to enhance the senator's public image.[32]

Another political discussion program, Longine's *Chronoscope,* aired from 1950 to 1955 on television stations with a CBS franchise. *Chronoscope* borrowed from the news magazine format. Interviewers (or "co-editors") with granitic foreheads steered the discussion along, including William Bradford Huie, publisher and editor of the ultra-right *American Mercury* magazine; Henry Hazlitt, a political economist and contributing editor of *Newsweek,* the publisher of *Freeman* magazine; and Larry Lesueur, a reporter for CBS News. Guests on *Chronoscope* included:

Adm. William H. P. Blandy (June 11, 1951): Former Commander-in-Chief of the Atlantic Fleet, oversaw the nuking of the Bikini Atoll.

Paul G. Hoffman (July 30, 1951): President of the Ford Foundation, a funding source for the Nazi migration from Germany.

William C. Bullitt (September 24, 1951): The pro-fascist former U.S. Ambassador to the Soviet Union and France.

Brig. Gen. Bonner F. Fellers (October 3, 1951): Strategist and psychological warfare expert.

Lt. Gen. Albert C. Wedemeyer-Weidenbach (June 18, 1952): National chairman, Citizens for Taft Committee, director of the U.S. Liberty Lobby, Nazi operative.

Senator Joseph R. McCarthy (R-WI) (June 25, 1952).

Robert Morris (July 2, 1952:): Special counsel, "Senate Internal Security Subcommittee," otherwise known as the McCarran Committee.

Thomas E. Dewey (October 15, 1952): Former Governor of New York with hidden ties to the Mafia, and 1948 Republican nominee for President. A founding investor in Cap Cities.[33]

Listen to the MOCKINGBIRD

The technology of early radio leap-frogged with the reverse engineering of sound equipment designed by the Nazis. In 1945, Col. John T. Mullin of the U.S. Signal Corps, assigned to a team investigating German electronics, was informed by a British officer of a tape-recorder discovered at a Frankfort, Germany radio station with unprecedented musical quality. The "Magnetophone" audio tape recorder/player was a vast improvement over the then current American counterpart. Professor Marvin Bensman, a historian at the University of Memphis, notes that the machine used "plastic tape impregnated or coated with iron oxide and the employment of a very high frequency mixed with the audio signal to provide 'bias.'"

"Hi-Fi" was born in Hitler's Germany.

As Dr. Bensman fine-tunes early radio history ...

The first two machines acquired were turned over to the Signal Corps and Col. Mullin disassembled two other machines and shipped them to his home in San Francisco. In 1946, Mullin re-wired and reassembled the Magnetophone machines and went into a partnership with Bill Palmer for movie sound-track work, using those machines and the 50 reels of tape he had acquired. In October of 1946, Mullin and his partner Palmer attended the annual convention of the Society of Motion Picture Engineers. He demonstrated the machine to the sound heads of MGM, 20th Century Fox and the chief engineer of Altec Lansing. Mr. Mullin was then invited to an Institute of Radio Engineers meeting in May of 1947 to demonstrate the German Magnetophone. It was there employees of Ampex saw and heard the tape recorder. Shortly thereafter, Ampex began its own developmental project.

In 1947, the technical staff of the Bing Crosby Show on ABC arranged to have Mullin re-record original disk recordings of the Bing Crosby Show on ABC onto tape and then edit them. Crosby had been with NBC until 1944, doing the Kraft Music Hall live but did not like the regimen imposed by live shows.

Since NBC would not permit recorded programs, Crosby took a year off and returned on the newly formed ABC network when his new sponsor, Philco, and ABC agreed to let him record on electrical transcriptions as long as his ratings did not fall below a certain mark.... In July of 1947, after the initial demonstration of editing, John Mullin was invited to give a demonstration of his equipment for Bing Crosby's producers by taping live side-by-side with transcription equipment the first show for the 1947–48 season in August at the ABC-NBC studios in Hollywood.

Bing Crosby Enterprises then negotiated financing for Ampex for exclusive distribution rights and Mullin was employed to record the Crosby show on his original German equipment until the Ampex machines would become available.

With the original German tape-recorders and 50 rolls of BASF tape, Mullin's first recorded demonstration show of August, 1947, was broadcast over ABC on October 1, 1947. In April of 1948, Alexander Poniatov and his team of engineers at Ampex in Redwood City, CA, introduced the first commercial audio tape recorder based on the Magnetaphone as Ampex Model 200. The first two, serial numbers 1 and 2, were initially presented to John Mullin and numbers 3–12 went into service at ABC. To meet the contract requirements, Mullin gave his machines to ABC and later received Nos. 13–14 for his contribution. Mullin joined Bing Crosby Enterprises in 1948 and recorded his shows and others at ABC until 1951. Bing Crosby Enterprises, as the exclusive distributor for Ampex products, sold hundreds of recorders to radio stations and master recording studios.

In 1951, Mullin and other engineers were spun off as the Bing Crosby Electronic Division to handle development of audio instrumentation and video recording. In 1956, the Electronic Division became the Minicom Division of 3M where Mullin served as head of engineering and Professional Recorder Development Manager until his retirement. [34]

The propagandists at Langley's House of Secrets proceeded to shape collective opinion with invisible chisels. The CIA's assimilation of old guard Nazis was overseen by the CIA's Operations Coordination Board, directed by Mockingbird C.D. Jackson. During World War II, Jackson had represented the Office of War Information, served as deputy chief, Psychological Warfare Branch of the Allied Forces HQ, 1943, and deputy chief, Psychological Warfare Division, Supreme HQ, Expeditionary Force, 1944–45. Jackson was also a former executive of *Time* magazine and Eisenhower's special assistant for Cold War strategy. In 1954, he was succeeded by the ubiquitous Nelson Rockefeller, who quit a year later, repulsed, he sneered, by the administration's political infighting.

Vice President Nixon succeeded Rockefeller as key Cold War strategist. "Nixon," writes John Loftus, at one time an attorney for the Justice Department's Office of Special Investigations, took "a small boy's delight in the arcane tools of the intelligence craft—the hidden microphones, the 'black' propaganda." Nixon especially enjoyed his visit to a Virginia training camp to observe Nazis in the "special forces" learning the arts of "spycraft" he so admired.[35]

One of the fugitives recruited by the American intelligence establishment was heroin smuggler Hubert von Blücher, the son of a German ambassador. Hubert often bragged that he'd been trained by the Abwehr, the German military intelligence division, while still a civilian in his twenties. He served in a reconnaissance unit of the German Army's 2nd Battalion until forced out for medical reasons in 1944. He worked briefly as an assistant director for Berlin Film on a movie entitled *One Day*, and finished out the war flying with the Luftwaffe—not to engage the enemy, but to smuggle Nazi gold bullion out of the country.[36] In 1948, he flew the coop to Argentina. Posing as a photographer, he immediately paid court to Eva Peron, presenting her with an invaluable Gobelin tapestry (doubtless a sample from the wealth of artifacts confiscated by SS from their victims). Hubert then met with Martin Bormann at Argentina's Hotel Plaza and turned over German marks amounting to $80 million. He later told investigators the loot financed the formation of the National Socialist Party in Argentina.

Three years later Hubert migrated to *El Norte*. The Nazi landed a position with the Color Corporation of America in California, and eked out a living writing scripts for Hollywood's thriving movie industry. His voice graces a film set in the Amazon, produced by Walt Disney. In 1951 he returned to Buenos Aires, then Düsseldorf, West Germany. He established a firm that developed not movie scripts, but anti-chemical warfare agents for the German government.[37] At the stately *Industrie* Club in Düsseldorf in 1982, Von Blücher crowed to journalists: "I am chief share-holder of Pan American Airways. I am the best friend of Howard Hughes. The Beach Hotel in Las Vegas is 45 percent financed by *me*. I am thus the biggest financier ever to appear in the *Arabian Nights* tales dreamed up by these people over their second bottle of brandy."[38]

Not exactly. Two of the biggest financiers to stumble from the drunken dreams of world-moving affluence were, in their time, Moses Annenberg, publisher of *The Philadelphia Inquirer,* and his son Walter, the CIA/mob-anchored publisher of the *TV Guide.* Like most American high-rollers, Annenberg lived a double life. Moses, his father, was a scion of the Capone mob. Both Moses and Walter were indicted in 1939 for tax evasions totalling many millions of dollars—the biggest case in the history of the Justice Department. Moses pled guilty and agreed to pay the government $8 million and settle $9 million in assorted tax claims, penalties and interest debts. Moses received a three-year sentence. He died in Lewisburg Penitentiary. Johnny Rosselli, years

The Imperious Walter Annenberg, by Andrew Wyeth.

before he was an intelligence asset, worked the gambling wire service operated by Annenberg, and remained in Hollywood, mingling with the most illustrious names in the business, after Moses died.

He once told another California Mafioso, Jimmy Fratianno: "I knew half the people in this town on a first-name basis. Jack Warner, Harry Cohn, Clark Gable, George Raft, Jean Harlow, Gary Cooper, I knew them all and enjoyed their company."[39]

Walter Annenberg, the *TV Guide* magnate, rose to the loftiest ranks of the Republican Party. On the campaign trail in April, 1988, George Bush flew into Los Angeles to woo Reagan's "kitchen cabinet." "This is the topping on the cake," Bush's regional campaign director told the *Los Angeles Times.* The Bush team met at Annenberg's plush Rancho Mirage estate at Sunnylands, California.

It was at the Annenberg mansion that Nixon's cabinet was chosen, and the state's social and contributor registers built over a quarter-century of state political dominance by Ronald Reagan, whose acting career was greatly enhanced by Operation MOCKINGBIRD.

Another trans-Atlantic student of Goebbels was Liz Noelle-Neumann-Maier-Leibnitz, whose presence as a visiting scholar at the University of Chicago caused a furor on campus in 1991 when her Nazi past was aired in the conservative Jewish quarterly *Commentary*.[40] At the outbreak of WWII, Noelle—a "visiting" scholar since 1978—claimed in her 1940 dissertation that Jews, "who have monopolized a large part of America's intellectual life, have concentrated their demagogic capacities on anti-German agitation.... the treatment of the Jews in Germany is portrayed by the American press in a completely distorted manner."

The dissertation was passed off in the U.S. under the title *The Spiral of Silence* as a contemporary study of "bandwagon" theory—based largely on the laboratory experiments of Solomon Asch, a social scientist who posited that people will often revise their own perceptions to agree with status quo opinions. "Mobs," Noelle claims, "are typically aroused by instinctive reactions.... It is on this basis that the Nazi minister of propaganda Goebbels was able to mobilize a full stadium with the rallying call, 'Do you want to have Total War?'"

In the 1930s, she'd been an activist and Hitler Youth leader. Noelle ran a series of Nazi student organizations, managed to survive arrest by the Army's Counter-Intelligence Corps in 1947 for her wartime propaganda efforts, and founded a public opinion polling agency, the *Institut fuer Demoskopie*. As late as 1991, a poll conducted by the agency asked Germans whether the Jews have "too much influence in this country."

She went on to become an adviser to Helmut Kohl and the 1990 recipient of the Helen Dinerman Award for "outstanding contributions of scholarship" to the World Association for Public Opinion Research.

In 1949, MOCKINGBIRD's Phil Graham and John Hayes, vice president of the *Post's* electronic media division, bought into CBS radio, an arrangement approved by FCC chairman Wayne Coy. It was Coy who negotiated the establishment of the CIA-anchored Radio Free Europe in Germany earlier in the year. Walter Cronkite, a former military intelligence officer, and in the postwar period UPI's Moscow correspondent, was lured to CBS by Phil Graham.[41]

The script for the charade of the CIA's propaganda war was written in 1955 by David Sarnoff, RCA's chairman of the board. Media historian Shawn Parry-Giles writes in the *Western Journal of Communication* that the 42-page plan, entitled "Program for a Political Offensive Against World Communism," recommended: "America's propaganda could be proliferated overseas via television and other media sources. Sarnoff argued that 'no means of communication should be ignored in America's propaganda efforts,' including official and private channels. Sarnoff's underlying assumption was that the 'best and surest way to prevent a Hot War [was] to win the Cold War,' [with] propaganda as the primary 'weapon.'"[42]

Television presented the intelligence world with unprecedented potential for propagandizing, even prying, in the age of Big Brother.

George Orwell glimpsed the possibilities when he installed omniscient surveillance technology in *1948,* a dystopian novel re-christened *1984* for the first edition published in the U.S. by Harcourt, Brace.

Operation Octopus was in full swing by 1948, a surveillance program that turned any television set with tubes into a transmitter with a range of 25 miles. Agents of Octopus could pick up audio and visual images with the equipment. Hale Boggs was investigating Operation Octopus at the time of his disappearance in the midst of the Watergate probe.[43]

The idea was revived in a Nixon administration study prepared by its Office of Science and Technology recommending the use of "telescreens" for surveillance purposes. The proposal was discovered by Congressman William Moorhead, who decried the plan to "manufacture and installation of special FM receivers in every home radio and television set, boat and automobile, which could be automatically turned on by the government to contact every citizen, whether awake or asleep." The drawback with existing surveillance devices, administration technocrats complained, was the lack of an essential "wake-up capability."[44]

Orwellian, obviously—but the programming of minds steeped in the "CIA culture" was equally intrusive, if a bit more subtle. A Hydra of private foundations sprang up to finance the propaganda push. One of them, Operations and Policy Research, Inc. (OPR), received hundreds of thousands of dollars from the CIA through private foundations and trusts. OPR research was the basis of a television series broadcast by public television stations in New York and Washington, D.C. in 1964, *Of People and Politics,* a "study" of the American political system in 21 weekly installments.[45]

Meanwhile, in Hollywood, the visual cortex of the Beast, the same CIA/Mafia combination that formed Cap Cities sank its claws into film studios and labor unions. Johnny Rosselli had been pulled out of the Army during the war by a criminal investigation of Chicago mobsters in the film industry. The CIA mob functionary, murdered shortly after his testimony at a closed

Watergate hearing, played sidekick to Harry Cohn, the Columbia Pictures mogul. Cohn visited Italy's Benito Mussolini in 1933, and upon his return to Hollywood remodeled his office after the dictator's.[46] The only honest job his pal Rosselli ever held was assistant purchasing agent (and a secret investor) at Eagle Lion productions, run by Bryan Foy, a former producer for 20th Century Fox. Rosselli, Capone's man in California, passed a fortune in Mafia investments to Cohn.[47]

Other Mafia dons found lifelong friends in Hollywood. Bugsy Siegel pooled gambling investments with Billy Wilkerson, publisher of *Hollywood Reporter*.[48] And in 1952, at MCA, Actors' Guild president Ronald Reagan—a movie idol recruited by MOCKINGBIRD's Crusade for Freedom to raise funds for the resettlement of East European Nazi Quislings in the U.S.—signed a secret waiver of the conflict-of-interest rule with the mob-controlled studio, in effect granting it a labor monopoly on early television programming.[49] In exchange, executives of MCA made Reagan a part owner of the company. The political bonds were tight. MCA Chairman Lew Wasserman was Reagan's agent in Hollywood and the studio's board of directors has been represented by politicians from both parties.

In 1987, historian C. Vann Woodward, writing in the *New York Times*, reported that Reagan "fed the names of suspect people in his organization to the FBI secretly and regularly enough to be assigned 'an informer's code number, T-10.' His FBI file indicates intense collaboration with producers to 'purge' the industry of subversives." [50]

The Mafia's hold on Hollywood periodically burst into headlines with politically-embarrassing results. In December of 1988, the president of MCA's Home Video Division, Eugene Giaquinto, was accused by the FBI of funneling corporate payoffs to Ed "The Conductor" Sciandra, believed to be Giaquinto's uncle and the alleged underboss of Pennsylvania's Buffalino crime family. FBI agents reported in sworn affidavits, based on wiretaps of the company's executive offices, that the money was laundered by North Star Graphics in Clifton, New Jersey, a company that held a $12–15 million a year contract to package MCA video cassettes. The FBI investigation centered on Giaquinto, Martin Bacow, a Hollywood labor consultant, and retired Los Angeles Police Detective John St. John, formerly an icon of the LAPDs organized crime intelligence section. A second connection to the LAPD was Giaquinto's attorney, Richard Crane, former chief of the department's Organized Crime Strike Force. Today, Crane is full or part owner of five gambling casinos in Nevada and Colorado.[51]

The wiretaps led the FBI to a self-described CIA asset, Robert Booth Nichols, a suspect in the murder of journalist Danny Casolaro, found slashed to death with a broken beer bottle in the bathtub of a West Virginia Sheraton hotel in 1991. Nichols, under oath, has described himself as an eccentric entrepreneur and intelligence genius. In March, 1993, in a civil suit waged against the L.A. Police Department, Nichols charged the cops with interfering in a huge overseas arms sale. From the witness stand he waved correspondence on White House stationery and photographs of himself in the company of foreign political and military dignitaries. He informed the jury that he had operated for nearly 20 years in the service of the CIA. The FBI affidavit alleges that during a July 15, 1987 stakeout on Sunset Strip, agents saw Giaquinto, then under investigation, hand a box to Robert Booth Nichols. The affidavit also mentioned that "Nichols may have been associated with the Gambino LCN [*La Cosa Nostra*] family in New York City."

The Justice Department inquiry set out to determine whether Giaquinto, Nichols and others were "buying or selling stocks by the use of manipulative or deceptive practices." In 1988, after Giaquinto resigned from the board of Meridian International Logistics, Inc., a firm controlled by Nichols, he took a sudden "leave of absence" from MCA, never to return.[52]

The name Robert Booth Nichols, reported the *Los Angeles Times* on March 21, 1993, also "surfaced in a House Judiciary Committee report on possible malfeasance in the Justice Department during the Reagan era. The report also linked Nichols to an aborted business venture at the Cabazon Indian Reservation in Indio which, he declared on the witness stand, dealt with the manufacture of machine guns to sell to the Nicaraguan Contras." To underscore his client's credibility,

Nichols' lawyer introduced in court a flood of paper indicating that he had worked on numerous ventures with prominent individuals. They included Robert Maheu, Howard Hughes' former right-hand man; Michael McManus, an aide to President Reagan; Clint Murchison, then the owner of the Dallas Cowboys, and George Pender, an executive with a worldwide engineering company. Nichols testified about discussions he had with a White House aide on the rebuilding of Lebanon while he was affiliated with Meridian's predecessor, Santa Monica-based First Intercontinental Development Corp., [a firm that] supposedly specialized in secret foreign construction projects for the U.S. government. Nichols also testified that he had no visible income for more than 15 years except for the living expenses he claimed he was receiving from unnamed CIA keepers.[53]

In 1988, the Justice Department assigned a seasoned criminal investigator to the U.S. attorney's office in Los Angeles. A year later he charged Hollywood spell-weaver Joseph Isgro, a record promoter and the executive producer of *Hoffa*, with fraud, among other charges. The trial got underway with the usual courtroom disputes and appeals, then stopped dead. There were no further developments in the case because, without a word of explanation to the press, a prosecutor in the case was quietly suspended in the Summer of 1995 and made the target of a criminal investigation himself. Isgro's attorney, Donald Re, an organized crime specialist, filed for dismissal, protesting that his client had a right to a speedy trial. The government countered that the delays were caused by the prosecutor's suspension. His office was sealed by dictate of the court.

The federal petition also claimed, somewhat lamely, that the probe of the prosecutor's own organized crime activity excluded the possibility of consulting directly with him about the Isgro case.[54] In fact, the Justice Department proved too soaked in its own corrupt practices to try Isgro. Six volumes of testimony from a government witness, Dennis DiRicco, conflicted with statements he'd made at his own trial a year before. Prosecutors withheld DiRicco's testimony from Isgro's defense attorneys. With the trial at an indefinite standoff, Judge James Ideman was forced to grant the motion for dismissal—"with prejudice" against the federal prosecutors for "outrageous government misconduct."[55]

Hollywood still crawls with operatives, not to mention organized crime. When Italian financier Ginacarlo Parretti set out to fund his purchase of MGM in October 1990, the deal was brokered by Joe Kelso, a self-styled financier with reported ties to the CIA (he appears in Oliver North's notebooks), and members of the Knights of Malta, O.S.J. in New York (a fraternal order unrelated to the eleventh-century Knights affiliated with the Vatican).[56]

Fox television has its roots in Metromedia Co., founded by German-born John Kluge, an Army intelligence officer in the Second World War. Kluge bought his first radio station in 1946 and went on to become one of the world's richest man with a personal fortune of $5.6 billion.[57]

In the print media, to quote former *Newsweek* editor Malcolm Muir to Carl Bernstein in 1977: "I do think in those days the CIA kept pretty close touch with *all* responsible reporters."

They continued to "keep in touch," throughout and beyond the Cold War, and so did their publishers. No one in the industry was more comfortable in the world of black bag jobs and foreign intrigues than Franklin Murphy, CEO of Times Mirror Square, the parent of the *Los Angeles Times*. Murphy was also the chancellor of UCLA throughout the 1960s, and he was a director of four multi-nationals—BankAmerica, Ford Motor Co., Hallmark Cards and Norton Simon,

Inc.. He was also the president of the Ahmanson Foundation, chairman of the J. Paul Getty Trust, a trustee of the University of Pennsylvania (like UCLA, a haunt of mind control research in the 1960s) and the Carnegie Institution. There was a decided editorial conflict-of-interest in his ties to the CIA and the Pentagon: The newspaper's ranking executive was a member of the Foreign Intelligence Advisory Board, the Federal Commission on Government Security, and served on the board of consultants of the National War College and the board of visitors of the U.S. Air Force Air University.[57]

The editorial pages were planted with "scholars" picking solemnly through national security issues in the "think tanks," propaganda machines that crank out pre-fab opinions to program public opinion for military-industrial clients. The American Enterprise Institute (AEI), a spook clearing-house, draws heavily on "scholars" from the intelligence pool. The current director of Asian studies at the AEI is James Lilly, a former assistant secretary of defense for security affairs, a veteran of the NSC and director of operations at the CIA with a total of 27 years under his belt. William Colby of the Phoenix Program was "an old friend."

In January 1996, Lilly told a Senate committee: "Journalists, I think, you don't recruit them. We can't do that. They've told us not to do that. But you certainly sit down with *your* journalists, and I've done this and the Station Chief has done it, others have done it—it's a *wonderful* way of finding out what's happening in a country, whether it's Steve Muffson or Patrick Tyler of the *Times* or Debbie Wong of ABC, you've *got* to keep in touch with these people."[59]

At the time of MOCKINGBIRD's conception by Allen Dulles, a bastion of social conditioning and disinformation was set up at Marquette University, the Interuniversity Consortium for Political and Social Research. The Consortium was an appendage of the Institute for Social Research at Michigan University. Early projects were funded by the military, including one Air Force study of the most effective approaches to propagandizing the Soviet Union.[60]

Newsweek, an early MOCKINGBIRD publication, was—and is—on cozy terms with the intelligence sector. In the 1950s, Dulles appointed an agent to deal regularly with the magazine's reporters. Muir declared, "I had a number of friends in the Allen Dulles organization."

The weekly dropped into MOCKINGBIRD's roost in 1961. The magazine was purchased from the Astor Foundation and New York Governor Harriman for a song. David Halberstam called it "one of the great *steals* of contemporary journalism." *Newsweek* was worth an estimated $15 million at the time, but ultimately no more than $75,000 actually changed hands.[61] As it happened, financier Gates W. McGarrah, the grandfather of Dick Helms, the Agency's director in the 60s, sat on the board of directors of the Astor Foundation. The Post's Ben Bradlee had been tipped that the magazine was to be placed on the block by his friend Helms—who'd heard of the sale from his grandfather.[62]

Any illusion that *Newsweek* exercises journalistic independence from the fetters of corporate and governmental influence is easily dispelled by a glance at the boardroom. *Washington Post/Newsweek* director Richard Simmons sits on the board of Union Pacific Railroad. James Burke, a director of IBM and the Prudential Insurance Co., recently sat on the board of *Newsweek's* parent company. In 1985, Cap Cities purchased ABC for $3.5 billion. Eighteen percent of the Cap Cities stock was transferred to the portfolio of Warren Buffett, a major investor in the *Post*. Barbara Scott Preiskel, *Post/Newsweek's* media conglomerate director, has been a director of Textron, General Electric and the Mutual Life Insurance Co.. The *Post* company and Cap Cities are both currently represented by the Wilmer, Cutler and Pickering law firm run by Lloyd Cutler, a Nixon crony, attorney to the Pharmaceutical Manufacturers' Association and the mentor of Clinton appointee Zoé Baird, whose bid to run the Justice Department was spiked by Congress to hoots of indignation over a minor tax violation.[63]

The CIA's infiltration of the media was such a stunning success that the executive branch established a propaganda machine of its own, Operation Candor, based on C.D. Jackson's recommendations for creating a "national will" in support of military objectives, created to perform what James M. Lambie, Jr., special assistant in the White House office, referred to as "a job of persuasion or indoctrination or propaganda." Shawn Parry-Giles, a professor of communications at Monmouth College in Illinois, combed through correspondence archived at the Dwight Eisenhower Library in 1996 and cobbled together the hidden history of a propaganda machine from its inception in the imagination of C.D. Jackson—a well-oiled machine that still thrums softly behind the headlines of the present day:

> [A] primary tactic of Operation Candor involved the domestic news media. A July 8, 1953 White House central files plan advised that the scope of Operation Candor be "extended to include ... support by newspaper and magazine publishers, editors, columnists and writers." In fact, the first initiative of this expansive campaign involved the "immediate exploitation [of] U.S. domestic press, radio, television, and newsreels." In order to achieve such exploitation, Abbott Washburn [deputy director of America's propaganda program at the time] requested that "top opinion molders [be] contacted." Those earmarked for inclusion were the heads of

national organizations, top journalists, columnists, commentators, educators. To further insure the requisite coverage, the campaign organizers planned a "confidential briefing at [the] White House of top media executives of TV and radio network presidents ... magazine publishers, etc." The media could provide what the organizers of the propaganda campaign refer to as a "multiplying effort" insuring the massive distribution of the administration's message.[64]

The shaping of a "public will" was undertaken by Eisenhower's contacts in the media, among them familiar publishers, advertising executives and network CEOs, including Henry Luce of *Time,* Helen Rogers Reid, owner of the *New York Herald Tribune,* William Robinson, publisher of the *Herald Tribune* and Arthur Sulzberger, publisher of the *New York Times.*"[65]

Over the years, Operation MOCKINGBIRD and its spin-off efforts have left a maze of tracks across the corporate media's Monopoly board. A quarter-century after the program was conceived, Representative Otis Pike (D-NY), chairman of the House Select Committee on Intelligence, pried open the lid on one of Langley's most sensitive black boxes—the takeover of the American press by the virtual government—in public hearings. The committee's findings proved so incendiary that the House voted down its release until the White House could censor it. Pike reports that the CIA's special counsel, outraged by the Pike Committee's to approval of the report, threatened to gutter his career. The counsel told one of Pike's principal investigators: "Pike will pay for this—you wait and see. I'm serious. There will be political retaliation. Any political ambitions in New York that Pike had are through. We will *destroy* him for this."[66] Both Pike and his fellow CIA inquisitor Frank Church were defeated in their bids for re-election, due largely to adverse publicity from MOCKINGBIRD's Op-Ed branch.

And with their defeat a republic rose from the window dressing of the "American Century." Then and now, most consumers of the corporate media were totally unaware of the influence the CIA has on their own beliefs. A network anchorman in time of national crisis is an instrument of psychological warfare in the CIA culture. He is a creature from the national security sector's chamber of horrors. For this reason, consumers of the corporate press have reason to examine their basic beliefs and attitudes about government and life in the parallel universe of these United States.

Notes

1. John Ranelagh, *The Agency—The Rise and Decline of the CIA,* New York: Simon and Schuster, 1986, p. 556.

2. Deborah Davis, *Katherine the Great: Katherine Graham and the Washington Post,* Bethesda, MD: Zenith Press, 1987, p. 138. Before his suicide, Philip Graham had been confined at Chestnut Lodge in Rockville, Maryland, a "private psychiatric hospital"—and a thriving mind control laboratory—immediately before he shot himself in the head. The hospital is staffed by military and CIA doctors, and researchers for the NIMH and the FDA. "In reality," wrote the late political researcher Mae Brussell in her notes, "Chestnut Lodge is a profit-making research prison.... Allen Dulles's son was confined [there] ... CIA personnel were assigned to 'nurse him.' Administrative head of the institution: [Col. Louis McColler] a retired Army colonel."

3. Davis, p. 139.

4. Carl Bernstein, "The CIA and the Media," *Rolling Stone,* October 20, 1977.

5. Daniel Sheehan interview, WBAI-FM, San Francisco, transcript posted to the alt.activism newsgroup, message ID: 1992Nov11. 124208.11887@murdoch.acc. Virginia.edu.

6. CIA Base entry from First Principles, August 1982 number, p. 11.

7. Fitzhugh Green, *American Propaganda Abroad,* New York: Hippocene Books, 1968, pp. 61–70.

8. Davis, p. 234.

9. David Wise and Thomas B. Ross, *The Invisible Government,* New York: Random House, 1964, pp. 325–27.

10. William Blum, *The CIA: A Forgotten History,* London: Zed Books Ltd., 1986, p. 114.

11. "An Insufficiency of Frankness," *Nation,* May 29, 1967, p. 678.

12. Matthew D'Ancona, "Why I am Still Fighting My Cold War," (Irving Kristol interview), *London Times,* April 9, 1993, p. 12.

13. Alexander Werth, "Literary Bay of Pigs," *Nation,* June 5, 1967, p. 678.

14. Philip Agee and Louis Wolf, *Dirty Work: The CIA in Western Europe,* New York: Dorset Press, 1978, p. 206.

15. Blum, pp. 127–28.

16. Murray Waas, "Covert Charge," *Nation,* June 19, 1982, p. 738.

17. Sean Gervasi, "CIA Covert Propaganda Capability," *Covert Action Information Bulletin* (32) Summer 1989, pp. 64–65. Also, "Micaj Sifry amd Robert Friedman, "From CIA Intern to '*The New York Times,*'" *Village Voice,* March 27, 1990, p. 31 on.

18. CIABase entry from *First Principles,* September 1977, p. 9. Also, *Washington Post,* September, 1977, p. 9.

19. George Seldes, *1,000 Americans*, New York: Boni & Gaer, 1947, p. 94.

20. George Seldes, *Never Tire of Protesting*, New York: Lyle Stuart, 1968, p. 91.

21. Fred Landis, "The CIA and Reader's Digest," *Covert Action Information Bulletin* (29) Winter 1988, p. 42.

22. Andy Boehm, "The Seizing of the American Broadcasting Company," *L.A. Weekly*, February 26, 1987.

23. Dan E. Moldea, *Interference: How Organized Crime Influences Professional Football*, New York: William Morrow, 1989, pp. 129 & 458.

24. Ibid., p. 458.

25. Ibid., p. 177.

26. Boehm.

27. Wise and Ross, p. 313.

28. Ibid., p. 317.

29. Bernstein.

30. John Loftus, *The Belarus Secret*, New York: Alfred A Knopf, 1982, p. 107.

31. George Seldes, *Witness to a Century: Encounters with the Noted, the Notorious, and the Three SOBs*, New York: Ballantine, 1978, p. 363.

32. Ibid.

33. Sarah L. Shamley, compiler, "Television Interviews, 1951–1955: A Catalog of Longine's *Chronoscope* Interviews in the National Archives," National Archives and Record Administration, Washington, D.C., 1990.

34. Marvin Bensman, "A History of Radio Program Collecting," University of Memphis Department of Commuication release.

35. Loftus., p. 132–33.

36. Ian Sayer and Douglas Botting, *Nazi Gold—The Story of the World's Greatest Robbery and its Aftermath*, New York: Congdon & Weed, 1984, pp. 92–93.

37. Ibid., pp. 221–22.

38. Ibid., p. 183.

39. Dan E. Moldea, *Dark Victory: Ronald Reagan, MCA, and the Mob*, New York: Penguin, pp. 84–85.

40. Leo Bogart, "The Pollster & the Nazis," *Commentary*, August, 1991, pp. 43–49.

41. Davis, p. 187–88.

42. Shawn Parry-Giles, "'Camouflaged' Propaganda: The Truman and Eisenhower administrations' covert manipulation of news," *Western Journal of Communication*, Vol. 60: April 1, 1996, p. 146.

43. John Judge interview, *Prevailing Winds Research*, Santa Barbara, CA.

44. David Wise, *The Politics of Lying*, New York: Random House, 1973, p. 186.

45. John S. Friedman, "Public TV's C.I.A. Show," *Nation*, July 19–26, 1980, p. 77.

46. Charles Rappleye and Ed Becker, *All American Mafioso: The Johnny Rosselli Story,* New York: Doubleday, 1991, p. 57. On Rosselli's status in the Mafia pecking order, see Ronald Brownstein, *The Power and the Glitter,* New York: Vintage, 1990, p. 163.

47. Ibid.

48. Ibid., p. 119.

49. C. Vann Woodward, "The President and Us," *New York Times Book Review,* January 11, 1987, p. 28. Reagan held on to the office of Guild president longer than anyone, from 1947 to 1952, and again, 1959–1960. "Under Mr. Reagan's leadership," Woodward noted, "the guild acted in concert with management allied with one union affiliated with the guild to break another and more democratic union also affiliated with it. Mr. Reagan seems to have acted [as a strikebreaker} doing the will of the producers."

50. Ibid.

51. Bob Feldman, "Newsweek Magazine's CIA Connection," *Downtown* (New York weekly), February 17, 1993.

52. "MCA Official Suspected of Funneling Funds to Mafia," *Los Angeles Times,* December 13, 1988. Also, Knoedelseder, Murphy and Soble, "Prosecutor Benched After Getting His Man," *Los Angeles Times,* January 20, 1989. Also, John Emshwiller, "U.S. Probe of Mob Influence in Hollywood is Stalled," *Wall Street Journal,* November 8, 1989. For more on Richard P. Crane, see Daryl Kelley, "Campaign Fund Laundering Probe Started," *Los Angeles Times,* June 23, 1993, p. B-1.

53. Henry Weinstein and Paul Feldman, "Trial Offers Murky Peek into World of Intrigue," *Los Angeles Times,* March 21, 1993, p. A-3.

54. John Emschwiller, "Federal Prosecutor in Los Angeles is Quietly Suspended Amid Probe," *Wall Street Journal,* April 22, 1996, p. B-9.

55. Jube Shiver, Jr., "Judge Abruptly Ends Payola Case Against Five," *Los Angeles Times,* September 5, 1990, p. A-1.

56. Alan Citron and Michale Cieply, "Financing Details Add Bizarre Twist to MGM Saga," *Los Angeles Times,* April 24, 1991, p. D-1.

57. Joe Taylor, "Nation's Richest Man Says He's Just Been Lucky," *Honolulu Advertiser,* October 14, 1990.

58. Myrna Oliver, "Franklin D. Murphy Dies; L.A. Civic, Business Leader," *Los Angeles Times,* June 17, 1994, p. A-1.

59. James Lilly testimony, transcript from the Hearing of the Commission on the Roles and Capabilities of the U.S. Intelligence Community, Room SD-106, Dirkson Senate Office Building, January 19, 1996.

60. Jim DiEugenio, "MOCKINGBIRD: The Next Generation," *Probe: Newsletter of the Citizens for Truth About the Kennedy Assassination,* vol. 3: no. 3, March–April, 1996, p. 13.

61. Feldman.

62. Ibid.

63. On Cutler, Robert N. Winter-Berger, *The Washington Pay-Off: An Insider's View of Corruption in Government*, New Jersey: Lyle Stuart, pp. 213–14. Also, on Baird and Cutler, Russ Baker, "CIA: Out of Control," *Village Voice*, September 10, 1991.

64. Parry-Giles cites *Memorandum on a public information program in support of Operation Candor*, (1953, July), White House Central Files (Confidential File), Box 12, Dwight D. Eisenhower Library, 1–6.

65. Ibid.

66. Agee and Wolf, p. 22. As for Pike's committee, it fell apart, according to Ranelagh: "President Ford paid particular attention to the demands for documents and information made by Pike, bringing in the attorney general on several occasions to advise if the demands should be met. When the attorney general said no, Ford witheld the requested information. The House Select Committee finally imploded with internal rivalries, its unfinished report leaked to the press in January 1976." *The Agency*, p. 595.

Addendum: MOCKINGBIRD UK, the Rise of Margaret Thatcher & the CIA's London Operations

England's answer to Operation MOCKINGBIRD was as ambitious an experiment in social conditioning as the original—and the stench of the CIA rose in England when the can of worms was peeled open by *The New Statesman* in March 1995:

> The political playing field of the postwar world was tipped to the right by the secret support of Whitehall's cold warriors for "politically correct" writers, academics and politicians. And, scandalously, the government is still refusing to reveal the extent of these operations. Key files are held back from the Public Records Office, long after they should have been released under the 30-year rule.
>
> The key agency in all this was the Foreign Office's Information Research Department (IRD), set up in 1948 as a secret anti-Communist propaganda department [with] 400 staff based at Riverwalk House on the South Bank, with an annual budget of £1 million.... It was also involved in various covert operations—attempting to influence the choice of leadership in the former colonial countries, interfering in domestic trade unions and mounting other black propaganda exercises that could in no way be described as anti-Communist.
>
> This continued well into the 1970s. For example, Colin Wallace, the former

British army information officer in Belfast, has told how IRD officers planted anti-IRA stories in the British and foreign press. These were straightforward disinformation, for example claiming that the KGB was running the IRA.

IRD was very much a creature of MI6. Many of its staff were intelligence officers. The last head of IRD was Ray Whitney, who later became a very dry Tory MP. (Within a few months of leaving Whitehall, Whitney was attacking the West's 'sell out to Marxists in southern Africa' in an article in *Free Nation,* an organ of the far-right National Association for Freedom.)

John Ogilvy Rennie, head of IRD from 1953 to 1958, later became head of MI6. IRD operations in Malaya during the crisis of the 1950s were run by Maurice Oldfield, then MI6 station chief in Singapore.

One of the most useful pieces of new evidence about IRD's activities is the recently published autobiography of *Brian Crozier, Free Agent—The Unseen War, 1941–1991.* Crozier, a journalist from the 1940s onwards, during the 1960s ran a London-based news agency, Forum World Features, which was later exposed as a CIA front. In his book, he describes how, after he left the *Economist* in 1964, he was also approached by 'Ronald Franks', an old friend from MI6. After lunch at Frank's club, the Athenaeum, Crozier was taken to MI6's then HQ at Century House.

Crozier: "Franks escorted me to the upper floor, where he introduced me to the head of his department, which dealt with Sino-Soviet questions. This was my first shock. I had met the man, Noel Cunningham (not his real name), several times. That day and on future days, I met a number of people whom I had talked to, in the Travellers and elsewhere, in the belief that they were 'Foreign Office' ... Later on, at Century House, I met a number of non-officials whom I had known for years, whose 'contact' with MI6 was similar to mine. They included academic friends of mine specializing in matters of interest to me, including Vietnam and the Soviet Union." Crozier was hired by MI6 as a part-time consultant for IRD.

IRD's roots lay in the wartime Special Operations Executive (SOE) launched by Winston Churchill to "set Europe ablaze." The great lesson SOE learnt about disinformation was that it worked only if it could be dropped into normally accurate news. Listeners and readers have to believe the output for the carefully placed lie to work. IRD set up a worldwide network of news agencies and radio stations, often connected to apparently independent news media.

One of the first agents recruited by the IRD was Soviet spy Guy Burgess, later fired for drunkenness, but not before he was able to pass on a full account of IRD's operations to Moscow.

Cord Meyer

Family and Personal History: Owned a fortune in sugar interests and real estate. Cord graduated from Yale in December 1942, and joined the Marines with the rank of lieutenant. A Japanese grenade took his sight in one eye while stationed in Guam. (Source: Philip Agee, *Dirty Work*)

In 1945, he attended the charter conference of the United Nations in San Francisco. Two years later he joined the United World Federalists. He was selected one of the ten most outstanding men in America in 1947. (Another was Richard Nixon.) Allen Dulles persuaded him to join the CIA in 1951. Meyer was assigned to the office of the Deputy Director for Plans and reported to Tom Braden (later a "liberal counterbalance" to Pat Buchanon on PBS's *CrossFire*).

Meyer was sent to London in 1973 and ran all CIA operations in Europe. From Ralph McGehee's *CIABase*:

Labor Infiltration: 1960–69. Cord Meyer's International Organizations Division assisted labor ops via AFL-CIO.

Funds to European Labor Unions: CIA opened mail of George Meany, Irving Brown and Jay Lovestone to ensure they were sending CIA funds to European labor contacts.

From Robert Moss, "Arnaud de Borchgrave, Robert Moss and Right-Wing Disinformation," *Covert Action Information Bulletin,* No. 10, pp. 40–41:

The CIA & the Rise of Margaret Thatcher

On his return to Britain, Moss became a speech-writer for a then little-known member of Parliament, Margaret Thatcher. Moss [a propagandist on the CIA payroll] wrote her speech attacking the "Sovietization of Britain," which gave Mrs. Thatcher the nickname "the Iron Lady." Moss became the leading light in the Institute for the Study of Conflict, [which] served as a way of bringing CIA journalists and military intelligence officers together.

Moss founded and became the president of a British version of the *Chilean Comando de Accion Gremial,* the National Association of Freedom. According to the *Guardian* (December 21, 1976), Moss organized the NAFF under the banner of halting the "Sovietization" of Britain through the Labour Government and the influence of the trade unions." It was this ISC that issued the disinformation (57 Labour MPs are Marxists, Soviet plan to Communize Britain, etc.) that provided the catalyst for the formation of the NAFF. The leaders of the NAFF then formed themselves into a Conservative shadow government that is today the Conservative Government.

In 1977, Moss and friends set up a would-be British Intelligence Station for Capitol Hill, a think-tank calling itself the Heritage Foundation....

The New York Times (December 1977) and former FWF writer Russell Warren Howe (*More Magazine,* May 1978) have identified Brian Crozier as a CIA contract agent, and Moss as his protégé. During the time Crozier was working for CIA, he used the journalistic covers of: defense correspondent of the *Daily Telegraph,* director of *Forum World Features,* founder of the Institute for the Study of Conflict, correspondent for *National Review,* publisher of the *London Economist* "Foreign Report," and correspondent for *Soviet Analysis.* As Crozier retired from many of these positions they were all taken over by Moss....

This propaganda was used as cover for two actual crises manufactured at this time—a series of insoluble strikes, and escalating terrorism and counter-terrorism in northern Ireland. From Moss's own handwriting we know that he had two mentors in fomenting these crises, Miles Copeland and Cord Meyer, Jr. Meyer was CIA Station Chief in London at the time and for many years the main figure in charge of the Agency's covert operations; Copeland was formerly head of the Gaming Room on the fourth floor at CIA headquarters, where simulations of strikes were acted out before being implemented in Chile.

NAFF's main activity was to turn strikes from symbolic ritual into covert war. It did so by turning each strike into a traditional testing ground of the ability to resist—not the normal economic demands of unions but "Communist encroachment."

Coordination with military intelligence was facilitated by a leading figure at ISC, Sir Peter Wilkinson who, according to the *Guardian* (July 16, 1976), "was recently the coordinator of intelligence on the Cabinet Office and formerly head of administration at the Ministry of Defense."

Through such contacts Crozier and Moss became instructors in military intelligence training schools.

Brian Crozier's CIA-funded Institute for the Study of Conflict and the British Labor Unions (Source: Philip Agee, *Dirty Work*):

The Institute prepared a special manual on counterinsurgency for the British police and regularly participated in training programs at the National Defense College and the Police College. The Institute's line appears to encourage preemptive surveillance and other measures against a broad range of 'subversives,' a term which could easily include law-abiding trade union militants and anti-establishment intellectuals.

Robert Moss, CIA/NET Propagandist

A sampling of Robert Moss's "conservative" propaganda for National Educational Television (Source NET Programming Press Release): Washington, DC March 17, 1996

AMERICA THE BANKRUPT?

(Commentary by NET President Paul M. Weyrich on *Dateline: Washington*) During NET's Eighth Wonder program this week, the thorny issue of entitlements was the subject of the entire program. Underwritten by the Vernon K. Krieble Foundation, producer ROBERT MOSS explored the explosive growth of entitlements over the past several decades as part of a three part special entitled "America the Bankrupt?"

Among the issues aired on this special broadcast is how the Social Security Trust Fund is handled. Currently that trust fund has a surplus. But that surplus is not invested on behalf of future recipients of Social Security. Rather, that surplus money is used to offset deficit spending in other federal government programs. Therefore, the so-called Trust Fund simply has some IOU notes from the federal government which may or may not be able to pay up when the time comes.

The way the United States handles Social Security is contrasted with the way the same issue is handled in Chile. In that country, where Social Security has been semi-privatized, real money is put aside and invested on behalf of each individual recipient. Needless to say, Chile's Social Security system is on a much sounder basis than our own.

The issue is very relevant to the moment because, as House Appropriations Committee Chairman Bob Livingston told us on Direct Line last week, great progress has been made in getting the non-entitlement portion of the budget under control. But not a thing has been done about the majority of the budget which consists of entitlements. And the growth of entitlements is what has put this nation on the road to bankruptcy.

President Clinton's own Medicare trustees have told the nation that Medicare needs reformation because it is headed for bankruptcy. Yet, President Clinton has refused to budge on any reformation of the system. He portrays himself as the savior of Medicare. But in truth it is quite the opposite. His refusal to even meet the Republican reformers half way on the issue is driving this nation ever closer to insolvency. Clinton is practicing politics of the moment, while some Republicans, at least, have sought to put the system back on a sound basis.

The issue of Social Security itself hasn't even been touched yet by either political party. But in a few years those surpluses, which have been used to hide the real size of the federal deficit, will end. At that point, payments to all Social Security recipients will be in grave danger.

Unless this President and the Congress tackle the issue of entitlements, the other cuts they may make in federal spending will be meaningless. In a few short years entitlements will overwhelm the entire federal budget.

The Vernon K. Krieble Foundation, under the able leadership of Helen Fuscuss, has done the nation a great service by putting the issue of entitlements front and center where it ought to be.

Now we can only hope that those in high office who can see beyond the next election will pay attention. Failure to do so will make these United States into a third world style nation in a very few years.

Re: Moss, Crozier and CIA propaganda in Chile (from Donald Freed, *Death in Washington*, Lawrence Hill & Co, 1980, p. 167):

The CSIS [Center for Strategic and International Studies] published ... *The Stability of the Caribbean*, edited by the British journalist Robert Moss. Moss's book was published jointly with the London-based Institute for the Study of Conflict, with financial support from the Tinker Foundation. Contributors to the book included James Theberge, Brian Crozier, head of the institute, and Moss himself, who was identified as the author of "the forthcoming book, *Chile's Marxist Experiment.*

In January 1977, *The Guardian* (London) and the *New York Times* identified *Chile's Marxist Experiment* as one of the propaganda books produced by the CIA. These articles also revealed that the entire second printing of Moss's book had been purchased by the Chilean military junta at a cost of £55,000, to be given away as part of a propaganda package.

VIRTUAL
GOVERNMENT

Alien Abduction,
Psychic Warfare
and Cult Programming

Military-Corporate,
Academic and
Quasi-Religious Fronts
for Mind Control
Operations in America

Vipers and Daydreams

He looses his hounds on us
Grants us a grave in the air
plays with his vipers and daydreams
     —Paul Celan, "Death Fugue"

Ed Dames, a proprietor of Psi-Tech—a "remote viewing" service in Beverly Hills, California founded by a clique of former intelligence officers—explains to late night radio talk show host Art Bell how the company's sole product—psi—works: "This is a very structured technique, the remote viewer sitting at a desk with a ream of white paper and a pen. Using [remote viewing] protocols, they first perceive a target. They're not told what the target is, only given a random number. Their unconscious minds are taught to do all the work, viewing the target first as sort of a *'thought-ball,'* if you will ...."[1]

"The next stage is sensory perceptions. They elaborate, download and objectify in words and sketches the colors, textures, the smells and taste, the sounds, the temperatures and the dimensions present at the site."

Dames lets on that his psychics constructed clay models of the Unabomber's bombs, "that sort of thing," for a "federal agency." It doesn't come to him that all of this may sound a bit far-fetched, grandiose, the paranormal hard-wired to the trappings of computer science—not to mention blatant disinformation. His firm built clay models when "remote viewing" could, if the "protocols" worked as advertised, have pinpointed the killer's location, supplied the "colors, textures," and so on, of the Unabomber's hutch, even his name. After all, insists Dames, "if the 'target' is a terrorist—Saddam Hussein or Abu Nidal—we go in through the back door. We can be in their minds, in their dreams."

A company brochure reports that Psi-Tech was founded in 1989, employing "a select, technically-qualified group of professional analysts who provide a unique data collection capability not available anywhere else in the world. We are a team of highly-trained remote viewing specialists [who've] developed applied remote viewing into a powerful investigative tool." The FBI and National Security Council have drawn upon the company's services.

Dames delivers a metaphysical Marvel Comics narrative, but assures us this is serious business. During the Gulf Crisis, one Psi-Tech client, "a large company with strategic oil interests in the Mid-East," called on Dames and his telepaths "to provide data and analysis on Saddam himself, his mind (intent, motivation, emotional and behavioral states), to penetrate his war room for information concerning battle plans, operations, force strengths and possible deception schemes, and to provide a six-month general outlook for the Gulf region."

Major Dames claims that human abductees are ferried to Mars for use as slave labor. He has "seen" all of this, of course, by remote viewing "alien" activity. But then, Dames is schooled in intelligence, the former commanding officer of the Army's "Psychic Espionage Unit," a cadré that operated under DIA and Army INSCOM charter.[2]

He is also a chronic confabulator, the chief Plumber of the "Stargate" psychic spying "scandal." He draws his intelligence background from the shadows like the priest's robes Jim Garrison recovered from the closet of David Ferrie. In the past, he acknowledges, "I have been involved in a lot of very, very deep, dark black occult projects." And he admits, "I have never been assigned to a unit that has suffered more ostracism, been looked upon with more *fear*."

He is on familiar terms with "aliens" and the "occult," but his resumé, published in Psi-Tech sales literature, qualifies him for covert military operations spiked with classified psychotronics:

Edward Arthur Dames joined the United States Army in 1967, enlisting as a paratrooper at the age of seventeen. After serving one year as an Airborne Infantryman, Mr. Dames transferred to the Army Security Agency, and was assigned to the Far East to support National Security Agency missions in that part of the world. In 1974, Mr. Dames returned home to attend college, quickly earning a four-year scholarship for academic excellence. After three years as an undergraduate at the University of California, Berkeley, where he double-majored in bioelectronics and Chinese, Mr. Dames joined Berkeley's ROTC program, becoming a Distinguished Military Graduate in 1978.

Newly commissioned as a second lieutenant in Military Intelligence, Dames was sent to be trained as a tactical electronic warfare officer and, for three years, was assigned to Germany to intercept and jam Soviet and Czech communications. From there he was recruited by a scientific and technical military intelligence "black unit," ultimately to direct clandestine operations against high-value foreign targets. He remained in deep cover, travelling worldwide under assumed identities....

Dames explains that he served with three "elite units." His familiarity with advanced technology includes highly-advanced espionage hardware, "boxes in the sky that look down and through buildings," precisely the sort used in certain covert operations, and quite possibly in "remote viewing" exercises as well:

The first [unit], beginning in ... 1980, had me as a targeting officer at the secretary of defense level, at the national agency level. My job there was to choose among America's intelligence collection priorities, mostly—those were weapons of mass destruction—and to select targets, and to engineer penetration missions using any means at my disposal. And *carte blanche*, when it came to funding, orchestrate the successful penetration of those targets—that is, facilities, programs, people, those kinds of things.... I'm talking about intelligence targeting.... They involved boxes in the sky that look down and through buildings, they involved agents underground and training case officers to manage those agents, they involved extremely sophisticated technologies.

But before all of this, in the late 1970s, Dames acknowledges, he served with a unit "associated with the occult. It gave the unit a bad name." [3]

And Dames as well. Wherever one stands in the ESP debate, Psi-Tech was formed in the caul of the intelligence underground's "occult" projects, a world of flying disks, cosmic telepathy, teleportation, out-of-body sojurns and communication with house plants. The "psychic spying" unit, Dames intones with pride (ignoring the compulsory secrecy oath?), has provided services to the CIA, NSA, DIA, DEA, Navy and Air Force under the watch of a board chaired by Army General Stan Hyman, one of several paranormal divisions run by the DIA and the Secretary of the Army, code-named Sun Streak, Grill Flame, Center Lane, Scanate and Stargate. [4]

Dames's allies in the military-metaphysical complex included General Albert Stubblebine, the retired director of Army intelligence (INSCOM), and a Psi-Tech co-founder. Another is David Morehouse, Ph.D, an executive officer of the Second Battalion and deputy of the 82nd Airborne Division until 1994, when he resigned. Morehouse is the author of *Comes the Watcher: The True Story of a Military Psychic Spy,* and *Peace Quest: Visions of Future War,* a glorification of advanced weapons. He is also the producer of a Hanna-Barbara cartoon series, *Peace Force: The Avalon Odyssey,* about aliens defending the galaxy with, again, advanced weapons. Morehouse is also a vice president at Paraview, a television production company with headquarters in Manhattan. [5]

Jim Schnabel, in a feature story about Morehouse commissioned but ultimately rejected by *Esquire,* notes that in the early 1980s the "psychic warrior" was a first lieutenant, [and] served briefly in Panama as the *aide de camp* to Brigadier General Kenneth Leuer. By 1986, Morehouse was a captain in command of a Ranger company. The following year, "apparently thirsting for a sexier assignment, he joined the Army's Intelligence Support Activity (ISA), a hush-hush unit that specialized in quick-reaction intelligence-gathering, covert action, and counter-terrorist missions." At least this is the account pedelled to the public. The ISA is the most secret unit in the Army, and reports of mind control activity have surfaced in connection with it (there is, for instance, a letter to me from a survivor in Atlanta, who reports that the ISA operatives handled her "more gently" than the CIA in a "Manchurian Candidate"-type mind control assignment. She may be disappointed to learn of the CIA watchers who insisted that the ISA was secretly run by the Agency all along, despite the usual denials to Congressional inquiries).

Morehouse is a graduate of the Army's Command and General Staff College. He moved on in 1992 to Fort Bragg—a base of military mind control operations with a long history of participation in projects that would make the Waffen SS pause (such as the Jeffrey MacDonald case, in which the physician's wife and children were butchered after he threatened to turn in members of a mind control cult engaged in heroin smuggling at Fort Bragg, according to his friends and supporters).

The wife of a subordinate, a driver, accused Morehouse at his dishonorable discharge hearing of aggravated sexual harassment. Schnabel writes that Angela Connor (a pseudonym) complained at the tribunal of Morehouse's "strange behavior." She testified that Morehouse slipped into blood-curdling moods. At the dinner table, "he liked to cut her food for her, and 'sometimes asked if he could feed me.'" On a few occasions, he bragged that he could kill her. Once during sex: "He was squeezing my neck with my jugular vein or something and I asked him, 'What are you doing.' He said, 'Oh, I was just rying to find your jugular vein. How does that feel? Do you know how easy it would be for me to *kill* you right now'" He was acting very strange that night and was kind of quiet, too. He kept looking around. I asked him, I said, 'What are you looking for? Why do you keep looking around?" He said, 'I'm looking for a good area, a good set of woods, so I can take you out and tie you up to a tree and murder you.'" A few minutes later, he "started laughing."

Schnabel tracked down witnesses to the sources of claims made in *Psychic Warrior* and found the book to be heavily "fictionalized":

> The book begins with Morehouse, guided by another remote viewer ... psychically visiting a friend who died in a helicopter crash. The anecdote, along with its description of remote viewing as a kind of vivid virtual reality game, is fictional, but it contains a grain of truth: A similar helicopter crash was targeted by Fort Meade remote viewers in the late 1970s. Morehouse presumably heard about the story and decided to make it his own....

To tag every piece of fiction in the Morehouse book would mean commenting on virtually every page. Indeed, both Mel Riley and Lyn Buchanan remember Morehouse telling them that they were not to worry, the whole thing was going to be a novel anyway. Or perhaps, as Ed Dames says, a screenplay, for there is lengthy screenplayish dialogue throughout, and the entire thing seems calculated to push all the New Age and *X-Files* conspiracy buttons in the Hollywood version of reality, from the repeated appearance of an angel to the cynical falsehood that the DIA was using remote viewers to monitor US troops' chemical weapons exposure in the Gulf War...

As I sifted back and forth through all this garbage the other day, with a borrowed copy of *Psychic Warrior,* the final thing to catch my eye was Morehouse's dedication: "To my darling wife Debbie, whose love has nourished and sustained me for longer than I can remember. We are together eternally." I have no doubt that Americans will buy that, in droves, not only at bookstores but in cinemas. Word on the street is that Sylvester Stallone wants to do the movie. People are talking about a budget of $70 million. I can already see Stallone's head trembling with paranormal effort as he tries to psychically scramble the mind of Saddam Hussein or some unlucky cocaine cartel boss. Perhaps blood will run from Stallone's nose, or his ears. And the audience will gape up at the screen, feeding themselves with popcorn, and somewhere Morehouse will be laughing, all the way to the bank.

Morehouse claims he was drafted as a "psychic spy" after he took a bullet in the head: "The son and grandson of military officers, Morehouse had been a straight-up-and-down soldier on a fast-track career in the elite infantry and had reached the rank of captain when he was hit by a stray bullet during a hush-hush training mission in Jordan. His Rangers helmet saved his life: he was knocked out cold, but the bullet did not enter his skull."

We are to believe that the injury endowed Morehouse with profound mental capabilities: "He came to, shook his head and carried on with the mock attack. By evening he had a headache. Later that night he awoke to a vision of dark souls wandering through the rocks, and spoke to an angel. He has been plagued with nightmares and spontaneous 'visions' ever since. His soldier's reaction was to tell nobody. He would scream and thrash about on his bed and would wake up on the lawn panting from fights with strange, demonic creatures. It was only after he was posted to a DIA unit dealing with dirty-trick spying that he let slip his torment to its psychiatrist. The psychiatrist seemed more intrigued than alarmed, and within weeks Morehouse found himself recruited to the ranks of the psychic spies."

> *I get these messages from other planets. I'm apparently some kind of agent from another planet, but I haven't got my orders clearly decoded yet.*
>
> William S. Burroughs

In *Psychic Warrior* there is discussion of the accident, but Schnabel learned that this story, too, is a fantasy. "Morehouse told colleagues about the incident," he found, "but mentioned that it had only given him a headache afterwards. In *Psychic Warrior,* the incident has been transformed into a turning point in Morehouse's life. The trauma from the bullet, we are now told, destabilized his brain and caused him to have a variety of psychic and transcendental experiences, including meetings with an angel."

The occult is a recurring theme in this milieu. "They have no idea what they're dealing with," complains Rod Lewis, a spokesman for the American Federation of Scientists. "Of course, the immediate speculation is that they're dealing with the demonic realm." *Demonic?* "It's a Greek word for 'disembodied intelligence.' Apparently it's something they take very seriously."

But the spirit realm takes a back seat to the technological marvels of the military-intelligence core of virtual government.

One corporation took part in coordination with the CIA, Scientific Applications International Corporation (SAIC), with corporate headquarters in San Diego. SAIC is directed by some of the highest ranking oligarchs of the DoD and intelligence groups: former NSA Director Bobby Ray Inman, former CIA director John Deutch, William Perry, Clinton's secretary of defense from ESL, Inc. (the corporate co-owner of Area 51), Melvin Laird, defense secretary under Nixon, and Donald Kerr, former director of Los Alamos National Laboratory. These men have in common a maudlin interest in advanced technology with military applications, *not* ESP.

The CIA "covets" remote viewing as a source of intelligence, Dames boasts.[6] In real life, the Agency covets his metaphysical cover stories, schizoid tall tales that direct attention from blatant human rights violations. The Taos Hum, he confides, is a 17 hz. "time beacon" that pumps pulses of gravity into space, an invisible lighthouse for time-travelling ETs. Psi-Tech's remote viewers, he says, have located and drawn diagrams of the "alien beacon" of Taos (and all along residents thought it was a classified electromagnetic device attuned to the brain's auditory frequencies). Mars is "super-important"—Psi-Tech's telepaths have supposedly discovered a breed of "alien" from Mars, ferried to earth by wayfarers from a remote civilization known as "The Federation." The time-travelling aliens store their mind control gear in "parking garages" on the moon's surface. Since Psi-Tech has "confirmed" that Bug-Eyes are abducting human beings, out goes the thesis that human scientists are conducting illicit biological experiments and dropping off the subjects with hypnotic/virtual-reality enhanced memories of "aliens" ...

Not to mention mental communication with "aliens" and—many abductees and mind control subjects, even ritual abuse survivors, report it—an awakened "remote viewing" ability. Are they "psychic?" Are "aliens," CIA researchers and cultists somehow stimulating the brain's "third eye?"

They are if the *technology* makes it possible. The mind control fraternity has had devices that broadcast images to the brain for some time, and the linkage of pulsed EM signals with digital "remote viewing" equipment produces this common symptom of "alien" abduction.

Basic components are current in emergent military technology. In England, the Army and RAF are working on a surveillance rig, mentioned briefly in the *Daily Telegraph* on October 9, 1996, that can peer far beyond enemy lines. The surveillance device "uses advances in digital imaging to provide standard and infrared images of the battlefield. It is capable of providing clear pictures from 20 miles and should replace reconnaissance cameras that use film"—and military technology in its class is primitive in comparison with classified exotica. "Remote viewing" devices exist that would make a true "psychic" queasy.

"Oscillatori Telegrafica"

Almost halfway through the Decade of the Brain, an interdisciplinary team of neurobiologists, computer scientists, physicists, and electronics engineers has devised an electronic version of the hippocampus—the brain's center for memory and learning. The research group, led by Theodore Berger, a professor of biomedical engineering at the University of Southern California, first created a computer program whose behavior is identical to the intricate neuronal firings of a rabbit's dentate gyrus, a region of the hippocampus. Next, they hardwired the program into a computer chip.

> *In principle, we have the ability to create an artificial hippocampus, one that might actually function in a living animal or replace a hippocampus damaged by trauma or disease in a human," explains Berger. Now, using neuron cell cultures, the team is working on ways to connect the electronics to living tissue.*
>
> —N. Sankaran, *The Scientist*, June 27, 1994

The paranormal fantasies spun by Dames, a veteran of the CIA's UFO "Working Group," could be interpreted as a blind for illegal mind control experimentation and the harassment of subjects or anyone falling into disfavor with the intelligence community. In fact, the deep history of Psi-Tech is a story of a much larger movement, one that thrives on the spread of religious programming, "alien" invasions and other forms of irrational belief. The surface of the underground movement swarms with seemingly delusional quasi-mystical savants. Beneath, a hidden world of terror—with origins in the waste of warstruck Europe and the beating hearts of some of Nazi Germany's most ruthless military scientists. From these cold chambers exploded many of the mysteries that have since riddled the postwar world.

One sector of the virtual government, the mind control and biocybernetics group, was born in academia. The goal of the research: to gain "control of an individual to the point where he will do our bidding against his will and even against such fundamental laws of human nature as self-preservation."[7]

The Agency's scientific contracts were first handed around by Barnaby Keeney, president of Brown University. In 1951, Keeney took a sabbatical to design a CIA trainee program and a system of fronts to finance covert operations. In 1962 he was named chairman of the Human Ecology Fund, the financial hub of MK-ULTRA.[8]

From "The Modern Era," a chronology of Brown University presidents issued by the school's public relations department:

> Brown President Barnaby C. Keeney was [an] "insider": He had joined the faculty in 1946 as assistant professor of medieval history, then became dean of the Graduate School in 1949 and dean of the College in 1953. But Keeney, a much-decorated combat veteran, [was] blunt and outspoken, and ... ambitious for Brown....
>
> President Barnaby Keeney got the equivalent of a standing ovation at his last Commencement exercises in 1966. The success of the building campaign was a testament to Keeney's skills as a fund-raiser (Wriston said that his "gift for charm-

ing money from flint-like men of substance ... is awe-inspiring") and to Brown's stature, which made it easier to attract large gifts. Citing its potential to "become one of the most important university centers in the country," the Ford Foundation twice honored Brown with major grants during the Keeney years, the first for $7.5 million and the second for $5 million.... Not all the money went into buildings, of course.... Plans for a medical school began to be discussed, and a six-year program leading to a Master of Medical Science degree was established in 1963. He went on to head the newly established National Endowment for the Humanities....

In *Black Issues in Higher Education* (January 11, 1996), former presidential contender Julian Bond discussed Keeney's role in defusing the civil rights movement—in concert with a covert state agency known as the Sovereignty Commission, a coalition of spies that kept files on thousands of civil rights activists—sweeping through Tougaloo College in Mississippi, an African-American academic sanctuary, in the mid-1960s:

Tougaloo was a movement center ... a safe haven that housed an interracial faculty.... Brown and Tougaloo had a cooperative arrangement which proved profitable for the small Mississippi school, securing support from Northern philanthropists. But Brown could not tolerate Tougaloo's involvement in the civil rights movement. Brown's president, Barnaby Keeney, managed to arrange the firing of Tougaloo President Daniel Beittel, who had encouraged students to take an interest in the world beyond their campus. Keeney also ended Tougaloo's association with a movement-inspired literacy project and its involvement in Mississippi's anti-poverty agency, which had long been a thorn in the side of the state's congressional delegation and local white leadership. The Brown president was also on the Central Intelligence Agency payroll, [and] the CIA connection is illustrative of the tangled web of government/academic/philanthropic connections and the Black struggle which remain largely unexplored today.

The newly-christened mind control initiative tended to attract academics of Keeney's caliber (and bigoted sensibilities, a reminder that one of four Nazi doctors participating in terminal experiments in the concentration camps hailed from leading universities).

The prospects for electronic control of the brain were explored in the laboratory sixty years ago, according to *Popular Electronics* (July, 1973), with the invention of a crude "brain-wave detector." In the 1930s, Professor F.

Cazzamalli published a series of papers on "radiations from the mind." Dr. Cazzamalli situated his subjects in a shielded room and shot VHF radio waves through their heads. He claimed to have picked up 'beat frequencies' using an untuned receiver equipped with a diode tube, a fixed capacitor, an antennae and a sensitive light-beam galvanometer: "He told an astounded world that his subjects would hallucinate when under the influence of his 'oscillatori telegrafica.'"

Tom Jaski, a highly-respected engineer of the 1930s, duplicated Dr. Cazzamalli's experiment with a low-power oscillator sweeping at 300–600 MHz: "His subjects could not see the dial. They were told to sound off as soon as they felt something unusual. At a certain frequency range—varying between 380MHz to 500 MHz—the subjects repeatedly indicated points with exact accuracy in as many as 14 out of 15 trials. At these 'individual' frequencies, the same subjects announced having experienced pulsing sensations in the brain, ringing in the ears and an odd desire to bite the experimenters."

Forty years later, the Department of the Army sanctioned the torture of civilians in a 1972 report entitled *Controlled Offensive Behavior—U.S.S.R.*, a review of Russian scientific literature based upon 500 studies on the biological effects of "Super-high frequency electromagnetic oscillations": "SHF may be used as a technique for altering human behavior. Lethal and non-lethal effects have been shown to exist. In certain non-lethal exposures, definite behavioral changes have occurred. There also appears to be a change in mammals when exposed to SHF in sensitivity to sound, light and olfactory stimuli."

The purpose of invasive electromagnetic brain experimentation, according to the report—which seems on hindsight to have cleared the way for experiments on unconsenting subjects—was perceived by the Pentagon as the creation of "one or more of several possible [mental] states in the conscious or unconscious areas of the brain. The ultimate goal of controlled offensive behavior might well be *the total submission of one's will to some outside force.*"

Two years later, Michael Shapiro, a professor of law at the University of Southern California, reported in the *Southern California Law Review:* "Psychotropic drugs, electrical stimulation of the brain (ESB) by electrodes, psychosurgery and organic conditioning techniques are now available for use by the state in controlling criminal, sick or otherwise aberrant or unwanted behavior."[9]

One 1982 Air Force study mustered then current data on bio-technology and EMR brain experimentation, predicting that "specially generated radiofrequency radiation (RFR) fields may pose powerful and revolutionary military threats. Electroshock therapy indicates the ability of induced electric current to completely interrupt mental functioning for short periods of time ... and to restructure emotional response."

Air Force officials warmed to the idea that "a rapidly scanning RFR system could provide an effective stun or kill capability over a large area," and cooed that low-level radio frequencies could be used to "sensitize large military groups to extremely dispersed amounts of biological or chemical agents to which the unradiated population would be immune."

The mind control syndicate has long been fascinated with the effects of extremely low frequencies (ELF) on human biology. Jack Anderson's column for July 31, 1986 notes: "For years, ELF research suffered under the cloud of 'parapsychology,' into which it was lumped with such cockamamie concepts as time-warp machines and intercontinental mind-reading. Unfortunately for the human race, there's nothing silly about the potential effects of very low-level electromagnetic radiation on the nervous system."

Most studies of mind control focus on experiments conducted 20–40 years ago—as if the CIA abandoned mind machines because a few loose secrets tumbled out in Congressional testimony. The clandestine operations branches are, in fact, very interested in EM brain manipulation. A 30-year lag yawns between declassified projects and the most advanced technology known to the American proletariat.

Contemporary military cybernetics dwarfs Orwell's most totalistic techno-fantasies.

Suddenly, as though machined from thin air, "dual-use" spin-offs from the mind control lab appear in the hands of law enforcement. One such device is the Passive Millimeter Wave Imager, an instrument with a range of 90 feet that can peer into clothing to find a concealed weapon or contraband. Two models of the Imager, a creation of the Millimetrix Corporation of Massachusetts, are under development. The large model, roughly the size of a shoebox, is mounted on a patrol car and pointed at an unsuspecting target. The gadget does not use X-rays; it collects electromagnetic waves emitted by human flesh. Anything that blocks the EM radiation—a pistol or knife—or emits an attenuated signal—a bag of cocaine or plastic explosive—is highlighted on a small screen in the patrol car. Walls do not block the signal.

Headlines like this one from the AP newswire on October 2, 1996 are increasingly common: "The Department of Health and Human Services awarded $1.9 million to the University of Pennsylvania this week to begin clinical trials of imaging processes developed to spot missiles. The federally funded trials will analyze at least 2,000 breast cancer cases, comparing standard mammograms to the digitally-enhanced pictures produced by the new technology."

Readers of *Physical Science Letters* for August 21, 1995 were treated to the latest plan for "a silicon implant with a lot of nerve," concerning the work of Drs. Peter Fromherz and Alfred Stett at the Max Planck Institute of Biochemistry in Munich, Germany. Fromhertz and Stett have developed a silicon chip that directly stimulates a single nerve cell without damaging it. By propagating a voltage pulse from a tiny spot on the cell membrane, a neuronal impulse can be triggered. Information flow in the opposite direction, from cell to chip, is accomplished using "neuron transistors" which pick up nerve impulses and transform them to electrical impulses on a silicon chip.

Victims of quasi-military EM experimentation report the transmission of crystal clear images and auditory effects.

From the Pentagon's classified psycho-technological arsenal came a "soft kill solution" promoted by Paul Evancoe, formerly deputy director of the State Department's counterterrorism division. The *Bulletin of the Atomic Scientists* reported in March, 1994 that Evancoe is eager to put non-lethals in the hands of SWAT teams and local police departments, although he warns their use could create legal complications: "Several 'disabling technologies' employ high-intensity strobe lights that flash at or near human brain-wave frequency, causing disorientation and nausea." Bystanders, of course, are not immune from the effects of the strobe.

The Yerkes Primate Center at Emory University has long been a busy hive for CIA mind control activity. In its heyday, the center was run by Dr. Geoffrey Bourne.

Bourne's family pedigree, from the notes of late political researcher Mae Brussell: "Trained at Oxford. Long career in intelligence related activities. Peter [his son] spent two years in Vietnam profiling U.S. special forces under stress, then set up counseling programs for turning veterans into Manchurian Candidate-type assassins *á la* John Hinckley. (Califano, partner of E.B. [Edward Bennett] Williams, Hinckley atty. [twice offered the position of CIA director; the mentor of Michael Tigar, an attorney in the Oklahoma City bombing case].)"

Dr. Peter G. Bourne, his son, was brought into the center by his father. Peter was a "special adviser on drug abuse" to the presidential administrations of Nixon, Ford and Carter. Dr. Bourne was forced to resign the office in 1979 when he was caught prescribing Quaalude prescriptions for Carter's staffers.

The timeline resumes: "Bourne met Carter, 1969: Carter, conservative, running for governor. Bourne directed mental health center in Atlanta ghetto. 1971: Asked Carter if he would 'run for president.' ... Bourne goes to Washington to work for Nixon on 'drug abuse' (Rebozo, Hunt, Liddy, Vegas, Sindona,

Marcinkus, Nixon, Italian mob). Mary King Bourne, $50,000 for ACTION, a director of Peace Corps. 1977: George Bush CIA director. Grenada, Medical school. 1978: Rep. Leo Ryan went to Guyana.... April, Prime Minister Bishop, elected in Grenada. London Attorney. CIA death plot on Bishop. Geoffrey Bourne, his father: Vice-chancellor, previously primatologist, expert on apes. Studying effects of drugs, sensory deprivation, behavioral modification on apes, surrogates for human beings. Bourne retained his affiliation to Yerkes Division of Pathology and Immunology even after he transferred to St. George's. Bourne views the black population of Caribbean as animals, equivalent to the apes he studied."

In 1978, Peter Bourne was accused by liberal activists in New York with the mystery murder of a physician-activist at the Lincoln Hospital drug detoxification program. The doctor had opposed Nelson Rockefeller's methadone maintenance proposals. Bourne was the last person to see the doctor alive, yet his possible involvement was never investigated. In 1977, Peter Bourne provided debriefing reports to the CIA after a trip to Southeast Asia and Pakistan. Details of the story appeared in the *Chicago Sun-Times* on July 23, 1978.

Peter Bourne ran the psychiatry division at the Grenada medical school at the time of the invasion—as it happens, the hospital was the only building on the island that was bombed (to destroy evidence of mind control experimentation?). Dr. Bourne advised the State Department and CIA at the time. He and Eric Gairy (voodoo practitioner, UFO watcher and petty despot) were close chums.

Press reports of the October, 1983 incursion were heavily censored. The American Air Force killed many of the inmates of the Grenada mental hospital. "It's hard to believe the bombing was accidental, given the technical sophistication of present day military targeting," writes Lenny Lapon, an independent reporter on psychiatric abuses, in *Mass Killers in White Coats:* "The Reagan government then sought $40 million in aid to Grenada—$360 per inhabitant—to rebuild the psychiatric institution. By comparison, the gross national product, counting the value of all goods and services produced in that tiny island country, was only $100 million in 1981, or $850 per person. Was the Grenada 'hospital' the scene of another Jonestown-style mind control experiment?"

Right-wing criminologists Barton Ingraham and Gerald Smith drew a timeline of their own: "The technique employed in electrophysiology in studying the brain of animals and man by stimulating its different areas electrically is nothing new.... [The technique has advanced] during the last twenty years ... as a result of equipment which allows the implantation of electrodes deep in the subcortical regions of the brain and the brain stem by stereotaxic instruments."[10]

The development of implants that interact with the brain and body was already underway in the academic haunts of the microwave mafia by the mid 60s. The Guiness world record for the most implants may go to Terry P., a subject in Toronto, Ontario left permanently disabled by dozens of foreign objects packed into his 42-year-old body. Terry, in a letter to Stone Angels, a Canadian network of mind control survivors, recalls forced psychosurgical vicimization at the age of fourteen:

> The pathology report reveals brain tissue removal. My mother was not informed of this. She was advised prior to the surgery that by 'removing scar tissue' they would lessen seizure disorder. In short, psychiatric brain mutilation was carried out under the guise of treating epilepsy. What I find confusing is the X-rays from Toronto General Hospital and St. Michael's Hospital, which reveal 43 metallic implants. Toronto Epilepsy Association states to my girlfriend that they can find no literature where metallic implants are used in surgical procedure [for] epilepsy.

The *Kugelblitz* Conundrum

It should be evident by now that those who deny that the spacecraft and space people are in our skies are agents of the Anti-Christ.
—George W. Van Tassel

The phenomenon reported is something real and not visionary or fictitious. There are objects approximating the shape of a disc, of such appreciable size as to appear as large as a man-made aircraft.
—Lt General Nathan Twining, Preliminary Report to USAF Commander, Air Materiél Command, Sept 23, 1947

The winged airfoil is not the only aerodynamic design in aviation history. An unpolled number of witnesses have observed flying disks performing wingless acrobatics, but they have not come bolting across time and space to torture humanity with genetic, biological and mind control experiments. The Federation has not arrived bearing brain implants. They are not "alien" in origin.

In 1917, a Dr. Nipher reported that the weight of a substance could be lightened by loading it with a powerful electrostatic charge.[11] One theory advanced by UFOlogists holds that the disks float on this principle—DoD documentation, however, only goes so far as to confirm positively that the EM propulsion has been an interest of the military since WWII.

Twenty years ago, Dr. Mason Rose of the University for Social Research published a monograph on the experiments of Dr. Paul Biefeld, a physicist at the California Institute for Advanced Studies in Pasadena, and his assistant, Thomas Townsend Brown. In 1923, Biefeld found that a high-voltage condensor is drawn to the positive pole when suspended in a gravitational field. The results of the Biefeld study were assigned to Brown, and a series of experiments led him to conclude that the field-propelled condensor opertated best when balanced in a disk-shaped housing. Three years after Biefeld's discovery, Brown published a paper detailing the design characteristics of his flying saucer.[12]

In 1930, he joined the Naval Research Laboratory and served as an officer in the Reserves, rising to Lt. Commander. Ten years later, he was hired as a radar consultant in the advanced design section at Lockheed. Yet he was unable to scare up funding to develop the electrostatic disk drive until 1952, after the Naval Research Labs conducted an exhaustive study of the propulsion system. Brown filed a report in 1956 on the USAF's Project Winterhaven, a joint undertaking of the Air Force and British military establishments to develop the Mach-3 Combat Disk, an aircraft with the classic design characteristics of a UFO.[13] At roughly the same time, he founded the National Investigations Committee on Aerial Phenomena (NICAP). His classified experiments continued into the 1970s at the Stanford Research Institute (SRI) (simultaneously the site of "remote viewing" experiments funded by the CIA, and as will become evident, the core of much of the chaos to come), in concert with the University of California at Berkeley and NASA's Ames Research Center.

Since the Biefeld-Brown experiments, the principle of electrogravitic propulsion has haunted the margins of establishment science. Townsend Brown fiddled with it until his death by lung cancer in 1985. Albert Einstein grappled with it.[14] Science fiction writers extrapolated its utilization in a multitude of bizarre forms. Theoretical possibilities gave rise to complex models for quantum EM wormholes, multi-dimensional gravity waves, space-time cross-currents, and some sought to wring from it a demonstration of Einstein's unified field.[15]

As late as 1990, SAIC, the corporate "remote viewing" folk, tinkered with electrogravitic propulsion for space travel on an Air Force contract.[16] A second study was conducted the following year at Phillips Laboratories in New Mexico, also for the Air Force, by Veritay Technology, Inc. entitled "Twenty-First Century Propulsion Concepts."[17]

Nazi scientists built similar electrostatic devices into German military prototypes. It is probably not the sole form of propulsion used in modern disks, but it was, at the very least, built into the Combat-13 and may still be an experimental engineering feature of the ubiquitous airborne vehicles.

Among the most avid American popularizers of Brown's theoretical work is Elizabeth Rauscher, a nuclear scientist and director of the Technic Research Lab in San Leandro, California. Dr. Rauscher is also champion of ELF for military applications. She has experimented with frequencies that induce nausea and play on the emotions. "Give me the money and three months," she boasts, "and I'll be able to affect the behavior of 80 per cent of the people in this town without their knowing it, make them happy (or at least they'll *think* they're happy) or aggressive."[18]

Rauscher appeared recently at a conference on Brown's theories with Harold Puthoff, formerly of the NSA and SRI, a parapsychologist and one of the principal hoaxers behind the promotion of Uri Geller. The ESP experiments at SRI were Puthoff's brainchild, and he pursued his quasi-academic interests with research partner Russell Targ. Both scientists engage in the R&D of advanced technology, while publicly engaged in zany forays on the paranormal. Like most of the merry pranksters of mind control, the SRI experimenters are not the addled occultists they appear. Puthoff designed a tunable laser. Targ is the inventor of a microwave-frequency plasma oscillator and an official of the International Association for Psychotronic Research.[19] As it happens, psychotronic devices that communicate directly with the brain are the hidden thrust of the current mind control program. Many survivors of the experimentation come to realize that psi and out-of-body experiences, like "alien" abductions, are hypnotic cover stories. Subjects are used against their will. They are often tortured in their own homes with advanced non-lethals of the type developed by the CIA's mind control crew.

In *The Search for Superman,* John Wilhelm mentions that Puthoff's psychics were funded by the Naval Electronics Systems Command in San Diego. These days, electronics are the beating heart of mind control because CIA scientists discovered years ago that any breakthroughs they may have enjoyed with hypnosis and drugs they could more easily and dependably reproduce with remote brain technology—and since the subject never lays eyes his tormentors, they need not fear exposure. EM stimulation of the brain and nervous system to control or punish a human guinea-pig is the perfect crime.

It is fitting that General Hans Kammler, the same Nazi who designed the Auschwitz concentration camp, should also have overseen the development of the "foo-fighter"—the predecessor of the flying disk and, later, a preferred kidnap and escape vehicle of the American mind control underground. The infamous Nazi compound and the disk have one thing in common: they are both used to conduct illicit medical experimentation.

Kammler, a protégé of Heinrich Himmler, was the highest ranking officer in Nazi Germany after the ministers in Hitler's cabinet, and he held more authority than any of them. "If Kammler had lived in ancient Egypt," British correspondent Tom Agoston wrote, "snobbish pharoahs, anxious to outshine previous dynasties, would undoubtedly have turned to him to build their pyramids."[20]

Kammler caught the eye of Hitler by pulling off construction projects considered impossible by many ranking Nazi engineers. Auschwitz, a state-of-the-art genocide machine, was his creation. A diplomat stationed in Berlin, shortly before the United States entered the war, described Hans Kammler as "always unpredictable. I have seen him soothe and tame a nervous unruly horse, using a magically gentle touch, and then minutes later order a negligent groom to be brutally horsewhipped."[21] The General was in command of the V-rocket campaign that terrorized London in 1944. He had the run of Germany's entire rocket program, the forerunner of NASA, and constructed the first bomb-proof underground aircraft factory in the world. One of them was the Nordhausen plant in the Harz mountains, a slave labor shop that turned out flying bombs, rockets and Messerschmitt motors.

Albert Speer distrusted and envied the man who built Auschwitz: "Himmler heaped assignments on him and brought him into Hitler's presence at every opportunity. Rumors were afloat that Himmler was trying to build up Kammler to be my successor. I had found Kammler absolutely brilliant, yet cold, a ruthless schemer, a fanatic in pursuit of his goal, as carefully calculating as he was unscrupulous."[22]

When the Reich was pummeled into defeat, Speer, technically the director of all new weapons development, watched the Nazi dream crumble. But work progressed in an underground factory deep within the Thuringian Forest.[23] It is well known that in the final months of WWII, Hitler promised his embattled troops that advanced weapons were on the way to turn the war around. To the Allies the boast seemed a last-ditch propaganda strategy. But the U.S. developed the A-Bomb in short order, and the scientists under Albert Speer were caught out at war's end with much more than a recipe for Buna rubber.

On January 2, 1945, the *New York Herald Tribune* blared: "Now, it seems, the Nazis have thrown something new into the night skies over Germany. It is the weird, mysterious 'Foo Fighter' balls which race alongside the wings of Beaufighters flying intruder missions over Germany. Pilots have been encountering this eerie weapon for more than a month in their night flights."

Most of the records of Nazi military science, advancements in nuclear, aeronautic and electronic warfare were removed to the Bavarian Alps or trashed. But intelligence reports describing a "circular German fighter without wings or rudder" survived, as did records of unusual test flights. One witness to carnage in the sky over Switzerland described "a strange flying machine, hemispherical or at any rate circular in shape." The machine overtook a formation of American airplanes, and "when it passed in front of the formation, it gave off a number of little bluish clouds of smoke. A moment later the American bombers mysteriously caught fire, exploding in the air, while the German 'rocket' had already disappeared over the horizon."[24]

Renato Vesco, the foremost aerospace engineer in Italy in the 1960s, traced the history of the Nazi flirtation with the flying disk to the U.S.. Albert Speer and the SS Technical General Staff, Vesco learned, had equipped the disks with a "proximate radio interference" capability—the most widely-reported electronic effect in postwar domestic UFO abductions—to disable the sensitive electronics of American night fighters: "Thus a highly original flying machine was born. It was circular and armored, more or less flat and circular, whose principles of operation recalled the well-known aelipile of Hero, which generated a great halo of luminous flames." The "fireballs" reported by Allied pilots over Germany were illuminated by "chemical additives that interrupted the flow of electricity by overionizing the atmosphere in the vicinity of the plane, generally around the wing tips or tail surfaces, subjected the H2S radar on the plane to the action of powerful electrostatic fields."[25]

The unmanned experimental disks were guided by remote television controls designed by *Telefunken,* in coordination with the German Institute for High Frequency Studies and *Blaupunkt.* The micro-television camera fitted by Kammler's technicians to the nose of anti-aircraft rockets was installed on the experimental prototype, which had but to fly within a hundred yards of an Allied bomber to knock out the ignition with a powerful electrostatic surge and send it spinning to earth.

The technology dropped into American hands with the Nazi surrender.

In the Pentagon, Assistant Secretary of War John J. McCloy, formerly a Wall Street attorney, used his authority to intervene in the executions of convicted Nazi war criminals. McCloy arranged to have Klaus Barbie sheltered from prosecution by the 970th Counter-Intelligence Corps at Oberamergau. His interest in the Nazis was obvious: McCloy represented Standard Oil and Chase Manhattan, both high-handed investors in Nazi Germany. Before the war, McCloy had been a legal adviser to I.G. Farben, the German chemical conglomerate that financially hoisted many in the Hitler regime to power and prospered by Jewish slave labor at Auschwitz and elsehwere.[26]

After the fall of Berlin, the Allies launched "Operation Lusty" to gather scientific papers, blueprints and experimental models hidden away in abandoned mines, ancient castles, caves and vaults buried throughout occupied Europe. The confiscation of German scientific files and prototypes was the chore of Allied "T-Forces," OSS and military operatives assisted by "Paperclip" personnel, playing escort to the Nazi thirst for bloodshed. In his review of Nazi technology, Colonel Donald Putt, assistant commanding officer of the Allied Technical Information Service (soon to serve in Operation Paperclip with a promotion to Lt. General), stated in July 1946 that fleeing German scientists had left behind, at Peenemünde, Wiener Neustadt (home of the famed Nazi Foo Fighters) and elsewhere, prototypical marvels of *future* air warfare.[27]

After the occupation, Colonel Putt toured the once-bustling R&D complex at Volkenrode. Kamikazé journalist Tom Bower reported in 1987 that Putt was "amazed." Strolling though the Nazi laboratories, the colonel "realized he was in the midst of [the] *most magnificent and lavish research facility ever constructed. The sheer abundance and extravagance of the instruments, subsidiary tools and testing equipment were awe-inspiring.*"

Theodore von Karmen, an American scientific adviser to the Air Force, was also struck by the show of German technical superiority. He was one of a small circle of military officials who, Bower reports, "forged the wartime marriage between the military and the scientists."[28] Von Karmen found employment after the war at Cal Tech, where he worked closely with Jack Parsons, the head of the Agape Lodge of the Ordo Templis Orientis (OTO), the occult lodge in Pasadena.[29]

A publicity release from Kelly Air Force Base touts Karman and Putt as originators of "a program to bring hundreds of Germany's best scientists and technicians to the United States."

Colonel Putt was a founder of the Air Force Scientific and Technical Intelligence Division. He was the deputy commanding general for intelligence in the Air Technical Service after the war. In 1995, the colonel was inducted into the Air Intelligence Agency's "Hall of Honor."[30]

Many were briefed on aspects of the Nazi migration, but two men knew all. The debriefing of Kammler and Speer took place in a pocket of history sealed and stricken from the record by the Pentagon. The fumigators converged on the moment. There survives no record that officials of the U.S. mission ever spoke to Herr Kammler—the man who built Auschwitz and Nordhousen—or even sought him out: an impossible oversight. Four entirely different accounts have been given of his disappearance on April 17, 1945.

Transcripts of the interrogation of Albert Speer by Allied officials are stored at the British Public Record Office. Their release has been *denied until the year 2020*, an exception to the standard 30-year rule.[31] A microfilm copy of the interrogation of Albert Speer is filed at the U.S. National Archives. Speer stubbornly denied knowledge of the Holocaust at Nuremberg, and Hollywood has depicted him as a blushing innocent, but a number of scholars have rejected his disavowals, including Matthias Schmidt in *Albert Speer: The End of a Myth* (1984), and Gitta Sereny in *Albert Speer: His Battle with Truth* (1995). He was denied a position in the postwar West German government because he was considered too tainted.[32]

Speer's memoirs (which briefly mention the development of flying disks) were best-sellers and made him millions.

Another welcome guest of the government was Dr. Hubertus Strughold, the "Father of American Space Medicine." When details of his past were declassified, the blowback was ferocious. On September 24, 1995, the Jewish Telegraphic Agency reported:

> The sadistic Nazi background of a late German scientist has resulted in plans to remove his name from a U.S. Air Force library. In 1993, soon after the scientist's background was first uncovered, his portrait was removed from a mural of medical heroes at Ohio State University.
>
> Scientist Hubertus Strughold, who died in 1986, was secretly brought to the United States in 1945 to work on the space program, even though he was sought for prosecution at Nuremberg. The library at the School of Aerospace Medicine at Brooks Air Force Base in Texas had been named to honor Strughold, who helped develop the pressure suits used by astronauts as well as the U.S. space capsule.
>
> As the head of Nazi Germany's Air Force Institute for Aviation Medicine, Strughold participated in a 1942 conference that discussed "experiments" on human beings. The experiments included subjecting Dachau concentration camp inmates to torture and death.
>
> Strughold had denied approving the experiments and said he learned of them only after World War II.

A Mind Control Octopus

Top Gun pilots chased a UFO across Europe to within five miles of the English coast, it was claimed yesterday. A Belgium F-16 Fighter locked onto the craft, but it swerved and vanished after accelerating from 230 mph to 1,700 mph in half a second. More than 13,000 people in three countries reported seeing the UFO in 1990. Now author Derick Sheffield is claiming a cover-up by the Ministry of Defence.

—The (UK) *Sun*, 4th September 1995

On numerous occasions, I was hypnotized to think that the helicopters I was forced to ride in were UFO's....

—K.S., "Alien" Abductee

Among the first of the technical hunters and gatherers was Major Clay Shaw, OSS, a spy under William Donovan who went on to become general manager of New Orlean's International Trade Mart, an import-export concern with a clutch of European war criminals on the board of directors. Shaw was the wartime *aide de camp* to General Charles Thrasher. After the war he rose to deputy chief of staff at a detainment camp for Nazi POWs. In *The Kennedy Conspiracy,* Paris Flammonde describes a fateful meeting:

Von Braun first met Clay Shaw in 1945 when he, Walter Dornberger [a Nazi, soon to become the CEO of Bell Helicopter] and about 150 other Nazi rocket scientists abandoned Peneemünde and traveled south to join the American forces in Germany close to the French border. The Nazis were brought to the Deputy Chief of Staff's headquarters where major Clay Shaw maintained their relationship over the years through their mutual connection with the Defense Industrial Security Command, or D.I.S.C., an operational arm of the counterespionage division of the FBI.

Shaw was arrested and tried for complicity in the murder of John Kennedy, acquitted on March 1, 1969, by a grand jury. When Shaw learned he was a suspect in the Garrison investigation, he immediately phoned Fred Lee Crisman, a veteran of Operation Paperclip and a covert contract "security" specialist for the ranking aerospace firms. In 1947, Shaw's contact supposedly found "metal slag" fragments dropped by a UFO over Maurey Island off Tacoma, Washington.[33] Crisman claimed to have given the fragments to two G-2 officers from Wright-

Patterson Air Force Base (a Paperclip stronghold run by General Twining) who'd witnessed the overflight. A few days later, The G-2 officers perished in a plane crash. The ensuing investigation concluded that the plane had been "sabotaged." Ever the good soldier, Crisman steered speculation over motive to the slag. Anthony Kimery, an investigative reporter in Washington, D.C., believes Crisman "knew a lot more about the aircraft [witnesses] saw than he acknowledged—aircraft some intelligence sources believe were hybrids of those designed early that decade by Nazi engineers who were brought to the U.S. under Project Paperclip."

Secret technology and mind control were themes in several lives close to the 1963 coup. Kerry Wendell Thornley, a Marine buddy of Lee Harvey Oswald, has alleged that while on active duty he was subjected to hellish electronic mind control transmissions. He maintains that a device planted without his knowledge in the base of his neck picked up the baleful "voices" of a "Nazi" covert operations unit toying with his head.

Another technological curiosity on the road to Dallas was the saucer found by Guy Banister, the FBI "counterterrorist" for Division Five who lurked at 544 Camp Street, a fierce anti-Communist alleged in conspiracy lore to have run patsy Lee Harvey Oswald through a self-implicating obstacle course on the periphery of the John Kennedy assassination. In 1947, Banister reported the discovery of a "flying disk" in Twin Falls, Idaho, according to a July 11, 1947, Associated Press report. The saucer measured roughly 30.5' across, and "appeared to have been turned out by a machine," possibly as a prototype.

Suspects in the John Kennedy assassination had a pronounced knack for stumbling onto the "unexplained" flying disks.

It is a commentary on the UFO/mind control/intelligence connection that the counterterrorist unit of the FBI already tied to Shaw and Crisman, Division Five—the Nazi division—also employed Guy Banister, and has been largely responsible for the development of a form of remote brain manipulation known as Ultrasonic Intra-Cerebral Control.[34]

Enter America's imperial clan, the Rockefellers. Laurance, vetted by the U.S. Naval Reserve, rose to the rank of lieutenant commander during the war, assigned to the Bureau of Aeronautics as liaison between the Navy and aircraft production plants—despite huge financial investments in Hitler's Holocaust machine by family-owned businesses, as documented by George Seldes and Charles Higham—who dreamed of transforming the postwar world with advancements in communications, nuclear power, aviation and computers. The defense industry fostered experimentation with new technologies and they intrigued Laurance, especially those with the potential to significantly transform everyday life.[35]

When Hitler's Germany rolled out the armaments to flatten Europe, young Rockefeller launched into an intense study of military aviation. He joined the Institute of Aeronautical Sciences, was a director of Eastern Airlines and a trustee of *Air Affairs,* a quarterly international journal. Laurance and his brother Winthrop organized the Air Youth of America, an aviation training program.[36]

Laurance may have been less visible than his brothers, but he was equally steeped in the sordid world of covert intelligence and propaganda. In the 1950s, he served on a panel that released a report written by Henry Kissinger, *International Security—The Military Aspect,* calling for successive escalations in defense expenditures of $3 billion per anum to 1965. In 1973 he was named a director of *Reader's Digest,* a fount of CIA cold war black propaganda. (To indulge in a bit of necessary guilt by association, Melvin Laird, a *Digest* officer, is also a director of SAIC, the "remote viewing" sponsor.) Rockefeller is a trustee of M.I.T., a director of the Alfred P. Sloan Foundation, Olin Mathieson, and so on.[37]

Renato Vesco traced the immediate postwar development of the Nazi disks to the UK. Vesco, the Italian Werner von Braun, plodded through a detailed investigation of the technology transfer in *Intercept, but Don't Shoot,* published in 1967. British defense officials, he discovered, hoped to barter advancements in saucer propulsion and design to the United States in exchange for classified nuclear research data. A priority was placed on making the aircraft faster, leading to experimentation with a number of rocket propulsion systems. Wind tunnel tests demonstrated the disks could easily slip through the sound barrier when the friction layer was drawn through a multitude of pinholes punched in the hull. Normally, the layer of air that builds along an aircraft's surface slows it. The air pulling on the craft, otherwise known as the buoyant layer, was eliminated in the saucer design with suction along the entire surface of the vehicle in place of the conventional jet design. The pinholes sucked away the buoyant layer and pumped the air through a jet thruster.

When the war ended, Laurance travelled to Europe, according to Alvin Moscow's martinized Rockefeller biography, "to examine the latest British experiments with *jet propulsion* for military aircraft. He looked into *the technology of the German Rockets* used in the blitz of London."[38] Moscow does not mention a visit to the British Air Force saucer section, but if developments were shared with anyone, it was surely Laurance Rockefeller, the wealthiest and most influential military aerospace scion in the world, gratis the spoils of war.

Laurance was a lavish godfather to UFO organizations that attributed saucer overflights and abductions to "alien" activity.

His business associates are familiar names in the security complex. Columbia, Missouri UFOlogist Val Germann writes in *Big Money and UFOs:*

> In 1947, there was talk of a Congressional investigation of Navy contracts vis-a-vis McDonnell during the period that Laurance was in the Navy. But, that investigation never seemed to get off the ground, no pun intended. Thus Laurance sailed on, later forming a consortium with family friends C. Douglas Dillon and Felix DuPont to make a fortune out of helicopter production during the Korean War. This consortium also owned Nuclear Development Associates, the original power behind civilian nuclear reactors, and a little company called ITEK, which would make the spy cameras for the U-2 and America's spy satellites. The capital for these ventures would come from brother David's Chase Bank, the very center of Rockefeller power.
>
> In 1950 Laurance hired Lewis Strauss, a former Kuhn, Loeb banker who had been an assistant to Herbert Hoover in World War I, an official in the 1930s of the company that later became UniRoyal, and the lawyer/banker who had helped Kodak market Kodachrome and later aided Dr. Land and his Polaroid. Strauss spent World War Two in the Navy and had been made an Admiral by his good friend James V. Forrestal. Funny how things like this worked out.
>
> In any event, in 1950 Strauss was overseeing the Rockefeller Brothers Fund and was heavily connected into the high-tech science world. He left Rockefeller employ to become the chairman of the AEC under Eisenhower, just as Laurance put together a company called United Nuclear which had the inside track on the development of civilian atomic power. Also at this time ITEK was created, begun when a Boston University scientist advised his good friend Laurance Rockefeller that Ike's Administration was going to liquidate Boston University's Physics Research Lab. Laurance bought the thing and put his good scientific friend in charge of it. It made millions out of the U-2 and the Discovery satellites, both of which were promoted relentlessly by Rockefeller operatives, including Nelson, inside the administration.
>
> Later on, Laurance would be a power behind LBJ's administration.

The number of aircraft defense firms swelled with an infusion of funds from Laurance Rockefeller. The most imposing is McDonnell-Douglas, founded in 1930 by a prodigy of aircraft design, James S. McDonnell of St. Louis.[39] McDonnell shares with Laurance Rockefeller the taint of war profiteering. Periodic postwar investigations of his aircraft company by the General

Accounting Office have exposed a deep, chronically over-funded well of fraud.[40] In 1967, the company merged with Douglas Aircraft, the primary subcontractor of Western Electric, an AT&T subsidiary.[41]

However cerebral, James McDonnell had one foot firmly planted in the occult. He was a principal donor to the famed J.B. Rhine psychic research center at Duke University, and supported psychic experimentation at Washington University in St. Louis.[42]

Professor Rhine and his wife Louisa joined the faculty of Duke University in 1927 to explore the paranormal with Dr. William McDougall, chairman of the psychology department. In a few years, according to Parapsychological Institute literature, "Dr. Rhine was conducting the groundbreaking research that demonstrated under rigorous, scientific conditions that certain persons could acquire information without the use of the known senses. He introduced the term extrasensory perception (ESP) to describe this ability and adopted the word parapsychology to distinguish his experimental approach from other methods of psychical research."[43]

Among the key early supporters of the Rhine ESP center was Medtronics, a medical technology firm in Minneapolis. The connection is chilling in the context of forced human experimentation. Bear in mind the horrors of the surgical table described by abductees, encircled by "alien" doctors, when paging through the Medtronics catalog: "The company's neurological business produces implantable systems for spinal cord stimulation and drug delivery.... The Itrel II spinal cord stimulation system is the most advanced and flexible implantable neuro-stimulation device on the market today."

Another financial supporter of the Rhine center was insurance magnate W. Clement Stone, whose name was the very first on Richard Nixon's list of presidential campaign contributors.[44]

The psi theme crops up repeatedly in abductee accounts. Dorothy Burdick, in her self-published study of electronic mind control, *Such Things Are Known* (1982), observed: "Recently, through TV and the news media, there has been an effort toward making parapsychology respectable.... The CIA has a program of 'disinformation' which may be a convenient cover for scientists working on programs which seem to the uninformed to border on the occult, such as bioplasma research and Kirlian photography."[45]

U.S. News & World Report recently featured a report on John Gittinger, a psychologist on a Human Ecology Fund contract, who admits to knowledge of ESP experiments in which subjects were given electric shocks when they responded to questions incorrectly.

The Agency had been interested in parapsychology well before ARTICHOKE, which grew out of the ESP experiments of the late 40s.[46] "Why," researcher Martin Cannon asks, "are paranormal phenomena always linked in governmental studies with mind control research? Why did the CIA study ESP as part of MK-ULTRA, and not as part of a separate program? Why are these two abilities—to read minds, and to commandeer minds—so closely linked?" [47]

Seymour Hersch, the acclaimed investigative reporter, was the first to expose in the public print classified bioelectromagnetic experimentation. He reported shortly thereafter that he began to receive long letters from subjects alleging to have participated in CIA mind control operations and telepathic links to "aliens."[48]

TEN STATES WITH THE HIGHEST INCIDENCE OF REPORTED SAUCER SIGHTINGS, June–July, 1947		
STATE	SIGHTINGS	WITNESSES
California	109	465
Washington	83	178
Oregon	54	110
Idaho	43	510
Illinois	40	74
Colorado	36	80
Ohio	29	150
Alabama	28	75
Wisconsin	27	58
Texas	27	50

Source: UFO Information Service

The paranormal is taken very seriously by many of the cults operating under the aegis of federal intelligence groups. Dr. Corydon Hammond's controversial "Greenbaum Speech" mentions a type of mind control subject called "Thetas," or "psychic killers," though much of his research remains unconfirmed.[49]

One abduction case has been traced by the subject herself directly to CIA operatives crouching behind a thinly-constructed "alien" blind. The woman had several contacts in the intelligence underground. She experienced the first of series of abductions after volunteering at an ESP testing laboratory. The experimenters advised her to join a local UFO organization, as were other test subjects. In the course of her abduction, two of her 'alien' kidnappers made the mistake of speaking to her—in English—and she recognized their voices. They belonged to her acquaintances in the CIA, one of whom had predicted the abduction. She confronted him. He explained that he'd known in advance because he had "ESP."[50]

Another abductee, identifying herself only as C.P., was so tortured by the microwave mafia that she sought asylum at a foreign embassy. Her experience, too, began with academic parapsychology experiments. There was nothing unusual about her life until 1983. C.P. had participated in the teaching of a parapsychology course at a West Berlin community college. Through students, she fell in with a circle of Americans with backgrounds in the intelligence field, among them Peggy Woolsey, former secretary to CIA director Richard Helms. Peggy was garrulous and often dwelt on her life in Iran.

One evening, at Peggy's apartment, C.P. noticed at least an inch of sediment at the bottom of her drink. Peggy explained it away as the residual sludge of "Berlin Water." On another occasion, Peggy took her along on a junket to East Berlin in a car with diplomatic plates. C.P. had crossed the border in the past to only to attend the opera and theater, or purchase books:

> I had the impression that something strange was transpiring. It was during this time that I was, on three occasions, at three different locations, talked to during my sleep by people I was acquainted with. On these occasions I had awakened abruptly during my sleep and became aware of what was transpiring. I went to the U.S. consulate and named names.
>
> After this I was harassed by a man in a white car who would drive by my apartment and when in close proximity, would zap me with an electrical field of some sort. He was very brazen. I would find my body pulsating during my sleep especially at the base of my spine, but my whole body would vibrate as well and I would see flashing lights on my wall. I had to go to the U.S. Consulate several times and they expressed disbelief in what I was saying, rudely stating: "Who would be interested in you—you have no important political or military contacts."
>
> Ultimately I decided to return to the U.S., and I had no idea what would be in store for me. I returned to a living hell and unbelievable torture, abuse and experimentation.
>
> In retrospect, the only conclusion that makes reasonable sense is that I must have exposed a CIA operation. I was then classified as a "write-off" or expendable as a human being. By some unfortunate decision I was designated for a constant monitoring, inhuman method of electronic incarceration utilizing intracerebral microwave induction of voices. This is one of several sadistic approaches they have used to destroy my life. So for 13 years now I have never known one moment of privacy or peace. My entire life has been stolen from me. My apartment serves them as the cage of a guinea pig. [51]

Kathleen S., an abductee in Atlanta, Georgia, described in personal correspondence the interplay of the politics and mind control in the Gingrich State:

"Several years ago, on an Atlanta talk radio station, I heard a very disturbing campaign advertisement. It promoted a candidate for the House of Representatives named Bob Barr. He was touted as the best candidate, since he already had experience in the government *as an employee of the CIA.* I did several double-takes. Did I hear correctly? Yes, he blatantly admitted, as if that made him *more* qualified to be a Georgia representative in D.C. The man won.

"Worse yet, he won AGAIN!"

"I saw the blurb about his background, etc. in the *Chattanooga Times* (November 6, 1996)":

U.S. HOUSE DISTRICT SEVEN

Counties: Bartow, Carroll, Chattooga, Cobb, Douglas, Floyd, Haralson, Heard, Paulding, Polk, Troup

BOB BARR

Hometown: Marietta

Career: Barr is a lawyer and CIA analyst.

Previous political involvement: He has served in the U.S. House since 1994.

On the issues: Barr represents a district that has become increasingly conservative. He voted against the minimum-wage bill, opposes gun control. He's opposed to gay marriages.

"District Seven has a spooky fox guarding an underground, black-marketing hen-house," Kathleen complains.

Her abduction occurred in or near Cobb County.

"Illegal activities are *rampant* in that part of Georgia," she says. "The county owes *its existence* to Lockheed/Martin-Marietta. Lockheed shares boundaries with Dobbins Air Force Base. I was drugged and guided through a 'space travel' scrambling memory on Lockheed grounds at least once. Lockheed and Dobbins AFB are in Cobb County. God help any survivor who begins to break away and contacts Barr's office for *assistance!*"

In the postwar period, universities housed the scientific and propaganda branches of the Pentagon. Harvard, Yale, Cal Tech, MIT, Princeton, UCLA and most other ranking academies in the Western hemisphere played host to the foundations. And the intelligence cells buried within them. From Cambridge, for example, came Ivan Sanderson from the wartime Navy Counter-Intelligence Corps (CIC). Charles Berlitz, co-author of *The Philadelphia Experiment,* was a Yale graduate recruited by the wartime CIC. UFOlogist Jaques Vallee was a student of Allen Hynek (Johns Hopkins, University of Chicago), worked for Shell

Oil and since the 1960s and has been a familiar face at Stanford, where he was engaged in computer projects for the Defense Advance Research Projects Agency (DARPA), the Project Pandora people: developers of direct microwave communication with the brain.

Charles Tart, a subject of the CIA's mind control program, met his wife at Duke's parapsychology lab and went on to become one of the leading authorities around on "ESP." Tart was born in 1937 and reared a Lutheran with an intellectual drive. In Dr. Rhine's lab, Tart, now 22, was given a massive dose of mescaline. At a young age he developed an unquenchable fascination with science, particularly electronics. In high school he obtained a first-class radio telephone license, and silenced his urgings for spirituality with books on the occult. He was admitted to the engineering school at MIT in 1955. There, Tart organized a psychic research club, met some of the leading psychics of the period. His extracurricular interests led him to declare a major in psychology.[52]

The abrupt change in career ambitions was accomplished with the help of Dr. J.B. Rhine. In 1957, the parapsychologist pulled strings and ushered Tart to Duke University. At the parapsychology lab he met Judy Bamberger and married her. He dropped mescaline a few years later.

The experiment was run by Dr. Ivo Kohler, a visiting professor from the University of Vienna who'd tested the hallucinogen on human subjects in Austria since the 1930s. Dr. Kohler visited the lab one afternoon and struck up a conversation with Tart, an aficionado of the British hallucinatorian Aldous Huxley. Dr. Kohler mentioned he'd never given the drug to an American and the curious student volunteered. It so happened that Kohler had a massive dose of pure mescaline sulfate on his person. It tasted like "vomit," Tart recalls.

He attended graduate school at the University of North Carolina in Chapel Hill a few years later, volunteered for experiments with LSD and psilocybin mushrooms funded by a private foundation with CIA moorings. He has since collaborated with CIA hucksters Targ and Puthoff on books and monographs popularizing ESP. Their high-toned theories of "anomalous phenomena" spurn an ambitious year-long Air Force psi research program known as VERITAC (named for the computer that calculated the results). The VERITAC study found any measurable "anomalies" to be "insignificant."

And compared to the EM weapons hidden in the DoD/CIA vault, they truly were: advances in brain research at UCLA were soon to render the quest for psychic abilities obsolete. Dr. Ross Adey, a neuroscientist who'd worked beside the Paperclip Nazis, is currently a brain researcher at Loma Linda University. The *New York Times* reported on January 1, 1973 that Adey had been accused of gross disregard in the testing of animals for NASA. He testified on his own behalf in a federal courthouse—and stated under oath that "the brain is insensitive to pain." Dr. Adey has participated in hundreds of brain experiments involving animals and humans, some funded by the CIA. He has stuffed electrodes deep within cerebral tissue to measure minute electrical impulses.

His early success at inducing calcium efflux in the brain have given rise to the "confusion weaponry" in the military's "non-lethal" arsenal. Adey was among the first scientists recruited by the DoD's Project Pandora, the quest for a psychoactive microwave. His work, researcher Anna Keeler explains, is "precise in inducing specific behavior. He has correlated a wide variety of behavioral states with EEG including emotional states (e.g. stress in hostile questioning) increments of decision-making and conditioning, correct versus incorrect performance etc. and he has [used] electromagnetic fields that look like EEG which have resulted in altered EEG and behavior."

In his own published accounts, Adey has shown it is possible to design a radio frequency carrier modulated at specific brain frequencies. He demonstrated that "if the biological modulation on the carrier frequency is close to frequencies in the natural EEG of the subject, it will reinforce or increase the number of ... the imposed rhythms and modulate behavior."[53] "Modulate" is a roundabout way of discussing the remote control of a human brain.

Paperclip Nazi Herman Schwann conducted similar experiments with microwaves at the University of Pennsylvania. Schwann was able to map out the electrical properties of human tissue stimulated by varying frequencies of microwave emissions.[54] The work continues to the present day, almost always in secrecy, sometimes camouflaged by innocent-sounding titles, like the $30,000 CIA study published in 1976 entitled "Novel Biophysical Information Transfer Mechanisms (NBITM)."

The technology of "biophysical information transfer" is so advanced that it is often passed off as "alien." In a lawsuit filed against the National Security Agency in a Disctrict of Columbia federal courthouse (civil action 92-0449) a private citizen, John St. Clair Akwei, described the ultimate in electronic surveillance, Remote Neural Monitoring (RNM). This device sends coded signals to the brain's auditory cortex, he claims, communicates directly with the brain "to debilitate subjects by stimulating auditory hallucinations characteristic of paranoid schizophrenia. Without contact with the subject, Remote Neural Monitoring can map out electrical activity from the visual cortex of a subject's brain [on] a video monitor. NSA operatives see what the surveillance subject's eyes are seeing. Visual memory can also be seen. RNM can send images direct to the visual cortex, bypassing the eyes and optic nerves. NSA operatives can use this surreptitiously to put images into a surveillance subject's brain while in REM sleep for brain programming purposes."

Hard physics meets the paranormal in telekinesis researcher Dr. Robert G. Jahn, dean emeritus of the Princeton Engineering and Applied Science Department. He is the recipient of an award from the American Society of Engineering Education for an experimental study of high-powered plasma discharges for spacecraft propulsion, a fellow of the American Physical Society and the American Institute of Aeronautics and Astronautics (AIAA), and (recalling the Biefeld-Brown effect) chairman of the AIAA Electric Propulsion Technical Committee. Jahn serves on the NASA Space Science and Technology Advisory Committee. He is also a director of Hercules, Inc. and chairman of the private spaceflight company's technology committee.[55]

The dean's work in spaceship propulsion systems is as futuristic as any fantasy offered by Puthoff's paranormal Pranksters. Jahn's investigation of pulsed electromagnetic gas acceleration, funded by NASA and the Air Force, examined how "high-power electrical discharges can be used to accelerate a variety of working fluids to very high velocities. These intense discharges and the plasma streams they produce are configured into magnetoplasmadynamic (MPD) thrusters which offer a desirable combination of high specific impulse and high thrust density for advanced space propulsion."

High-energy plasma has apparent uses in UFO technology. Connect the Paperclip UFO/CIA mind control dots in this excerpt from Dr. Jahn's resumé:

ENGINEERING ANOMALIES RESEARCH

Investigators: R. G. Jahn and B. J. Dunne

Support: The McDonnell Foundation, The Fetzer Institute, Laurance S. Rockefeller, Donald C. Webster, and The Ohrstrom Foundation.

This program addresses the interaction of human operators with low-level information processing devices and systems. This program combines appropriate engineering facilities and techniques with a selection of protocols and insights drawn from modern cognitive science to explore certain aspects of human/machine interactions known to yield anomalous effects currently inexplicable on the basis of established physical concepts and statistical theory.

"Human/machine interaction" on a "cognitive" wavelength is a round-the-block euphemism for mind-linked cybernetics, with "ESP" supposedly acting up as a ghost in the works. Obviously, the ability of a psychic to jerk a molecule—Jahn claims it has been done in his laboratory—pales by comparison.

The hybrid of cybernetics and radio transmitters oscillating on the brain's frequencies has made possible horrific new forms of assault. Why allow this priceless technology to molder around the shop?

Princeton conducted its share of early experiments with psychoactive devices. The hoarding and reclassification of the university's scientific data on infrasound by the Pentagon led Eliot Handelman, a researcher at McGill University, to post his frustration on an academic computer bulletin board: "I'm trying to locate research on the biophysical effects of infrasound," Handleman complained. "A few years ago I collected a series of citations—about 25 from *JASA,* primarily from the late 50s and early 60s. Princeton cataloged several of these but they were all *missing.* It turned out that these papers were reclassified during the 1980s, and my efforts to get them through the DoD met with no success, supposedly because Princeton did not wish to comply with DoD's restricted materials protocol. Can anyone tell me what is so interesting about the biophysical effects of infrasound that merit classification?"[56]

Among the responses: "It's really a very powerful tool for mood manipulation ... you'll feel very giddy, your face will flush red ... if you're drunk you'll become much more drunk ... you'll lose about 20% of your IQ and about 15–20% of your ability to balance yourself ... it makes your chest vibrate ... it makes your eyes shake so much that you can't see clearly anymore."

Like most acoustic weapons, the effects of infrasound vary as a factor of frequency. The military potential is mind-boggling. In 1983, Russian scientists at the Leningrad Institute beamed rats with a scattering of infrasonic frequencies for three hours a day over a period of 45 days. The exposure produced spasms in the main blood vessels, resulting in lesions, especially in the range of 10–15 Hz.[57] The low-frequency, high-decibel sound resonates in body cavities, blurs vision and causes nausea. As the decibels rise, effects range from general discomfort to permanent damage and death.[58]

According to a brochure from a subsidiary of Mankind Research Unlimited (MRU) in Los Altos, California, a CIA proprietary, the company's psychoacoustical infrasound emissions invade the brain cells *"and wipe them clean."*[59]

The Power

In a 1975 speech, Leonid Brezhnev refers to novel weapons systems
"more terrible than anything the world has known."

—James Mills, *The Power*

The Russian and U.S. governments fill the air with low-frequency
sound waves meant to control us.

—Steve Carlton, *Sports Illustrated*, April 18, 1994

The work of the German aeronautical scientists was kept under wraps. If anyone knew the background of the UFO sightings of the early 1950s, it was American military personnel drawn into the Operation Overcast and Paperclip Nazi emigration projects. One of them, Brigadier John Samford, a graduate of West Point, was an eager participant. When Colonel Putt filed a memo with the Brigadier, pleading for measures to "improve the morale" of incoming Nazis, Samford tore off a letter to the DoD requesting "Immediate action in this situation." The German scientists, it seems, were a bit down in the mouth. Some of them were even suicidal, Samford lamented. It was the Pentagon's responsibility to make the fugitives comfortable, he pointed out, "if we are to divert the services of valuable scientists from France and Russia to the United States."[60]

Dissolve from Samford's collaboration with "valuable" Nazi scientists to the *London Times*, July 29, 1952:

AERIAL OBJECTS OVER WASHINGTON AIR FORCE INQUIRY

The *Times* reported: "a group of unidentified aerial objects [has been] observed on radar screens at Washington National Airport. This is the second time in a week that such objects have been reported in this area." The overflights squeezed the Democratic National Convention from the headlines (and this may well have been the intended aim since the Nazis who migrated to the U.S. were ensconced in the Republican Party). A pilot reported he'd been unable to intercept the "glowing lights" seen near Andrews Air Force Base. (Most residents of Washington chalked it up to experimental aircraft.) So who should step forward to brief the press but John Alexander Samford, fresh from a promotion to director of Air Force intelligence (and four years later to the highest office of the National Security Agency).[61]

Major General Samford, with other officers, discussed the investigation of the reported phenomena for an hour and a half this afternoon and answered innumerable questions. The result was largely "an explanation of an inability to explain," but General Samford did say definitely that Air Force inquiries made since 1947 had revealed "nothing constituting a danger." The radar blips, he said, were probably "phenomena associated with intellectual and scientific interests."

Pentagon spokesmen made no attempt to account for the report of one agitated woman in Oregon, according to *Newsweek* (April 17, 1950), that "she had seen a whole squadron of disks maneuvering in the sky. The hovering UFOs spelled out: **P-E-P-S-I.**

A detailed accounting was given by radio commentator Henry J. Taylor in a series of broadcasts. Taylor announced that the flying machines were "wonderful news," highly advanced "*secret weapons.*" One of the aircraft was "roughly circular," a variation on the Phantom Jet with engine louvres arrayed across the aircraft's shell. The other vehicles sighted were *saucer-shaped.* The Pentagon, of course, denied the reports.[62]

But the lights of Peenemünde flitted in the sky from Seattle to Washington, D.C.

Pentagon spokesmen smoothed away any exposures of Operation Paperclip, not to mention saucers, for decades. It was therefore inevitable that the very first "investigative" panel assembled in 1953 to investigate UFO sightings was chaired by Dr. Howard P. Robertson, another Princeton physicist—wouldn't you know, the same intelligence officer charged with directing the Consolidated Advance Field Teams (C.A.F.T.s) assigned to locating Nazi Germany's technical secrets after WWII.[63]

Dr. Robertson was also instrumental in the transplanting of Werner von Braun and his fellow Nazi fugitives from Peenemünde to the United States.

For the next 20 years he designed weapons for the CIA and DoD. In the mid-1950s, he jumped ship to the California Institute of Technology and joined the science advisory board of the NSA under Director John Samford.[64] Another scientist from the Robertson Panel, Lloyd Berkner, was a technical adviser to the CIA for 20 years.[65]

J. Allen Hynek, an astronomer, had already found fame as an "authority" on the growing "saucer psychosis." His own 1947 UFO committee probe had, according to Vesco, an unstated objective: "to attribute the sightings either to nonexistent things or to mistakenly identified things that already existed: psychopathic hallucinations, hoaxes, optical illusions, weather balloons, perihelia, lenticular clouds, meteorites, ordinary planes flying at high altitudes ..."[66]

From the Robertson Panel's recommendations came a policy of "debunking" all flying saucer sighting reports: "The 'debunking' aim would result in reduction in public interest in 'flying saucers' which today evoke a strong psychological reaction," the panel concluded. "This education could be accomplished by mass media, [especially] television, motion pictures and popular articles." The panel advised that mental health professionals familiar with mob psychology should design the "education" program. It also recommended that UFO organizations should be *surveilled* "because of their potentially great influence on mass thinking if widespread sightings should occur. The apparent irresponsibility and the possible use of such groups for subversive purposes should be kept in mind."[67]

Ordo Templis Intelligentis

UFO mythology was launched in a big way in the 1950s, wrapped in gaudy pulp covers and flashed on the silver screen. Jack Parsons, the CalTech rocket pioneer and high priest of the Ordo Tempis Orientis Agape Lodge in Pasadena—and one of the first Americans to report sighting a UFO—was addicted to science fiction. He regularly attended meetings of the L.A. Fantasy and Science Fiction Society, where, in 1945, the adept (he took "the Oath of the Anti-Christ" in 1949) met Lt. Commander L. Ron Hubbard, who made "alien" visitations an integral part of a religious doctrine he called Scientology.[68]

The OTO was founded between 1895 and 1900 by a pair of powerful Freemasons, Karl Kellner and Theodor Reuss. Politically, the order was right-wing in the extreme, proposing the creation of a pan-German world based on pagan spiritual beliefs. Kellner died in 1905, and Reuss, a former spy for the Prussian Secret Service, assumed the office of High Caliph. While living in the UK, Reuss spied on German socialist expatriates. In 1912, he made the acquaintance of Aleister Crowley and appointed him head of the OTO's British chapter.[69]

But The Beast's political loyalties have always been an open question. While living in the States, he penned a series of pro-German diatribes for a pair of fascist publications, *The Fatherland* and *The Internationalist*. After the war there were calls for his head. Crowley offered that his pro-German stance was a ruse concocted by MI6, England's military intelligence apparatus. In 1912 he had informed the secret service of his correspondence with Reuss, the German spy. Throughout the 20s and 30s, Crowley gathered intelligence on European Communists, the Nazi movement and Germany's occult lodges.[70]

Crowley died in 1947, willing the copyright for his books and unpublished manuscripts to the OTO and leadership of the order to Karl Germer, otherwise known as Frater Saturnus X., formerly Crowley's Legate in the United States. Germer was born in Germany, served in WWI and was reportedly tossed in prison by the Nazis for his involvement in Freemasonry. (Crowley believed Germer to be a Nazi spy but admitted him to the OTO anyway.) He settled after the war in Dublin, California and died on October 25, 1962 "under horrifying circumstances," according to his wife in a letter to Marcelo Matta, an OTO official in Brazil. She informed him that Germer, on his death bed, had insisted Matta succeed the German as the Outer Head of the occult order.

However, the mantle did not pass to Karl Germer's chosen successor because the CIA orchestrated a coup. But not as one OTO spokesman tells it: "Recently the United States government has legalized our opinion.... [Outer Head Grady McMurty's] leadership of the Ordo Templi Orientis rests on several rather clear letters of authorization from Crowley himself. They met while McMurty was a young First Lieutenant during World War II. He had been admitted to the OTO in 1941 [by] Jack Parsons."[71] In fact, the choice of McMurty was not "clear" at all. Matta's advocates insist that the court decision was based on the perjured testimony of Grand Poo-Bah Grady McMurty and a clutch of attorneys on the CIA dole. And the cult's position is irrelevant since, according to charters signed on March 22, 1946 and April 11, 1946 by Crowley, The Beast had left it to Germer to veto or amend his choice of a successor.

As Matta saw it, no one had a legitimate claim to the title but he. Unfortunately, Herr Germer died during the period the CIA had chosen to move mind control experimentation from academic and military labs into the community. An inner circle of Heironymous scientists experimented on cult devotees, and sometimes collaborated in mass murder to silence the subjects (Jonestown, SLA, Solar Temple). It was a marriage of convenience. Occult societies are secretive. They follow direction. They exist in corners of a society that ignores them.

A number of intelligence agents with occult interests already had their hooks into the OTO. One of them was Gerald Yorke, a veteran British intelligence agent working, an advocate of Matta argues, "with American intelligence in an attempt to absorb the OTO into the ideological warfare network of the political right."[72]

Before the horns of Thelemite succession were bestowed upon Grady McMurty, Yorke the prelate spy "misinterpreted" Germer's will and named Joseph Metzger, a ranking Thelemite (and the son of a former Swiss intelligence chief), to the office of High Caliph. One order adept, Oskar Schlag, was an alleged "psychological warfare" specialist from Israel. Even McMurty (with his degree in political science) was a State Department bureaucrat on the day Herr Germer died.

The coup was sealed while Marcelo Matta, a writer for Brazilian television, fended off operatives of the CIA bent on destroying his sanity and leaving him financially crippled. It was a ritual that subjects of mind control conditioning would come to know well. Strangers approached his friends and filled their ears with lurid stories of debauchery. He was suddenly unable to find work. His mail was opened.

Matta took a job teaching English, studied self-defense.

"He had begun to doubt his sanity," the Matta advocate says. "He constantly suspected people who approached him. He saw in himself all the clinical symptoms of paranoia."

After a few years of harassment and squabbling over the leadership of the OTO, Motta came to the realization that the McMurty junta and "the American 'intelligence' network behind them had a worry, and a pressing one; "Motta's proposed *New Manifesto* [did] not mention ... Grady at all. Since their purpose was to create an American 'intelligence' tool at the expense of a religious organization, it was necessary to either bring Motta to concede Grady further authority or discredit Motta completely."

They did what they wilt. In 1967 Germer's entire occult library and manuscripts were stolen from the home of his widow. Without the royalties these raked in, Mrs. Germer was destitute and literally starved to death.

Matta was cast out of the OTO.

Trouble brewed in the cult's cauldron. At least one Son of Sam killer passed through a deviant offshoot.[73]

The OTO's Solar Lodge in San Bernardino was founded by Maury McCauley, a mortician, on his own property. McCauley was married to Barbara Newman, a former model and the daughter of a retired Air Force colonel from Vandenberg.

The group subscribed to a grim, apocalyptic view of the world precipitated by race wars, and the prophecy made a lasting impression on Charles Manson, who visited the lodge on occasion. In the L.A. underworld, the OTO spin-off was known for indulgence in sadomasochism, drug dealing, blood drinking, sexual child abuse and murder. The Riverside OTO, like the Manson Family, used drugs, sex, psycho-drama and fear to tear down the mind of the initiate and rebuild it according to the desires of the cult's inner-circle.[74]

On the East Coast, a series of murders created an atmosphere of fear in New

York City. Before the world had ever heard of Son of Sam, an obscure Vietnam veteran named David Berkowitz moved into an apartment on Pine Street, a rotting gantlet of hovels in Yonkers. Like much of the bloodshed for which he is known, Berkowitz did not make the decision to live on Pine Street. Key decisions in his life were made by the leaders of a religious group based in Westchester, a hybrid of OTO members and acolytes from the Process Church of the Final Judgment. Members of the cult mingled with others in Manhattan and Brooklyn, and had contact with similar groups across the country. The leader of the Westchester "family" was a real estate attorney with a practice in White Plains. He was active in local politics. Balding, lean with years, the attorney directed Berkowitz and his "brothers" to kill in the name of an ancient cause.

The group's meeting place was an abandoned church, a decrepit hulk on the grounds of the abandoned Warburg-Rothschild estate. The church, partially eaten by fire, was the group's "eastern Headquarters." Most of the pews had been removed from the church long ago. On one wall was hung a large silver pentagram, festooned with silver insets in the shape of Waffen SS lightning bolts.[75]

MK-ULTRA and the Godfather

The interaction of the CIA with organized cult crime is a natural, and it's hardly unprecedented. Other, more traditional crime "families" also have connections in spyworld.

James "Whitey" Bulger, the most notorious gangster in Boston, has achieved mythic status in his hometown with the help of the the FBI. His past is a study of the national security underground insinuating itself into a typical metropolitan criminal network.

On January 1, 1994, the *Boston Globe* ran a story on Bulger's introduction to the CIA:

James (Whitey) Bulger, the reputed gangland leader, is uniquely qualified to comment on the burgeoning scandal over the government-sponsored use of human guinea pigs." From 1956 to 1959, while serving a sentence at Atlanta federal penitentiary on a bank robbery conviction, Bulger received a reduction in sentence for volunteering to be a subject in LSD experiments sponsored by the CIA. In an interview with *Globe* reporters," Senate President William Bulger said he had discouraged his brother from participating in the experiments in letters the two siblings exchanged in the late 1950s. Those who know Whitey Bulger say he continues to suffer side effects from the experiments, including nightmares and insomnia.

"Who knew about LSD then?" recalls State Senator Bulger. "But I was very apprehensive about it. Imagine, three days a month [dropped from his sentence] for running that risk. There were only 8–10 of them and two guys went stark raving mad.... You couldn't go through something like that and come out improved."[76]

Whitey read voraciously in prison. The bank robber was especially fond of books on military history, strategy and intelligence operations. Whitey's reading contributed to his survival in the mob wars of the 1960s. His legendary ability to manipulate federal agents was, one local reporter noted years later, "a study in Cold War political strategy."

After his release from prison in 1965, Bulger rose to prominence in organized crime in Boston's south side. The 1986 President's Commission on Organized Crime declared him a killer. Bulger, the *Globe* reported on September 20, 1988, rose steadily in the past decade to the top of the underworld with 'nary a scratch': "I can't tell you that anybody I've worked with has any idea what kind of muscle he has," a former prosecutor says, "just that everybody's scared to death of him." In 1981, the bugging of the Angiulos Mafia family led to the discovery that they could call on Bulger and Flemmi, if need be, anytime, to *kill* for them.

"I'll tell you right now, if I called these guys ... they'd kill anybody we tell 'em to," underboss Gennaro Angiulo claimed. When Angiulo was placed under arrest in 1983, Bulger became the most powerful organized crime figure in Boston. It was rumored that Whitey fed leads to the FBI, resulting in Angiulo's downfall. With the competition scrubbed, Bulger became the ranking mobster in South Boston.

Whitey led the charmed life of a godfather with an uncanny intuition for evading arrest. Local police complained that he always *seemed to know* when there was a listening device in the room. Bulger was somehow aware of the sleuthing and either talked nonsense when monitored by FBI agents, or said nothing at all. On one occassion he unearthed $50,000 in electronic equipment and federal agents begged him to return it while Bulger drowned out their voices with a good-cop, bad-cop parody.

For thirty years, he managed to maintain an unblemished police record.

Bulger was a sensitive subject around city hall. Police Commissioner Francis

Roache refused to discuss him. There was internal dissension at the FBI over Bulger's untouchability, much of the protest arising from blowback over his relationship with John Connolly, an agent of the FBI's organized crime unit. But James Ahearn, the special agent in charge of the Boston office, flatly rejects any suggestion that the FBI was protecting Bulger. He also instructed Connolly not to talk to reporters about his friendship with South Boston's most powerful mobster.

"It really made you think, why won't the FBI do this guy?" one high-ranking DEA official complains.

More chaos in local law enforcement ensued when state police discovered a small proviso tagged to state budget legislation in 1991, The attachment would have forced all supervisors of the department's intelligence division to "*retire immediately.*" It was purged from the budget, but police were unable to determine exactly who in the state capital had slipped the item into the state budget. Many in law enforcement felt the proviso was a message to the state police officials who ordered the Lancaster Street investigation of Whitey Bulger.

The whole unexpurgated story of the mobster's federal connections leaked out slowly over a period of five years. The *Globe* took notice on March 5, 1995 of "ill will arising from Bulger's role as an informant and his uncanny ability to dodge electronic surveillance used by the Massachusetts State Police and US Drug Enforcement Agency."

The FBI "informant" had friends in high places, that much was clear. There was, in 1991, for example, Bulger's $1.9 million in state lottery winnings—the Justice Department discovered five years later that Bulger had obtained his share of the winning $14 million lottery ticket in a mob money-laundering scheme.

Charges that he received a "tribute" on all drug profits from the mobs of South Boston arose when 51 residents of the area, otherwise known as the Winter Hill Gang, were stung in a DEA investigation and indicted on drug charges. Bulger, their boss, quietly lit out of town and went into hiding. His partner in organized crime, 'Cadillac Frank' Salemme, escaped at about the same time. In August, 1995 the FBI caught up with Salemme, who had presided over the entire New England Mafia. The don was arrested in West Palm Beach, Florida and held without bail.

In 1996, the FBI completely reversed itself and formally acknowledged that since the 1960s (not the 80s, as FBI officials confessed a few years earlier), James Bulger had been a valued "informant." That is, while local, state and federal police—even the FBI's own agents—doggedly pursued him, the most feared man in Boston had friends in the Bureau. They granted him a license to run drug-trafficking operations in Boston, even to knock out competitors by turning state's evidence against them.

As of this writing, James Bulger remains at large.

The Mafia's Savona-Profaci family was drawn into the obscure world of intelligence and mind control when a young member of the clan became a guinea-pig in trauma-based mind control and covert radio-frequency brain experimentation. Thomas Savona was convicted after a two-day trial—in which the complainants, an uncle and aunt on his mother's side, were the only prosecution witnesses—by the New York State Supreme Court. The charge was the attempted murder of his uncle. Savona testified on his own behalf on the advice of his attorney. Three eyewitnesses for the defense were not called. Savona's attorney explained to him that his own testimony would be sufficient to win an acquittal. It wasn't. Thomas was sentenced on September 30, 1991.[77]

The question of exceptional circumstances was never addressed by the court: "Ever since my teenage years, I have been trying to prove that I am being victimized," wrote Savona from the Sullivan Correctional Facility to New York's *City Sun* on February 19, 1994, "by [the CIA's] brain wave frequency sector, twenty-four hours a day, seven days a week." Savona complained that parties unknown had tapped his "thoughts, vision, hearing and other sensory wave frequencies, detecting and tuning into them, modulating them."[78] His complaint was ignored by the court and examining psychiatrists, though he asked repeatedly for an MRI scan and medical tests to prove that he'd been implanted with a bio-chip.

Until the age of six, Thomas Savona was raised by black Muslims. He still does not eat meat or fish. He doesn't take drugs. One day, Savona recalls, the Muslims "disappeared," and his Uncle entered, or "infiltrated," the picture. The uncle was a cultist, Savona says. The boy suffered ritualized, trauma-based conditioning—in the course of a prolonged war waged against the Mafia family by local "blood cults" with ties to "the elite power structure and government."

Young Thomas turned to Carmela Profaci, his great aunt and the mother superior of Regina Pacis Church in Brooklyn, New York, to protect him from the abuse. She hid him when the cult attempted to subject him to further abuse.[79] In high school, he was generally considered to be honest and hard working. Dr. Adolph Goldman, a court-appointed doctor, noted in is 1988 report that the accused "had no history of psychiatric problems." Thomas's brother Philip entered the family business, organized crime. The first arrest came in 1979—although, according to parole officers, he spoke of occultism and electronic brain monitoring months before the police hauled him away. As he tells it, Thomas and his uncle, said to be a high priest in a local satanic cult, had a heated argument after the latter refused to ship heart medication to Thomas's father in Sicily, where it was unavailable. The uncle produced a gun and Thomas struggled with him. The gun went off while still in his uncle's hand. The weight of the testimony (from his aunt and uncle) heard by the jury was against him. Savona was convicted in 1979.

He was sent to Marcy State Hospital. Thomas had become "delusional," according to Dr. Goldman: "He [Thomas] remembered being at Marcy for 14 days, but he couldn't really give an explanation for this. 'I was trying to explain to people that my brain was monitored.' He has a theory that the brain gives electrical waves which can be picked up. "I know I'm monitored ... through biofeedback."[80] The patient was incarcerated at the mental hospital for 45 days and "refused any medication," insisting he was a target of electronic mind control and harassment. After his release in 1985, Savona fired a gun at his much-despised uncle on two occasions, "in self-defense," he says, and was again charged with attempted murder in 1988.

Court-appointed psychiatrists diagnosed Thomas as a "delusional psychotic," yet concluded he was "fit to stand trial and be sentenced." The diagnosis is questionable since Savona was verbally articulate, and while incarcerated maintained a 3.5+ grade point average at a local community college.[81] He has been consistently denied the MRI scan he has requested since the mid-80s. Like most victims of EM experimentation, Thomas has written letters to anyone who might help him prove that he is a target of electromagnetic attack, including Governor Mario Cuomo, the Martin Marietta Corp., the Brain Research Foundation, IBM Research Department, the Department of the Navy, and so on. None of the respondents have offered technical assistance. He is currently a prisoner at a the Fishkill high-security medical facility in Beacon, New York.

Occult Politics

One can safely predict that techniques for controlling behavior and modifying personality will grow more efficient by the year 2000. Thousands of experts at conditioning are now trying out their behavior-changing technology on tens of thousands of people—in classrooms, prisons, mental hospitals, day-care centers, factories, nursing homes....
    —*Journal of the American Academy of Arts and Sciences* (Summer, 1967)

The CIA's s use of cult cut-outs was advanced by a visit to Elizabeth Kubler-Ross, whose knowledge of the occult underground served as the map for forging alliances. Cults sprang up and proliferated throughout the 1960s, many with links to the munitions and intelligence empires.

The cults were on the rise. In San Francisco, Anton LaVey's "Magic Circle," the forerunner of the Church of Satan, was an elite secret society comprised of assorted eccentrics. They enacted Egyptian rituals in celebration of Osiris, seances, black masses. LaVey's Magic Circle included, according to LaVey biographer Burton Wolfe:

> The heir of the Vickers munitions empire, a [crony] of arms dealer Basil "Death Merchant" Zaharoff in the days when the war profiteer had a mysterious black chapel in his chateau; Carin de Plessen, inaccurately called "the mad countess" by her neighbors in Marin County (she was an authentic baroness who grew up in the Royal Palace of Denmark) because she kept a compound of Great Danes at her rustic, isolated house on a knoll in Woodacre; novelist Stephen Schneck, author of *The Night Clerk;* anthropologist Mike Harner [headed for professorships at Columbia, Yale and Berkeley, also the chair of the New School for Social Research]; investment broker Donald Werby [a billionaire accused of pederasty in 1990] and his wife Willy, son-in-law and daughter of the man who owns Chock Full O' Nuts; underground filmmaker Kenneth Anger ....

And a gaggle of others, not to mention Shana Alexander (current director of the National Women's Political Caucus); a dildo manufacturer; the grandson of an American president; several popular science fiction writers and "various physicians, attorneys, artists, writers, policemen and policewomen."[82]

Like so many others in this inventory, the direction of LaVey's life took a drastic turn with exposure to the castrated Hitler regime. In the spring of 1945, LaVey's uncle took "Tony" along on a sojourn to Germany to rebuild blasted airstrips. On this junket, the impressionable youth stopped at a military post long enough to watch confiscated Nazi horror movies, thinly-veiled depictions of Nazi occultism. The gothic trappings of LaVey's postwar notoriety had their beginnings in rumors circulating in Germany, grim accounts of a Black Order operating within the Nazi Party.[83]

The shamanic beliefs of the cults were formed by national security gurus spinning capricious spiritual self-indulgence into blinds for CIA mind control operations. In 1961, Dr. Timothy Leary of Harvard directed a program that tested hallucinogens on prisoners in Massachusetts to determine whether the drugs had an effect on criminal tendencies.[84] State officials fired him for inciting inmates to rebellion, but in a tape-recorded interview in 1975, Leary admitted he was a "willing agent of the CIA." He refused to discuss how he was paid.[85]

In an unpublished manuscript, mind control researcher Walter Bowart invokes documents indicating that Leary "had received money channeled by the CIA through various government agencies. The files showed that, in all, there were eight government grants paid to Leary from 1953 to 1958, most of them paid through the National Institute of Mental Health, now known to have 'fronted' for the CIA."

Another psychedelic priest of the period was Charles Tart, the LSD-dropping protégé of Dr. J.B. Rhine. Tart received his Ph.D in psychology from the University of North Carolina. His academic interests included personality theory, dreams and hypnosis. Tart's *Altered States of Consciousness*, published in 1969, was widely considered a ground-breaking study of meditation, yoga, drugs, hypnosis and dreams. His work is greatly influenced by the philosophy of G.I. Gurdjieff, and he has mingled with cults founded on the teachings of the Russian mystic and spiritual guide of Karl Haushofer, the Nazi strategist. Professor Tart taught at the University of California at Davis for 30 years. (The Davis campus is a stone's throw from Vacaville Prison, where psychotropic drugs were tested on prisoners by the CIA, sometimes against their will and often as punishment. The adjacent town is Dixon—one of two sources, according to an FCC report, of the famous "Soviet" ELF hum that rumbled through Eugene, Oregon in 1978.[86] A second signal was detected with a source offshore. Who should step forth to "explain?" Pentagon spokesman William Perry, until recently secretary of defense, an SAIC board member, falsely blamed the Soviets for the ringing ears, nose-bleeds and head pains caused by the EM transmissions.)

One of the savants who did the most to fill the heads of credulous seekers with addled metascientific proselytizing was Andrija Puharich, the CIA mystic who discovered Uri Geller, the Cyprus-born Israeli "psychic." Puharich was born in 1918. He received a medical degree from Northwestern University in 1947. Upon graduation, Puharich developed a slavish interest in clairvoyance and dabbled in theories for electronically enhancing and synthesizing psychic abilities. He joined the Army and took part in certain "parapsychology" experiments.[87] The *Washington Post* reported in 1977 that Puharich also worked in the Army's Chemical and Biological Warfare Center at Fort Detrick, Maryland, and has "lectured the Army, Air Force and Navy on possibilities for mind warfare. Expert in hypnotism as well as microelectronics."

Puharich took a fatal fall down a flight of stairs in January 1995. Researcher

Terry Milner peeled away the cover stories and found that the true Puharich bore little resemblance to the hallucinatory shaman touted by his devotees:

> Throughout his life Andrija performed many outrages on four legged inhabitants of earth, slicing and dicing them as he saw the need to do so all in the name of science. Dogs were a favorite. One of life's little mysteries is why he belonged to the Kennel Club, but he did.
>
> It was while he was at Northwestern that Andrija put his mental-pedal to the mental-metal and came up with his Theory of Nerve Conduction. The theory proposed that the neuron units radiate and receive waves of energy which he calculated to be in the ultra-shortwave bands below infrared and above the radar spectrum. Therefore the basic nerve units—neurons—are a certain type of radio receiver-transmitter.
>
> The theory got passed around and glimpsed by various high personages of 1940's science. Among them was Paul Weiss, a neurophysiologist at the University of Chicago. José Delgado, the guy who tortured animals by putting electronic implants into their brains to influence their behaviour, liked Paul Weiss and you can find his grateful acknowledgment to the man in his "ve know vat's goot for you" book, *Toward a Psychocivilized Society.*
>
> While his nerve conduction manuscript was circulating, Puharich headed out for California to do his internship as a medical researcher. He spent a year or so at the Permanenté Research Foundation. During that time he carried out research into the effects of digatoid drugs, funded by Sandoz Chemical Works. Sandoz.
>
> Andrija's wife Virginia, who had been an editor at the Office of War Information during the war, came with him and worked at the same facility.

Puharich is the inventor of an implantable, "miniature tooth radio, sold to the CIA."[88] He admits to involvement in "LSD work for the CIA in 1954." (Biological warfare researcher Frank Olsen, injected with a massive dose of MDA, a potent hallucinogen, plummeted twelve stories and was killed in an operation run by agents from Ft. Detrick at New York's Statler Hotel a year before.) Immediately upon his ostensible release from the service, Puharich set up a laboratory to study clairvoyance. He was also the founder of the Intelectron Corporation, a medical electronics firm (recalling the J.B. Rhine/Medtronics combination).

The electronic wizardry of Dr. Puharich was the source of the unpleasantness experienced by David B., a mind control subject who had implants surgically removed ...

X-rays revealed a metal object on the left side of my skull under the jaw in the soft tissue of my neck. In May 1996, I finally had it removed, I asked many doctors about the possibility of it falling there during an extraction—they said, "possible, but remote." Most of them thought it punctured my neck from the outside. I sent X-rays to Dr. Sims, and he arranged removal. The strange thing that came out of this was discovery of the small object in my shoulder. Dr. Leer called after receiving my X-rays and asked if I had ever broken my shoulder, if I had ever been in an explosion. I replied no. He said the reason was that the X-ray clearly showed a screw in my left shoulder. He said it looked like an operation for a broken shoulder. I have never broken a bone to my knowledge, and called my mother to ask. She said I'd had no operations as a child. This part is a complete mystery,

During the first six months of torture (extreme at that time), I went to a dentist and reported pain under my new dental bridge, installed a few months before the assault. He removed it and I was still in contact. So I wrote off my teeth and concentrated on my throat, wrongly. In my X-rays and CAT scan, one tooth is very bright and in one frame of the catscan it shows rays of white emanating from it. People I asked said it was probably an interference effect with the metal.

A researcher commented by mail recently: "The tooth implant I have followed was to be used as a send-receive unit or a hearing device. I have no idea what its current appearance would be. Back then it required using the tooth's nerve as a pathway. It was developed by Dr. Andrija Puharich and a dentist named Joe Lawrence." He also said there was a Government interest in the doctor's work.

In his books, Puharich echoed the schizy Blavatsky efflux of his fellow mind control operators. Uri Geller ("tested" and approved by Targ and Puthoff at SRI) had profound mental abilities "beamed to him," Puharich claimed, from "a distant galaxy." The source of the radio signal that allowed Geller to bend silverware was an "extraterrestrial race" known as "the Hoovians," under the command of a powerful alien council he called "The Nine." Most impressive was Geller's ability to "teleport" himself across great distances in the blink of an eye and "dematerialize" small objects. Puharich complained that the "E.T.s" buzzed him in flying saucers and left obnoxious messages on his answering machine. One summer, at his Ossning, New York complex, Puharich put together a cult of "Gellerings" called the "Space Kids," twenty adolescents from seven countries supposedly graced with the same abilities as Uri Geller. They claimed to be of "alien" origin. A 14-year-old participant reports his suspicions were aroused when he was asked to take part in a "remote viewing" exercise—to spy on the Kremlin, among other sensitive political targets.[89]

Russell Targ, an instigator of all this—the most unlikely cover story in history—affects the trappings of hard science in his books on the paranormal. But his work is laden with more fantastic tales that conceal his efforts on behalf of the CIA. Targ claims that the public is hobbled from an understanding of psychic functioning by a wide variety of religious cult leaders who "profit and flourish by attracting a continuous flow of recruits who believe their claims [of] enlightenment and power ... derived through special knowledge about the inner-workings of reality and the mind."[90]

In 1979, as director of the Human Freedom Center in Berkeley, Targ devoted several months 'interviewing and counseling' former cult members" (bear in mind that he is a physicist, not a therapist), and "I found that many individuals had joined cults as a result of their having either experienced or witnessed what they believed were psychic occurrences."[91] All well and good, but Targ somehow neglects to mention that the Human Foundation Center was a direct link to the CIA mind control operation known as People's Temple.

The UC Berkeley counseling center that employed Dr. Targ was founded by Elmer and Deanna Mertle, Jones's public relations officers. The Mertles changed their names to Al and Jeannie Mills after leaving the Temple in 1975.[92] The Mills clan pulled out of the Jones operation with a group of Caucasians who made up the inner-circle of People's Temple, lieutenants of Jim Jones reborn as Concerned Relatives, a support group. The core of the group had in fact conspired with Dr. Lawrence Laird Layton at UC Berkeley, the hidden hand of the CIA medical experimentation compound in Guyana, and "Minister" Jones in mass murder.[93]

Al and Jeannie were unwilling participants in People's Temple. Jones had forced their loyalty by reminding them of the confession of criminal acts they'd signed before the couple and their children were permitted into the fold. Eventually, Al and Jeannie came to like their positions of rank in the Temple. Once out of it, they were instrumental in luring Congressman Leo Ryan, who'd been investigating CIA ties to the cult, to Guyana, where he perished among the 1,200 murder-victims of Jonestown.[94]

Al and Jeannie Mills set up the Human Freedom Center in a ramshackle house in Berkeley. Russell Russell Targ joined the Center in March, 1979, four months after the People's Temple slaughter.[95] He counseled survivors for almost a year, then returned to his psi research position at Stanford Research Institute, from whence he had come.

On February 26, 1980, shortly after Targ resigned, an unidentified killer entered the Center and executed Al, Jeannie and their teen-aged daughter with gun shots to the head. The building was not burglarized. A friend of the Mills family arrived at the local police station a few days later to report that a psychiatrist once employed at the Center had committed the murders.[96]

Vipers and Daydreams (Reprised)

The California university system was a minor West Coast Pentagon of covert planning of psychological warfare programs that tended to overlap with CIA mind control operations. Experimentation on the People's Temple flock was directed by Dr. Layton, a Berkeley scientist. A decade earlier, in the winter of 1969 to be exact, Dr. Arthur A. Jensen, a professor of educational psychology at UC Berkeley, turned the science of eugenics on its ear with the publication an article in the *Harvard Educational Review* reviving discredited notions of race and IQ.

Almost instantly, Jensen became the darling of the corporate media. Jensen's position that the genetics of race determines intelligence was treated by the press, independent scholar Allan Chase recalls in *The Malthus Legacy*, "as the greatest scientific development since the first nuclear device was exploded at Los Alamos." Feature stories lauding Jensen's incarnation of Nazi-style eugenics were published in *Newsweek, Time, Life* and *U.S. News & World Report* and elsewhere.

On March 31, 1969, *Newsweek* summarized Jensen's "findings": "Dr. Jensen's view, put simply, is that blacks are born with less 'intelligence' than most whites.... The reason, he argues, is that intelligence is an inherited capacity and that since a prime characteristic of races is that they are 'inbred,' blacks are likely to remain lower in intelligence."

The notion that African-Americans were not as smart as Caucasians (and even engaged in "in-breeding") led Jensen to ask the rhetorical question, "Is there a danger that current welfare policies, unaided by eugenics foresight, could lead to the genetic enslavement of a substantial segment of our population?"

Welfare, Dr. Chase emphasizes, "was the basic point of the Jensen testament—not education. Nor intelligence. Jensen's article was nothing more, and nothing less, than a propaganda tract for eugenics."

The Pioneer Fund has made Jensen's theories the academic backbone of its anti-welfare campaign. The right-wing organization exerts unheard of influence on public policy for a political fringe group. Its platform—ending welfare, halting immigration, cutting funds to educational programs, scaling back entitlements and affirmative action—fuels federal and state ballot measures.

Marek Kohn, in *The Race Gallery* (1995), traced the history of the Pioneer Fund: founded in 1937 to promote higher reproduction by American whites and "research 'race betterment.'" The fund "disburses around a million dollars a year. In the second half of the 1980s, its main beneficiary was Thomas Bouchard's twin study project, which was given more than $500,000. .... Between 1971 and 1992, Arthur Jensen received more than one million dollars."

The Pioneer Fund was set up, according to IRS documents, to raise money to fund the study of racial purity. On December 14, 1995, *El Sol Del Valle* reported:

> Their literature was quoted by Nazi war criminals as the basis for the "Final Solution," that is, the extermination of the Jews. Yes, at the Nuremberg War Crimes trials, German war criminals actually quoted Americans and their study of "eugenics" as the basis for Nazi racial views and policy.
>
> The Pioneer Fund led American groups in advocating the use of German "eugenics." It still does. The Fund responded to Dr. Tanton's requests with over $700,000 in seed money to fund FAIR [an activist front that advocates population control]. FAIR is a group founded by ... Dr. John Tanton. For start-up money, Tanton went to the Pioneer Fund.... Dr. Tanton claims he knows nothing of the Pioneer Fund's pro-Nazi background. It has financed such racially charged and directed projects as the famous Dr. Shockley studies that tried to prove that "negroes" are inferior to white people and, more recently, it is reported, funded the infamous *Bell Curve* studies of Charles Murray.

The Pioneer Fund has granted liberal support to Roger Pearson ($787,400 by 1993), editor of two widely distributed journals advocating racial purity, *Mankind Quarterly,* repeatedly cited in *The Bell Curve,* and *The Journal of Social, Political and Economic Studies,* which publishes articles by Jensen and his fellow "conservative" eugenicists. Pearson was once an organizer for The Northern League, the UK neo-Nazi movement that recruited senile officers of Hitler's SS.

Pearson moved to the U.S. in 1965 to edit *Western Destiny,* a jorunal published by Willis Carto of the Liberty Lobby. The editorial board of the "academic" journal included Austin App, the pro-Nazi leader of the German American National Congress and a leading Holocaust revisionist. Pearson went on to become the editor of the American Security Council's *Journal of International Relations* and served on the board of the Council's American Foreign Policy Institute. The council is headed without exception by military-industrial hawks, and high on the council's agenda is the promotion of military spending, thus the molding of public opinion with Dr. Jensen's genetic IQ theories, a "scientific" rationale for stanching the welfare coffers and diverting tax revenue to the DoD. (It is a testament to the ASC's political clout that presidential candidate Robert Dole boasts Council credentials).

Thirty years after Arthur Jensen's revival of fascist eugenics hardened racial attitudes, he sits on the "Scientific Advisory Board" of BrainTainment Resources, Inc. (BTR) in Laguna Beach, California. BTR sales literature boasts that Dr. Jensen is the country's "most highly esteemed scientist in the field of IQ measurement and intelligence analysis." Incorporated in January 1995, BTR set up a core development team of cognitive scientists, computer technicians, teachers and psychologists. John H. Kranzler, PhD, formerly a research associate of Arthur Jensen's, is the company specialist in intelligence testing, or "cognitive chronometrics." Kranzler received his doctorate, also from the University of California at Berkeley, in 1990. He is currently an assistant professor of the School of Psychology at the University of Florida. His research turns on the "assessment and development of cognitive abilities."

BrainTainment, Inc. claims that ThinkFast, computer software advertised on the Internet, utilizes "the underlying technology of psycho-interactive intelligence to perk up tired brains, clear out foggy heads and focus in scattered minds." After all, "why not have fun while educating and empowering your brain?" The company suggests that "real brain power should be measured much like muscle-power, that is, with an 'ergometer' that dynamically challenges ('loads') the full capacity of the 'muscle.' We call it *psycho-interactivity.*"

But the interaction of mind with computer, the essence of electronic brain manipulation, is not advertised on the Net. It is squandered by the "national security" underground. Chris Bird, a CIA psychological warfare specialist, and Peter Tomkins, an OSS veteran, authors of *The Secret Life of Plants* (Harper & Row, 1973), are also steeped in the moral wasteland of the CIA's mind control sector. The book was largely concerned with the experiments of Clive Backster, a lie detector operator who took galvanic readings of houseplants and claimed to have produced fluctuations that coincided with his thoughts. Cornell experimenters were unable to duplicate his results (although Paul Sauvin, a minister at the Psychic Science Temple of Metaphysics, claimed that the "Backster Effect" was easily evoked in his own lab). As usual, the technology behind the ruse is a dead give-away—Sauvin, according to Bird, was a "pacifist, abhorrent of the use of thought controlled weapons ... though he has taken out business certificates on such devices—which put him on record as the owner."[97]

Bird himself has bona fidés that scream EM mind control. After the Vietnam

War, he found employment as a representative of the Rand Development Corporation (a front similar to the Human Ecology Fund), chaired by H.J. Rand, the son of the CEO of Sperry-Rand, the munitions builder. Bird partook of an early exchange of advanced scientific information with the Soviets. He was also a "biocommunications"—cyber-clairvoyance—specialist at MRU, the CIA proprietary engaged in the development of "psycho-acoustical" biotechnology.[98]

The "New Age" (still dripping with occult beliefs reminiscent of the "New Age" in proto-Nazi Germany), saucer mythology and drugged clairvoyance are blinds for involvement in extreme human rights violations. The gamut of zany cover stories combine in the enigmatic C.B. Scott Jones, yet another military intelligence officer who, as a Navy pilot in the Korean War, happened to witness a UFO overflight.[99] It has long been suspected by abduction researchers that Jones is a veteran of electromagnetic mind control operations.

Angela Thompson, once a fixture at Jahn's psi research lab at Princeton, reports that Jones's primary metaphysical pursuit is "dream-projection" (á la John Alexander and his much ballyhooed "Jedi Project," the DoD's "New Age Army"), the supposed ability to entrain and manipulate the thoughts of others.

Thompson was a consenting target. Jones, then an aide to Senator Claiborne Pell, entered the picture in the late 1980s and linked "psychic" research to military intelligence brass, including Laurance Rockefeller. Pell's mentor was Averell Harriman. The Pell presence in American politics antedates the American revolution. "Clay" has long been a career politician. He attended the organizing session of the UN in San Francisco and spent seven years in the State Department, assigned to the Foreign Service. He has a strong interest in the paranormal.

He is also a closet homosexual. Attorney Robert Winter-Bergen, in *The Washington Pay-Off*, relates that he was summoned in June 1964 to release Senator Pell from jail after he'd been arrested in a Greenwich Village gay bar:

> If Senator Pell had had any identification with him, the police would have entered his name in their record of the raid [and] it would have become a matter of public information, available to anyone. In politics, the opposition will go to any lengths to obtain information that can be used to pressure, even to blackmail, a candidate, no matter how innocent the circumstances may be. I realized that only a person of influence would be able to resolve the problem without leaving any traceable evidence, and the only person I knew with such power was Carmine DeSapio, then the Democratic leader of Manhattan's First Assembly District South. I had come to know DeSapio through Julia Skouras. DeSapio had been a good friend of Pell's father, Herbert Pell, a prominent New York socialite and Democratic Party leader.

Despite the hour, I telephoned DeSapio, whom I had known slightly for several years, and after I explained the situation to him he offered to meet me at the police station in an hour. We arrived at the same time. While I waited in the main room, DeSapio went down a hall and evidently talked to whoever is in charge.

He returned in a few minutes and told me: 'Everything's okay.' Almost immediately, Pell came out of a large room at the back of the station. The moment was not conducive to chit-chat, so there were some embarrassed thank-you's and we all went our separate ways.

Scott Jones is founder of the Human Potential Foundation (HPF), a UFO "watchdog" organization in Washington, D.C. In October 1995, *Common Cause* reported that Laurance Rockefeller donated some $700,000 to the Foundation.[100]

Scott Jones was recruited by the Navy in 1946, trained as an aviation midshipman and rose to officer rank as a pilot in Korea. He has degrees from George Washington University, the University of Maryland and American University. He was with Naval intelligence for 15 years, assigned as an "assistant attaché" in New Delhi and Katmandu. And while still an intelligence officer, Jones worked at Kaman Tempo, Inc., a subsidiary of the Kaman Sciences Corporation. In 1983, a branch of the company, Kaman Tempo, a "think tank" that performs intelligence analysis for the virtual government, hosted a seminar on "applications of parapsychology." The minutes of the seminar were edited and published by Jones. In them, he mentions a network of intelligence contacts.[101]

Dr. Cecil Jones "retired" from Naval Intelligence in 1976. Turn down the volume when he talks. Like his fellow psyop agents, emergent neuro-cybernetic technology lurks behind the shaggy-dog "aliens" and psychic excursions.

The Kaman Corporation is a sprawling, diversified military contractor. Company officials include Admiral Huntington Hardisty (ret.), former commander-in-chief of the U.S. Pacific Command and director of operations for the Joint Chiefs of Staff.[102] Former Secretary of Defense Frank Carlucci, a Kaman director, also sits on the boards of several companies known to have built radio-frequency "mind control" weapons (Westinghouse and Bell Atlantic). He is chairman of the Carlyle Corporation, former secretary of defense (1987 to 1989), a director of Texas Biotechnology and other founts of advanced military technology. Among other things, Kaman manufactures airborne laser electro-optical imaging systems for military operations, and provides "advanced technology services to a number of customers, including all branches of the armed forces and various government agencies." Kaman's technical services include "various types of artificial intelligence systems," the heart of modern mind control.[103]

The company Jones keeps reveals, a social register of oily political operatives:

Congressman Charlie Rose (D-N.C.): Best remembered for his investigation of Banco Nationale Lavorro (BNL) and American companies that conspired to stock Saddam Hussein's $100-billion armaments base—ironic, since Rose was himself tarred by the scandal. In August 1989, the congressman from North Carolina threw his weight behind a lobbying group, led by the Bush administration, that pressured Eximbank—chaired by William Draper III, a friend of George Bush at Yale and the son of a Dillon, Read executive who advanced the Nazi rearmament effort between the wars[104]—to relax restrictions on military exports to Iraq. The lobbyists, including Representative Rose, convinced Draper to stretch Iraq's line of credit against the advice of the bank's own analysts, who pointed out that Hussein was the world's worst credit risk.

On April 15, 1991, Rep. Henry Gonzales of the House Banking Committee wrote in a memo, "at present, the U.S. government owes various U.S. and foreign companies over $2 billion because of Iraqi default."[105] Rose chaired a House committee investigation of the Bush administration's role in Iraqgate, a gross deception since he was among the scandal's key participants.[106]

The Congressman has long been an advocate of the Pentagon's "parapsychological" pursuits.

"Some people think this is the work of the Devil," he observes, "other people think it's the work of the Holy Spirit." The comment prompted James Mills, author of a novel about the DoD's "psychic warriors," to complain: "I think it's very dangerous for even an individual to be toying around with the occult. When you see nations doing it as a matter of national policy, that really gets scary."[107]

Rose moves in the Pentagon's mind control underground like an old hand. His friend Ira Einhorn, a counter-cultural Jabberwocky, was forced to flee the country after police in Philadelphia discovered his girlfriend's cadaver stuffed in a trunk. Jack Sarfatti of the Esalen Institute caught a glimpse of the underground on a visit to Einhorn, then "very concerned about what he called 'Soviet breakthroughs in psychotropic weapons of mind control at a distance using ELF and sound waves.'" This is just the sort of rationale that leads to classified domestic weapons development. Einhorn was attempting to pull together a study group to meet the Soviet threat. "He said he had support from the local telephone company and from the Bronfmans [the Canadian liquor

Family that held an interest in Clay Shaw's Trade Mart] to link up visionary scientists like myself.... Ira mentioned that he was working with Congressman Charlie Rose of the House Select Committee on Intelligence. Rose confirmed his connection to Einhorn in a telephone conversation."[108]

Hill & Knowlton: An intelligence clearinghouse, the most frequently exposed CIA proprietary in the District of Columbia.

Dick Farley, formerly an assistant to Jones at HPF, informs us ...

Here is a 'Jones link' to Hill & Knowlton that I can confirm. In 1990–93 or so, a former Capitol Hill staffer by name of Janet Smith (well, she said that's her name) was one of those receiving money passed through the Human Potential Foundation. Janet would visit Jones for a few hours from time to time, with office door closed and locked (according to Jones's secretary at the time), and then Janet would emerge with a nice check in the $5K or more range to tide her own little non-profit group over for a while. Janet was "into" alternative medicine, and she had a "donated" office at Hill & Knowlton. I was there a few times, as H&K also hosted some "alternative medicine" kinds of meetings, filled with cultists of the New Age sort, both the true and the gullible, as well as the manipulators.

Janet Smith is a devotee of Indian mystic Sai Baba, and she visited him regularly in India. Jones also is a scholar of India and particularly its military (subject of his doctoral thesis at American University), and of course Jones served in India.

Theodore Rockwell: Scott Jones has conducted "ESP" studies with Rockwell, a nuclear engineer from the Oak Ridge Lab (home of radiation experiments on children, etc.) and vice president of the U.S. Psychotronics Association, an organization that passes off absurd cover stories as legitimate science—the Association's 1989 conference in New York on the "Cosmicgate Conspiracy" explored the following "topics": how UFO abductions are permitted by government "in exchange for extraterrestrial technology," inter-dimensional warfare, astrological weather forecasting, the Illuminati, CFR, the world "super government" and "the prophecy of Americas economic collapse in 1989."[109]

Prince Hans Adam of Liechtenstein II: In pursuit of "aliens" and the paranormal, C.B. Scott Jones has a kindred spirit in Prince Hans Adam of Liechtenstein II, the most autocratic ruler in Europe and one of the last of ruling princes. One conservative German magazine opined that the Prince governs the tiny principality of Liechtenstein, wedged between Austria and Switzerland, "according to his wishes." He lives in imperial style: the prince once proposed dismantling the government and reigning like a monarch from his medieval castle. When he inherited power in 1989, Hans Adam went so far as to dissolve the parliament because it balked at giving him a museum for his famous art collection. His Highness owns a lion's share of the richest bank in Germany, the Bank of Liechtenstein, and his assets are valued at an estimated $2.5 billion.[110]

Hans Adam's fascination with UFOs may seem plebeian, but he has bankrolled some of the dizziest operatives in UFOlogy to fan a smokescreen for abductions by the mind control underground. In this context, traipsing after flying saucers is as imperious and arrogant as one might expect. In 1995, Prince Hans Adam was an "anonymous donor" to a conference on "alien" abductions at MIT. The conference drew about 100 abductees, scientists, doctors, psychiatrists and a pair of admitted intelligence agents.[111] The itinerary featured a lecture by John Mack, the Harvard psychiatrist Pulitzer Prized for his biography of Lawrence of Arabia, famed for his work with "alien" abductees. Less well-known is his deep background in psychoanalyzing fear and trauma in children, leadership in political organizations with CIA ties, an obsession with Werner Erhard's mind control techniques, and a $200,000 donation from Laurance Rockefeller, channeled through C.B. Scott Jones's Human Potential Foundation to fund his therapeutic work with "alien" abductees.[112]

John Alexander: Connect the Metaphysical-Industrial dots—UFOlogist Robert Durant mentions names and cover stories already examined in connection with "non-lethal" EM technology:

> Scott's friend, Colonel John Alexander, was Jones's fellow researcher on anomalies in the Bahamas, and has displayed a long term interest in the paranormal. Alexander has actively promoted psychic metal bending among government personnel using the techniques pioneered by Jack Houck of McDonnell-Douglas.
>
> Alexander is a former president of the International Association for Near-Death Studies, and he worked with Elizabeth Kubler-Ross. Alexander also served as the military liaison to the National Research Council's panel evaluating parapsychological applications.
>
> Reportedly, he had access to classified government material on parapsychology. Alexander had a 32-year career in the Army, including a stint as director of the Advanced Systems Concept Office, U.S. Army Laboratory Command. Alexander

also was chief of the Advanced Human Technology Office of the Intelligence & Security Command (INSCOM)."[113]

Alexander and Janet Morris, research director of the U.S. Global Strategy Council, teamed up with Newt Gingrich on his first book, *Window of Opportunity,* released in 1984. "Gingrich acknowledges in the book that Janet Morris, research director of the U. S. Global Strategy Council, coached the congressman through the book and gave form to his ideas. Former Jones staffer Richard Farley offers: "It was Janet's more recent 'nemesis,' her once friend and colleague John Alexander in 'non-lethal' weapons R & D, who helped Newt get his 'thinking cap' straightened out. Alexander taught them NLP (neuro-linguistic programming)." NLP, of course, is a form of hypnotic behavior modification.

Alexander ran the "non-lethal" weapons lab at Los Alamos in New Mexico. Non-lethals are a scientific bull market for virtual government technocrats. A monograph from Los Alamos ponders the bioeffects of EM radiation, or "friendly force":

PHYSIOLOGICAL RESPONSES APPLICABLE TO DEVELOPMENT OF LESS-THAN-LETHAL WEAPONS

Sponsored by National Institute of Justice, Oak Ridge National Laboratory

Less-than-lethal weapons have a variety of applications in law enforcement, including rescuing hostages, stopping fleeing felons and quelling prison disturbances. The National Institute of Justice is sponsoring a broad program to develop new techniques for "friendly force" as an alternative to the use of deadly force. As part of this program, Oak Ridge National Laboratory (ORNL) is examining approaches based on known physiological responses to certain types of stimuli. These "weapons" would temporarily incapacitate an individual or a group with no lasting physiological damage. These concepts are based on ORNL's experience and expertise in biological-based systems and biophysical responses, particularly in evaluating the physical responses of humans to a variety of chemical, physical and radiological agents....

ORNL has already examined several possible concepts for less-than-lethal weapons based on known physiological responses to energetic stimuli, including a thermal gun, a seizure gun, and a magnetophosphene gun. A thermal gun would have the operational effect of heating the body to 105 to 107°F, thereby incapacitating any threat, based on the fact that even a slight fever can affect the ability of a person to perform even simple tasks. This approach is built on four decades of research relating radio frequency exposure to body heating. A seizure gun would use electromagnetic energy to induce epileptic-like seizures in persons within the range of a particular electromagnetic field. The magnetophosphene gun is designed around a biophysical mechanism which evokes a visual response and is thought to be centered in the retina, known as magnetophosphenes. This effect is experienced when a person receives a blow to the head and sees "stars." This same effect can be produced with electromagnetic energy.

British reporter Armen Victorian concluded that Alexander is an active operative assigned to a covert military group "specializing in dissemination of disinformation," collectively known as the "Aviary."[114] ("Remote viewers" Ed Dames, Hal Puthoff, David Morehouse and Courtney Brown are also Avarians.)

The *Albuquerque Journal* reported on March 10, 1993 that Alexander had organized a national conference in Santa Fe devoted to research reports of "ritual abuse, near-death experiences, human contacts with extraterrestrial aliens (sic) and other so-called 'anomalous experiences.'"

"Something's happening that's impacting on the psyché of America," Alexander told the *Journal*. "That's for sure."

Nomenclature of a Brain Trust

There is no doubt that the original Laurance Rockefeller, now 85 years old, is the power behind much UFO research in the United States. This man, one of two surviving grandsons of the first John D. Rockefeller, has been a true major league player in the affairs of the United States since the 1930s. If he is interested in UFOs, then they are indeed very, very important.

—Val Germann

You couldn't miss it. Brightly-lit saucers barreled across the sky and folks periodically disappeared to pop up again with horrific tales of "alien" abduction, mental telepathy and macabre experimentation. Cults, many distributing narcotics, roamed the cities. And then there were the "zombie killers."

A typical example was Tyrone Mitchell, who mowed down a group of young children in a school-yard across the street from his L.A. home on February 24, 1984. He managed to murder one ten-year-old girl and wound thirteen other children before killing himself. His rampage was attributed to drugs and the torment he suffered after his parents, a brother and four sisters were killed at Jonestown, the cloistered CIA concentration camp conceived by U of C

Berkeley's Dr. Lawrence L. Layton. Mitchell had been at Jonestown, too. But the press did not speculate that the cause of his murderous tantrum may have been related to mind control programming conducted in Guyana, or rage-inducing brain stimulation back home.

Mitchell was a bodyguard at the People's Temple for Beatrice Grubbs, formerly a legal secretary for the Internal Revenue Service. She was also one of Jim Jones' most trusted sidekicks. Grubbs narrowly escaped the carnage of Peoples' Temple because she'd been in nearby Georgetown for a dental appointment, accompanied by her bodyguard.

Tom Grubbs, her husband, a psychologist from the University of California, allegedly died in the massacre—but his body was not identified among the dead. Grubbs had been the principal of the People's Temple school.

He also designed Jones's personal sensory deprivation chamber, an implement of torture known as the "box." Experimental subjects (children) were forced inside the chamber, and lowered into a root cellar to simulate the effect of being buried alive. Jones appreciated Grubb's traumatizing "box" so much he ordered a complete set of coffin-shaped models.[115]

Jones researcher Michael Meiers: "Early Temple experiments in sensory deprivation are not well documented, but it is known that Jones imparted his expertise to Donald DeFreeze, who utilized the technique to brainwash Patricia Hearst." Subjects "interred in the boxes were totally deprived of all sensory input." Sans input, the subject emerges from the ordeal in a receptive state for mind control conditioning.

The Peoples' Temple arrived in Ukiah, California in 1965. *The Psychic World of California,* a paranormal handbook by David St. Clair published seven years later, highly recommended Jim Jones's "psychic healing" abilities to all New Age seekers.[116] The Peoples' Temple flock believed in them as well, but then most were patients from Mendocino State Mental Hospital. (The hospital had been systematically infiltrated by the cult until every employee of the institution was also a parishioner of the Temple. When Governor Reagan scaled back funding for state psychiatric institutions, most of the patients were released to the supervision of the Jones commune—so many, in fact, that the hospital was nearly emptied. It was the first mental hospital in California closed by order of Governor Reagan as a "cost-cutting" measure.

Familiar behavior modification techniques were applied in Guyana. Children were subjected to electric shocks to keep them in line. University of Miami psychologist José Lasaga described Jones's hold on his followers as "mass hypnosis at a social level ... a unique process of group regression that led to a full acceptance of the leader's delusional system."[117] Drug experimentation was conducted with a surfeit of supplies from leading chemical companies, offshoots of I.G. Farben, the German drug conglomerate fused by a complex series of patents and investments with the Rockefeller family's Standard Oil. Jonestown was built on land leased by an attorney for Farben, once the landlord of Auschwitz, like its successor in Guyana a center of inhumane medical experimentation with a mass murder queüe.

In 1978, People's Temple became People's Tomb. Among the public figures to release statements concerning the massacre was Albert Speer, resurfacing in Bonn, West Germany. Speer stated flatly that ODESSA was playing out a strategy to "take control of the U.S."[118]

Keith Harary, a research associate in psychiatry at Maimonides Medical Center in Brooklyn, abruptly resigned and relocated to San Francisco to "investigate" the workings of the cult and direct a year-long counseling program for former cultists. He was employed by leading experimental laboratories for 25 years before he was, by his own account, suddenly gripped by an urge to become a clinical psychologist. A year later, he signed on to the CIA's Stargate "psychic spying" project at SRI, Russell and Targ's stomping grounds, funded by SAIC. Harary holds a Ph.D. in psychology and has published eight books on altered states of consciousness, perception and "coercive influence" (or practical mind control techniques to influence a subject short of violence. Many CIA mind control propagandists focus on "persuasive coercion technology" as a diversion from the advanced methods and machines perfected by the Agency and commonly employed by the intelligence cults.) He is known in occult circles for his contributions to a Duke University study of out-of-body flights. In 1982, Harary founded Delphi Associates with Russell Targ to sell "clairvoyance" to the private sector.[119]

Harary has extensive laboratory experience in the physiology of altered states of consciousness and has developed techniques for inducing them. He is the co-author of a book, *Who Do You Think You Are? Explore the Many-Sided Self,* which has sold 100,000 copies since its release in November, 1995. He has lectured to the International Association of Law Enforcement Intelligence Analysts, the UN, Stanford University, UC Berkeley, the University of Edinburgh, drawn audiences in Europe, Canada and Russia. He is the research director of the Institute for Advanced Psychology in Tiburon, California.[120]

The media, late in 1995, strained public credulity to the breaking point by reporting Stargate's far-fetched cover stories without a smirk. In a shower of CIA disinformation, all objectivity eroded at the *San Francisco Examiner:*

Keith Harary, alone in the white room, had been given an assignment: "Describe the condition of Subject X." Given no other details, he began to concentrate, striving to clear his mind of everything save making "a connection" with this unseen stranger.

Soon, Harary was describing an "extremely ill person" who had a "physical disease that was affecting his mental state." The subject, he said, may be suffering from multiple sclerosis. In any case, he predicted, the person "would be on a plane in the next two to three days."

Two days later, in July 1980, American diplomat Richard Queen, one of 53 Americans being held hostage in Iran, was released from captivity. He was flown to a military hospital in West Germany—where he was treated for neurological problems later diagnosed as multiple sclerosis.[121]

From top to bottom of the virtual government's paranormal corps, invasive mind control weapons are bound to lurk nearby. The SRI's "psychic" experiments were duplicated at the Navy Electronics Laboratory in San Diego, not in a tarot parlor—the test runs may well hve been technological, not paranormal. This much is strongly suggested by declassified, internal SRI documents identifying Puthoff and Targ as experimenters in "perceptual augmentation techniques" for the Institute's Electronics and Bioengineering Laboratory.[122]

Concrete evidence that electronic mind control was an object of study at SRI was exposed by the *Washington Post* on August 7, 1977. When the Navy awarded a contract to the Institute ...

The scientific assistant to the Secretary of the Navy, Dr. Sam Koslov, received a routine briefing on various research projects, including SRI's.

As the briefer flashed his chart onto the screen and began to speak, Koslov stormily interrupted, "What the hell is that about?" Among the glowing words on the projected chart, the section describing SRI's work was labeled,

ELF AND MIND CONTROL

"ELF" stands for "extremely [low] frequency" electromagnetic waves, from the very slow brain frequencies up to about 100 cycles per second.... But the "Mind Control" label really upset Koslov. He ordered the SRI investigations for the Navy stopped, and canceled another $35,000 in Navy funds slated for more remote viewing work.

Contrary to Koslov's attempt to kill the research, the Navy quietly continued to fork out $100,000 for a two-year project directed by a *bionics* specialist.[123]

Mind control is not a humanitarian pastime: it is military. As a rule, test subjects are treated with the same thorough disregard for human rights as the radiation tests conducted at the height of the Cold War.

The treatment subjects have received at the hands of their own government would be considered atrocities if practiced in wartime.

Mind control was also used in domestic covert operations designed to further the CIA's heady ambitions, and during the Vietnam War period SRI was a fount of covert political subterfuge.

The Symbionese Liberation Army, like the People's Temple, was a creation of the CIA. The SLA had at its core a clique of black ex-convicts from Vacaville Prison. Donald DeFreeze, otherwise known as "Cinque," led the SLA. He was formerly an informant for the LAPD's Criminal Conspiracy Section and the director of Vacaville's Black Cultural Association (BCA), a covert mind control unit with funding from the CIA channeled through SRI. The Menlo Park behavior modification specialists experimented with psychoactive drugs administered to members of the BCA. Black prisoners were programmed to murder selected black leaders once on the outside. The CIA/SRI zombie killer hit-list included Oakland school superintendent Dr. Marcus Foster and Panthers Huey Newton and Bobby Seale, among others.[124] DeFreeze stated that at Vacaville in 1971–72, he was the subject of a CIA mind control experiment. He described his incarceration on the prison's third floor, where he was corralled by CIA agents who drugged him and predicted that he would become "the leader of a radical movement and kidnap a wealthy person."[125] After his escape from Vacaville (an exit door was left unlocked), that's exactly what he did.

EM mind machines were championed at SRI by Dr. Karl Pribram, director of the Neuropsychology Research Laboratory: "I certainly could educate a child by putting an electrode in the lateral hypothalmus and then selecting the situations at which I stimulate it. In this was I can grossly change his behavior." *Psychology Today* hailed Pribram as "The Magellan of Brain Science." He obtained his B.S. and M.D. degrees from the University of Chicago and at SRI studied how the brain processes and stores sensory imagery.[126] He is credited with discovering that mental imaging bears a close resemblance to hologram projection (the basis for transmitting images to the brains of experimental subjects under the misnomer "remote viewing"?).

The Institute is joined incestuously to military-industrial sponsors. Former SRI Chairman E. Hornsby Wasson, for example, was a director of several major companies, including Standard Oil of California; he went on to become chairman of the Chamber of Commerce, and CEO of Pacific Telephone & Telegraph.

The SRI/SAIC psi experiments were supervised at Langley by John McMahon, second in command under William Casey, succeeding Bobby Ray Inman, the SAIC director. McMahon has, according to Philip Agee, the CIA whistle-blowing exile, an affinity for "technological exotics for CIA covert actions."[127] He was recruited by the Agency after his graduation from Holy Cross College (also the alma mater of CIA contractees Edward Bennett Williams, attorney, and Robert Maheu, hit man). He is a former director of the Technical Services Division, deputy director for Operations, and in 1982, McMahon was appointed deputy director of Central Intelligence. He left the Agency six years later to take the position of president of the Lockheed Missiles and Space Systems Group. In 1994, he moved on to Draper Laboratories. McMahon is a director of the Defense Enterprise Fund and an adviser to congressional committees.[128] This is not exactly the resumé of an eccentric spiritualist.

Many of the SRI "empaths" were mustered from L. Ron Hubbard's Church of Scientology. Harold Puthoff, the Institute's senior researcher, was once a leading Scientologist. Two "remote viewers" from SRI have also held rank in the Church: Ingo Swann, a Class VII Operating Thetan, a founder of the Scientology Center in Los Angeles, and the late Pat Price. Puthoff and Targ's lab assistant was a Scientologist married to a minister of the church. When Swann joined SRI, he stated openly that fourteen "Clears" participated in the experiments."[129] At the time, he denied CIA involvement, but now acknowledges, "it was rather common knowledge all along who the sponsor was, although in documents the identity of the Agency was concealed behind the sobriquet of 'an east-coast scientist.' The Agency's interest was quite extensive. A number of agents of the CIA came themselves ultimately to SRI to act as subjects in remote viewing experiments, as did some members of Congress."[130]

"If you recall," astronaut Edgar Mitchell, another participant in the experiments, reminded radio disinformation broker Art Bell on April 30, 1996, "back in the early 70s, I did work at SRI with Harold Puthoff and Russell Targ and Uri Geller, and I was invited to brief the CIA on our results. George Bush was head of the CIA at that time." (Mitchell was preaching to the choir—Bell's own background is strongly suggestive of military intelligence and advanced weapons involvement: his mother was a Marine drill instructor, his father a Marine officer. Bell served in the Air Force for a dozen years as a microwave electronics technician. He has also been employed by ITT in Nutley, NJ, a manufacturer of sophisticated radar and navigational devices for the military. The participation of ITT in cloaked CIA misadventures is widely documented.)

Mitchell spins a cocoon of metaphysical yarns as outrageously far-fetched as any of his SRI cronies. He claims to have traced the brain's center of ESP to native creativity, a "relationship that exists in nature, it's responsible for our inner-experience.... It involves the zero-point field, quantum physics, mystical experience, para-psychological functioning." The ubiquitous "aliens," he insists, are at the heart of the federal UFO cover-up, visitors from a civilization "a few million, or even a few billion years older than we are." His book *The Way of the Explorer* is chock-a-block with the astronaut's rambling metaphysical cover stories.

The Agency was reportedly so taken with the SRI experiments that the bankroll for "human augmentation" research swelled. Millions of dollars were thrown at "Grill Flame" under (DIA) and Navy auspices. The projects at SRI were augmented by a parapsychology team at Fort Meade in Maryland under INSCOM and the NSA. Military intelligence personnel were recruited, including Major Ed Dames. General Stubblebine ran the project and broadened it to include tarot cards and the channeling of "spirits." By this time, Puthoff and Swann left the Church of Scientology to join a spin-off religious movement. The DIA inherited Project Grill Flame.

A reporter for the BBC (requesting anonymity) offered a glimpse of the Army's remote viewing project at Fort Meade. He declares that he was given the "Official Line"—that is, "we were about to be used for disinformation. As soon as I started asking hard questions, the project was taken away from us and [given] to a far more docile broadcaster."

The British correspondent learned on the tour that medical oversight for the "remote viewing" experiments was provided by Dr. Louis Jolyon West, a retired professor of psychiatry at UCLA, one of the most notorious CIA mind control specialists in the country. Apart from monitoring the health of subjects, according to SRI spokesmen, Dr. West conducted his own experimental studies of the "phenomenology of dissociative states," or multiple personalities, at SRI. Dr. Colin Ross, a specialist in dissociative disorders, confirms that Dr. West's work for the CIA centered on the biology or personality of dissociated states.[131]

In "Pseudo-Identity and the Treatment of Personality Change in Victims of Captivity and Cults," "Jolly" West details the creation of "changelings," or dissociative personalities. "Prolonged environmental stress," UCLA's own CIA mind control specialist observes, "or life situations profoundly different from the usual, can disrupt the normally integrative functions of personality. Individuals subjected to such forces may adapt through dissociation by generating an altered persona, or pseudo-identity."

Patricia Hearst (examined by Dr. West for trial) hosted an alternate personality named "Pearl," he reports. The newspaper heiress was subjected to a corpus of trauma-based programmimg of a sort developed by CIA specialists (e.g. Dr. West):

> [Patricia], violently abducted by members of the [CIA-mustered] Symbionese Liberation Army in February of 1974, [was] brutalized, raped, tortured and forced to participate in illegal acts beginning with the bank robbery for which she was later (in our view wrongly) convicted. The traumatic kidnapping and subsequent two months of torture produced in her a state of emotional regression and fearful compliance with the demands and expectations of her captors.

> This was quickly followed by the coerced transformation of Patty into Tania and subsequently (less well known to the public) into Pearl, after additional trauma over a period of many months (Hearst & Moscow, 1988; *The Trial of Patty Hearst*, 1976). Tania was merely a role coerced on pain of death; *it was Pearl who later represented the pseudo-identity* which was found on psychiatric examination by one of us (West) shortly after Hearst's arrest by the FBI. Chronic symptoms of PTSD were also prominent in this case.[132]

Many survivors of CIA-sponsored experimentation have been left with multiple personalities induced at a tender age, and it is reported by subjects that the CIA can trigger electronically from a remote source to commit any act on cue—the ultimate Manchurian Candidate.

In *Such Things are Known*, electronic mind control subject Dorothy Burdick discusses one of Dr. West's writing partners, Dr. Jerome Siegal, another UCLA psychiatrist—the creator of FOCUS (the Flexible Optical Control Unit Simulator), a machine that projects images directly on the retina, rendering the image indistinguishable from reality. In 1968, Siegal published a monograph, "A Device for Chronically Controlled Visual Input," which describes a device that broadcasts visual images to the brain via the optic nerve.

Dr. William Sweet of Massachussetts General Hospital, another psychiatrist from the Louis J. West mind control circle, implanted four electrode strands in the brain of Leonard Kille, a referral misdiagnosed by Sweet and his colleagues as "epileptic" after losing his temper at his wife after learning that she'd been carrying on an affair with a boarder.

Dr. Sweet didn't lack credentials. He is the co-inventor of the PET scan, and he lists among the many accomplishments in his vitae the development of "the most frequently used procedure for the treatment of trigeminal neuralgia (radiofrequency lesioning of the trigeminal ganglion)." But Kille didn't know he'd been selected as a mind control test subject in Sweet's radio-frequency experiments, or that his doctor had no intention of treating his "disorder." The subject was partially paralyzed for life.

Oblivious to the destruction he'd visited upon Leonard Kille, Dr. Sweet crowed in medical journals that the procedure was a stunning success.

In 1995, Dr. Sweet's morbid medical curiosity caught the attention of the corporate media. Reporting was spotty. Dr. Sweet was not identified as a CIA asset.

RELATIVES PREPARE SUIT OVER BRAIN TUMOR TREATMENT
(*New York Beacon,* October 4, 1995)

Cancer patients who underwent experimental radiation therapy blamed for killing at least 10 of them were unwitting pigs for doctors who knew it was useless, according to suit prepared on their behalf.

Relatives of two patients who died in 1961 after brain tumor treatment at Massachusetts General Hospital and the Massachusetts Institute of Technology prepared the suit for filing today in U.S. District Court in New York.... The idea was to destroy tumors by injecting them with boron and exposing the chemical to a beam of neutrons, but the treatment was found to also kill brain tissue and blood vessels.

"The early experiences were very unfortunate," Dr. Victor Bond, head of the medical department at Brookhaven, said in a 1982 interview cited in the suit.

The suit maintains that none of the patients was told enough about the procedures to give consent....

"It is a monstrous crime that Dr. William Sweet did, and I'm glad that he is still living so that he can be exposed, not as a great scientist, but as the monster that he is," Evelyn Heinrich [said].

Sweet's patients were treated to cancer-eating streams of boron radiation at the Brookhaven reactor. They were stretched out in a coffin-like trench in the concrete floor, their heads positioned over a hole and a nuclear reactor that blasted neutrons through their brains.

In his current resumé, Dr. Sweet boasts that he is a "major proponent of Boron Neutron Capture Therapy for brain tumors."

"We were really completely in the dark," Sweet told journalist Pete Carey from *U.S. News & World Report* (September 18, 1995), "as to what was going to happen." He is still in the dark, but that hasn't stopped Massachussetts General from reviving the experiments more than 30 years later. "Last September," Carey discovered, "researchers at Brookhaven National Laboratory in New York began treating 28 cancer patients with the procedure. Scientists there have developed an improved boron compound and a new neutron energy beam, reviving hopes for the treatment. More recently, a consortium of physicians leased an idled government nuclear reactor in Idaho. Their plan: to use the reactor [for] treatment of brain tumors. Despite those developments, critics say, [the] treatment is as *useless* now as it was 30 years ago."

Dr. Sweet's theories of brain surgery are not exactly geared toward healing, either, according to Peter Schrag in *Mind Control 1978*):

> Between 1968 and 1972, Vernon Mark, William Sweet and Frank Ervin reported on a series of cases purporting to show the effectiveness of psychosurgical procedures. One of them was a woman who, after two such operations, became enraged and refused any further psychosurgery. The doctors dismissed the rage as "paranoid," but they removed the electrodes and, noting her good mood and "high spirits," released her from the hospital to go shopping. She went directly to a phone booth, called her mother to say good-bye, took poison and killed herself. The doctors interpreted the suicide as an indication that she was functioning and therefore getting well, a "gratifying result of the operation."

Vernon Mark, Dr. Sweet's partner in psychosurgical crime, is currently the director of the Center for Memory Impairment and Neuro-Behavioral Disorders in Brookline, Massachussetts, and author of *Brain Power: A Neurosurgeon's Complete Program to Maintain and Enhance Brain Fitness Throughout Your Life* (Houghton Mifflin, 1989).

Under Dr. West's tutelage at UCLA, parapsychology experimentation of a sort was conducted by Kirlian aura researcher Thelma Moss, a writer for television and a human guinea-pig herself in LSD experiments conducted by the CIA in 1957. Three years later, as a UCLA psychology student, she designed protocols for her own LSD experiments under the supervision of Dr. Oscar Janiger.[133]

The CIA, of course, could not be far away. Dr. Janiger's supplier of the drug was the legendary Captain Al Hubbard, the "Johnny Appleseed of LSD." "Nothing of substance has been written about Al Hubbard," Janiger once said, "and probably nothing ever should."[134] Hubbard, a convicted rum-runner, had a knack for electronic communications. He was recruited by the OSS by agents of Allen Dulles and almost certainly reported to the CIA thereafter. Hubbard, an arch-conservative, joined SRI at the urging of Willis Harman, director of the

Institute's Educational Policy Research Center, ostensibly as a "security guard." Harman, an LSD experimenter himself, admits, "Al never did anything resembling security work." Hubbard was employed on the Alternative Futures Project, a "corporate strategy program."

"Al had a grandiose idea," a co-worker recalls, "that if he could give the psychedelic experience to the major executives of the Fortune 500 companies, he could change the whole of society."[135] Hubbard was a major supplier to universities sponsoring experimentation, and flooded the youth subculture he despised with LSD in the 1960s. The massive drug-dealing operation—at least as large as the government's—had Harmon's full support.

Among the labs closed in 1966 with the criminalization of LSD was Dr. Janiger's.[136] His protégé, Thelma Moss, continued to experiment with the hallucinogen as a psychotherapeutic tool, and later an ESP trigger and for experiments in "behavior modification."[136] Her increasingly bizarre interests led her to Kirlian photography and she christened a lab at UCLA under Dr. West.[137]

At least one volunteer in Moss's experiments alleges to have been led down a blind alley to lifelong torture. D.S. (requesting anonymity) appeared on Moss's doorstep in 1978. After the experiments, she was stricken by "back-to-back psychic experiences"—not true ones, she realized, but precognitive dreams "that had to be fed to me." (Subjects of EM assault frequently complain that their dreams are commandeered.) For fifteen years she walked through a barrage of novelty effects. The "psychic" episodes gradually gave way to torture, including head pains and endless hours of "persuasive coercion," the art of psychological paralysis honed by the CIA in the prison system. In 1994 she began to receive non-stop audio transmissions that still torment her, cybernetic "voices" registering on her brain's "primary frequency allocation," her own mental "channel."

The resident "psychic" at Moss's parapsychology lab was graduate student Barry Taff. Moss recalls that Taff had "the special gift" of falling into a trance at will. He is also a certified hypnotist.[138]

Israeli Schlomo Arnon, an electrical engineer on loan to Moss from the UCLA Physics Department, suggests on hindsight that Taff was familiar with the development of "non-lethal" weapons of the sort used in CIA mind control operations—decades before they were popularized by John Alexander and the military-intelligence "alien"-touting Aviary.

"In all the conversations with Taff, he and I were always on the same 'frequency,'" Arnon recalls. "Except for one occasion: He told me a story I will never forget, because it was so unusual. He said he was present in a military experiment, where a tank had been blown out by a laser beam at a distance of a few hundred yards. And this is in the mid-seventies! Now, I have never known him to lie to me. He did not have to tell me anything. I was never interested in anything else outside of the paranormal. If he really saw it, this is a technology that *even today* we don't admit that we have."[139]

The cryptic Barry Taff has gone on to become a noted UFOlogist, parapsychologist and screenwriter (*UFO Cover Up, Live!*).

Val Bankston, an abductee, met Taff in the course of seeking answers to her abuse by the ubiquitous "aliens."

"You may recognize the name Barry Taff," she says. "He consulted on a movie called *The Entity.* Shortly after we met, I was assaulted by a disembodied 'entity' during broad daylight [a "novelty effect' of electromagnetic harassment], who engaged in sexual acts with me. At the time, I believed that it was an incubus. Now, knowing what I do about Barry—the fact that he is a certified hypnotist, for one—I believe that Barry hypnotized both me and the other subject of his research leading to the movie *The Entity* into having these experiences. I believe that this woman and I may have been sexually assaulted, and caused to remember the sensations at a later date than the activities actually occurred. He probably did several women this way, and picked the one that was the best at bolstering his book and movie scheme."[140]

Another indication that military biotechnology, cyber-psi, was focal in Stargate research was the Agency's choice of the American Institutes of Research (AIR) in Washington, D.C. to evaluate the validity of "remote viewing." AIR could be counted on to keep the secrets. In the 1970s, the Army's Office of the Inspector General released declassified files disclosing a series of CIA-DoD behavior modification experiments conducted in prisons, mental hospitals and campuses from 1950 through 1971. The documents identified 44 laboratories enriched with public tax funds for secret, inhumane brain research. The first on the list was AIR.[141] SRI also received funding. An in-house "study" ensured CIA personnel would not be dragged in from the "cold."

Some of the aims of the research:

- ◆ Inducing toxic psychosis, terminal cancer, stress, sleep, headaches and chemical lobotomies.
- ◆ Developing foods that taste normal but stimulate fear and anxiety.
- ◆ The concoction of drugs to facilitate the brainwashing of civilians.
- ◆ Using LSD-25 and electrodes in the brain to pinpoint pain centers.

A number of SRI spin-offs have taken "remote viewing" into the private sector. A brochure for the Farsight Institute promotes the "alien" diversion:

> The Farsight Institute (TFI) was founded by Courtney Brown, Ph.D, in 1995, evolving from a research program that he conducted in the early 1990s, described in his book *Cosmic Voyage: A Scientific Discovery of Extraterrestrials Visiting Earth* (Dutton 1996). Dr. Brown's investigations began with his training in a remote viewing technology that had previously been used by the U.S. military during highly classified operations in the 1980s and 90s.
>
> Historically, the principal breakthroughs with this technology were made at Stanford Research Institute in the 1970s and 1980s by the gifted artist and natural psychic, Ingo Swann. The vision of The Farsight Institute is to promote the continued research and development of the most modern and effective forms of this continually evolving technology.

Other "remote viewing" gurus from the SRI program have sprung up like poison mushrooms around the country, ranting about the paranormal, scapegoating "aliens." The rhetoric is a serious development in mind control—cult programming for mass consumption. The populace is now subjected to the same crazed systems used to indoctrinate recruits of the mind control cults. Psi-Tech founder Ed Dames claimed on Art Bell's syndicated radio program that his company can comb the "collective unconscious" for answers to such mysteries as the origins of the AIDS virus. By scanning the "Global Mind," Dames claims, "we perceived massive global weather changes that preclude growing crops, a tremendous problem with epidemics and pandemics in Third World countries because it appears the ozone problem is increasing the mutation rate. We're perceiving a bovine AIDS that kills a lot of babies.

The future "gets grimmer after that."[142] It certainly did for the Rancho Santa Fe cult believing in Dames's "remote viewing" of the "Hale-Bopp spaceship"—"fantastic proof" of the group's far-fetched religious cosmology—they suicided.

Parapsychology, E.T.s and the "End Times" are not just for the tabloids anymore—the intelligence community wants you to believe ... *believe* ...

Like so many Cold War propagandists. In fact, current mind control disinformation has its foundations in anti-Communist propaganda. Lt. Col Thomas Beardon, an Army Reservist, was made to order in magazines published by the "Committee to Restore the Constitution" and other ultra-conservative organizations. Beardon had a loyal following. He made a career of writing about emergent Soviet EM mind control technology, but somehow it rarely seemed to cross his mind that the U.S. might be pursuing the same initiative. Beardon warned that the Soviets were developing weapons that generate "time-reversed (TR) electromagnetic waves," and were capable of launching a "TR Blitzkrieg War" of awful proportions. He warned grimly that the black-hearted Communists had their hands on "time-reversal" weapons that could "take Europe." A single flying Soviet "TR wave weapon," he claimed, was capable of knocking out all British and American radars. It could "kill personnel wholesale."[143]

Return of The Cabalistic Reich

There is a growth industry in electromagnetic assaults on the brain. "Some of the people trained for this computer science type of control," concludes San Francisco mind control researcher Elizabeth Russell-Manning, "are Werner Erhard graduates (EST), as well as students from many of the ivy league schools (University of California, Stanford M.I.T., etc.)."[144]

Jack Sarfatti, a physicist with a degree from Cornell—home of the CIA's Human Ecology Fund, the mind control funding pool—class of 1960: "I did graduate from an Ivy League school, where CIA finds many of its 'academics,'" Sarfatti says. "Couple that with the fact that my former professors at Cornell are the guys who built the bomb in the Manhattan project and that I was a National Defense Fellow. Just put two and two together and read between the lines the remark of British agent, Dennis Bardens, to me in 1974 at the Blue Boar Inn in Cambridge, England: 'Doctor Sarfatti, it is my duty to inform you of a psychic war raging across the continents between the Soviet Union and your country.'"

Connect the dots in Jack Sarfatti's recent journey through an Oz of mind control "mystics" and old-guard Nazis:

I was back in Paris several weeks later [at] the swank Ritz Hotel. We waited in the lobby and a guy who looked like Richard Gere in a jump suit walks in with a woman. He says: 'Hi, I'm Werner Erhard.'... We flew to New York. Sharon and I spent a few days with Uri Geller, Ira Einhorn, Bob Toben, Sir John Whitmore and Andrija Puharich at Puharich's large house in Ossining.

Sarfatti stayed with his "literary agent," Ira Einhorn, and his "doomed girl-friend Holly Maddux." Einhorn took him on a junket to Arthur Young's mansion. Young, the inventor of the Bell Helicopter, had been a close friend of Charles Lindbergh, the pro-Nazi aviator. Young landed Paine a position at Bell Aircraft under former Nazi General Walter Dornberger, who oversaw V-2 development for the Nazis and was snatched from a death sentence at Nuremberg by the United States Air Force.[145]

Young was married to an heiress of the Forbes Steel fortune. He was also the sugar daddy of the Institute for the Study of Consciousness in Berkeley, California. The melange of cultists at Young's mansion was rife with intelligence intrigues and Nazi plots. Sarfatti:

> The estoids all seemed to be glassy-eyed and very creepy. I was not at all subservient to Werner in his presence like most of the academics that surrounded and apparently adored him.... Werner had fifteen loyal estoids in the Carter White House. [He] was very active with trainings of government people in Washington D.C.... Werner used remote-viewing in his training and he also contributed money to SRI for that project....
>
> Werner had me meet with several Stanford and U.C. faculty before he set up the Physics Consciousness Research Group at Esalen with me and Michael Murphy as co-directors. Michael arranged for Jean Lanier to supply me with money. Jean was a close friend of Laurance Rockefeller who would telephone the Nob Hill flat looking for her....
>
> I attended the est April Celebrity Training of 1975.... Sterling Hayden quickly walked out calling Werner a "Nazi" as he pushed away some estoids who tried to block his passage.... I was getting suspicious of Werner, especially after I heard the rumor that he said he changed his name from Jack Rosenberg to Werner Erhard to *"give up Jewish weakness for German strength."*
>
> I received a phone call from a man named George Koopman during one of our Esalen seminars in 1976.... He provided money through military contracts with the Air Force and the U.S. Army Tank Command funneled through his company Insgroup in Irvine, California.... I found out through one of my girlfriends that Koopman succeeded in spying on the Arica organization.... Arica was started in Chile by high ranking fugitives from the Third Reich who were masters of the occult. Many of the regulars at Esalen including some of our group like Dr. John Lilly and Claudio Naranjo had been in the first Arica training in Chile. Timothy Leary was released from prison. Leary became part of my group at Esalen. Leary was a close friend of Michael Murphy....
>
> I walked into the Caffe Trieste one day in 1979. A young girl Maiti said she had written a poem about me. We soon started dating. She said her father [Robert Dickson Crane] was a "senior policy planner" in the government.... She showed me a photograph of her grandfather who was German [Nazi] General Hans Rudel during World War Two [and an ODESSA leader]. Her father had

met her mother while on Army duty after the war.... Her father was an Arabic-speaking expert in Middle-East affairs with high level contacts... She also said that her father was a close friend of conservative Pat Buchanan....

My adventures with two more women during this period are worth mentioning.... One named Crystal picked me up in the Caffe Trieste. She was a statuesque blonde in a low cut green evening dress. Crystal said she belonged to a Coven of Beautiful Witches who wanted me to be their Warlock. I later found out that Crystal knew another girl friend of mine from Esalen named Betty Andreason. I have since heard of a woman by that name who claims to have been abducted by UFOs....

Was Jan telling the truth about the Fourth Reich using Arica to influence the New Age? Brewer was part of the original Esalen group of forty that went to Chile for the first Arica training.[146]

Sarfatti makes no bones about the involvement of the CIA in his "occult" projects. He has identified the late Harold Chipman, a former CIA station chief, as the middle-man in funding to SRI's remote viewing lab and even Uri Geller.[147] Chipman served in Laos in the mid-1960s. In Vietnam, he was the director of all CIA operations in Nha Trang. After the war, he was assigned to Moscow, Berlin and Miami.[148]

Sarfatti looks back on his involvement with the mind control sector as if he has severed all bonds. "I was then simply a young, inexperienced, naive 'useful idiot' in a very very sophisticated and successful covert psychological warfare operation run by the late Brendan O. Regan of the Institute of Noetic Sciences and the late Harold Chipman, who was the CIA station chief responsible for all mind-control research in the Bay Area in the 70s. Chipman (aka 'Orwell') funded me openly for awhile in 1985 when he was allegedly no longer in the CIA, and covertly before that, and told me much of the story. In fact, he even introduced me to a beautiful woman adventurer-agent who was one of his RV subjects who later became my live-in 'significant other.'"

In fact, Chipman was one of Sarfatti's numerous contacts in the murky intelligence world. His resumé boasts that he was "consulted" on the physics of "remote-viewing," Strategic Defense Initiative, and other classified matters for several U.S. intelligence agencies and policy think tanks (e.g., A.L. Chickering of the Institute for Contemporary Studies in San Francisco, and CIA propagandist Robert Conquest of the Hoover Institution at Stanford on the new paperback edition of *Special Tasks* by former KGB officer Sudoplatov)." Conquest was exposed in 1967 as a CIA disinformation agent for Melvin Lasky's Congress for

Cultural Freedom, the publisher of *Encounter,* a pasty academic loaf of white-bread political commentary, during the Cold War. Conquest currently grinds out slippery pro-business tirades disparaging Soviet Communism and the American Left,[149] a genré of opinion-shaping that went out with the Wooly Mammoth but has been resurected with the "conservative" propaganda onslaught of the 1990s.

The Arica Institute bills itself as "a mystical school" for "spiritual transformation" through meditation, gymnastic "psychocalisthenics" (sic), nonverbal communication and group theater.[150] Oscar Ichazo, the institute's founder, teaches a hodge-podge of Zen, Sufism, Yoga, I Ching and Buddhism. The symbol adopted by Ichazo for Arica resembles a top-heavy pentagram, known as the Enneagon, representing "a body of practical and theoretical knowledge in the form of a nine-level hierarchy of training programs aimed at the total development of the human being."[151] Ichazo held his first Arica seminar in Chile in 1971. It was attended by Charles Tart, LSD experimenter Lilly (then studying on a fellowship at the Center for Advanced Study in the Behavioral Sciences in Palo Alto), Naranjo and about 45 Sufi poseurs. Since, some 40 training centers have surfaced in the U.S., South America, Europe and Australia.

Arica is a small cloud in a big sky. But as the Pentagon's psychotronic arsenal proliferates, so do the victims of illicit experimentation and harassment.

Meanwhile, back in the USSR, Georgey Georgyevich Rogozin, a former Soviet undercover officer and occultist, was named a ranking general in May, 1995 by Boris Yeltsin. It was said that Rogozin "terrorized" Kremlin bureaucrats. He was given free reign in his occult studies, which included 'reading thoughts at a distance, obtaining information by way of analyzing man's biological electric field.'" The CIA has followed these developments closely ...[152]

Notes

1. Interview, Art Bell radio program, December 7, 1995.
2. "Ed Dames Challenges Government on Remote Viewing," CNI News, vol. 13, part 1, ISCNI News Center, December 7, 1995. Also, ABC Nightline, November 28, 1995.
3. Psi-Tech literature and Bell interview.
4. CNI Report.
5. Leonard Buchanon, "Who is Dave Morehouse, Ph.D.?" a hand-out from ProblemsSolutions-Innovations (PSI), a "psychic viewing" firm in Mechanicsville, Maryland run by Buchanon.
6. Debby Stark, "Talking to Ed Dames," *Mufon News,* nos. 6 & 7, June–July 1993.

7. *CounterSpy,* Spring 1980, p. 46. Listed in Ralph McGeehee's CIA-Base.

8. *Counterspy,* Spring 1980, pp. 45–46.

9. Michael H. Shapiro, "Legislating the Control of Behavior Control," *Southern California Law Review,* vol. 47, February 1974, no. 2, p. 240.

10. Barton Ingraham and Gerald Smith, "The Use of Electronics in the Observation and Control of Human Behavior and its Possible Use in Rehabilitation and Parole," *Issues in Criminology,* vol. 7: no. 2, Fall 1972.

11. *Science,* Sept. 21, 1917, p. 173.

12. Townsend T. Brown, "How I Control Gravity," *Science and Invention,* August 1929, and *New York Times,* February 18, 1929. Also of note: "The Townsend Brown Electro-Gravity Device — A Comprehensive Evaluation by the Office of Naval Research," September 15, 1952, and Gaston Burridge, "Another Step Toward Anti-Gravity," *American Mercury,* June 1958, p. 77. "After the mid-1950's to the present, no other information regarding the technology of electrodynamics and its effect on gravity have been [found] in any of the unclassified U.S. literature." — James Hartman file, Future Science Administration.

13. Hartman file.

14. Paul Arthur Schilpp, *Albert Einstein: Philosopher-Scientist* [3rd ed.], LaSalle, Ill., Open Court, 1979, pp. 522–23.

15. See, for example, Marco Cavaglia, "Quantum Electromagnetic Wormholes and Geometrical Description of the Electric Charge," *Plain Tex, Report* no. SISSA 92/94/A, 13 pp., and Racz Istvan, "Maxwell Fields in Spacetimes Admitting Non-Null Killing Vectors," PACS nos. 04.20.Cv, 04.20.Me, 04.40+c.

16. Dennis L. Cravens, "Electric Propulsion Study," AL-TR-89-040, Scientific Applications International Corporation (SAIC) for the former Astronautics Lab, Air Force Space Technology Center, Edwards AFB, August 1990.

17. R.L. Talley, "Twenty-First Century Propulsion Concept," PL-TR-91-3009, Air Force Systems Command, Phillips Laboratory, Propulsion Directorate, Edwards AFB, May 1991.

18. *Orvotron Newsletter,* March/April, 1994.

19. Ken Lawrence, "Flim-Flam," *Covert Action Information Bulletin,* no. 21, Spring 1984, p. 44. Also, Targ and Harary's *Mind Race.*

20. Tom Agoston, *Blunder! How the U.S. Gave Away Nazi Super-Secrets to Russia,* New York: Dodd, Mead & Co., 1985, p. 4.

21. Ibid., p. 9.

22. Ibid., p. 8.

23. Renato Vesco & David Hatcher Childress, *Man-Made UFOs, 1944–1994,* Stelle, Illinois: Adventures Unlimited Publishers, 1994, p. 110.

24. Ibid., p. 134.

25. Ibid., pp. 85–86.

26. Mae Brussell, "The Nazi Connection to the John F. Kennedy Assassination," (1983) in *A Mae Brussell Anthology,* Prevailing Winds Research, Santa Barbara, California.

27. Vescoe & Childress., p. 162. For Colonel Putt's promotion of the Nazi scientists to higher-ups, see Tom Bower, *The Paperclip Conspiracy: The Hunt for the Nazi Scientists,* Boston: Little, Brown & Co., 1987.

28. Bower, pp. 89 & 155.

29. Mike Davis, *City of Quartz,* London, Verso, 1990, pp. 59–62.

30. "Eight Inducted into AIA's Hall of Honor," Air Force Intelligence Association Headquarters, Kelly Air Force Base, Texas, a publicity release concerning ceremonies held on September 30, 1995, highlighting the reunion of the Freedom Through Vigilance Association.

31. Agoston, pp. 58–59.

32. Milton Goldin, "Speer Carrier," *The Intelligent Guide to Jewish Affairs* (a biweekly newsletter), no. 54, January 3, 1996. Speer consistently denied that he was privy to the Holocaust. Yet he was, on a daily basis, "wide awake and in constant touch with Himmler and SS chiefs intimately involved with mass murder, robbery and slavery. He constantly demanded more slaves for his factories, made deals with the SS to obtain them, and visited camps where all he claims to have noticed were prisoners hard at work."

33. Anthony L. Kimory, "The Secret Life of Fred L. Crisman," *UFO Magazine,* vol. 8: no. 5, 1993, pp. 34–38.

34. SKBI (a group of involuntary subjects exploited in electromagnetic mind control experiments or harassed for falling into disfavor with the intelligence sector) Report, *Intelligence Community's Use of Mind-Control and Thought-Manipulation,* pp. 44–45.

35. Alvin Moscow, *The Rockefeller Inheritance,* New York: Doubleday, 1977, p. 178.

36. Ibid., p. 126.

37. Ferdinand Lundberg, *The Rockefeller Syndrome,* Secaucus, New Jersey: Lyle Stuart, 1975, pp. 266–68.

38. Moscow, p. 178.

39. Moscow, pp. 126–27. Among the aircraft firms and suppliers in which a sizable share is held by Laurance Rockefeller, count Airborne Instruments Laboratory, Wallace Aviation, Marquardt Aircraft, Flight Refueling, Airborne Instruments Laboratory, New York Airways, Eastern Airlines, Piasecki Helicopter and so on. Lundberg, p. 267.

40. Richard F. Kaufman, *The War Profiteers,* New York, Bobbs-Merrill, 1970, p. 27.

41. Ibid., p. 89.

42. Richard S. Broughton, communications specialist for the Institute for Parapsychology, Rhine Research Center, Duke University, personal correspondence, January 29, 1996.

43. "History of the Rhine Research Center," Duke University Parapsychology Lab public release.

44. Bruce Oudes, *From: The President—Richard Nixon's Secret Files*, New York: Harper & Row, 1989, p. 142.

45. Dorothy Burdick, *Such Things Are Known*, New York: Vantage Press, 1982.

46. Michael Rossman, "On Some Matters of Concern in Psychic Research," in *Psychic Warfare: Fact or Fiction*, Guildford, Surrey, Aquarian Press.

47. Martin Cannon, "Selections from a DIA Report on Soviet Parapsychology Research," *Mind Control: A Reader Compiled by the Editors of Prevailing Winds Research*, Santa Barbara, Prevailing Winds, 1994, p. 69.

48. Rossman, p. 142.

49. D.C. Hammond," "Hypnosis in MPD: Ritual Abuse," delivered at the Fourth Annual Eastern Regional conference on Abuse and Multiple Personality, Radisson Plaza Hotel, Mark Center, Alexandria, Virginia, June 25, 1992, .

50. Martin Cannon, unpublished chapters from *The Controllers*, February, 1996. "The 'ESP' connection is suggestive," Cannon argues. "The MK-ULTRA documents betray an astonishing interest on the part of the intelligence agencies in matters parapsychological."

51. C.P., "A Victim of CIA Mind Control: Political Asylum," *MindNet Journal*, vol. 1, no. 33, December 4, 1995.

52. Ralph Losey, "The Problem of the Subtle Sybil Effect," ms.

53. Keeler essay.

54. James and Joyce Frazer, "How Radiofrequency Waves Interact with Living Systems," *21st Century*, March–April, 1988, p. 51.

55. Resumé of Robert G. Jahn, professor and dean, Princeton University Engineering Quadrangle.

56. Eliot Handelman, "Biophysics of Infrasound," request for information posting, WWW, McGill University, January 27, 1994.

57. S.V. Alekseev, et.al, "Myocardial Ischemia in Rats During Exposure to Infrasound," *Zabolevaniia*, August 1983, pp. 34–38. Abstract on file at the NASA Life Sciences Division.

58. Gerald Frost and Dalvin Shipbaugh, *GPS Targeting Methods for Non-Lethal Systems*, Rand Publication, RP-262, 2-1-94, p. 3.

59. A. J. Weberman, "Mind Control: The Story of Mankind Research Unlimited, Inc.," *Covert Action Information Bulletin*, no. 9 (June 1980), p. 16.

60. Bower, p. 160.

61. James Bamford, *The Puzzle Palace: Inside the National Security Agency: America's Most Secret Intelligence Organization*, Middlesex, UK: Penguin, 1982, p. 98.

62. News item, "DELUSIONS: Flying Saucers Again," *Newsweek,* April 17, 1950, p. 29.

63. Bower, p. 86. Also see, Val Germann, "Know Your UFO Players!" *UFO,* vol. 10: no. 1, February 1995, p. 24.

64. Bamford, p. 427.

65. Germann, p. 24.

66. Vesco, p. 18.

67. Timothy Good, *Above Top Secret: The Worldwide UFO Cover-Up,* New York: William Morrow, 1988, pp. 336–38.

68. Davis, pp. 59–62.

69. Michael Howard, *The Occult Conspiracy: Secret Societies—Their Influence and Power in World History,* Rochester, Vermont: Destiny, 1989, p. 112.

70. Ibid., p. 133–34.

71. Frater Cernunnos, "The OTO After Crowley's Death," from the secretary's office, OTO's Albion Lodge, London, England.

72. Anonymous., "Intelligence Services are Not So Intelligent, or The OTO Since Crowley's Death," undated pages from *The Oriflame,* c. 1987.

73. Maury Terry, *The Ultimate Evil: An Investigation into America's Most Dangerous Satanic Cult,* New York: Dolphin, 1987.

74. Lucian K. Truscott IV, "Even in Arcadia" *Vague,* London, England, no. 18–19, Spring 1989, p. 128. Truscott writes that the sado-masochistic sex was part of the cult's personal brand of "perverse sacraments, practices that the [Manson] Family held in great esteem. At the Tate house, Susan Atkins licked the blood of Sharon Tate off her fingers."

75. Terry.

76. Background information in this section was culled from stories about James Bulger appearing in the *Boston Globe* for September 20, 1988; January 1, 1994; March 5, 1995; August 1, 1995; August 15, 1995; January 5, 1996; January 27, 1996.

77. *West's New York Legal Supplement,* second series, 176 A.D. 2d 362, People v. Savona case file, N.Y.S.2d 595 (A.D. 2 Dept. 1991), pp. 595–596. Also, Dr. Adolph Goldman, M.D., New York Supreme Court-ordered psychiatric evaluation, March 10, 1988.

78. Thomas Savona, letter to Maitefa Angaza c/o the *City Sun,* New York, January 19, 1994.

79. Thomas Savona, letter to Cardinal O'Connor, April 15, 1992.

80. Goldman.

81. Student transcript of Thomas Savona, Sullivan County Community College, January 3, 1994.

82. Burton H. Wolfe, *The Devil's Avenger: A Biography of Anton Szandor LaVey,* New York: Pyramid Books, pp. 66–67.

83. Blanche Barton, *Secret Life of a Satanist: the Authorized Biography of Anton LaVey,* Los Angeles: Feral House, 1990. p. 23.

84. "Leary Gave prisoners Drugs, Newspaper Says," *Orange County Register,* January 2, 1994, p. 24, after a story that appeared in the *Boston Globe* a day or two before.

85. "Leary Admits He was CIA Agent," *Freedom,* May, 1975 (the interviewer was Walter Bowart).

86. "EPA Joins Probe of Odd Signals," *Chico Enterprise-Record,* March 28, 1978, p. 1.

87. Steven Levy, *The Unicorn's Secret: Murder in the Age of Aquarius,* New York: Prentice Hall, 1988, pp. 128–29.

88. John L. Wilhelm, "Psychic Spying?—The CIA, the Pentagon and the Russians Probe the Military Potential of Parapsychology," *Washington Post,* August 7, 1977.

89. Levy, pp. 166–67.

90. Russell Targ and Keith Harary, *Mind Race: Understanding and Using Psychic Abilities,* New York: Ballantine, 1984, p. 121.

91. Ibid., p. 124.

92. Michael Meiers, *Was Jonestown a CIA Medical Experiment?: A Review of the Evidence,* Lampeter, Dyfed, Wales, Mellen House, UK, 1988, p. 468.

93. Ibid., p. 468–69.

94. Ibid.

95. Targ and Harary, p. 127.

96. Meiers, p. 470.

97. Weberman.

98. Ibid.

99. R.F. Haines, *Advanced Aerial Devices Reported During The Korean War,* Los Altos, California, LDA Press, 1990, p. 54.

100. Deborah Lutterbeck, "White House Alien Policy," *Common Cause,* October–December, 1995.

101. Robert J. Durant, "Will the Real Scott Jones Please Stand Up?" Paranet Information Service, Denver, Colorado, September 5, 1993.

102. "Admiral Hardisty Elected President of Kaman Aerospace International," Kaman Corp. press release, September 18, 1995.

103. Kaman SEC report, March, 1996.

104. Howard Watson Ambruster, *Treason's Peace: German Dyes and American Dupes,* New York: Beechhurst Press, 1947. p. 386.

105. Kenneth Timmerman, *Death Lobby: How the West Armed Iraq,* New York: Houghton Mifflin, 1991, pp. 359–61.

106. Richard Lacayo, "Did Bush Create this Monster?" *Time,* June 8, 1992, p. 41.

107. James Mills, interviewed by Ray Briehm, KABC-AM, Los Angeles, October 19, 1990.

108. Jack Sarfatti, "In the Thick of It!" Internet posting by Jack Saratti, p. 3.

109. Durant.

110. Andrew Giarelli, "The Last Prince," *World Press Review,* January 1, 1994, p. 28. For information on the $200,000 donation from Laurance Rockefeller to John Mack, see Deborah Letterbeck, October, 1995 number of *Common Cause.*

111. Paul McLaughlin, "ET: The Extraterrestrial Therapist," *Saturday Night,* vol. 110: June 1, 1995, p. 44.

112. "The Harvard Professor and the UFOs," *Psychology Today,* March/April 1994.

113. Durant.

114. Armen Victorian, correspondence with Gilbert Ortiz, Los Alamos, NM, February 14, 1994.

115. Meiers, p. 390.

116. D. St. Clair, *The Psychic World of California,* Garden City, New York: Doubleday, 1972, p. 315.

117. Joel Greenberg, "Jim Jones: The Deadly Hypnosis," *Science News,* vol. 116, December 1, 1979, p. 378.

118. Meiers, p. 320.

119. Russell and Targ, p. 310.

120. Promotional literature for *Neuro Transmissions,* a newsletter edited by Harary on "emerging topics in psychology, neuroscience, and many other fields." Also, Julian Guthrie, "Tapping Our Psychic Powers," *San Francisco Examiner,* December 24, 1995.

121. Guthrie.

122. Harold Puthoff and Russell Targ, final report on perceptual augmentation experiments for the period January 1974 through February 1975, Project 3183, SRI, Menlo Park, CA, approved for release, July 1995.

123. Wilhelm.

124. Mae Brussell, "Why was Patricia Hearst Kidnapped?" *The Realist,* undated copy from 1974.

125. Brussell, undated taped lecture in 1974.

126. Elizabeth Russell-Manning, ed., in *Mass Mind Control of the American People: Conspiracy & Cover-Up of the State & Federal Government,* published by the author, 1993: 1600 Larking Street, San Francisco, California 94109, p. 16.

127. Philip Agee and Louis Wolf, *Dirty Work: The CIA in Western Europe,* New York: Dorset Press, 1978, p. 307.

128. Lockheed Co. press release, "Missiles & Space Company, Inc., Founders and Presidents."

129. Wilhelm.

130. Ingo Swann, "The Emergence of Project SCANATE—The First Espionage-Worthy Remote Viewing Experiment Requested by the CIA (Summer, 1973)" ms., sci.psychology.misc. newsgroup, posted January 24, 1996.

131. BBC reporter, correspondence with the author, January 29, 1996.

132. Louis Jolyon West, "Pseudo-Identity and the Treatment of Personality Change in Victims of Captivity and Cults," in *Dissociation: Clinical and Theoretical Perspectives,* Lynn, SJ and Rhue JW, eds. (Guilford Press, 1994).

133. Thelma Moss, *The Body Electric: A Personal Journey into the Mysteries of Parapsychological Research, Bioenergy and Kirlian Photography,* Los Angeles: St. Martin's, 1979, pp. 27–8.

134. Todd Brendan Fahey, "The Original Captain Trips," *High Times,* November 1991.

135. Ibid.

136. Moss, p. 33.

137. Moss, p. 124.

138. Val Bankston, an abductee, correspondence with the author, July 7, 1996.

139. Shlomo Arnon, correspondence with the author, July 7, 1996.

140. Bankston.

141. Mae Brussell, "Why Did Allen Dulles Buy 100,000 Doses of Acid?" *Mind Control,* Santa Barbara, CA, Prevailing Winds Research, 1994, p. 7.

142. Bell program.

143. Thomas Beardon, "Soviet Phase Conjugate Weapons: Weapons that Use Time-Reversed Electromagnetic Waves," *Bulletin* (Committee to Restore the Constitution newsletter), January 1988, p. 1.

144. Manning.

145. Letter from Mike Coyle, editor of *MindNet,* to Jack Sarfatti, January 26, 1997.

146. Sarfatti. On February 21, 1995, Nightline reported that a cultist borrowing from the Werner Erhard formula of huckster psychologizing conned an excess of $1 million from the Federal Aviation Administration (FAA). Gregory May, a disciple of the Ramtha sect (whose leader supposedly channels the wisdom of a 35,000 year-old master), dressed exactly like Erhard and closely imitated his speech and gestures.

"Was a cult training government employees?" asked the ABC program listing for February 21, 1995. "*Nightline* will reveal the results of a forthcoming investigation by the FAA Inspector General. FAA employees had bizarre training techniques imposed on them by an outside contractor with clear connections to the Ramtha cult located in Washington State. Gregory May was hired to train senior executives of the FAA. ABC News *Nightline* has learned that over five years, May put executives through bizarre training rituals; had control over appointments and was able to continue being funded without competitive bidding."

147. Sarfatti Internet post, "Harold Chipman and Remote Viewing," September 9, 1995.

148. Ralp McGeehee's CIABase.

149. "An Insufficiency of Frankness," *Nation,* May 29, 1967, p. 678. Also, Matthew D'Ancona, "Why I am Still Fighting My Cold War," *London Times,* April 9, 1993, p. 12, and Alexander Werth, "Literary Bay of Pigs," *Nation,* June 5, 1967, p. 678.

150. Arica Institute brochure, "The Arica System of Spiritual Transformation," an introductory program sponsored by the Associates for Inner-Maturity in San Diego.

151. "Arica Institute, Inc., Plaintiff v. Helen Palmer and Harper & Row," no. 771, docket 91-7859, U.S. Court of Appeals, Second Circuit, January 30, 1991 (a trademark dispute).

152. Martin Sieff, "Reputed Rasputin Advises Yeltsin—Ex-KGB Officer Dabbles in Occult," *Washington Times,* 24 May 1995, A-16.

The Search for the MANCHURIAN Preschooler

In September 1995, a psychology conference held in Los Angeles explored the treatment of children subjected to experiments by the CIA's mind control fraternity. Topics on the conference itinerary included discussions of torture-based programming, the treatment of multiplicity and the remote control of human automata ...

Time Machine: Singed Synapses, Muffled Scream

The debris of Berlin smoldered. The American intelligence "services" quietly courted Nazis and their Quislings in the Soviet satellites. Some 5,000 European "anti-Communists," according to the *Washington Post* for June 9, 1982, quietly emigrated to the United States. In the early days of television, young Ronald Reagan's fund-raising acumen was tapped by the "Crusade for Freedom," a CIA front. The then "liberal" celluloid cut-out and FBI informant appeared in a cameo spot to talk viewers out of their hard-earned dollars to fund the migration of East European "freedom fighters" to the United States—these paragons were really diehard Nazis. The CIA, Pentagon and an army of Nazi recruits have since consummated an ideological bond that has held in sickness and in stealth.

In 1950, the Agency tooled up for a battery of mind control experiments on human guinea pigs, underwritten by a network of scientific foundations and academic fronts. Neuropsychiatrists at Tulane, McGill, Yale, UCLA and Harvard, some of them laboring beside the Nazi imports, researched the use of brain implants to control behavior. Dozens of books and articles have since appeared describing grim laboratory experiments—none chronicle the use of children in The Firm's mind control initiative (in part, presumably, because journalists never imagined children could be used in such a bloodthirsty way).

An article written in the 1960s by Dr. José Delgado, a Yale psychiatrist hailing from Franco's Spain, detailed his experiments on an 11-year-old boy with electrodes implanted in his brain. Dr. Delgado stimulated his young subject's synapses with a radio transmitter at a range of 100 feet. The boy was immediately stripped of his sexual identity, reporting that he wasn't sure if he was a boy or a girl.

One survivor recalls that she'd been instructed to address her CIA programmer as "Herr Doctor."

Some of the children subjected to the experimentation, according to New Orleans psychologist Valerie Wolf, were fragmented by trauma-based programming into a spate of alternate personalities. "Most of these patients responded to certain sounds," Wolf reported in testimony to the President's Advisory

Committee on Radiation Experiments on March 15, 1995, "clickers, metronomes or just clicking the tongue or hand clapping. Patients would vacillate from calm to robotically asking, 'Who do you want me to *kill?*'"

They were triggered to attempt suicide and attack the therapist, or march out of the office in a fugue state to assassinate somebody.

Claudia Mullens, a survivor of the experiments, testified at the Advisory Committee hearings about a trip in 1959 to the Deer Creek camp in Maryland, then used to train child prostitutes for sexual blackmail operations. At the camp, she was the "guest" of a Mr. Sheiber, an alias of the CIA's notorious LSD*meister* Dr. Sidney Gottleib:

> Most of the men I came to know well were either there as observers or volunteer targets. We were taught different ways to please men and at the same time ask questions to get them to talk about themselves. Then we had to recall everything about them....
>
> After this trip, I mainly went to hospitals, Army or Air Force bases or universities or the hotels in New Orleans and a place called the TRIMS facility in Texas.

The sole CIA official not briefed on the cabin and Dr. Gottlieb's child prostitution ring was John McCone, a former director who might have objected to the use of seven-year-old girls to gather information and ply their training in sexually "coercive techniques."

Weeping in the Playtime of Others, by former Princeton scholar Ken Wooden, describes a mental institution near Dallas, Texas that conducted freakish sensory deprivation experiments on retarded children of military personnel:

> On the grounds I noticed a strange structure with heavy, black plastic covering all the windows. That evening, a former house parent told me it was the private domain of a Dr. Snapp, who believes that the children are not retarded, but that their intellectual development has been aborted by birth.
>
> Dr. Snapp believes he has restructured the mother's womb with totally darkened rooms, and he places the child there to grow.
>
> Donna Parrish came close to dying in her "womb." When her parents removed her after four weeks in this atmosphere, they found her body covered with sores.

"Most patients," Wolf testified at the Advisory Committee hearings, "reported neo-Nazi alter personalities who believed in the coming of the next Reich."

Other symptoms of survivors include grand mal epileptic seizures with a temporary cessation of breathing. Doctors managed to strap one survivor to an EEG machine in the midst of a seizure—his brain waves registered normal—in other words, the fit was not a true grand mal, but a body memory of electric shocks years after the torture occurred.

ECT, the invention of Dr. Ugo Cerletti, another Spanish fascist, was often applied to various parts of the body, Wolf says, "usually the physical places that do not readily show or in tissue that heals quickly." High technology was combined with drugs, hypnosis and torture to create alter personalities. Years before Silicon Valley introduced virtual-reality computerware, children by the score told psychotherapists they'd been forced to wear goggles that flashed 3-D images of horror and death.

Cult Abuse of Children and Mind Control Programming

In the mid-1960s, Langley's spychologists feared exposure. Newspaper reporters had caught wind of Auschwitzian behavioral modification research funded by the government. Congress was asking questions. The thugs at Langley scratched their heads. It was only a matter of time before an inquisitive reporter exposed the rot of mind control.

The solution: CIA scientists bugged out of the laboratory. The experiments were moved into the community, hidden, like the flying saucers, in plain sight. Eccentric religious groups were organized or co-opted by intelligence operatives, including the People's Temple, the Symbionese Liberation Army, Ordo Templis Orientis (OTO), Finders, Solar Temple and the Bhagwan Shree Rajneesh Movement, among others.

In 1966 Charles Buckey built a preschool in Manhattan Beach, California. Buckey was an engineer at Hughes Aircraft (a household crack of the period: "Hughes *is* the CIA").

The McMartin mind control operation was reportedly the work of an intelligence cult.

The sect is said to be a cut-out of the American security elite's mind control fraternity. It isn't unique. There is much intermingling. Janet Morris, for instance, a science fiction writer and charter member of the Association for Electronic Defense, is a member of the Subud sect, an interdemonational group with roots in Indonesia. She is also research director of the U.S. Global Strategy Council, a Washington "think tank" founded by ultra-conservatives Claire

Booth Luce, Gen. Maxwell Taylor, Gen. Richard Stillwell, former CIA Deputy Director Ray Cline and the abrasive Jeanne Kirkpatrick, among other representatives of virtual government. In 1991, Morris traveled to Russia to study a technological marvel that transmits subliminal command messages over the low frequency infrasound band. Political researcher Armen Victorian discovered that with the Russian "psycho-correction" transmitter, "subliminal messages bypass the conscious level and are effective almost immediately." Another prominent member of the Subud sect, according to informants, is an executive of Mattell—a leading maker of virtual reality computer games for children, similar to the ones used by CIA scientists to traumatize young subjects. Children at the school mentioned balloon rides, elephants and clowns—were these virtual reality episodes, like the ones reported by Valerie Wolf? Other Subudians include executives of TRW and Hanna-Barbara, a cartoon company founded by OSS agents.

The CIA's hired guns in the media, and front groups like the False Memory Syndrome Foundation (with its shadow chairman Martin Orne, a veteran of the Agency's pedophile/blackmail ring, according to Claudia Mullens), have mustered support for the defendants in the McMartin case by distorting the children's testimony in the press.

It is conveniently forgotten that after the hung jury verdict was delivered in the second trial of Ray Buckey, *all* jurors at a press conference raised their hands when asked by reporters if they believed children had been abused at McMartin. It had simply not been proven that Buckey was the perpetrator, they said.

Tunnels unearthed beneath the preschool in 1990—60 feet of them, according to *five* independent scientists from local universities—corroborate the testimony of the children.

The McMartin disclosures to parents and psychologists are identical to those of children victimized in the formative years of the CIA's mind-splintering laboratory experiments.

Oliver Stone was drawn into producing a film, *Indictment,* conceived by screenwriter Abby Mann and aired by HBO earlier this year. Mann, the Emmy-winner, is also credited with the writing of *Judgment at Nuremberg*—unfortunately, there was no justice at the Nazi war crimes tribunal. Mann's specialty as a manipulator of public opinion is damage control of blowback from the Nazi diaspora. One of the best-selling Hollywood biographers in the country offers that Abby Mann does not really write screenplays but employs ghostwriters to produce the scripts in his name, an allegation confirmed by researcher Donald Freed.

Indictment conceals the fact that ritual child abuse is a legacy of The Firm's work in torture-based programming.

Treating Mind Controlled Children

On September 30, about 100 psychologists, mostly from the western states, convened at the Biltmore Hotel in Los Angeles for a three-day conference on "Mind Control, Multiplicity and Ritual Abuse." Each of the therapists have patients who have been tormented by cult cut-outs. Conference organizer Catherine Gould, a child psychologist from Encino, California, gave the keynote tour of a programmed multiple's "landscape of alters."

"In most instances," she said, "the alters are cult aligned. They are caught up in the underworld of mind control and know no other life. It isn't unusual for a patient to have an alter who reports to the cult everything said in the last therapy session."

But programmed alters are not the enemy. "They have experienced horror. Sexual abuse may be only one part of the traumatization pattern. Mind control is originally established when the victim is a child under six years old. During this formative stage of development, the perpetrator systematically combines dissociation-enhancing drugs, pain, sexual assault, terror and other forms of psychological abuse in such a way that the child dissociates the intolerable traumatic experience. The exception is the child who cannot dissociate and has been exposed to horror, disintegration and psychological death. The worst perpetrator is rage-based, disconnected from the core personality, and in the course of programming disdain for the victim is instilled in the alter personality. The mother herself may be a cult multiple and an amnestic. "

Mind control programming is deeply embedded, triggered by code words and sounds, sometimes inaudible ones. The alter personalities frequently "live" in the part of the body that has been traumatized. If a child was tortured in the shoulder, this is where an alter will reside. "The psychologist's job," Gould said, "is to map the alters and neutralize 'booby traps'—including suicidal impulses—left by the programmer as a monkey trap in the therapeutic process. The patient is ready to work with conscious memories of the trauma and begins healing when he can move around freely in the system of alters."

Vicki Graham-Costain, Ph.D., a clinical child psychologist, discussed the treatment of character pathologies that accompany mind control conditioning, and the sudden "flooding" of memories of childhood torture lurking behind post-hypnotic obstacles to recall, and in some cases, repression. Dr. David Neswald took up programming neutralization strategies, and common roadblocks to overcoming mind control conditioning. "Survivors are told they will be shunned by 'decent' people," Neswald says, "that people will be repulsed by and never accept them."

The treatment of mind controlled kids is a growing field, despite the call for public denial from the corporate press. Cult abuse of children, Gould wrote in *The Journal of Psychohistory* in the Spring of 1995, "is considerable in scope and extremely grave in its consequences. Among 2,709 members of the American Psychological Association who responded to a poll, 2,292 cases of ritual abuse were reported. In 1992 alone, ChildHelp USA logged 1,741 calls pertaining to ritual abuse; Monarch Resources of Los Angeles logged 5,000; Real Active Survivors tallied nearly 3,600; Justus Unlimited of Colorado received almost 7,000; and Looking Up Maine handled around 6,000."

Leading scientists in the Company's mind control academy have all at one time or another spoken of creating a "psycho-civilized" society. If this is the grand design, it is built on a bed of torture. Civilization is not the idea.

The Captains of Industry want our heads.

McMartin
Preschool

REVISITED

PART I.
Welcome to Manhattan Beach

Paul Bynum graduated from college in 1972 and joined the Hermosa Beach police department a year later. At 31 he was promoted to the rank of chief detective. He was not a typical investigator—a fellow detective observes that Bynum was "too bright to be a cop." Off duty, he drove an MG and mixed with the 60s survivors at the Sweetwater Café. In 1976, Bynum was assigned the investigation of the Karen Klaas murder. Klaas was the divorced wife of Bill Medley, a vocalist for the Righteous Brothers. She was raped and murdered one morning about an hour after dropping her five-year-old son off at the McMartin preschool in Manhattan Beach.

Neighbors told police they'd been alarmed at of a menacing stranger spotted before the murder wandering through the neighborhood. Police later entertained speculation that Klaas had been stalked. Throughout the week her body was found, this same stranger had popped up several times on her street corner. A neighbor phoned Karen to warn her. She didn't answer the phone. When friends entered the back door of the house, concerned for her safety, they found a Caucasian male with a beard, about 5′ 7″, about 28-years-old, dressed in a long olive green coat with a tunic collar and boots, exiting through the front door. Klaas was found naked and unconscious. She died five days later.

Nothing was stolen. Police had no indication that Klaas knew her killer.

In 1984, shortly after indictments were handed down to defendants in the McMartin child molestation case, Gerald Klaas, her husband, drove off a cliff in Oregon and was killed. Children alleged in a grand jury hearing that teachers at the preschool had threatened to kill family members if they disclosed abuse. It was rumored that the Klaas deaths and the McMartin case may have been related.

But police insisted there was no connection. "We have no leads, no suspects and we're not coordinating with Manhattan Beach," Hermosa Beach Lt. Mike Lavin told reporters.[1]

In 1979, Paul Bynum was forced out of the police department without an explanation despite an unblemished record. After the detective completed an investigation of a series of murders of teenage girls in nearby Redondo Beach—culminating in the arrest and conviction of serial killers Roy Norris and Lawrence Bittaker—police chief Frank Beeson pressured him to take a stress leave. Bynum was still haunted by the serial murder investigation, but he remained confident in his emotional stability and refused the leave. The chief obtained an order from the city manager, and Bynum was forced out on indefinite disability leave.

He chalked it up to internal politics, "paranoia," a purging of all potential detractors in the police department.

Bynum told local reporter Kevin Cody: "When the papers reported that Beeson had shown up apparently drunk at his first Hermosa [city] council meeting and dropped his revolver on the floor, he thought we had tipped reporters." Beeson was apparently unaware that reporters routinely attended meetings of the city council.[2]

Bynum found a new career as a private investigator. In March 1984, he was retained by the Buckeys' defense attorney, Danny Davis, and in the course of his investigation came to the conclusion that children had been abused at the preschool. Bynum found the videotaped interviews of the children by child therapists "credible." One afternoon, outside the courtroom, Cody mentioned to Bynum that hundreds of children had alleged abuse took place at the preschool. A dark cloud of distress passed over Bynum's face. He stammered that he had no idea so many children were involved.

In 1986, Bynum was called to testify at the trial of Ray Buckey by prosecutor Lael Rubin. The morning he was to appear, a juror's home was burglarized and the private investigator's testimony was rescheduled for the following morning.

"Neither side is going to like what I have to say," he confided to Cody.

For one thing, there was the matter of Bynum's lost citation books, records he'd kept as a detective in Hermosa Beach. When the police arrested Ray Buckey on child molestation charges, the "lost" books were discovered on the preschool attendant's desk.

What were official police records doing in Buckey's home?

Rubin meant to ask Bynum about a map turned up by investigators from the District Attorney's office in March 1986, pin-pointing the location of turtle shells Bynum had unearthed at the lot adjacent to the McMartin preschool. (The children claimed teachers had killed turtles to demonstrate what would happen to them and their families if they talked about the molestations. Bynum, while retained by the defense, had managed to corroborate a key point in the testimony of the children.)

Bynum's court appearance was pre-empted by his "suicide," although the timing left some parents in the case convinced he'd been murdered.[3] His body was discovered by his wife at 5:45 in the morning. Bynum died of a head shot from a .38 caliber pistol.

"None of the half dozen people questioned who were close to Bynum could think of any reason why his involvement in the case might have driven him to suicide," reported Kevin Cody in the *Easy Reader* in Manhattan Beach. "Paul was kind of a worrier," said Stephen Kay, a deputy district attorney and friend of the Bynum family, "but there was no hint of suicide. He was very upbeat about his wife and new daughter, both of whom he adored."[4]

The belief that Bynum had been murdered was fueled by the memory of another odd death, the alcohol toxicity that claimed the life of Judy Johnson, the first mother to speak publicly about child molestation at McMartin. Sympathizers of the Buckeys in the press have gone to great lengths to portray Johnson as "crazy." There is no indication that her life was inverted the day her son returned home from the McMartin school, bleeding from the anus. Threatening strangers entered her life. She believed she'd been poisoned. (In 1992, therapists at the L.A. Commission for Women's Ritual Abuse Task Force also insisted they'd been poisoned, and corroborated their allegations with medical reports—the *Los Angeles Times* was given the reports but shunned them, alleging the therapists were paranoid fantasists with "hysterical" delusions.[5]) She lived in fear and felt it necessary to keep a gun in the house. Her estranged husband appeared to have joined in the harassment campaign. Johnson took to alcohol. She was allergic to alcohol.

It poisoned her.

Wendy Hoffman, "Child's Drawing," 1990

The death of Judy Johnson was met with howls of laughter in greater Los Angeles. She will be remembered as the delusional paranoiac who set in motion an implacable wave of child abuse "hysteria" carried through southern California by a sensational press and out across the mountains and plains, contaminating lives and decimating families everywhere, a groundless "witch-hunt." This was the explanation given by "experts" from leading universities.

Nevertheless, children who attended the preschool *still* insist they were abused. And the detailed memories of their parents are sharply at odds with the simple caricature of the case repeated endlessly in the press. They recall the long hours of testimony by dozens of children, the telephoned death threats, how some of the children suffered deep emotional problems requiring hospitalization. Knowing child pornography to be a highly lucrative business, they frown at the snickering over the children's disclosures that they were forced to play "naked movie star" games. They haven't put aside as anomalous accident the first exhibit in the case: a physician's report that one of the children suffered "blunt force trauma" of sexual areas.[6] The parents were left to ponder why some of the toddlers in the care of the McMartins had chlamydia, a sexually-transmitted infection.[7]

Where was the humor in all of this?

Open Season

The parents questioned, like everyone else, the incredibility of the charges'— some said the children were lying— yet had to wonder about Peggy McMartin's testimony that she had only worked at the school for a few weeks, when payroll records revealed that she had been employed there for years. To the families, the final verdict of Ray Buckey meant it was now "open season on children."

The world was told repeatedly that ABC's Wayne Satz, the reporter who broke the case (felled by a heart attack in December, 1992 at age 47), and therapist Kee MacFarlane, had had an affair—as if this had any bearing on the children's allegations. Even Oliver Stone took to the bandwagon with a film made for HBO, written by Abby Mann, reinforcing the already widespread belief that "hysteria" in Manhattan Beach was kindled when a child returned home from school one afternoon with "a red bottom"—this would be the son of Judy Johnson, and he hadn't been spanked—he was bleeding. This hardly constitutes a little media "spin." It is conscious participation in a felony. The account of the case pounded into collective memory by media repetition goes that far to distort the facts. The widespread media coverage was, according to *Los Angeles Times* editor Noel Greenwood, "a mean-spirited campaign" organized to discredit the children and their therapists.[8]

But why should certain members of the corporate press and segments of the legal and psychiatric professions go to such lengths to suppress evidence of organized child abuse at McMartin preschool? Because the traumatic crimes reported by the children bear an uncanny resemblance to mind control programming, a specialty of certain classified federal agencies and cultists on the black budget payroll.[9]

The children are often ridiculed because some of their charges are thought to be impossible. Tunnels under the preschool? Too far-fetched to consider. But, in fact, there were tunnels, confirmed in 1993 by a coalition of five earth scientists from leading universities.

The unearthing of the tunnels, like much of the critical evidence, never made it to the courtroom. They have been discreetly filtered from newspaper accounts.

To fill the void, Debbie Nathan, a widely published skeptic of ritual abuse, heaped scorn on the tunnel allegations in the *Village Voice* in June 1990. She maintained the McMartin site had been "painstakingly probed for tunnels" once before. "None were found."[10] Nathan's account is a fabrication. In fact, recalls Dr.

Wendy Hoffman, "Child's Drawing," 1990

Roland Summit, who contributed to the final report on the tunnel excavation, parents started digging and prosecutors, reluctantly forced to a showdown, "commissioned a superficial search of open terrain." District Attorney Ira Reiner then declared the tunnel stories unfounded "without going under the concrete floor of the preschool." Once the tunnels were officially discounted, attempts to explore for an underground reality were instant targets for ridicule.[11] Archeologist Gary Stickel was retained to lead the excavation on the recommendation of Dr. Rainier Berger, chairman of UCLA's Interdisciplinary Archeology Program, by parents of McMartin children.[12] Initially Stickel sided with the Buckeys, believing the abuse allegations to be so much moonlight for hysterics. However, he'd heard of late homicide detective Paul Bynum, the first to dig at the site:

> "Bynum apparently conducted his informal digging in February," 1984 (*Daily Breeze*, 1987). "It is significant to note he did unearth some buried animal remains, 'numerous pieces of tortoise shells and bones'" (*Daily Breeze*, 1987). "There was keen interest at the time since it was reported that the children testified that tortoises, rabbits, and other small animals were mutilated to terrorize the children into keeping silent" (*Daily Breeze*, 1987).[13]

But "authorities" courted by the press snaffled at the suggestion that animals were killed to frighten children at McMartin and other preschools around the country. It was not until 1993 that a study by the National Center for Child Abuse and Neglect confirmed that children are not only threatened in day care settings, but most threats are "specific in terms of what the consequence of disclosure will be and how the threat will be carried out.... The use of such severe threats is obviously quite frightening to young children and is effective in preventing disclosure. In fact, it appears that threats used in day care center cases may go beyond what is usually needed to silence victims, and may in some instances be made for purposes of psychological terror in and of itself."[14]

Into the Grotto

Most reporters in Southern California pooh-poohed the notion that the children had been threatened into silence, but there was a great, gaping silence in the media when the tunnels were found.

"I asked my daughter," recalls Jackie MacGauley, a mother of two children who attended the preschool, "'how could they have taken you to these places without being seen?' And she answered me as though I was silly to ask such a question. She said, 'through the *tunnels,* of course.'"

For a month, the *Los Angeles Times* ran a spate of feature stories ridiculing the excavation team—until actual evidence of tunnels was discovered. Then the *Times* ran a one-paragraph news item, dryly noting that "evidence" of tunnels had been found. The *Times* never mentioned the subject again.

Only the local *Beach Reporter* covered the story without an embarrassed grin.

Parents began to dig with shovels in an area pointed out by a nine-year-old former charge of the McMartin preschool, who told them to dig behind a cement planter in the northeast corner. When parents unearthed several broken turtle shells and a few bones, they stopped digging and notified the District Attorney's office.

Once the entrance was exposed, Stickel used remote ground sensing equipment to read the terrain conductivity of the empty lot next to the preschool. The survey was conducted by a respected geophysicist, Robert Beer, working with an electromagnetic scanner. The tunnel opening was found precisely where children said it would be.

Stickel: "Some of the children had stated there had been animal cages placed along that wall and that they had entered a tunnel under the cages." A foreign

Wendy Hoffman, "Child's Drawing," 1990

soil deposit was found near the foundation. Clearing the anomaly with a back-hoe, they found the roots of an avocado tree cut to clear a path for the tunnel. The roots had been cut with a hand saw and torn away, and shreds dangled on either wall of the tunnel.

This is precisely the moment editors at the *Los Angeles Times* chose to pull reporters off the story: once "evidence" of tunnels was found, the story was no longer deemed newsworthy. All other news outlets rapidly followed suit.

But the excavators cleared the foreign soil and followed the tunnel anyway. The passage "meandered under Classroom No. 4 and then most of Classroom No. 3.... There is no other scenario that fits all of the facts except that the feature was indeed a tunnel," they concluded. "The date of the construction and use of the tunnel was not absolutely established, but an assessment of seven factors of data all indicate that it was probably constructed, used and completely filled back in sometime after 1966 (the construction date of the preschool)."[15]

Dr. E. Michael, a specialist in forensic geology in Malibu, was called to examine a cavity in the underground passage. Together with Dr. Herbert Adams of the geology department at Cal State University, a ground resistivity reading of the tunnel was followed from the preschool to a triplex next door, a traversing section parallel to the north wall of the school, 5 feet away, extending 20 feet eastward, 10 to 15 feet beneath the surface.[16]

Gerald Hobbs, a local tree surgeon for 25 years, did much of the actual digging. Hobbs reports that the children told two different stories about the tunnels:

> One, that they had gone through the tunnel and came up in the house next door, and two, they had come up in the garage, which blocked the house from the street. At any rate, the tunnel went in that direction.... That evening I went to the house next door and followed the walk between the school and the house, only about 4 1/2 feet apart. I went about 30 feet down between the buildings and found a crawl space under the house. I bellied my way toward the southwest corner of the house. After going about 20 feet, I found an area inside the west wall of the house where the floor was cut out. If I remember correctly, the area of floor that was missing was 36" x 38" x 41" [17]

The use of tunnels to conceal criminal activity is not unprecedented. One SRA/mind control survivor in Atlanta, Georgia (identified as Kathleen H. in Daniel Ryder's *Cycle of Abuse*), grew agitated when asked to comment on the above account of the McMartin dig. As it happens, an organized kidnap ring in Cobb County, GA, she recalls, had

... caged and killed and sold children in underground systems of tunnels, some under their own neighborhoods. They had also used the tunnels to conceal drug laboratories and for munitions storage. Such people will most likely never be caught, because [their] activities are literally underground. One of them was a retired Presbyterian minister who owned a house where I and his grandchildren independently showed adults where the tunnel access was, but he'd had time by then to seal off the entrance from behind a wall—in the grandchildren's playroom.

Police, Kathleen says, "scratch their heads after doing searches *above-ground*. More law enforcement officials should be informed of the widespread usage of underground tunnels, old bomb shelters, abandoned S.A.M. missile sites, and more sophisticated equipment could be made available to law enforcement personnel to help them to detect such tunnels."[18]

But there is still much snickering in Los Angeles over the tunnel allegations—even after a subterranean complex of passageways was discovered in Brooklyn, an underground arms caché that linked the safe houses of a political sect that conditioned recruits with sleep and sensory deprivation, rudimentary forms of mind control, in its indoctrination sessions. On November 13, 1996,

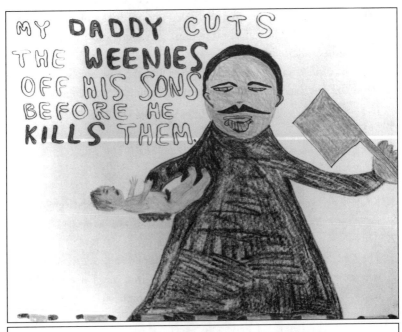

Wendy Hoffman, "Child's Drawing," 1990

the *Times of London* described the "MAZE of tunnels and underground 'dungeons' containing rifles, machineguns and explosives [found] in a residential district of New York. Police said the bizarre find in Brooklyn's Crown Heights area could indicate the presence of an urban militia which may have been using three adjoining houses."[19]

A total of 77 animal bones were found buried at the McMartin site, a assortment of the osteo-remains of domestic cattle, chickens, dogs and a single rabbit.[20]

However, Debbie Nathan, the hide-bound "skeptic" of ritual abuse and a widely published advocate of the False Memory Syndrome Foundation, tells another story: "[The McMartin] parents have invested years believing in demonic conspiracies and underground nursery tunnels. (Until recently, the parents were still digging. They came up with Indian artifacts)." No mention of Bynum's independent findings. No mention of the dig as it happened in the real world. She reserves much of her ridicule for former FBI agent Ted Gunderson and Jackie MacGauley. In fact, these two brought in Stickel and his geological team to defuse accusations they were directly engaged in the dig. They weren't. The search for the tunnels was independent, and scores of volunteers pitched in.

Nathan's refrain of "no evidence" is hollow. She has been known to contort the facts of ritual abuse in a grotesque parody of journalism and is frequently blind to critical evidence. Nathan continues to find "no evidence" of abuse at McMartin, despite the nightmares, the acting-out, medical molestation reports and sexual infections. The tunnel excavation, she assures with psychic certainty (and a sniff of condescension), is a "*hoax.*"

Nathan's disingenuous attacks on children and their advocates, repeated in the *New York Times* and a host of other corporate publications, happened to conceal a classified mind control operation the CIA and Pentagon had undertaken 30 years before....

Notes

1. Kevin Cody, "Former HB Officer's Suicide Adds Questions to McMartin Mystery," *Easy Reader* (Manhattan Beach tabloid news weekly), November 17, 1987.
2. Ibid.
3. The *Easy Reader* obituary declares: "none of the half dozen people questioned who were close to Bynum could think of any reason why his involvement in the case might have driven him to commit suicide. But the timing of Bynum's death and the controversy already surrounding the McMartin case ... inevitably spawned speculation that a link existed between his suicide and his pending testimony."

4. Cody.

5. The medical reports were reprinted in Alex Contantine, *Psychic Dictatorship in the U.S.A.,* Portland: Feral House, 1995, pp. 97–111.

6. McMartin trial record, exhibit one.

7. Interviews with parents.

8. Constantine, "Ray Buckey's Press Corps and the Tunnels of McMartin," pp. 77–96.

9. Ibid.

10. Debbie Nathan, "What McMartin Started: The Ritual Abuse Hoax," *Village Voice,* June 12, 1990.

11. Roland Summit, M.D., "Introduction," *Archeological Investigations of the McMartin Preschool Site,* Manhattan Beach, California, unpublished report by archeologist Gary Stickel of the McMartin Tunnel Project, 1993, p. ii.

12. Gary Stickel, foreword to Archeological Investigations.

13. Ibid.

14. Kelly, Brant and Waterman, "Sexual Abuse of Children in Day Care Centers," *Journal of Child Abuse & Neglect* (17), 1993, p. 74.

15. Stickel, Archeological Investigations, p. 95. The assessment of the tunnel's age was corroborated by Dr. Jon Michael, a geologist on the McMartin project.

16. Dr. E. Michael, letter to Dr. Gary Stickel, July 2, 1992, pp. 2–3.

17. Gerald Hobbs, "Notes on Investigation of the Neighboring Triplex," in Archeological Investigations, p. 176.

18. Kathleen H., personal correspondence with the author, August 29, 1996.

19. Quentin Letts, "Arms cache found under New York," *Times of London,* November 13 1996.

20. Charles Schwartz, Ph.D., "The McMartin Preschool Osteological Remains" (2nd report), *Archeological Investigations,* June 15, 1990, p. 1.

PART II.
Bad Apples

Federally funded biomedical and behavioral research has resulted in major advances in health care and improved the quality of life for all Americans.
—Bill Clinton, February 17, 1994

Intelligence officials contort through hard questions so gracefully that their appearance at investigative hearings is always lively with outraged congressmen bellowing in disbelief. A spy is a liar by definition, so no one listened in 1964 when CIA director Richard Helms, in a letter to the Warren Commission, made reference to Langley's interest in a cyborgean form of "biological communication."

"Cybernetics," Helms explained, "can be used in molding of a child's character ... the amassing of experience, the establishment of social behavior patterns..."—What was that? Machines? Molding character? No one at the Warren Commission thought to ask the CIA official what he was talking about—"... control of the growth processes of the individual ..."[1]

Helms wasn't exagerrating. At McGill University, Georgetown, Cornell and some 40 other upper-crust academic institutions around the country, psychiatrists and engineers on the CIA payroll R&D'd the technology of remote "biological communication." But the breathtaking potential of the devices has been marred by the bloodthirsty protocol of CIA-military experimentation.

One subject of the experiments in the 1960s, a psychologist living in Germany today, recalled in a letter to the Freedom of Thought Foundation, an organization of researchers and survivors of CIA-DoD mind control experiments, his grim history as a guinea pig. The experience was horrifyingly similar to the abuse later described by hundreds of toddlers in southern California. He suggests that far-fetched cover stories (ritual abuse, "psychic" spying experiments, "alien" abductions, poltergeists, etc.) routinely conceal EM assaults on mind and personality, as detailed by one subject of nonconsentual mind control experimentation:

> The functions of torture ... associate the original personality of the victim with pain, panic and horror—the desired personality is conditioned with pleasure afterwards, to function as aversive conditioning to establish new behavior patterns, establish a panic-controlled mechanism of amnesia ("If you remember, you will try to betray us, but we will be informed before you succeed in managing this, because we are everywhere, then you will be tortured again, so you will not remember."), produce an artificial, controlled multiple personality disorder (which is, under natural conditions, a result of traumatization).
>
> And by the way, torture itself, even if not combined with mind control techniques, elicits amnestic disorders or memory blocks.... With heavy electroshocks the victim is regressed to a state of an infant. Then the torture resembles psychologically the ill-treatment in childhood. Rape is common, too, as an equivalent of sexual abuse in infancy.
>
> Being a human robot means to be mentally ill, means to be a person suffering from Multiple Personality Disorder (MPD). The difference between a "natural" MPD and a artificial, mind controlled MPD is that the latter was consciously tailored by the controllers to whom the victim is tied by invisible unconscious chains.
>
> Many students in the field of psychology and psychiatry don't believe that

mind control is possible ... and that is probably because they haven't understood the basic concept: MPD produced by a stimulation of the natural conditions of its causes. This is very important: Only if the natural conditions of the causes of MPD are reproduced [will] a human robot work reliably. And that is a "must" in all clandestine actions.

You may ask why I can be so sure. There are two reasons: As a psychologist I know a little bit about the mechanisms of mind and behavior, and I am a victim.

As far as I can remember, I was the victim of a program with the aim to delete my personality—literally to dissolve my personality and extract it from my nervous system. They told me that I was sentenced to death and that they have found a method to execute me, but leave my body alive. In short: They tried to make a human robot or a slave out of me [with]:

- Classical hypnosis, drugs and so on.
- Electrical torture of my genitals. They used a device which I call a torture trouser. This is a sort of loin-cloth made of leather and steel bonds by which an electrode is fastened to the genitals of the victim. For electric supply they use a cable or a battery so that you can freely move and if the torturer wants to torture you he sends an electric signal to the battery using a transmitter. This is a very practical device for aversive behavior modification....
- They gave me a drug that induces near-death experiences. When I was clinically dead a voice suggested to me that he was God and that he had decided that I have to be born again as a slave. Then I was reanimated.
- They used electromagnetic fields to induce panic, fear, depression and pleasure. By this means they conditioned me very effectively. They used ESB too, but it was not so effective. They conditioned my EEG.
- They obviously have found a wavelength with hypnotic effects so that they could give me post-hypnotic orders. I wasn't able not to obey.
- My memory was erased by electroshocks, radiation and the described torture mechanism.

As far as I can remember all this happened between 1972 and 1982. There are some reminiscences making me believe that the first manipulations started earlier, 1967.

Some other reminiscences furnish evidence that they began to dissociate my mind when I was a little child living in an orphanage, younger than three years old.

I am not a mad man. I am 43 years old. I am a psychologist and a doctor of the economic and social sciences. I am working for a network of facilities treating drug addicts, and I am responsible for public relations. I am strongly convinced that I am out of danger now. I don't know whether they used modern electronic mind control methods. I can't believe that they implanted brain transmitters into my skull, but who knows.

I don't know why they chose me for this program. There are lots of more or less nonsensical cover stories ... being a man from outer space, having dangerous paranormal (psi) faculties, being able to unmask spies by using these methods....[2]

"Averse conditioning ... electric shocks ... rape is common"—years later, the McMartin children would also testify they were" tied by invisible unconscious chains" to morbidly cruel adults engaged in traumatic "clandestine actions." Another survivor of the experiments of the 1960s has memories nearly identical to those of the McMartin children: "hypnosis, electroshock, sensory deprivation, by isolation—in closets, in underground dirt rooms, in graves, underwater, death threats to self, others and animals, use of drugs ... seduction and black-mail...."[3]

At the preliminary McMartin hearing, 14 children testified for 88 days. They described 45 threats to them and their parents.[4] The tactic is debated. One psychologist will frown at threatening children. Another will dismiss the very mention of death threats as a hysterical aberration or a "false memory."

Guess which psychologist has a security clearance.

Virtual Hell

Walter Urban, a defense attorney for the Buckeys, told *New York Times* reporter David Hechler in 1988 that the "stories" of children at McMartin were impossible to believe, "such as: 'I was molested.' Where did it occur? 'In a hot-air balloon over the desert.' 'In a speed boat, where sharks were all around, and they told us that we were going to be thrown to the sharks if we didn't agree to be molested.' That kind of stuff."[5] Other children swore they'd witnessed teachers at the preschool "flying."

Kids do say the darnedest things. Anyone with a grain of sense rejects these claims out of hand. Then again ...

Chris de Nicola would keep Amnesty International's entire staff occupied for a year. Born in July, 1962, Nicola was used at the age of four in federally-sponsored hypnotic imaging experiments at Kansas City University. "I was strapped down," she recalls. A doctor festooned her head and body with electrodes, "used what looked like an overhead projector and repeatedly said he was burning different images into my brain while a red light flashed, aimed at my forehead." Electric shocks and drugs were applied in each sequence, "and [he] told me to go deeper and deeper, each image would go deeper into my brain, and I would do whatever he told me to do.... When it was over, he gave me another shot. The next thing I remember I was with my grandparents again in Tucson."[6] The McMartin children also spoke of adults slipping them drugs, and electric-convulsive shocks are a recurrent theme of cult abuse claims. The "doctor" in this instance was L. Wilson Greene. With a little research, the girl's therapist discovered that a man with this name was the scientific director of the Chemical and Radiological Lab at the Army Chemical Center.[7]

Children forced into participation in the experiments have spoken of wearing virtual-reality goggles. Thirty years after the inhumane treatment Nicola received, the beaming of images to the visual cortex is stock-and-trade stuff in the mind control underground. The virtual-reality goggles were described by young mind control subjects years before they were commercialized. In the CIA experiments, the children reported they were made to view threatening images, or convinced they'd participated in murder, cannibalism and other horrific crimes.[8]

In January 1996, the full-grown director of a support group for ritually abused children in Los Angeles (she has worked closely with the families in the McMartin case) experienced first-hand the same virtual-reality episodes induced at the preschool when local mind control technicians targeted her for torture from a remote source. The experience began with a splitting headache, "like needles" boring into her cranium. The pain was not stationary, like the average headache, but moved around in her head. The attack continued for seven or eight hours. She was reduced to screaming and crying and took to bed. When she closed her eyes, her head teemed with technicolor images of figures in robes moving in a circle. She opened her eyes and the figures still swarmed in the darkness in front of her. She switched on the light. The images were still there.[9]

She wasn't hallucinating. And the McMartin children weren't suffering "false memories." These days, the images—frequently combined with an electronic form of hypnosis—are projected to the brain's visual pathways, received with perfect clarity.

There are innumerable examples of helpless private citizens who've had the misfortune to fall prey to the whims of the radionics crews.

One of them was Patrick Warden, a high-potential high-achiever who scored in the 98th percentile of his high school intelligence test in 1969, an accomplishment repeated in his graduate record exam at the University of California at Berkeley. In 1980, a CIA recruiter approached him. In short order, invasive "voices" spoke to him. They told him that the Agency wanted him to become a public relations officer for the Agency's "mental telepathy system." The "system," he discovered by scouring obscure journals and the few books on CIA mind control available, is "operational," employing "technology that operates apparently by radio and microwaves, and can broadcast voices, visual images and somatic sensations, and affect the autonomic nervous system across distances.... Though in its primitive form the MTS mimics psychic phenomena, it involves man-made technology."[10]

There are innumerable instances of ritual abuse accompanied by exotic "psychic" images, voices, sensations, special effects of the type generated by technology described in case histories of CIA mind control.

There is the case of Chad Ingram, the son of confessed ritual abuser Paul Ingram of Olympia, Washington. Lawrence Wright, in a 1993 *New Yorker* story attempted to dismiss ritual abuse as a therapeutic aberration and exonerate Ingram based on opinions of psychologists from the False Memory Syndrome Foundation. The CIA shrinks dismissed the boy's memories of abuse out-of-hand because "he had heard voices in his head."[11]

A doctor at one of Stockholm's most prestigious hospitals states that young children were used for experiments involving advanced mind control technology to evaluate their "thought activity and reactions."[12] This line of R&D quite naturally evolved into tinkering with the transmission of virtual-reality images and voices to the brain.

The devices have been around for decades. And they weren't produced in the dog-star cluster, shipped by flying saucer to earth, though the CIA, military intelligence sector and certain psychologists (with a CIA pedigree) have convinced hundreds of millions that "aliens" travel from untold light-years away to stick CIA implants in human heads, the most transparent cover story ever told—one passionately defended by many of the very same skeptics who drown allegations of ritual abuse in condescending snorts of laughter.

Richard Helms was acknowledging his own deepest ambitions when he told the Warren Commission of the Agency's experiments in "molding a child's character" with cybernetics.

Notes

1. Walter Bowart, *Operation Mind Control,* New York: Dell, 1978, p. 256.

2. Anonymous letter, *Free Thinking* (Freedom of Thought Foundation newsletter), pre-publication review copy, vol. 1: no. 4, March 1995.

3. Marcia Chambers, "Bail is Rejected in Child Sex Case," *New York Times,* December 20, 1986, p. 34.

4. Renee Bright, correspondence to the President's Advisory Commission on Human Radiation Experiments, March 9, 1995, p. 2.

5. David Hechler, *The Battle & the Backlash: The Child Sexual Abuse War,* Lexington, Massachusetts: Lexington Books, 1988, p. 334.

6. Chris De Nicola, statement to the President's Commission on Human Radiation Experiments, April, 1995 hearings, p. 1.

7. Valerie Wolf, letter to Presidential Advisory Commission on Human Radiation Experiments, March 12, 1995, p. 3.

8. Valerie Wolf, "Report on Behavior and Activities Reported by My Patients from 1988 to Present," Presidential Advisory Commission hearings.

9. Interview with author, January 24, 1996. Compare this virtual-reality vision with the memory of Paul Ingram in the Olympia, Washington ritual abuse case: "Ingram began seeing people in robes kneeling around a fire. He thought he saw a corpse." Lawrence Wright, "Remembering Satan—Part I," *The New Yorker,* May 17, 1993, p. 73.

10. Patrick A. Warden, "Mind Control and Mental Telepathy," *MindNet Notes* (electronic journal), August 1, 1993.

11. Wright, p. 74. Often, as the German subject points out, post-hypnotic suggestion is used to dissolve a child's memory of the trauma, protecting the identities of his tormentors. It's not uncommon for a subject to resort to self-mutilation, an impulse that is programmed in by hypnotic command, when recalling blocked memories of childhood abuse in therapy sessions. Similar programming could explain the sudden comatose state of Chad Ingram when confronting certain memories: "Chad produced a memory of being assaulted by Ray Risch [a mechanic for the Washington state police and a drinking buddy of the boy's father] in the basement of Ingrams' house when he was ten or twelve years old. At this point, Chad leaned forward in a trance-like state.' Sometimes he would go off for 5–10 minutes without saying anything." Wright, p. 77.

   "A major part of the mind control experimentation [on children] was involved in wiping out the memory of the subject through electric shock, trauma and drugs."—Valerie Wolf, in a report to Clinton's Commission on Radiation, March 12, 1995, p. 4.

12. Robert Naeslund, a victim of Swedish mind control research, original ms. of Brain Transmitter, a privately-printed appeal.

PART III.
The Wall

One much-maligned school of psychology holds that a day-care center operated by a mind control cult specializes in dissociative conditioning, a regimen of physical and psychological beatings that give rise to a cluster of pseudo-identities. The first stage of conditioning, they maintain, insults the child's most primitive reflexes, a repetition of torture that overloads the child's neurological complex and forces the adoption of protective alters. Most very young children rapidly learn to dissociate, a learned reflex that the group exploits as the child grows—often into adulthood—by accessing the alters. They can be called upon at any time and used in criminal enterprises. Dissociative programming is sort of a psychological hard drive: it occurs when the victim is very young and is the bed of future programming.[1]

But the study of dissociative conditioning in traumatized preschool children did not reach these conclusions until 1990 (with the work of Dr. Steven Ray, Frank Putnam and others)—nearly a decade after the first charges of abuse at McMartin were filed.

Before techniques for multiplicity programming were understood by psychologists treating survivors of ritual abuse, a lively debate of distinguished, smartly-groomed psychologists was kindled by the McMartin trial. An early champion for the defense was the late Dr. Nahman Greenberg, a prominent psychiatric consultant on child abuse. With a grant from the National Institute of Mental Health in 1971, Dr. Greenberg once designed a psychological profile to identify the personality characteristics of abused children. For twenty years, while still an associate professor at the University of Illinois's psychiatry department, he was director of child development in the clinical and research unit. In 1975, he founded CAUSES (Child Abuse Unit for Studies, Education and Services) at Illinois Masonic Hospital. His office glittered with numerous honors from federal and state government agencies.[2]

Dr. Greenberg was retained to make sense of the McMartin allegations. He studied the questioning techniques of therapist Kee MacFarlane and generally seemed to agree with her findings. But in public pronouncements Greenberg later stated that MacFarlane coerced accusations of abuse from the children, goaded them into making slanderous allegations. The argument, endlessly repeated by the media, has since tainted McFarlane's credibility.[3]

But Greenberg's subsequent career is revealing. His next ritual abuse case came shortly after his consultation on McMartin. Beth Vargo joined Believe the

Children shortly after witnessing it.

In April 1984, Vargo suspected that her four-year-old daughter had been sexually abused at the Jewish Community Center (JCC) preschool in Chicago. Several other children detailed abuse. They described "strangers" engaging in sexual escapades at the center and elsewhere. But this time it wasn't only children who spoke of sexual abuse. Adult staff members of JCC stepped forward to fill gaps in the children's allegations with their own testimony.

Vargo was referred to Dr. Greenberg by the local Department of Child and Family Services.[4] The name rang a bell, and after a moment of reflection she recalled where she had heard the name before—the family doctor had warned her to steer clear of him.

Dr. Greenberg did not believe in "involving" the "police or prosecutors in child abuse cases, but preferred to work with the child victims and adult perpetrators to repair relationships damaged by sexual abuse," she recalls. "Since our case involved extra-familial abuse, not incest, my husband and I made other therapy arrangements for our daughter."

At a meeting called by the center to address parents' concerns about the investigation, Greenberg recommended that they and the teachers attend a retreat to "share their feelings." The psychiatrist empathized primarily with the teachers' "stress," not the children's trauma, and engaged in heated arguments with therapists treating them. He refused to accept the word of the JCC's own staff that the toddlers had been abused at the school, and when asked, refused to cooperate with police.[5]

The case was a repetition of McMartin. During questioning, two mothers reported that their daughters had told them the teachers had threatened to kill their families if they talked. The children insisted that they'd been beaten, stuck with needles and screwdrivers. In fact, parents reported unexplained scratches and bruises. The preschoolers also said that teachers at the center organized "naked games."

"This will be with us forever," one mother lamented. "It will never be wiped away."[6]

In 1987, Dr. Greenberg's consultation in another aborted child abuse investigation—the child pornography operation run by the Finders cult—exposed an unshakable bias in favor of ritual abuse perpetrators—and his role in a CIA cover-up. The Finders, as most cult observers are aware, was a CIA-anchored circle of ritual abusers engaged in operant mind control conditioning, child pornography and kidnap. At first, Langley officials admitted to custom agents in Tallahassee, Florida that the CIA "owned the Finders."[7]

Marion David Pettie, who retired from the Air Force in 1956 and defined himself as a "political powerhouse," was the guiding light of the cult. He denied any connection to the CIA—yet his late wife was an employee of the agency and his son a veteran of Air America, the opiate courier. Confidential sources told police the Finders conducted "brainwashing" sessions and "explored satanism."[8]

Police in Tallahassee were called off the case after Dr. Greenberg examined the children and found "no evidence of recent physical harm." Nonetheless, two Florida policemen stood by their statement that they'd found visible evidence of sexual abuse. The original arrest file, as one investigating Treasury agent complained in an internal report, was "classified *secret* and not available for review." Customs service agents in Washington discovered on the group's premises directions for kidnapping children and photographing them. Yet the case was guttered, largely due to Dr. Greenberg's denials that children could possibly be used by an occult group with an active interest in mind control programming.

Another ritual abuse "expert," an oft-cited debunker, has FBI credentials. Agent Ken Lanning of the Quantico Behavioral Science Laboratory has provided "skeptics"—mostly pedophiles, CIA propagandists and mind control operatives in academia and the press—with an illusory pillar of debate. (The unit had three founders hailing from the Justice Department, among them Mark Richard, who went on to become a key advisor to Janet Reno in the Branch Davidian stand-off. According to Lanny Sinkin, writing in the *Portland Free Press:* "In a recent interview, Daniel Sheehan, general counsel for the Christic Institute, noted that Mr. Richard has a long history of [closing] down investigations [that] might expose covert operations," among them, "assassinations, drug smuggling and other criminal activity, pursued under the guise of combatting terrorism.")

Fatal flaws in Lanning's "research report," a denial that the cult abuse of children exists, were exposed as a cover-up by a fellow law enforcement "insider":

I have spoken to Ken Lanning, I know others who have spoken to him and we all take issue with Ken's "opinion" and how this report is being used.

It should also be stated that I work within the System in some capacity and have some experience in investigations. Neither am I too pleased by what I have been learning about the atrocities that are occurring, the reasons for it, and the artful skewing of perceptions....

Ken Lanning is an armchair analyst and he has "not" personally investigated many cases of RA. Law enforcement and others sometimes "consult" with him about cases and how to proceed. He is not aware of all RA cases. The FBI,

Children's Services and law enforcement do not keep statistics on ritual crime. No one is keeping track; therefore no one can say with authority how prevalent ritual abuse is. The DAs are not bringing evidence of RA into cases unless they really have to because of freedom of religion issues and reports like Lanning's.

He has a confusing, difficult time defining RA. He has told others that he prefers to categorize RA under "sex rings" or "gang violence." Someone like him cannot deal with or understand metaphysical intent. Few people can. Nor can he officially acknowledge ritual abuse because of various governmental entities which have been implicated.

There are mechanisms being put in place to make the RA claims "incredible." The FBI has been implicated in at least "botching" some RA case investigations and in some instances covering up the evidence. The CIA has been implicated in far worse fashion.... There are many cases of ritual murder and brainwashing.

Lanning professes not to know of any.[9]

The science of mind control has benefited enormously from experiments on young children. The horror stories told by toddlers at McMartin did not arise in a historical vacuum. Comparable outrages, foreshadowing McMartin by thirty years, filled Lynne Moss-Sharman's childhood as an unconsenting guinea-pig:

I am a survivor of military torture and experimentation as a young child in the 1950s. It is very difficult to write about my experiences because of the military's use of electricity and binding on my right hand to assure I could or would not communicate through printing, writing or drawing for decades. One of the sessions involved huge amounts of electricity applied to my right hand; then it was tied to my back, and I was made to walk around on my knees, using my left hand for support, "like a dog." Their other torture techniques and devices took care of the possibility of talking.[10]

The preschoolers in Manhattan Beach provoked scorn and giggles when they claimed they'd been whisked off to military bases. But numerous examples from classified federal files could confirm that children have been tortured in biomedical and behavior control research since the prime of D. Ewen Cameron. Military bases are a common theme.

One mother of children attending McMartin alleged that employees of TRW, a local defense contractor based in Southern California, paid regular afternoon visits to the school.[11]

In 1989, nearly a year before the verdict of the second trial was delivered, a

McMartin mother took note of a van parked in front of her home. Two strangers sat inside the van. A few hours later, they were still there. When two of the mother's strapping male friends arrived, she complained of the surveillance. Her friends strolled out to the van. They couldn't help noticing that the walls of the vehicle were lined with advanced electronic surveillance equipment. The stake-out team was dragged out of the van and questioned—but not by police. More than one child in the household had attended McMartin. A compromised justice system and a hostile media had forced the families to find answers anywhere they could. And this pair of snoops with their high-tech gear would do fine.

But they refused to answer questions. One of the interrogators hit on an idea frowned upon by most law enforcement authorities—sodium amytal. The drug was administered. In a few minutes, the pair gazed blankly and began to answer questions. Who were they? Members of a religious cult. Where did they call home? San Diego. Who else belonged to this cult? They named several prominent officials in the defense establishment.[12] The pair were released after questioning.

Of course, none of this reached the jury.

Lee Coleman, a California psychologist who delivered the keynote address at the Second National Conference of VOCAL (Victims of Child Abuse Laws)—a now-defunct organization notorious for recurring scandals among its leadership involving pedophilia—testified that the McMartin children had indeed been abused—not by teachers at the preschool, but by unnamed law enforcement "officials" who'd "brainwashed" the children into "believing" abuse had occurred at McMartin.[13] Coleman's theory has evolved into a combative branch of psychology based on "false memories" a "syndrome" that lends its name to an organization of accused child abusers directed by veterans of the CIA's mind control fraternity, the False Memory Syndrome Foundation.

The "syndrome" is widely accepted as fact. But at Carleton University, a group of graduate researchers recently concluded a study of the so-called "false memory syndrome," a theory promoted by psychologists who appear frequently on talk shows to denounce therapists for filling the heads of children with recollections of horrific abuse. One of the most prominent figures on the board of the False Memory Syndrome Foundation (FMSF) was Dr. Ralph Underwager, formerly a director of VOCAL, a clinical psychologist and minister who once insisted that it was "God's will" adults have sex with children and suggested to a group of British reporters in 1994 that most women who are raped "enjoy the experience."

The researchers at Carleton were unable to find any evidence that an insidious pathology, the "confabulation" of memories, exists, a charge the FMSF has been making about ritual abuse for years—to conceal the participation of CIA psychiatrists in the torture of young children, a regime of trauma used to condition the minds of young children to mind control programming.

The Ottawa Survivors' Study searched for evidence of the false memory syndrome in 113 adult women who, as children, reported they'd been sexually molested. Four sets of questions concerning symptoms of false memory were drawn up. The women were asked about the type of therapy they received, problems with personal relationships and subsequent patterns of stress. A detailed evaluation of their responses also sought the presence of pseudo-memories, the core of false memory theory.

The study was headed by Connie Kristiansen, a professor of psychology at Carleton who proposed that the university examine statistical claims of the Foundation widely repeated in the press. The FMSF claims that 25 percent to all recovered memories of child abuse are completely false, in contrast to the results of the Ottawa study. About half of the subjects remembered abuse. The other half had, as adults, eventually recalled buried memories of abuse. The responses of the two groups were evaluated—only two of the 51 women with recovered memories had symptoms that met the false memory criteria, leading the researchers to conclude that the syndrome does not exist as defined by the Foundation, and may not exist at all.

They advised that false memory "syndrome" should not be used in the courtroom to discredit recovered memories of abuse until the validity of false memory theory can be demonstrated.

Notes

1. David Neswald & Catherine Gould, "Basic Treatment and Program Neutralization Strategies for Adult MPD Survivors of Satanic Ritual Abuse," *Treating Abuse Today,* vol. 2: no. 3, p. 5.

2. Obituary, *Chicago Tribune,* June 4, 1991.

3. Correspondence, Beth Vargo, executive director of Believe the Children, Gary, Illinois, to John Boyd, Ph.D., August 28, 1995.

4. Vargo.

5. Ibid.

6. Carolyn Lenz, "Parents: Abusive Teachers Still at JCC," *Rogers Park Edgewater News,* May 23, 1984, p. A-1.

7. U.S. Custom and Treasury Department documents.

8. Witkin and Martinez, "Through a Glass, Very Darkly," *U.S. News & World Report,* January 3, 1994, p. 30, and Saperstein & Churchville, "Officials Describe 'Cult Rituals' in Child Abuse Case," *Washington Post,* February 7, 1987.

9. Anonymous, "Re: FBI/Ritual Abuse," alt.pagan WWW newsgroup, March 7, 1996.

10. Lynne Moss-Sharman, "Nancy Drew Meets the Exorcist," *MindNet* (electronic journal), January 20, 1996.

11. Interview, August 22, 1988.

12. Interviews with participants.

13. David Hechler, *The Battle and the Backlash: The Child Sexual Abuse War,* (1988: Lexington, Kentucky), Lexington Books, p. 255.

The Notebooks of Lynn Moss-Sharman: In a book of drawings recalling a childhood of experimentation in the 1950s, predating McMartin by thirty years, the allegations are strikingly similar:

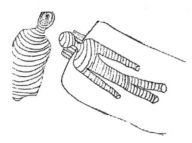

"First we make you. Then we break you." A series of techniques. They dislocated my arms at the shoulders, then wrapped me up in bandages. It is a portable sensory deprivation unit. You know who is boss after this. Most of the other "breaking" techniques involved electricity, boxes and other containers.

There were always sacrifices and rituals involving children. The small angel is my internal "observer." Whenever the "angel" showed up, somebody usually got killed. The same man who did the experiments in the hospitals and at the military bases were part of the group of men who went to the rituals and pedophiles.

Sexual bait to blackmail men: I was used for sexual purposes as part of the programming as a little girl. The robotic quality of "I can walk, I can talk" is a result of a series of torture-programming techniques utilizing sensory deprivation, electricity, drugging.

Acclaimed 1991–92 San Diego Grand Jury Child Abuse Report Demonstrated to be Fraudulent by Subsequent Grand Jury

An Organized Child Abuse Cover-Up

In 1992 some 2,300 copies of a report on child abuse were mailed by a San Diego County grand jury to congressmen, newspaper reporters, social service agencies and college faculty. The report, *Child Sexual Abuse, Assault and Molest Issues,* was touted on network television and in the public print. Even the liberal *Mother Jones* magazine, in its July 1996 issue, lauded the efforts of Carol Hopkins, deputy forewoman of the original San Diego grand jury and organizer of the mailing campaign, for courageously taking on the sensitive issue of "unfounded allegations" of child abuse. The *Mother Jones* story, written by Judith Levine, was typical of the publicity given the report, which claimed that mindless "panic" over child abuse "seems to sprout from the desert soil of San Diego as abundantly as neon fuchsia succulents and bougainvillea":

> The county has been the scene of a string of highly publicized false allegations of molestation, including satanic ritual abuse, going back to the 1980s. In 1992, a major grand jury investigation found the county's child welfare agencies and juvenile courts to be "a system out of control," so keen on protecting children from predation that it took hundreds of them away from their parents on what turned out to be false charges. The report called for "profound change" throughout the system.

Verbatim copies of the report are available from men's rights organizations and legal advocacy groups on the Internet promoting the "false memory" bromide of ritual child abuse. Defense attorneys representing accused pedophiles and ritual abusers have quoted from it in the courtroom.

And much of the report is a hoax, sheared from whole cloth and sewn into a legal parachute for child abuse defendants facing conviction. In a second, unpublicized grand jury inquiry into claims made in the 1991–92 report. it was discovered that the first grand jury, chaired by retired Navy Captain Richard Macfie, had blatantly misrepresented case histories, cooked courtroom testimony and ignored physical evidence of sexual abuse to arrive at the erroneous conclusion that a "family crisis" exists in the justice system, that a break-up of families is endemic, aggravated by overzealous social workers and a profusion of unfounded accusations.

The 91–92 "Families in Crisis" report concluded that the issue of child molestation has "suffered from excessive, sometimes bordering on hysterical, media attention, reporting of inaccurate or questionable statistics, and the failure to define and identify child sexual abuse accurately." And the panel's own handling of facts and statistics can, ironically enough, be interpreted as an attempt to generate hysteria, to arouse parental fear of child protective services and reinforce the ongoing backlash against ritually abused children and their advocates.

The April 1993 report of the San Diego County Commission on Children conflicts flatly with the original grand jury's argument that "children lie about these issues." On the contrary, the commission's study, cited in the second grand jury's review, refutes the "false memory" argument and the original panel's suggestion that children frequently "lie" about sexual predation :

> Goodman (1986, 1989) and Saywitz (1989) on children's memory and on the reliability of children's allegations of sexual abuse ... demonstrate:
> 1. It is uncommon for children to make false allegations about being molested.
> 2. Children's memories are relatively good when compared to adult's memories.
> 3. Errors by children in the recall of events are usually those of omission, rather than commission.
> 4. While children may be more suggestible with respect to their memory of peripheral details, their recall of significant events that they have experienced, rather than things they have merely observed, cannot be easily changed or manipulated.

The second grand jury protested that its investigation was "hampered by missing 1991–92 files." The files, they discovered, "had been removed from the grand jury offices" by members of the original jury. A total of "fourteen files were returned on June 14, 1993 following a court hearing." The review panel's report, completed in 1993, details serious "flaws" in the 91–92 findings, and uncovers an unmistakable pattern of gross misrepresentation, arriving at the false impression that families are routinely torn asunder by groundless accusations of abuse.

A review of the original report found more falsifications in the presentation of abuse histories from county files, obvious in the following excerpts:

THE 1991–92 GRAND JURY REPORT

"[A] school teacher was tried for child abuse after pushing a child. A jury found her not guilty. It was acknowledged by the supervising Deputy D.A. that this was a weak case, prosecuted "'to teach a lesson, test the parameter of the law, educate the public.'"

REVIEW FINDINGS

"The 1992–93 Grand Jury found there were seven victims [not one]. The defendant was *not charged at all* due to technical complications (statute of limitations and lack of witness availability). One child had been lifted by one arm and thrown into his desk, another was slapped hard on the head. She also had her hair pulled. A third child was slapped twice on the head and a fourth was hit on top of the head during a school assembly.

"The children said that the defendant called them such names as 'stupid' or 'idiot.' This teacher's personnel file showed that she had received ten notices complaining about her inappropriate use of physical discipline on 8-year-old children. One of [the complainants] suggested termination."

THE 1991-92 GRAND JURY REPORT

"A teenager was prosecuted for felony child molestation upon an allegation by a foster child in his mother's home. There was no physical evidence. The D.A.'s office prosecuted despite its awareness that this child's DSS file contained references to previous unfounded allegations as well as psychological evaluations of the child as a pathological liar."

REVIEW FINDINGS

"The case was based on a report by a 12-year-old boy to his social worker. He said that the defendant had molested him numerous times during a two-year period by oral copulation, sodomy and masturbation/fondling. The abuse began about one month after the victim was placed in foster care at the defendant's mother's house. The victim described weapons the defendant had either used or threatened to use, including a whip, a knife, brass knuckles and a rifle. These weapons were found in a subsequent police search of the defendant's living quarters. The examining physician detailed physical findings which supported the victim's claim of having been sodomized.

"The victim was borderline retarded, had sociopathic behaviors and psychological problems, but no reference to a report that the victim was a pathological liar was found.

"The defendant pled guilty to Penal Code 647.6 (child molestation). The 1991–92 report makes additional comments about this case ... and alleges that the District Attorney's "decision to prosecute was based solely on the child's accusation." The files that were reviewed contained references to far more physical evidence, and in a civil suit brought by the victim against the County of San Diego, an award of over $1 million was made. This fact is a positive indication that the County felt their the case was valid, and that the victim was truly a victim."

THE 1991–92 GRAND JURY REPORT

"A step-grandfather was prosecuted for the felony child molestation of his 11-year-old granddaughter. He and the family adamantly denied the allegations. Again, DSS files available to the D.A. contained contradictory information and evaluations of the child as a pathological liar. There was also a child molest report involving the natural father and the child. None of this information was revealed to the defense. The child testified at the preliminary hearing but was not cross-examined. At the time of trial, the D.A. stated that the child could not be located. The preliminary hearing testimony of the child was entered. The step-grandfather was convicted. Between conviction and sentencing the defense became aware that the child's whereabouts were known, and had been known, by the D.A. The defense asked for a retrial. It has been granted."

REVIEW FINDINGS

"This case involves the molest of a nine-year-old girl by the boyfriend of the girl's grandmother. After trial, he was convicted of eight counts of violating Penal code 288(a) and he was sentenced to six years in a state prison. His motion for a new trial was denied. No reference in the reports contained in the dependency file contained any reference to the victim as a 'pathological liar.' The girl's grandmother did accuse the girl of being a pathological liar. No police report was ever made regarding a molest of the victim by her father, after a report by the brother of an ex-landlord who said that he once saw some "messing around" between the father and the victim, but the incident was written up by the San Diego Police Department and referred to Child Protective Services.

"The statement that the victim was not cross-examined at the preliminary hearing is untrue, and the preliminary hearing transcript shows such cross-examination. The prosecution found out where the victim was after the trial, when the victim's grandmother told the deputy where she was. Prior to this time, the prosecution had no information on the whereabouts of the girl. The defense did ask for a new trial, but the motion was denied and the defendant was sentenced to prison."

Among other many "flaws" in the 1991–92 child abuse report, the grand jury cited the statement that a chief deputy county counsel pressed subordinates to file charges in cases based on false allegations. The counselor in question, however, states that she had overruled deputies on only four petitions of child abuse, and all four petitions were in fact sustained by the court.

The initial San Diego grand jury report also quoted the director of Child Protection Services in San Diego, who denied that he had ever made the statement, "I don't think I'm as good as some doctors at maintaining an objective outlook, but I do the best I can." This was based on a misquote in a newspaper story. He emphasizes that errors in "non-intervention" far outnumber "intervention" errors. The 92–93 grand jury review confirmed the observation with statistical analysis demonstrating that, if anything, the system is far from "out of control," but errs most often in favor of abusive parents:

> Of the current annual level of 68,000 plus calls entering the San Diego Child protection system, most are closed without action, many result in children being referred to "diversion" or left at home relying on "family preservation" programs, with only 1,500 (at current rates) resulting in removal of the child and dependency court petitions, less than half the number three years ago.... Complaints may be expected from adults who feel deeply offended, regardless of the merits of the removal from the viewpoint of the best interests of the child. The adults may be articulate, or at least have articulate counsel. Adults can organize politically, contribute to campaigns, issue press releases, grant interviews to the media, testify before the legislature and attempt to persuade the grand jury. In fact, adults have done so—particularly those accused of sexual abuse of their children.

And who speaks for the 64,000 cases of reported child abuse in which no action is taken?

> Here, there is no articulate spokesperson. Even where there is counsel for the child, that counsel is circumscribed by rules of confidentiality, meant to protect the child. In addition, no civil remedy for the child exists where the state fails to remove—even where failure to do is gross negligence by the state."

The result of the original jury's "investigation" has been, according to the subsequent grand jury report, that San Diego Children's Services Bureau employees "were caused unneeded difficulty in performing their jobs." Morale was "seriously affected." Prosecutors and social workers identified by job title in the original report and "accused of misconduct or worse have suffered greatly. And, because of the prestige associated with the imprimatur of the grand jury, the reports are now held up as authoritative proof of a malaise in child protection services generally, and by implication, those associated with the process."

The review panel also blamed the 91–92 child abuse report and attendant media coverage for creating an atmosphere in which "errors are more likely to be made in the failure to remove children than in their inappropriate removal," rendering abused kids defenseless. Contrary to the widely reported findings of the original panel, the most significant flaw in the system was determined to be a failure to "adequately investigate and intervene where there is an indication of serious child abuse." The intransigence of child services was found to contribute to "substantial numbers of errors in failure to remove, failure to intervene, failure to treat," with the result that many children are "condemned to years of suffering."

Failure to separate a child from parents suspected of abuse can culminate in tragic circumstances:

> There has been a great deal of attention placed on voluntary diversion {family agrees to CSB contract terms in return for having children left at home} in the last few months. The family of Tiffany C. was offered a voluntary contract, which the father signed, agreeing that he would move out of the house, attend anger management classes, and never be alone with the children (Tiffany and her sibling). Two months after the contract was signed, Tiffany was dead of injuries sustained in her home.
>
> Natasha B.'s mother has borne six children. The youngest, and the only one still in the mother's custody is Natasha, now six months old. When Natasha was 11-days old, her mother signed a voluntary services case plan. On two separate occasions since, Natasha has suffered head injuries inflicted during her parents' domestic disputes.

The original jury detailed the handling of one child, Alicia Wade, which has since become something of a cause *celebré* in the "men's rights" movement. The review panel acknowledged that errors were made in the deputy D.A.s investigation—but as a result of statements made by Alicia and her parents themselves, and by confusion in verifying the identity of the true perpetrator, not an inquisitional campaign of persecution waged by the San Diego D.A.'s office, as the 91–92 report claimed. There was no question that Alicia had been sexually abused. She sustained serious injuries, conclusively. But the first grand jury report neglected to mention this fact and treated the molestation charge as frivolous:

1991–92 GRAND JURY REPORT

"In the case of Alicia W., the father persisted in denying allegations of molest, but the mother was repeatedly told by her attorney and social worker that her only chance to reunite with Alicia was to say that she believed her husband did it. The child, who persistently described a strange perpetrator, was not believed. In order to allow her 'the freedom" to remember' without trauma, visits with her parents were terminated until she could come up with 'a more believable story.' This child was kept in court ordered therapy for two and a half years, twice a week, 'dealing with the molest.'"

REVIEW FINDINGS

"Albert Carder [ultimately determined to be Alicia's abuser] was charged with [four] child molests ... in July 1989. The deputy district attorney assigned to the case filed charges against Carder alleging molestations of these children. Carder pled guilty just before his preliminary hearing. Although the deputy D.A. had heard of the incident involving Alicia, which had occurred in May 1989, no evidence had been presented to her requesting additional charges against Carder since no evidence was known to the police connecting Carder to that case at that time.

"In the case of the four victims mentioned above, the deputy D.A. learned that Carder knew the victims and their mothers. The attacks did not result in serious injury as they did with Alicia.... The explanation given by Alicia's parents for her injuries was odd. Mr. W. told police that if he had done it, he did not recall it. The detective assigned to the case had received a report that Mrs. W. had told another person that her husband had committed the molest.

"The grand jury report on Alicia W. unleashed an attack on the deputy district attorney, accusing her of ethical violations. She was threatened with criminal prosecution. This harmed her professionally, socially and emotionally. "

It is a cutting irony, in light of the many sexually-abused children neglected by the legal system, that the false findings of the original grand jury report have been gleefully aired by the media, while the critical grand jury examination issued in 1993 has been widely overlooked.

It is serious enough that the 1991–92 "Families in Crisis" jury report defrauded San Diego's legal system into adopting policies inimical to the lives of abused children. Equally outrageous was the *plagiarizing* of the report by a grand jury in Merced County, a farming community in California's central valley. *The San Diego Union-Tribune* reported on July 9, 1992 that the original hoax was revisited in the Merced report, "uncannily similar—virtually word-for-word in most sections—to the San Diego jury's report. Even some of the testimony quoted by the San Diego panel appears in the Merced jury's report." The pirating was discovered when officials of Merced's Human Services Agency compared the documents, and concluded that at least three-fourths of the Merced report had been cribbed from the deception cobbled together under the watch of Captain MacFie in San Diego.

Oh, what a web ...

BLEAK HOUSE

A Case of Nazi-Style Experimental Psychiatry in Canada

by Steve Smith and Alex Constantine

After 20 years of frustrated efforts to do anything whatsoever about the night-marish "treatment" Steve Smith received in a Canadian mental institution, the paperwork began to in.

In 1991, Smith requested his clinical records from the archive of the Oak Ridge Mental Hospital and received a grand total of 15 pages. Predicated on these, Smith filed a complaint with the College of Physicians and Surgeons about an illicit, sadistic regimen of psychiatric "treatment," euphemized by his handlers as "Defense Disrupting Therapy." The College investigated and blunt-ly denied that Oak Ridge had ever conducted experimental studies on Smith or anyone else.

Smith appealed to Canada's Health Professions Board and submitted the hos-pital records to support his complaint. The Board ordered the College of Physicians and Surgeons to open the investigation. In a 19-page letter, the Health Board demanded a thorough investigation. "I have copies of the corre-spondence between the Board and the College," Smith says, "and they have become quite critical, applying to the former such terms as 'not serving the pub-lic interest.'"

It can only serve the public interest to report Smith's submergence in a hor-rifying world of brutal psychiatric experimentation and the men who presided over it, particularly Dr. Elliot T. Barker, the psychiatrist who supervised Smith's "treatment" at Oak Ridge. The selection of experimental psychiatric subjects is often arbitrary when sanctions are handed around by secret bureaucracies, and the involvement of the CIA is suggested by Dr. Barker's experimental psychiatric method and sponsorship of a patient cum Rhodesian mercenary. Experimentation on human subjects in violation of the Nuremberg agreement is ongoing. Like Steve Smith, subjects may struggle for decades to assemble a case documenting their exploitation. His account is not unique. Anyone is a prospective subject to a scientific underground founded on absolute disregard for human rights.

—A.C.

Steve Smith's Story

In the winter of 1968 I left high school, and no one seemed bothered by that. An adolescent urge to wander set me on the road to California. At that time I was learning to drive and getting a driver's license was the most important thing in my life. I'd sometimes swipe my mother's keys and drive around the back streets of my neighborhood. My parents were divorced when I was ten. My brother and I lived with my father in Sudbury, Ontario. My mother ran off with a tough, good-looking bartender, and my father's life was rapidly overtaken by alcohol and self-destruction. My brother and I were left to fend for ourselves in a house that was neglected and often without food. The decimation of my father took about a year, and we were sent to live with my mother and Bill. These were years of physical and emotional abuse. We were all victims of Bill's drunken rages. He committed suicide in 1987. My mother lives out the declining years of her life alone with her dogs and cats.

After a few brushes with the Sault Ste. Marie police, and a system of justice that dealt with the local counter-culture in a heavy-handed way, I headed for the west coast.

My friend Ben and I hit the road in the dead of winter, no funds, no plans. The first hitch took us to WaWa, Ontario. We spent the night in the basement of a church. The next morning was freezing cold and hitching a ride was punishment. We hitched on to White River, the "coldest spot in Canada."

Our choice was to walk or die. We reached Marathon sometime in the night, desperately cold. Everything in town was closed. There was no point in looking for an open restaurant. We didn't have enough money between us for a cup of coffee. Ben and I found a small used car lot on the outskirts of town and stole a car. We drove to the next town and arrived just before dawn, abandoned the car at a service station. As we were climbing out, the police pulled in behind us. Five minutes earlier or later, and the course of my life would have been entirely different.

A child of the times, I had in my shirt pocket two tablets of LSD I'd planned on taking when we reached Vancouver. The tabs were about the size of a match head. The trip to Vancouver was ended by our arrest, so I swallowed the tablets and thus began my trip into a hell that was to last eight months and haunt me the rest of my life. My recollection of the next 24 hours is fuzzy, but much is unforgettable:

I am in a black steel cell covered with lurid graffiti, handcuffed, standing in front of a doctor. The floor is rolling like a wave.

In a hospital emergency room large men hold me down, dodging and maneuvering to insert a plastic tube in my nose. I am struggling. A glass of what looks like red wine. I drink and within seconds I am violently throwing up. I am overdosing, very sick, more frightened than I have ever been in my life.

The next several hours are a blank. I remember standing in a court room full of skeletons in black robes. The judge took one glance at me and I was bundled off to 30 days of observation at the local psychiatric hospital.

The first day I was confined to bed with little or no contact with anyone. The next week was uneventful. I was interviewed a few times but I don't remember if I told anyone about the LSD. I had the impression they either believed me to be faking or drugged. Within a short time I was given my clothes and permitted to wander about the hospital. I was not locked in, and I suppose I could have walked out. I met a girl from another ward and she invited me to a dance that evening. I was leaving my ward for this rendévouz when I was stopped by an attendant who objected to the way I was dressed, very 1960s counter-culture, beads, the usual accoutrements. The attendant was hostile. He pushed me against the wall and pawed at my jeans, blustering something about proper dress.

I made another big mistake. I fought back. He dragged me to the floor in short order. Reinforcements came running, and in an instant my pants were around my ankles and I was injected with something painful. I was dragged down the hall, tossed into an empty room and locked inside. I was furious. The girl was waiting for me and here I was, naked, locked in this little room. I pounded on the door and screamed until my lungs were aching.

There is an entry in my clinical record, dated April 26, 1968, a few days after this incident: Steve Smith "... tends to become resentful, hostile and uncooperative when he is not able to have his own way...." Of course, I didn't realize how dangerous an outburst of defiance could be. Never get mad in a mad house. The next day I was informed that I was to be sent to Penetang Hospital for the criminally insane. I have no words to express the fear that swept over me at that moment. Penetang was notorious. It's the end of the line, you never get out. I was in big trouble, but not insane. The next day I was dragged onto a train in handcuffs by two burly guards who made it clear that they would take no nonsense from me. They showed me a billy club and a large syringe. We traveled in a private berth. Neither of my traveling companions shifted their gaze from me.

We reached Midland, Ontario. There was a car waiting for us. A short drive later, I was at the front gate of Oak Ridge Hospital, which resembled a prison. The iron gate rang behind me and I was not to see the outside world again for eight months. I was struck by the size of the guards. I have never in my life seen such a collection of oversized homosimians. As far as I knew, no one knew that I was there. I had disappeared off the face of the earth, and never felt more alone and helpless. No one said a word to me. I was treated like a slab of meat. Stripped naked. My hair, mouth and armpits were probed for concealed weapons or contraband. My head was shaved. I was sprayed with a disinfectant that burned, given a heavy canvas gown and locked in a cement cell with nothing but a blanket. Not a word from anyone. The door slammed shut.

I don't know how many days passed. It occurred to me that I could be incarcerated for the remainder of my life. If there was anything in that cell I could have used to kill myself, I believe I would have done so.

The light was on 24 hours a day. I ate from paper plates. No utensils, not even a plastic spoon. The only escape was sleep, and I forced myself to do as much of it as possible. Men strolled past my cell dressed in street cloths. I thought they were doctors or hospital staff, and tried to talk to them, find out what the hell was going to happen to me. No one even looked my way. I was completely ignored. I don't know how many days this went on.

One day the door slid open and a Dr. Elliot T. Barker entered. He was charming, soothing, smiling, his arm around my shoulder. He addressed me by my first name. It seemed I'd never known contact with another human being. I fell for it, not knowing what this man had in store for me, the torture and degradation I was to suffer.

"Do you think you are mentally ill?"

"No, I do not."

He grinned, his arm around my shoulder.

"Why do you think you are here?"

"I don't know."

"Well, I'll tell you. You are a very *sick* boy," Barker told me. "I think you are a very slick psychopath, and I want you to know that there are people just like you in here who have been locked up more than 20 years. But we have a program here that can help you get over your illness. If you volunteer for this treatment, it will improve your chances of release—but you must cooperate fully with the program."

He told me that being a psychopath was essentially an inability to communicate with others, and that beneath the reinforced surface was a deeply rooted psychosis. What he proposed to do, through the use of LSD, methedrine and other drugs, was to bring out this "hidden psychosis" and treat it. In other words, to cure you I must first drive you mad.

I was locked in a cold, brightly-lit cell, numb with cold, clutching a blanket. Anything would be better than this. I agreed to cooperate.

The "consent" form that I signed on the 27th of December, 1967, obtained under freedom of information, proposed an unusual approach to "psychotherapy":

REQUEST FOR COMPRESSED ENCOUNTER THERAPY

Realizing that my chances of recovery and release are improved considerably by intensive treatment, I request admission to the Compressed Encounter Therapy Unit on "F" ward. I am ready to meet the conditions of treatment specified below:

1. Commitment to an indefinite period of group interaction under conditions of the most stringent security.

2. Agreement to take such medications as the ward psychiatrist may judge likely to hasten or otherwise assist in my treatment. Such medications might include scopolamine, methedrine, mescalin, psilocybin, sodium amytal, dexedrine, etc....

I was released from my cell, given a shower, khaki pants and shirt, escorted to the "Sun Room," an unfurnished vestibule occupied by six or seven men (boys) about the same age as myself. They had all been in this room for a week or more. Dr. Barker informed me that he was locking me in with them without prior "conditioning" to "shake things up a bit." I watched them for a few days without saying much. Nothing they did was rational. The patients seemed to be playing some kind of psychotic game, talking like doctors. When their attention shifted to me, I was forced by ringleaders to concede that I was mentally ill. The pressure was intense, unrelenting. Here I was imprisoned in this snake pit of a hospital, encircled by rapists and killers determined to convince me that I was insane.

I was the only character in this equation who wasn't deluded. My sole possession in the world at this stage was my sanity, and I wasn't about to give it up. I was soon to discover that these mental patients had more resources at their command than group pressure. After a few days of silent resistance, the other patients concluded that I needed some drugs to "loosen" me up—THE PATIENTS PRESCRIBED THEM. They recommended I be given methamphetamines. Dr. Barker signed his approval. Two attendants and a nurse entered and chased me around the room until I was cornered and dragged to the floor. I put up a good fight but they finally managed to slip the needle into my arm. The drug hit me within seconds. I lived for that drug for the next five years. I would do anything to have it.

Dr. Barker's program was run by the inmates. The staff observed and approved their decisions. What followed was a systematic bombardment of drugs intended to break my resistance and to bring out the so-called "hidden psychosis." I suggest that these potent drugs did not reveal something that was already there, but in fact created a drug-induced psychotic state. In his published papers, Dr. Barker describes the drugs he used and the results that he hoped to obtain, but reports nothing about the horrors suffered by the victims of these experiments.

I will try to relate some of the effects of the drugs forced on me over a sustained period. During the drug treatments, it was standard practice to handcuff patients together with seatbelts and padlocks. It was also common for any patient resisting the injections to be choked into unconsciousness by twisting a towel around his neck. This was done to me a few times before I realized that I was more likely to stay alive if I submitted to the drugs. I remember a direction that I was to be an "observer," that I must stay awake all night to watch the other patients sleep. To aid me in this task I was given as much Benzedrine as I wanted. I was supplied with a log book and a pencil stub and told to record everything that happened. I wrote all night.

The hallucinations began after a few days of sleep deprivation, smoke at the edge of my peripheral vision, and eventually thousands of bugs crawling on my skin. I tried to show these bugs to other patients and the attendant who brought us our our meals. Everyone would take a close look and start laughing. Two attendants came in and without a word put me in handcuffs and leg restraints.

Then paranoia, not the generalized anxiety that is so common in current language, but the real thing, full-blown psychotic paranoia. I thought everyone just out of my range of hearing was conspiring to kill me. I remember laying on a mattress on the floor with a blanket pulled over my head. I assumed the two patients next to me were prying a staple out of the log book to impale my eye.

I lifted a corner of my mattress. The floor was seething with bugs and worms. That was it. I jumped up in a panic, attacked the two patients next to me. I tried to wrench my arm around one of them, and with the seatbelt straps locked around my wrists strangle him before anyone could stop me. This outburst was the result of chemical torture and sleep deprivation, otherwise known as "Defense Disrupting Therapy."

A series of drugs was forced on me. I remember something called scopolamine, a so-called truth serum. I was told that it was used by the Nazis as an effective means of chemical interrogation. The effects of this drug are so overwhelmingly horrifying that I am at a loss to describe them. It was administered in three injections, about an hour apart. After the first, my mouth dried up completely. The throat constricts to the size of a pinhole. When you try to swallow you hear a dry, clicking sound. One side-effect is a very high pulse-rate (160 sitting down) and a sense of suffocation and anxiety. After the second injection you begin to slip in and out of delirium. Time sense and continuity are disrupted. The third injection is followed by an 8 to 12 hour period of complete delirium, incoherence, restlessness, hyperventilating.

Patients undergoing this study in medieval degradation were handcuffed to two other patients throughout the ordeal. It was the job of these observers to stop the subject from bashing himself into walls and hyperventilating to death. No training was provided. The life of another patient could be in the hands of people who themselves were on the same drugs a few days before. I think I was given scopolamine three times during my stay in the "sun room" and a continuous diet of methamphetamines and "goofballs."

I don't recall much about the months that followed. I slipped further into a drug-soaked existence, punctuated by incidents of extreme brutality. Dr. Barker came into the sun room with a small can of something. He flipped it from one hand to the other and described a wonderful new invention he called "mace." With no justification but a as test of its effectiveness, he let loose with this spray and blasted us all to the floor. That's the kind of man he was: very curious and always willing to try a little hands-on experiment. I think I was in the sun room for about two weeks when Dr. Barker moved me into the regular program.

At this point I was resisting everything, and fought Barker's attempts to morph my mind with drugs so he could reshape it to his own idea of normalcy. I was moved to a cell with a real bed and my own sink and toilet.

Shortly thereafter, a patient-teacher came to my cell with a stack of psychological tests and insisted I take them. He was dressed in street cloths and conducted himself like hospital staff. I'd had enough of this. I told him to take his tests and shove off. He came back with two attendants who strangled me with a towel and injected me. My clothes were peeled off. I was thrust into an empty cell.

My inmate-instructor returned with the tests and said with a smile, "are you ready to do this or do you need a little more prompting?" I was so drugged I could not keep my eyes open. I started to write and fell asleep, face down on the paper. I woke up with someone squeezing a nerve point on my heel. I started to write again. It was impossible to concentrate. Math questions, logic questions. What's wrong with this picture? I fell asleep again and came to under an ice-cold shower, locked in place by attendants at each arm. This was torture and I screamed. Back into the cell, dripping wet and turning blue.

Do the tests or submit to more torture. I turned to the tests.

Hospital records claim that my IQ is roughly equivalent to my shoe size. I don't remember completing these tests, but eventually I was permitted to sleep.

The next day a formal brainwashing program was underway. Every minute of the day was structured. The basic idea was to force patients to memorize long papers dealing with defense mechanisms and some kind of twisted logic. A rule of silence was strictly enforced. Inmates were not permitted to talk to one another outside the groups. No warnings were given. Any breach of the rules was met with immediate punishment. This could be anything from having your cell stripped, leaving nothing but a blanket on the floor, to strapped incarceration and drugging that went on for days. An infraction of the rules could be something as simple as turning your eyes to the ceiling in a gesture of disbelief. After a week of this discipline I was a whipped animal, docile and cooperative. I followed Dr. Barker's dictates like a robot.

We were forced to perform military exercises three times a day. When the whistle blew, we dropped for push-ups. Put your heart into it or take punishment. I never knew what the next phase was going to be, but throughout the ordeal of drugs, handcuffs and humiliation came authoritarian "psychic driving." I gave the answer expected of me when asked if I was mentally ill.

I suppose I had truly been driven mad.

I had seen LSD used in massive doses on selected patients. There were beatings and murders. I remember the names Matt Lamb, Peter Woodcock and others.

All of this under *the direct control of inmates*. This in itself makes this story all the more difficult to write. It sounds so absurd. That's how it was. And I couldn't request a review of my case by hospital administrators—this required the approval of a panel of mental patients.

Dr. Barker's "treatment" program was devised to drive young men into a drug-induced psychosis, and through fear and discipline from within the group, create a self-sustaining system of docile mental patients. How any doctor could view this as a benefit to the mentally ill is beyond me.

But in light of what I have since learned of CIA-sponsored LSD experiments, and the part Canada played in the Agency's MK-ULTRA program, my story is placed in a context that is far from outrageous. Much of what occurred in Oak Ridge was comprehensible only after I began to fit it with pieces of the CIA mind control puzzle.

For example: a cut-throat world of covert operations lurks in the subtext of this report from the *Toronto Globe & Mail* on the premature release and death of the homicidal Matt Lamb, a "rehabilitated" Oak Ridge patient:

ARMY CLASH WITH GUERRILLAS

TWO KILLED IN ONTARIO, CANADIAN SLAIN IN RHODESIA

A Windsor man who spent seven years in an Ontario mental hospital after killing two people has been slain in action with the Rhodesian army. Lance Corporal

Matthew Charles Lamb, 28, died in a clash with black nationalist guerrillas seeking to oust Rhodesia's white minority government.

Dr. Elliott Barker, a psychiatrist who treated Lamb for several years in the hospital and befriended him, said he was not recruited but traveled to Rhodesia about two years ago with the purpose of joining the army. Lamb was released in 1973 from the maximum security section of the Penetanguishene Mental Health Center, where he had been sent after the shotgun slaying of two young people walking with friends on a Windsor street. Lamb visited relatives and went to see Dr. Barker at his farm near Penetanguishene while on leave last summer. "He knew when he went back he probably would be killed," Dr. Barker said yesterday.

A communiqué issued by the Rhodesian security forces yesterday said that the Canadian and eight blacks identified as guerrillas were killed in clashes during the past 48 hours. Dr. Barker said he was advised that Lamb was killed on Sunday.

Last month another Canadian serving with the Rhodesian forces, Trooper Michael McKeown of Dartmouth, N.S., was sentenced to a year in prison for refusing to fight. He said he was recruited in Canada. Lamb was 19 in January, 1967 when he was found not guilty by reason of insanity on a charge of murdering 20-year-old Edith Chaykoski. She was in a group of young people walking toward a bus stop when a man stepped out from behind a tree and began shooting. Three other people were wounded, and one of them a 21-year-old man, died later.

During court proceedings in his case, Lamb made two unsuccessful attempts to escape.

In 1965, when he was 16, Lamb served 14 months in the penitentiary after he robbed a suburban store and exchanged shots with a policeman. After his 1967 committal to Penetanguishene, Lamb was treated by Barker, who was then head of the therapeutic unit at the hospital's maximum-security division.

He was released in 1973 by order of the Ontario Cabinet, acting on a recommendation of an advisory review board. "He was given a clean bill of health," Dr. Barker said in an interview. "The advisory review board felt he was no longer dangerous. He had been sick and he was no longer sick."

During his two to three years in the hospital, he was one of the patient therapists, and they looked up to him.

After he was freed, Lamb lived with Dr. Barker and the psychiatrist's family for a year on their 200-acre farm near the hospital, earning his keep as a laborer....

Fortunately for me, the laws governing committal to hospitals were changed during my stay at Oak Ridge. A review board was created to give patients an avenue of appeal.

I remember sitting in a chair before five or six bureaucrats. They were my last chance at reclaiming my life. The interview lasted less than half an hour, and in the end they told me that I would be released as soon as arrangements could be made. It was out of Barker's hands. Within days I was on a bus to Toronto. It ended as suddenly as it began, but the consequences of my months as Dr. Barker's guinea pig were to affect the direction of my life for years to come. I had tried LSD twice, and the second time precipitated my forced incarceration. Like most people my age in the 1960s, I experimented with drugs. But after Oak Ridge I was addicted to amphetamines, my slide into self-destruction revisiting my father's decline.

Before Oak Ridge, the thought of sticking a needle into my arm was repulsive. But when you want amphetamine, the quickest way is the only way. It came to living in the back of an abandoned car, using a refill from a ball-point pen for a fix. Barker left me shipwrecked on the shore.

But there came a time when I was able to reclaim control of my life and determine my own direction, because that's who I am. Today I have my own business. I have a little sailboat and I go skiing when I can.

Many others were left incurably wounded. I have found some of them. Dr. Barker devastated our lives. I saw murder in Oak Ridge. I saw torture that one would only expect to see in the most squalid Third World country. I have been over this for years, and it seems that every question inevitably leads to more questions. I want answers from Oak Ridge and Dr. Barker.

The Hollywood/Florida Mob Connection, the CIA and O.J. Simpson

PART I:
Pizza Drippings on the Courtroom Floor

"Here, take a good look." He tossed it across the desk. Chuck [Giancana, brother of the Mafia's Sam Giancana] caught the coin and instantly realized it was old, ancient in fact. Chuck fingered the coin, turning it over and over again, and then tossed it back to his brother.

Mooney [Sam Giancana] leaned forward. "Look, this is one of the Roman gods. This one has two faces, two sides. That's what we are, the Outfit and the CIA ... two sides of the same coin."

—Sam (Jr.) and Chuck Giancana

The shadow of Joey Ippolito falls across the courtroom floor, seeps into every crack in the Simpson case. Yet his name is seldom mentioned.

His father, Joseph Ippolito, Sr., was in the pay of the syndicate's Meyer Lansky and a soldier of Sam "the Plumber" DeCalvacante, who brought Joey into the league. "Little Man" Lansky, of course, was no homunculus. He led the mob into an alliance with the intelligence sector of government in WWII and loomed above the Combination until his death in 1983. Today, Meyer Lansky's foot soldiers march in step with Langley. CIA denials have been scuffed by too many tongues over the years to be taken seriously (Campbell, Hoch, Pizzo, et. al.).

Joey Ip's Murder, Inc.

Joey Ippolito is second generation Mafia, one of several powerful successors of Meyer Lansky. He was born to a brood of nine children. Joey's brother Frankie perished of a heart attack unloading a crate of marijuana from an Eastern Airlines plane in New Jersey. His brother Louie is a convict (Burdick).

Ippolito's influence in the Mafia is felt from Philadelphia to Dade County, Florida to Southern California. Joey received a medical discharge from the U.S. Marines in 1968, and went to work for his father, the proprietor of Ippolito Construction in New Jersey. A few years later he was charged with counterfeiting federal reserve notes and served a single year, hard time (Medvene). Joey, a one-time U.S. Powerboat Champion, was forced out of racing after a competing boat veered out of control and hurtled across his own, crushing one hand and killing Ippolito's best friend. In 1988, after completing a 40-month prison sentence for marijuana smuggling, he spent a year rebuilding his family's motel in New Jersey, then headed for California. Ippolito's brothers purchased a restaurant in Malibu, the PCH Bar & Grill, and Joey undertook its renovation and management (Medvene; Anastasia & Jennings).

For at least eight years, he retained a burly African-American bodyguard, one Allen C. Cowlings, then an assistant to the president of Jonathon Martin Dress Company in L.A. On August 24, 1994, the *Boston Herald* reported that O.J. Simpson's chum was a "close associate" of the mobster when he "was running a popular restaurant—and a thriving cocaine-dealing business—until last year. Telephone records from the restaurant, confiscated by federal prosecutors and the FBI in Los Angeles, also show calls from Ippolito's restaurant to O.J. Simpson's Brentwood estate, where the tense freeway drama ended."

Los Angeles law enforcement enjoys publicizing its efforts to frustrate the attempts of organized crime to gain "a foothold" in Los Angeles (a Hooverism, since the Mafia established roots in Southern California decades ago). The Organized Crime Intelligence Division (OCID) boasts that it maintains a squad of operatives at L.A. International Airport to intercept incoming mob figures at the turnstile and send them packing (Lieberman). Presumably, Ippolito slipped into town and opened a restaurant in an exclusive area without drawing the attention of the OCID's watchdogs.

Another explanation, of course, is that certain Mafia figures are permitted to flourish in Los Angeles. There is even a question as to whether the OCID gives a fig about organized crime. The division evolved from a unit called the Public Disorder Intelligence Division, a highly political unit, and retired OCID detective Mike Rothmiller maintains that the priority is still politics, not the Mafia. After resigning from the department, Rothmiller gave a deposition to the ACLU and six lawsuits were promptly filed charging the PDID's subversives squad with illegal spying and undercover political provocations. In his deposition, Rothmiller charged that OCID officials had instructed him to find "dirt" on "at least a half-dozen" public officials. One source to the department recalls: "They had files on almost everybody. They were interested in people who could hurt the government, publishing companies, media people, show business people, people like that" (Lieberman & Berger). The division kept no files on organized crime at the time of Rothmiller's resignation, but did target liberal activists for surveillance, spied on police in rival departments, harassed opponents of former police chief Daryl Gates and performed local services for the CIA (Rothmiller & Goldman).

Among the notables to emerge from the OCID into the headlines:

- In 1988, one OCID detective agreed to take an early retirement after he was questioned by police upon receiving information that he had tipped the Mob's labor negotiator to a federal investigation. The detective's OCID partner was suspended for thirty days for failing to inform department heads of the impropriety (Lieberman & Berger).

- Former police detective Michael D. Brambles, an acclaimed mob investigator, convicted to 102 years in state prison for a string of stickups and sexual assaults in 1994. The 47-year-old OCID veteran exhibited "no remorse whatsoever," Superior Court Judge John W. Ouderkirk observed from the bench (Abrahamson & Lieberman).

Among Ippolito's narco-goons was bodybuilder Rod Columbo, his life ended with three shots to the back of the head on January 7, 1992. Columbo himself had been the leading suspect in the murder of cocaine dealer Rene Vega in 1989. Columbo worked at *Cent'Anni's*, a restaurant owned by Ippolito until it folded in 1991. At this time Columbo began to travel extensively. His body was found slumped over the wheel of a 1984 Cadillac in southern New Jersey. LAPD Detective Lee Kingsford told reporters that it was the West Coast consensus the murder had been "drug related."

A few months before to the Columbo killing, Ippolito fell under the scrutiny of Los Angeles police and the FBI. The timely death of a leading distributor eased his legal difficulties considerably.

Dante's Circle of Ippolito associates is not a lonely place.

Another ranking member of the Ippolito syndicate on this plane of existence was John Steele, formerly the mayor of Hallendale, Florida. Mayor Steele once placed a police station at the sub-division where Meyer Lansky lived, at the gangster's request (Burdick). Joey Ippolito, who also lived in the high-security subdivision, was arrested in Long Island in the early 1980s with a dozen other marijuana smugglers running eight tons of cannabis from a ship anchored offshore (Burdick).

Yet another cog in Joey's dope machine was Donald Aronow, a friend of George Bush and designer of the famous Cigarette speed boat, a high-speed favorite of cocaine runners everywhere. Aronow, a wealthy Casanova with more testosterone in his blood than Earnest Hemingway, built racing boats for numerous financial outlaws, including the Shah of Iran, Robert Vesco and Charles Keating. (Convicted of securities fraud in 1991 by Judge Lance Ito.) Keating's extensive CIA ties were never mentioned by prosecuting attorney William

Hodgman, who incidentally, acted as a trial strategist in the Simpson case.

Aronow was gunned down in his parking lot on February 3, 1987. Throughout the week prior to the fatal ambush, he held a series of lengthy telephone conversations with Vice President George Bush (Burdick). It was rumored about Miami that Aronow, who'd been questioned by police about cocaine trafficking a few days before, intended to turn state's evidence. A subpoena was to be served on him the day after the shooting.

Ippolito once broke parole after an eight-year prison term to visit actor James Caan of *Godfather* fame in Los Angeles. The actor was also friendly with Ben Kramer, the convicted Bell Gardens, California casino owner and marijuana smuggler. Kramer is married to Meyer Lansky's niece (Burdick).

The syndicate lurking behind the O.J. Simpson case is a closed circle. Actor James Caan was a regular at the exclusive Turnberry Island resort, twelve miles south of Fort Lauderdale, Florida's Bacchanalian playground for wealthy men (daily rates for a suite range from $275 to $2,100) with teeming hormones.

Turnberry Isle is the Floridian stomping ground of Robert Evans, once Denise Brown's paramour. (He still dotes fondly on erotic memories elicited by the photo of Denise that hangs on his wall.)

Bill Mentzer and Alex Marti—the convicted killers of fledgling Hollywood producer Roy Radin (the godson of Johnny Stoppelli, a soldier in the Genovese crime family)—accused Evans from the witness stand of complicity in the murder. Evans was subpoenaed. He pled the Fifth and went home.

Alex Marti hails from an Argentine death squad. *Newsday's* Steve Wick writes that Marti "loved guns, had a fascination with violence, craved money and hated lots of people, but particularly Jews. A watercolor portrait of Adolph Hitler adorned one wall of his Los Angeles home, and he was a collector of books and writings about the Third Reich.... His most quoted remark was that to really put someone away, you had to shoot him in the back of the head. That was the way the *Nazis* did it" (Wick).

CIA mind control operations overlap with the activities of this family of cocaine distributors and contract killers.

Tally Rogers, a coke courier who had the misfortune of falling in briefly with the Mentzer/Marti circle, is currently serving a prison sentence for child molestation. He claims: "They are frying my brain with microwaves. It's some kind of government *plot,* and I don't understand it" (Wick).

In the early 70s, Robert Evans, according to author Maury Terry in *The Ultimate Evil,* gave orders to the "Son of Sam cult" in New York, a heavily-armed death squad that recruited Bill Mentzer, Marti's co-conspirator in the

Radin murder, to participate in the contract killings.

Evans, cut his teeth in syndicated crime at the gaming tables of Batista's Cuba. He boasts in his autobiography of his friendship with Henry Kissinger. Bill Mentzer, a cocaine courier, bodybuilder and hit man, belonged to the Sams and took part in the killings attributed to David Berkowitz, according to Maury Terry. His neo-Nazi partner, Alex Marti, opened a private investigative service in Los Angeles and hired the late Rod Columbo before the cocaine distributor found employment with Joey Ippolito, another regular at Turnberry Island, James Caan's friend and the employer of Al Cowlings.

Other regulars at Turnberry Isle: Jack Nicholson and Tommy Lasorda. Statuesque hostesses, employed by Don Soffer, the resort's developer—the "Don" who received a fond farewell in O.J. Simpson's suicide letter (Ruiz)— have included model Donna Rice, Lyn Armandt (the wife of a Miami drug dealer alleged to be a friend of Lansky's great-nephew Ben Kramer; her phone call to the *Miami Herald* finished Gary Hart's presidential ambitions), and a clutch of heart-breakingly beautiful hookers with pasts in CIA sex trap operations.

On the afternoon Donald Aronow was gunned down, his chum Soffer received a telephone call at Turnberry's central office, informing him: "You're *next*" (Burdick).

Chris Darden's book tells the tale of one Beth Reed, who phoned the Simpson trial prosecutor from the Bahamas to volunteer that a store clerk had informed her O.J. Simpson was due, shortly after the Brentwood murders, to arrive in the Bahamas for a rendévous with a yacht dubbed the "Miss Turnberry." Darden writes that he checked Simpson's address book and found a reference to "Turnberry Associates" and the name, "Don Soffer." Darden flew to the Bahamas to check into the story, and met the boat's captain, who adamantly denied the story despite the insistence of several witnesses that Simpson had planned to meet there with Soffer's subordinates.

Parenthetically, the resort is the home of the Wolfsonian Museum, named for Miami business tycoon Mitchell Wolfson, Jr. The museum opened in 1995 with an exhibition titled, "The Arts of Reform and Persuasion," drawn from Wolfson's permanent collection, an endless labyrinth stuffed full of historical objects promoting ideas of modernism. "There were," wrote a reporter for the *Nashville Business Journal* on February 12, 1996, "Norwegian tapestries celebrating romantic nationalism ... and posters from Germany and Italy exploring how the Nazi and fascist propaganda machines there penetrated all aspects of life and art."

PART II:
Meyer Lansky's Migratory Birds of Prey

"It seems like all the LCN [La Cosa Nostra] drug interests are interconnect-ed," I suggest. "I'm thinking that you just chopped off one arm of an enor-mous octopus."

[Assistant U.S. Attorney Bill Norris] nods. "That's usually what we do," he says in a somewhat resigned tone. "And it turns out to be more like one arm of a starfish, so it regenerates."

—Thomas Burdick, *Blue Thunder*

Meyer Lansky's attorney Mel Kessler was a suspect in the investigation of Joe Ippolito's drug smuggling venture. Kessler was suspected of being the brains of the operation (Burdick). Hollywood, Florida vice squad officials suspect that Kessler arranged the shipment of 200 kilos of cocaine from Bolivia and was involved in a smuggling operation based in San Juan, Puerto Rico with stopovers in the Caribbean. Telephone records revealed that Ippolito's fellow mobster, Ben Kramer, an investor in the Bicycle Club in Southern California, consulted with Kessler almost daily (Burdick). Kessler has also been linked with "Little Ray" Thompson, another Lansky associate, indicted for drug smuggling with Steadman Stahl, a Dade County judge groomed for the post by state prosecutor Richard "One Eye" Gerstein, a former Watergate investigator who doubled as Kramer's attorney and a business partner of F. Lee Bailey.

He lived in Meyer Lansky's back pocket. Gerstein was elected in 1956 to the first of six terms as state attorney, generally considered to be the second most powerful office in Florida, after the Governor's (Myers). He was also the most popular prosecutor in Dade County history.

PART 1:
F. Lee Bailey, "Bad Eye" Gerstein and BCCI

In 1982, stormy Dick Gerstein was investigated, but not indicted, after accept-ing drug money intended for laundering in Panama.

He has long been a crony of F. Lee Bailey. In fact, O.J. Simpson's celebrated attorney hung a shingle in Florida with him: Bailey, Gerstein, Carhart, Rushkind, Dreskick & Rippingille.

At the time of Bailey's migration to Florida, he represented the families of the passengers of Korean Airlines Flight 007, downed by the Soviets in 1983, in a wrongful death suit. A few years later, the families' steering committee sued Bailey himself for misrepresentation after making "a personal pledge" in his letter of acceptance to "work full-time as required" on the case. In five years, Bailey clocked only 97 hours on pretrial preparation, compared with 6,311 hours put in by the two other law firms retained by the families. In a court brief, Bailey cited the move to Florida, allowing his wife Patricia to be near her "ailing parents," as his rationale for not assisting the families he'd been hired to represent—although he had no qualms about charging full-time legal fees. In 1993 a federal court in Washington ordered Bailey to return a share of his ill-gotten fees to the families (Felsenthal).

Bailey and Gerstein were the directors of CenTrust Federal Savings Bank, a failed satellite of the Bank of Credit and Commerce International (BCCI), the CIA's preferred money laundering franchise (Truell & Gurwin; Bender suit). A major share in CenTrust was secretly owned by BCCI—in fact, a full quarter of the bank's shares were snapped up by Saudi tycoon Ghaith Pharaon, a BCCI front man who maintained daily contact with CenTrust President David Paul between 1984 and 1988, when the S&L was declared insolvent (Truell & Gurwin), and Paul was convicted on 68 charges of bank fraud to a maximum prison term of five years. Paul's financial strategies included illegal bond deals with Charles Keating and false entries in the S&L's accounting books (*New York Times,* November 25, 1993).

CenTrust Savings, the largest thrift in Florida, made handsome contributions to the campaign funds of several Congressmen, including Joseph Biden (Truell and Gurwin) and Newt Gingrich (FEC Report). When it defaulted, taxpayers were saddled with $2 billion in debts (Truell & Gurwin). The co-trustee named in lawsuits filed against CenTrust was Citibank and its president John Reed, a banker with extensive ties to the CIA (Thompson & Kanigher).

Bailey was Dick Gerstein's legal and business partner. The prosecutor's Family chum, Joey Ippolito, never wanders far from the Simpson case. Nor do his mob associates. Simpson's well-connected attorney brought in retired New York investigator John E. McNally to look into the Brentwood murders. McNally, the *Los Angeles Times* reported, was, in 1989, accused by federal investigators "of being part of the 'security department' of Gene Gotti, the younger brother of notorious mobster John Gotti." Prosecutors in New York believe McNally screened prospective employees for the Mafia (Newton). Also hired to investigate on behalf of Simpson was Pat McKenna, a Palm Beach gumshoe, and a veteran of the William Kennedy Smith rape case.

Attorneys on both sides of the case have been an odd assortment. Robert Baker, Simpson's attorney in the civil trial, specializes in wrongful death suits with an emphasis on medical malpractice and product liability. "He has fought on behalf of doctors accused of killing or injuring patients," reported Stephanie Simon in the *L.A. Times* on September 10, 1996, "manufacturers blamed for dangerous products and corporations suspected of producing toxic waste. In a tribute to his top-notch reputation, Baker has also defended some of L.A.'s most powerful lawyers against clients claiming malpractice." His fuse is short: under questioning about drug use, O.J. Simpson repeatedly spurned Baker's advice to stop talking. Baker snapped out: "Am I a potted plant?"

Of the original "Dream Team," Simpson chose to bring along to his civil trial F. Lee Bailey.

The plaintiff's attorneys had little experience trying murder cases. Daniel Petrocelli, an attorney from Mitchell, Silberberg & Knupp, represents Occidental Petroleum. Arthur Groman, a Yale graduate and a senior partner in the same firm, is a director, with Al Gore and John Kluge, of Occidental (1995 company FEC report). The Petrocelli team boasted two former New York prosecutors and an appeals consultant. Also, a criminal defense attorney whose client list includes Radovan Karadzic, the Serb leader accused of orchestrating genocide in Bosnia (Simon, September 9, 1996). The latter attorney would be Petrocelli's law partner, Edward Medvene, who has also represented Marlon Brando and Ruben Zunoi Arce, the Mexican businessman who spear-headed the 1985 kidnap and murder of DEA agent Enriqué Camarena (Weinstein).

Again, the CIA and drugs enter the Simpson orbit. Scripps Howard reported on October 4, 1990 that the CIA "trained guerrillas at a ranch owned by a Mexican drug lord" convicted of killing Camerena:

> A DEA report filed in a Los Angeles federal court quotes informant Lawrence Harrison, 45, as saying representatives of Mexico's now disbanded Federal Security Directorate were at the ranch to give the CIA "cover." According to the report, Harrison said the directorate was working with drug traffickers to move narcotics from Mexico to the United States. The House Government Operations Information Subcommittee has held two closed-door hearings on the matter and plans to question Justice Department officials at another private hearing (Bennett).

The CIA's Mark Mansfield bluntly denied any connection. "The whole story is *nonsense,*" he swore. "We have not trained Guatemalan guerrillas on that ranch or anywhere else." Naturally, the Agency's interaction with Guatemalan death squads has since turned up with nauseating regularity in the "mainstream" press.

So, in this tale, does Joey Ippolito. In his 1992 court battle on cocaine distribution charges in Los Angeles, Joey retained Edward Medvene—two years later an attorney for Fred Goldman in the wrongful death trial—and his partners Robert DiNicola and Scott Bauman, to represent him (*U.S. v Lorenzo et.al.*). On November 16, Ippolito fired the Medvene team and hired Cowlings attorney Donald Re. But the conflict-of-interest in Medvene's role as a forensics specialist in Simpson's civil trial is staggering: The plaintiffs hired an attorney for a mobbed-up cohort of O.J. Simpson, the employer of Al Cowlings, a suspect in a score of murders.

PART 2:
Joey Ip's Nubian Wiseguys and Denise Brown, the Grieving Gunsel

"Fred Goldman's lawyer said Wednesday that there is 'not a single shred of evidence' linking the murders of Ronald Goldman and Nicole Brown Simpson to ... drug activity, as O.J. Simpson has alleged."
—*Los Angeles Times*, February 18, 1996

Nicole Simpson's sister, Denise Brown, was squired about L.A. for several years by an Ippolito recruit. When Joey was arrested, police questioned his bodyguard and chauffeur, Allen Cowlings, who was visiting the mobster when police entered his residence to make the arrest (Harrell). In a sworn declaration submitted to the federal district court of Los Angeles in September 1992 on behalf of Ippolito, Cowlings claimed that he'd met the drug dealer "four or five years" earlier (*US v Lorenzo* et al). However, the AP reported in August, 1994 that Joey knew Cowlings "for up to 20 years, [and] that Cowlings was once a bodyguard and driver for Ippolito" (Deutch).

Organized crime investigator Steve Bertellucci told ABC News that Ippolito was a "principal player in major narcotics trafficking." Yet Al Cowlings maintained in his sworn declaration that Ippolito was "opposed" to cocaine use: "Joe became very upset when he learned that I was a free-base cocaine addict," he wrote. After years in the public spotlight as a professional football player, Cowling confessed: "I was having difficulty adjusting to life in the real world. I had entered a drug rehabilitation center a couple of years before, but I couldn't kick my habit. When Joe moved to Los Angeles, he took it upon himself to help me overcome my addiction." The situation was "so dismal that I know if it were not for Joe, I probably would have died" (Cowlings deposition).

Ippolito's roommate, Ronnie Lorenzo, was the owner of Splash, a chic Malibu restaurant, and a fraternal member of the Bonnano crime family, a perennial target of organized crime probes.

In 1987, LAPD detectives investigating Lorenzo found themselves on a dizzying trail when they discovered that Splash had recently changed ownership in a sale handled by an Encino company, Richman Financial Services, and that Lorenzo's Pontiac had been registered by the firm's president, Maurice Rind, a principal shareholder with Barry Minkow in L.A.'s ZZZZ Best Carpet stock fraud scandal—once described by LAPD officers, in congressional testimony, as an organized crime figure with ties to all five Mafia families (Lieberman). (As a New York stockbroker, Rind was sentenced twice on fraud charges. In the ZZZZ Best case, however, only one of nine suspects, some of them felons with lengthy rap sheets, was indicted, namely Barry Minkow, though Police Chief Daryl Gates had, in a press conference, accused all nine of stock fraud and the laundering of Mafia proceeds. Minkow made the Mafia the main thrust of his defense, testifying that he had had been "a puppet" under "duress." Maurice Rind, called to testify for the defense, pled the Fifth no less than 92 times and went home. Stockbroker Donald A. Johnson refused to testify because Rind had "threatened" him. He pled the Fifth as well.)

Kidnap and extortion were two of many charges filed against Lorenzo. James Caan offered his home as collateral toward the $2 million bail and appeared as a character witness for his "dear friend" (Lieberman, Connolly). The government case centered on Lorenzo's obscenity-strewn comments, captured on tape as he and Robert Franchi, an FBI informant, bought five kilograms of cocaine in Brentwood and Santa Monica from a source arranged by Lorenzo: Joey Ippolito. The narco-restaurateurs were both sentenced to ten years hard time for distributing cocaine in Santa Monica and Brentwood (Lieberman, February 27, 1993).

Joey escaped from the minimum security prison to which he was sentenced *three weeks before the brutal murders* in Brentwood. The prison was located on a MILITARY BASE in Pensacola, Florida (Harrell). The Mafioso was seen escaping in an automobile driven by an African-American male, according to news reports.

Bullish Bostonian Robert Franchi, the aforementioned FBI informant turned to the Bureau's investigation of organized crime in L.A., learned of Ippolito's stroll to freedom at Eglin Air Force Base and immediately ran to the FBI, demanding to know why the mobster had been interred at a minimum security prison. Franchi was convinced that Joey would attempt to kill him in retaliation for turning state's evidence. The feds told Franchi that they had "allowed Ippolito to escape," and "tracked his movements" to "learn who his contacts might be." The FBI claimed to have known of Ippolito's whereabouts at all times, traced all telephone calls and learned of an ex-girlfriend, who claimed to have been physically abused by the mobster and agreed to cooperate with investigators. As a fugitive, the agents told Franchi, Ippolito made numerous calls to O.J. Simpson. What's more, Franchi reports that, Ippolito had a "sit-down meeting" with Simpson two weeks before the carnage on Bundy Drive. The nature of the meeting is not known. On August 24, 1995, Ippolito was recaptured and placed in the custody of U.S. marshals in New York City. He has since been released from custody and turned as an "informant" for the FBI (Bosco).

What does Ippolito know of the killings? A source in the LAPD confirmed for Donald Freed, the author of *Killing Time,* an examination of the evidence untainted by courtroom strategy, that an organized crime figure had ordered the killings.

Someone besides Nicole's estranged husband took an intense interest in her.

O.J. Simpson consort Paula Barbieri's Toyota 4 X 4 was stolen from a Beverly Hills parking lot on January 24, 1994. The Toyota was used to follow Nicole. Police in Newport Beach recovered the car after it was involved in a traffic accident a week later and arrested one William Wasz, who insisted when questioned by police that he was unaware Barbieri owned the vehicle.

Simpson, said the miscreant, did not hire him. He refused to divulge the identity of the mystery man who did.

Inside the vehicle was found a 3″ x 5″ notebook with scribbled references to two weapons, including a 9mm pistol. The first page mentions "Nicole's sched." The notations make reference to "the Gym ... Westwood," and at "11:00," Nicole's stop at "Litchfield Toys, Westwood." At "12:00 noon," she eats at "Tony Roma's, Ventura Blvd. Encino." The note ends with "9 PM Viper Room" (Tinney).

A gun and a crack pipe were also found in the stolen Toyota. Nicole Simpson had apparently been someone's obsession. Allegations have also been made that Anthony Pellicano, a veteran military-intelligence officer, the so-called "Gumshoe to the Stars," had staked out Nicole's house. Pellicano has more mob connections than J. Edgar Hoover. He was hired by Howard Weitzman in the John DeLorean case, his first assignment upon moving to Los Angeles in 1983.

In 1976 he resigned under fire from the Illinois Law Enforcement Commission after local newspapers publicized the $30,000 loan he'd received from Paul "the Waiter" Ricca, the son of mob boss Paul de Lucia—the godfather of Pellicano's daughter. He was credited as technical adviser in the making of *The Firm* (Hubler & Bates). Pellicano also provided an inventive but ultimately unconvincing alibi for singer Michael Jackson (of child molestation and Nazi video fame) with his "frame-up" plea.

Since the start of the Simpson trial, the busy Denise Brown was the smiling paramour of Tony "the Animal" Fiato, a marmoset-eyed mob enforcer and FBI informant in a probe of the murder of Hollywood's Frank Cristi, another actor with a *Godfather* credit. The lead investigator of the Cristi murder case was Detective Tom Lange, a Florida veteran of the Marine Corps and Vietnam, assigned to the "elite" LAPD Homicide Special Section (Van Derbeken and Hardy). Lange was also assigned, with Detective Phillip Vanatter, to the Simpson case. Tony Fiato's testimony was directed at Norman Freeberg, who attempted to hire Fiato on the contract. The "Animal" rejected the offer. Two alleged collaborators were indicted.

On March 23, 1995, the *San Francisco Examiner* broke ranks with the press gang and noticed Ms. Brown's latest love interest:

> Two convicted murderers filed for retrial Wednesday because Anthony Fiato, a key prosecution witness and shadowy mob informer, emerged from hiding in a public relationship with Nicole Brown-Simpson's sister. The Superior Court retrial motion was filed by attorney Barry Levin on behalf of Ronald Coe and Alan Betts, who were convicted Feb. 3 of killing tough-guy actor Frank Christi in a murder-for-hire scheme.... Prosecutors told jurors that Norman Freedberg hired Coe, Betts and Harvey Rosenberg to kill Cristi because of a dispute over a woman.
>
> Defense lawyers were blocked from delving into Fiato's background because prosecutors said revealing his whereabouts would endanger the federally protected witness. Photographs of Fiato and Denise Brown have appeared recently in newspapers and supermarket tabloids.

Denise Brown's ties to ne'er-do-wells surfaced again with her much-ballyhooed domestic abuse "charity," run by Jeff Noebel, a 40-year-old S&L swindler from Dallas, Texas.

Noebel was a convicted con artist and accused spousal batterer, described in a restraining order filed by his wife as presenting a very uncharitable "clear and present danger to his estranged wife and two children." The polyamorous Denise Brown met the convicted felon by way of her contact with Randall England, an actor in "General Hopsital." She'd met England at their mutual modelling agency on L.A.'s west side. They dated and England became a close friend of the Brown family. He was a pall-bearer at Nicole's funeral.

On July 10, 1995, the *Los Angeles Times* reported that Noebel, the "dapper, smooth-talking" president of the Nicole Brown-Simpson Charitable Foundation, had blazed a trail of white-collar crime from Texas to California. Dreading a conviction, he agreed to cooperate with police. Noebel pled guilty to one count of making a false statement to federal banking regulators. In exchange, he was granted a reduction in a maximum two-year prison term.

Despite all of this, Randall England, a longtime cohort of Noebel's, claimed to have "no knowledge" of his legal or domestic problems:

Denise Brown, the organization's spokeswoman and chief executive officer, did not respond to repeated requests for an interview.

Noebel's life was complicated by ... matters that seemed at odds with his charitable work. While he was busy strategizing with the Browns—who he contends knew about his troubles—Noebel was under federal indictment in Texas for a scam that allegedly bilked 14 investors out of $875,000.

According to court records, Noebel and several cohorts were accused of duping the investors into buying dubious shares of a Florida savings and loan....

Court documents also show that Noebel's estranged wife has accused him of a pattern of stalking and abuse that came to head in June, 1994, just days after Nicole Brown Simpson was killed.

Under his guidance, by all appearances, the organization got off to a rollicking start. A news conference was called at the swank Rainbow Room, high atop New York's Rockefeller Center.

Speaking for the family was Denise Brown, 37, a near mirror-image of her slain sister, whose portrait was blown up on one wall. After reading a brief statement, which Noebel says he co-authored, she held up a giant-sized check for $50,000, courtesy of jeans-maker No Excuses.

No Excuses had snatched up Donna Rice as a spokesmodel after her rendezvous with then-presidential candidate Gary Hart, then anointed Marla Maples as its pitchwoman after her tryst with Donald Trump (Lopez and Katz).

In defense of the Foundation, Denise responded to reporters on July 19, 1995 that media reports were "overblown" (Reyes).

This is one accusation that will never be leveled at Ippolito's camaraderie with Al Cowlings and another long-suffering Buffalo Bill.

The mobster considered O.J. a sterling source for inside information on the football industry, enhancing his stake in the gambling pools, according to tabloid profiles.

That Simpson and Cowlings had formed an alliance in the black market and had more in common with Joey Ippolito than point spreads became evident with the arrest of Tracey Alice Hill, alias Amanda Armstrong, a 32-year-old stripper from Santa Monica. in February, 1995. Hill was seized by police in Dunsmuir, a small town in northern California, with 40 pounds of cocaine stuffed in her suitcase. Police also found a vial of pills prescribed to one Al Cowlings in her purse. Hill's computerized address book listed the telephone numbers of both Cowlings and Simpson.

She was booked in Eureka and flown to Sacramento. During the fight, *she twice attempted to leap out of the plane while it was airborne.* (Simpson, during the Bronco "chase," also attempted suicide, according to Robert Kardashian.) On March 3, Ms. Hill was indicted by a grand jury on a single count of possessing cocaine with intent to distribute.

The Associated Press reported that Donald Re, Cowling's attorney—and Joey Ippolito's, also a former law partner of Howard Weitzman— denied any connection whatsoever to Ms. Hill (March 25, 1995). In fact, the denial is a direct contradiction to the snappy admission issued by Cowlings' attorney to the *Contra Costa Times* that "Ms. Hill is a *friend* of Al Cowlings. He is *upset* she was arrested" (Ginley & Porterfield).

Moreover, Cowlings visited the stripper's apartment on Pier Avenue, a stone's throw from the beach, after her arrest, a few days before federal agents searched it, according to a neighbor. Within two days of Cowling's visit, a moving van arrived. The movers were still crating and hauling Hill's belongings when the police pulled up, cordoned off the apartment and conducted the search. But it is likely any evidence that might connect Ms. Hill and her cocaine to Cowlings and Simpson had vanished by this time.

The *Contra Costa Times* reported on the 24th that police "refused to say what they found. Patrick Hanley, an assistant U.S. attorney assigned to the case in Sacramento, would not discuss the matter, saying he couldn't confirm or deny Cowling's involvement."

Robin Meiss, the neighbor, told the *Times* that Ms. Hill "was a quiet tenant whom Cowlings visited often." Meiss's husband offered: "He [Cowlings] was dating her."

Simpson has been involved with the mob since his glory days as running back for the Buffalo Bills. In his prime, local police accused him of selling cocaine. Simpson also ran with a real estate swindler in Florida with mob affiliations.

One of Simpson's Mafia friends back in Buffalo, Casimir "Butch Casey" Sucharski, visited O.J. in Brentwood a few weeks before the Brentwood murders. Sucharski himself and two women in his company were shot repeatedly in the head and neck in Miramar, Florida two weeks after Nicole Brown-Simpson and Ron Goldman were murdered.

Eerily enough, other Southern California murder cases are linked to the Simpson case, including the March 19, 1995 murder of O.J.'s friend, record company promoter Charles Minor in Malibu, California, Ippolito's stomping grounds. Suzette McClure, one of Minor's many paramours, was charged with the murder. Simpson's attorney Robert Shapiro attended the wake (Haring).

Bobby Chandler, another chum of O.J.'s, was in blooming health in the summer of 1994. By the end of the year, he contracted lung cancer and was dead (Ruiz).

Yet another muffled death scream resonating with Nicole's belonged to Brett Cantor, the proprietor of the Dragonfly, a Hollywood nightclub. Nicole and Ron Goldman were regulars at the Dragonfly. Cantor was murdered on July 30, 1993, in a vicious knife attack nearly identical to the one that took the lives of Ron Goldman and Nicole Simpson. The club owner had been cut from behind. The killer started on the lower left side of the neck, drew upward and away to the right. Both Goldman and Cantor were stabbed repeatedly on the arms and chest. In both cases, the knife had a long, thin blade. At one point, Shapiro planned to argue that the same killer was responsible for the bloody melée on Bundy Drive, but the LAPD announced (with psychic certainty) that there was "no connection" between the two cases (La Fontaine). A close friend of the Cantor family reports that the club owner's parents believe firmly that the cases are linked.

The Syndicate has been a quiet participant in the Simpson case since the opening knock of the gavel. Howard Weitzman, the first attorney to speak for Simpson, studied white-collar crime in law school. He represented Tom Dragna, a racketeer, in 1980. Three years later he lost a vigorous defense of Barbara Mouzin, currently serving a 25-year prison term for her role in the Grandma Mafia cocaine-trafficking case. Weitzman's client roster includes "conservative" S&L stinkbug Charles Keating, John DeLorean, Marvin Mitchelson, Michael Jackson (who once quit a party attended by Robert Shapiro after receiving word that his brother Tito's ex-wife, who loathed swimming, had been found dead at the bottom of a pool with numerous *bruises* on her body—the coroner ruled that she'd drowned to death), and rock geek Ozzy Osbourne (West). The grizzled Hollywood lawyer's bona fidés also include a stint as lecturer at Georgetown Law Center, long a haunt of the CIA.

As the first Simpson trial wrapped up, Weitzman took an executive position at the Music Corporation of America (MCA), the Mafia-ridden black tower that looms above much of the entertainment industry in North Hollywood (Moldea). MCA also employed Simpson's crony and parttime counsel Robert Kardashian as president of the Radio Network at Universal Studios from 1987 to 1990 (Karabian).

Johnny Cochran's post-trial legal career also entered familiar territory: Murderville, USA. A particularly well-heeled, politically-connected client of Johnny Cochran's, in the aftermath of the "Trial of the Century," was Calvin Grigsby, founder of Grigsby Brandford & Co., the largest minority-owned bond underwriting firm in the country. His investment company sank $200 million into returning the Raiders to Oakland. For more than ten years, Grigsby Brandford handled all municipal financing for Alameda County, California. Grigsby drew the interest of federal investigators in Miami when they looked into his incursions in local municipal bond markets. Also under investigation was Dade County Commissioner James Burke, a business partner of Grigsby's. Burke was caught up in a sweeping probe of corruption known as Operation Greenpalm after he had given Grigsby an assist in landing lucrative Miami bond deals. When reporters called for comments, Grigsby immediately resigned as chairman of his own firm. His departure was hastened by a $5,000 fine imposed by the California Fair Practices Commission for improper contributions in an Oakland mayoral race. Cochran refused to take telephone calls concerning Grigsby's influence-peddling in Dade County (Sinton & Howe).

The statistically-striking incidence of murders on the edge of the Simpson case were an overlooked sideshow. During the criminal trial, Judge Ito's bailiff was shot dead without a squeak of speculation from the press regarding a possible connection to the case. With few exceptions, the murder of Ron Goldman's friend Michael Nigg shortly after the verdict was announced went unreported. The *Los Angeles Times* did not find Nigg's death newsworthy, although the newspaper dealt at length with trial minutiae and duly published leaks from the LAPD concerning "blood-smeared trench tools," and such. The *San Jose Mercury-News* reported Nigg's murder on September 11, 1995:

FRIEND OF RONALD GOLDMAN KILLED

LOS ANGELES (AP)—A waiter and aspiring actor who befriended Ronald Goldman when both worked at the Mezzaluna restaurant was shot to death after refusing to give money to two robbers.

Michael Nigg, 26, was killed Friday night in a parking lot as he and his girlfriend were going to a restaurant, police spokeswoman Cherie Clair said Monday....

Nigg was from Colorado and worked as a waiter at Sanctuary, a Beverly Hills restaurant. He recently appeared on the syndicated TV show "Liars."

Nigg had worked at Mezzaluna in nearby Brentwood, where he and Goldman, another waiter, were good friends. Nigg quit Mezzaluna in May 1994, just a month before Goldman was slain along with Nicole Brown-Simpson.

Nigg had just stepped out of his car at the Hollywood parking lot Friday when two thieves approached and demanded money. He was shot in the head after he refused, Clair said.

She didn't know if the thieves got any money.

Nigg's girlfriend, Julie Long, was still in the car and was not injured.

The thieves fled in a car driven by a third suspect, police said.

Michael Nigg was one of several employees at Mezzaluna who fell under armed assault. Another, a waiter, was nearly killed in a car bombing. The national media did not find either story newsworthy. Locally, the murder received scant mention on the evening news. It was not until "sweeps" month, November 1996, that the television news industry in Los Angeles realized that Ron Goldman and Nicole Simpson were but two links in a chain of murders. KCOP, an independent television station, ran a series on the Mezzaluna carnage, but cautioned viewers that the station's own investigation found "no connection" to the Simpson case, echoing police sources—despite the LAPD's exceptionally, chronically flawed handling of the related cases.

In an interview, conducted by KABC-AM's Michael Jackson on November 26, Steve Cohen, KCOP news director, positively ruled out the possibility of conspiracy in the Simpson case—yet acknowledged repeatedly that the station's own investigation was not, in fact, all that "definitive":

Cohen: Michael Nigg was a waiter at Mezzaluna. He was approached by three men, apparently a robbery attempt. They demanded money from Mr. Nigg. He refused to hand over his wallet and they shot him in the head. He died on the way to the hospital. Within a month the police had three men in custody, and one of them confessed. That's what our sources say. What we learned is that the prosecutors never filed a case against the three men.

Jackson: Why?

Cohen: Well, there was some problem in terms of the nature of the informants they had.

Jackson: But if one of the three confessed, the other two were his associates, surely they [the police] had sufficient information...

Cohen: They had sufficient information, but they had what I guess I would call tainted sources that brought them to the case. And the prosecutors were not feeling good about the nature of the confession and how it was obtained. The result was that the L.A. prosecutor's office decided that they would not bring charges against these three people. However, right now the LAPD has continued to appeal to the District Attorney's office to see if they could do something...

Jackson: Again ...

Cohen: Now, Goldman and Nigg ...

Jackson: Just one second. Again, that includes the man who *confessed?*

Cohen: That's correct. Now, Goldman and Nigg were definitely friends, and they hung in the same circles.... We have not been able to determine anywhere that there was any connection between any of these three fellas that [are] alleged to have murdered Mr. Nigg.

Jackson: So at this stage it's all just a horrible, sad, sick, criminal coincidence.

Cohen: Correct. There's another gentleman, 25-year-old Brent (sic) Cantor, who also was a friend of Ron's and also of Mr. Nigg's....

Jackson: The other guy, what happened to him?

Cohen: Well, he was 25 years-old. His name was Brent (sic) Cantor. He also was a friend of Ron. And he eventually had a record company of his own. He signed bands like Rage Against the Machine, pretty well-known bands. He promoted shows at a place called the Dragonfly, which is an "underground" nightclub.... And on the night of July 30, 1993, which was eleven months before the deaths of Ron and Nicole, someone walked up to Cantor's apartment ... which was just off the Sunset Strip ... rang the bell and was buzzed inside. So we guess that it was someone that he knew. And he was murdered brutally, by how many assailants no one knows. He was stabbed repeatedly, and his throat was slashed.

Jackson: Did they take anything?

Cohen: No, no. The case file is sealed in this one. And, again, this is the case of Brent (sic) Cantor. The Simpson defense team did have the opportunity to examine the Cantor file prior to the beginning of the original O.J. case, the criminal case. His throat was deeply slashed, just like Nicole Brown's. But as far as we can determine—again, this is our independent investigation—that's where the similarity ends. We haven't had access to the file; we've not seen the details of the autopsy report.

Jackson: If I worked there, I'd be in hiding.

Cohen: Well, again ... but ... but ... I know this is hard for everyone, especially our viewers and your listeners, but it does seem, as far as we can tell, ballistically, that there doesn't seem to be any specific tie, except some darn, pretty bad luck that comes out of the kind of the kinds of circles that these folks lived in. I guess that's the only ...

Jackson: But it is fodder for those who see a "conspiracy" in everything.

Cohen: Yeah. Well, sure. And I want to go a little further here just to clean up the record. Phil Vanatter and Tom Lange did meet with the detectives investigating the Cantor case, because of course the similarity—the use of a long knife, multiple stab wounds, etc. THEY concluded that there was nothing further for them to pursue in the case. Now, the "Dream Team" did try to enter Cantor as evidence into the preliminary hearing in the criminal case with O.J., and Ito said, "No. We're not going to have it. It's irrelevant."

Now, there is one other individual who is alive I think your listeners might be interested in. They probably know about it. His name is Keith Zlombowitch. And Keith was the director of operations at Mezzaluna, and he was also a former lover of Nicole. He did appear before a grand jury, and his testimony is a matter of public record that he was her lover, and that he was scared to death, as he put it, of O.J.'s having found out about that. And he went to Aspen to run the Mezzaluna there, then went to Florida. We have been unable for the last two months of this investigation to find him. When we have it that he disappeared, he *disappeared.*

There also was another incidence of a fella who was a waiter for a short time, in the same period of time. His car was firebombed. He was just working at Mezzaluna. He's okay, but his car was blown up.

Unsolved murders, the release of a confessed killer for nebulous reasons, similar murder weapons, sealed autopsy reports, disappearing witnesses and carbombings do not add up to the conclusion there is "no connection" between the murders and the under-reported backstage carnage.

Despite the fact that there have been no convictions for any of the above slayings, Cohen closed off the interview with the ironic observation, "I think it's very seldom that the system doesn't work."

But then, the opinions of a news director are all too often susceptible to the influence of the corporate executives who sign his paycheck. KCOP is owned by Chris-Craft, a CIA front that once had auto-cocaine wizard John DeLorean on its board of directors (Levin). Another director of the company that owns KCOP, until his death by brain cancer on December 6, 1996, was Alvin "Pete" Rozelle, the retired commissioner of the Mafia-ridden National Football League (see *Interference: How Organized Crime Influences Professional Football*, by Dan Moldea, 1989).

According to the *New York Daily News* on May 6, 1996:

> O.J. Simpson's buddy Al Cowlings was called before a grand jury probing one of the largest sports gambling rings in Southern California.... Cowlings, an ex-pro football player, appeared before the secret panel in the Criminal courts building April 23, a date squeezed among his three days of questioning last month in the wrongful-death civil suit against Simpson....
>
> The grand jury also wanted to question Simpson's lawyer buddy Robert Kardashian, according to our law enforcement source. But last week Kardashian said, "I don't know anything about it. I don't gamble" (Freed).

In a telephone conversation in June, Donald Freed informed this writer that the grand jury looked not only organized into gambling, but also drugs and child pornography as well.

The Rumor and the Phoenix

After the Brentwood murders, a rumor circulated in Beverly Hills night spots. It explains more than the average corporate media courtroom glossover, and pulls together significant loose ends. Simpson and his estranged wife were immersed in the adrenal world of Joey Ip and the Combination. The rumor accounts for motive, is correct in essential details, and fills some gaps in the trial testimony regarding Simpson's secret life in the Ippolito syndicate.

This account holds that O.J. Simpson had financed a wholesale cocaine distributorship employing a network of Fast Eddys and aspiring celebrities on the Hollywood fringe. It is said that suppliers (Mr. Ippolito and Mr. Lorenzo?) entrusted him, over a period of several months, with a sizable quantity of cocaine, on credit. And Nicole was not exactly the thriftiest of wives with her designer, danger-high-voltage wardrobe and jet-set vacations ...

Barry Hoestler, a private investigator hired for the Simpson case by Robert Shapiro, contended that Nicole entertained the notion of becoming financially independent by opening a restaurant with Ron Goldman as her partner and financing it with cocaine profits (Frost). Hoestler also said that Nicole and her friends were "over their heads with some dope dealers."

As one Beverly Hills resident put it, Simpson and his circle were under intense pressure but "optimistic—entering a tough street business, fueled by a jolt of the goods from time to time."

Simpson's inability to make good on cocaine debts, run up largely by Nicole's circle, was not viewed lightly.

When Simpson's suppliers insisted on payment, Nicole Brown-Simpson and friends suddenly found reasons to leave town. O.J.'s suppliers were attempting to control him by controlling his finances.

This was done by manipulating the habits of Nicole's circle. He attempted to patch up the marriage and failed.

"Simpson wanted her to straighten up and come home," an adherent to the rumor maintains. "Unfortunately for her, O.J. was not in the mood to pick up her 'bar bills' while some young stud was driving the Mercedes he bought for her. He told her that explicitly.... He refused to pay for the wholesale purchases she and her friends made for their new 'business' venture. When O.J. was threatened by her "bill collector," he balked because it was not the debt he agreed to back, and it was more than he could raise."

Simpson's debtors did not buy his excuses. He went to Chicago to pay a call on "the man whose Family, even though not in Los Angeles, has always been the 'patron saint' of a particular part of the movie industry. The people in Chicago tried to step in. They asked for a meeting, but it's a new Family that owns the streets of Los Angeles these days. That only made it worse, because the L.A. boys took the interference as an insult. They've been beating the Chicago crowd for years, even in South Chicago and all over Indiana, where they have spread their operation."

Nicole Brown-Simpson was living precariously. Her best friend was a cocaine addict. Next door when she lived on Gretna Green Way, lived Carl Colby—son of William Colby, a former CIA director and guiding force of the PHOENIX program, the notorious mass-murder operation in Vietnam that targeted suspected and potential Viet Cong collaborators in the South. Carl's sister starved herself to death. It is widely thought that she slowly dwindled away to protest her father's role in the war, according to David Corn in *The Blond Ghost* (1995).

Colby's wife, Catherine Boe, took the stand first to testify that she'd often heard O.J. Simpson, at the time of his separation from Nicole in early 1992, argue with her about their respective sex lives. Nicole, she said, "was upset about his womanizing." O.J. fumed that Keith Zlombowitch, the Mezzaluna manager, had been sleeping at Nicole's in a spare bedroom.

Repeatedly, Mrs. Colby—who asked to be addressed as "Miss Boe" (probably to distance herself from the name "Colby" and the CIA) continued to answer the prosecution's questions after Shapiro and Cochran raised objections.

Glaring, Simpson's attorney barked for a sidebar conference:

Shapiro: Your honor ... we have no discovery on this. I have called this lady and asked to talk to her and she refused to talk to us.
Darden: You just really never know what you are going to get from Mrs. Colby,
Cochran: It might be helpful if you talked to her.
Darden: I have, but I believe she is going to testify that ...
Cochran: She is an ALIEN from another planet!

The *Los Angeles Times* (February 4, 1995) reported that Carl Colby's testimony at the preliminary hearing was "disjointed and confused." Colby testified that he "spied [sic] a suspicious man" outside his house one evening in 1992. It was Simpson. Colby called police, "because he found it odd that a person of Simpson's description was in the neighborhood at that hour. As he said that, a black alternate juror rolled his eyes toward the ceiling, and another alternate, also black, chuckled to herself."

The *Times* did not find it worth mention that Nicole happened to live next to the son of a necrotizing CIA official.

Nicole Brown-Simpson had been tethered to Simpson throughout her adult life. She feared her husband's periodic rages. He followed her ("Oh my God, it's O.J.!") and knew her whereabouts at all times. She had escaped a suffocating marriage. Her newfound freedom was exhilarating.

Why glance back?

PART III:
The Catspaw Precursor—A Mirror Image of the Simpson Case

Because the Simpson case is a carefully concerted reenactment of another double-murder: Before the legal throes of O.J. Simpson, there was embattled Murray Gold.

The Brentwood slaughter was foreshadowed in 1974 when 71-year-old Irving Pasternak and his wife Rhoda were brutally stabbed to death in Waterbury, Connecticut. All in a few moments. Gold was charged. There were no witnesses.

Mr. Pasternak, before his retirement, was legal counsel to the Motion Picture Producers and Distributors of America (MPPDA), a Hollywood labor union once run by Pat Casey, an "undercover agent" of mob boss Johnny Rosselli (Moldea). (Already the "Catspaw" case has struck familiar territory: Murderville.).

A glance at Mafia history links the two cases.

Rosselli, like Lansky, had one foot in the underworld, the other in Langley, Virginia. By his own testimony before the Church Committee in 1974, Rosselli was once handed a CIA contract on the lives of Fidel Castro, Che Guevara and other Latin American rebels. Rosselli went on to link Las Vegas casino interests with Howard Hughes, Moe Dalitz and Jimmy Hoffa (Kohn).

John Rosselli was an asset of the intelligence sector, per his own admission before the Church Committee on Assassinations. Charles Rappleye, in a biography of Rosselli, describes the gangster's initial appearance as Congress attempted to unravel criminal interconnections of the Watergate debacle:

> Hoping to get to the bottom of the Nixon administration burglaries, the Watergate prosecutors turned to John Rosselli. Leslie Scherr, the Washington D.C., attorney who appeared with Rosselli at the closed hearing, recalled, "It was so convoluted, you really had to be John Le Carre to follow it." But judging from the questions posed to Rosselli, Scherr said, the prosecutors felt that "the reason why the break-in occurred at the Democratic Party headquarters was because Nixon or somebody in the Republican Party suspected the Democrats had information as to Nixon's involvement with the CIA's original contract with Rosselli" (Rappleye & Becker).

In July 1976, Rosselli's dismembered body was found—shortly after a Congressional appearance—stuffed inside a 55-gallon oil drum bobbing in the intercoastal waters of Biscayne Bay, off Miami, near Donald Aronow's speedboat factory.

Lansky and Aronow were both questioned by police about the murder (Burdick).

The indictment of Murray Gold, a Jewish survivor of the Holocaust and former son-in-law of the Pasternaks, hung entirely on circumstantial evidence. There was, for one thing, the tell-tale slash on the index finger of Gold's left hand. The prosecution made a fuss over the finger. They argued in court that Gold had injured himself in the course of killing the Pasternaks. His defense team—a coalition of world famous attorneys, soon to include F. Lee Bailey—ushered to the stand an expert witness who testified that it was improbable a slasher could frenetically wound his victims and stab himself without inflicting more damage than a minor flesh wound.

Witnesses passing the Pasternak home the night of the murders gave police a description bearing no resemblance to the accused.

Bruce Sanford, a friend of the Pasternak's daughter who enjoyed sleeping in graveyards, fit the description in all particulars. Sanford was known to wear Catspaw boots consistent with the feral heelprints stamped in the blood of the Pasternaks. Sanford had a long, sordid criminal history: a heroin addict, he once attempted suicide by *eating glass*, admired Charles Manson and belonged to a motorcycle gang called the "Peddlers of Death." On two occasions, he openly confessed to friends of committing the murders, yet Waterbury authorities covered for him, at one point going so far as to testify in the courtroom that Sanford had been safely locked away in a jail cell the night of the murders when, the defense learned, he had not.

Yet the name Sanford did not turn up on the list of suspects, because on December 12, 1974, he cut his own throat. Murray Gold argued that police and prosecutors had set him up and were deliberately overlooking Sanford's guilt to win a false conviction.

The prosecution dogged Murray Gold through *five* murder trials before a guilty verdict was finally handed down—ten years after the crime took place. It was a textbook frame-up.

On the jury sat a secretary for the Attorney General of Connecticut, the same office that indicted Gold (just as a secretary for the D.A.'s office turned up on the jury in the second Simpson trial), a woman with two first cousins on the police force, another who admitted upon questioning to have "extensive contact" with the police, a juror who spent "23 years in government service," an employee of a state agency, and an alternate with a son employed as a "corrections officer" (Nizer).

Yet Gold's claim that he was the target of a "police conspiracy," lightly dismissed by the state's prosecutrix, Marcia Smith, was treated by the court as proof of diminished capacity.

The jury found Gold guilty of the murders, but at a post-trial hearing the verdict was set aside with a false finding that Gold was mentally crippled, that an irrational fear of courtroom "conspiracies" had decimated his sanity. The judge concluded that Gold was entitled to a *sixth* trial. In the meantime, evidence that Sanford committed the murders mounted. Gold was released after a defense argument about suppressed evidence at the post-trial hearing.

PART IV:
A Killer's Brain Frequencies & A Few Words About CIA/Mafia Clean-Up Operations

Gold was not the slasher—but he was an ideal cut-out for a CIA/Mafia killing. Gold once held a top-security position at Grumman Aerospace. He had worked on secret defense projects (Nizer).

Grumman's personnel office would have kept a comprehensive file on Gold. His history would be an open book to any intelligence operatives—including the period when he was incarcerated at Mount Sanai Hospital in New York, where he received shock treatments for depression.

Mount Sanai shares with other leading hospitals around the country the distinction of employing psychiatrists moonlighting in the scientific/psychiatric netherworld of CIA mind control. Dr. Harold Abramson (hand-picked for the mind control program by Sidney Gottlieb of the CIA's Technical Services Division) conducted LSD research at Mount Sanai—unusual in itself because Abramson had no formal training in psychiatry. His research was funded by the Macy Foundation, a CIA shell (Marks). Abramson is best known as biochemical warfare specialist Frank Olson's therapist—before the CIA mind control subject plummeted from a tenth-floor office window.

At Mount Sanai, too, the Agency would have easy access to detailed information concerning Murray Gold. His professional and psychiatric profile spelled p-a-t-s-y.

The backroom presence of CIA mind control in the Simpson case explains the break-in at the office of Dr. Ameli and other therapists retained to temper the emotional aches of the Simpson crowd.

A chilling indication that the CIA's mind control fraternity exercised a hidden influence on the trial was the breakdown of juror Tracy Hampton in early May, 1995. Before she was released by Judge Ito, Ms. Hampton had been observed *sitting motionless* in the jury box. Jurors reported that she had taken to staring at a blank television screen for *hours* at a spell. Hampton was removed from the jury on May 3, after complaining to Judge Ito, "I can't take it anymore."

Hard Copy reported that Hampton had been "hearing voices," a detail over-looked in newspaper accounts. The CIA's mind control fraternity has, for at least 20 years, transmitted words to subjects snared for experimentation in mental institutions, prisons and even society at large. After she was ousted from the courtroom, Hampton tried to commit suicide by eating glass—an allusion to the Catspaw case—specifically the attempted self-immolation of suspect Bruce Sanford, who also bolted down a mouthful of glass. Paramedics carted Ms. Hampton from her home on a stretcher. She was hospitalized. After her release, she denied attempting suicide.

Prosecutor Christopher Darden also seems to have had a close brush with mind control. In April 1995, Duarte, California artist Steve Hardy related a grim story of CIA brain manipulation and death to reporters of the *Los Angeles Sentinel*. The "subject" was Sonji Taylor, an elementary school teacher shot by police on a medical center rooftop in Los Angeles on December 16, 1993. Taylor was discovered in a stairwell at the medical center at about 8 PM by a jan-itor, who summoned security guards. They found Taylor—a church choir singer, devoted single mother, a former homecoming queen—holding her son in a head-lock, clutching a knife. A hospital dispatcher called 911 at 8:25 PM and reported that Taylor had threatened to stab anyone who approached.

"Sonji Danese Taylor," Hardy said, "was an involuntary human experi-mentee. Advanced technologies using microwaves can make people hear voices":

> Officials do not know how, when or why Taylor arrived atop the medical cen-ter. She moved to Los Angeles in 1991 with dreams of becoming an actress or model. Neither she nor her son, Jeremy Jamal, 3, had ever been a patient or received any treatment at the center.
>
> Taylor was working as a substitute teacher at K.L. Carver and William L. Valentine elementary schools in San Marino....
>
> Shortly after [a] 911 call, Los Angeles Police Department officers Sgt. Michael Long, an 18-year veteran, and Craig Liedahl, a 15-year veteran, arrived on the scene....
>
> Taylor was holding her son in her left arm and using her right to make threat-ening gestures with the knife and yelling "For the blood of Jesus!"
>
> The heliport lights were off and the only illumination was provided by the street lights below and by adjacent structures.
>
> Taylor failed to respond to repeated commands to release her son and drop the knife. The officers later said Taylor was swinging the knife dangerously close to Jeremy and they feared she might stab him.

Long sprayed Taylor twice with pepper spray and the second application forced her to release Jeremy, who was grabbed by another officer and rushed from the immediate vicinity.

Long and Liedahl said Taylor then lunged at them with the knife and both officers shot her, Long firing twice with his nine-millimeter automatic and Liedahl seven times with his weapon. Jeremy witnessed his mother's death.

Although nine shots were fired, the autopsy revealed Taylor sustained ten bullet wounds, seven in the back. The coroner speculated the tenth wound was caused by a ricochet.

Hardy said he became intrigued with Taylor's case because her last minutes on earth were so unlike everything that preceded it.

"Something seemed wrong," he said. "She wasn't on drugs, she wasn' t drunk and she had no mental health problems. She was a good mother and a law abiding citizen. She came from a stable family and she had a little boy. Then, suddenly, she goes crazy. No one has any idea why she was there [at the medical center] or what she was doing."

If Taylor was an involuntary human experiment of microwave experiments, all of her odd behavior is explained, Hardy said....

Hardy said people will not participate in experiments if they know the outcome of certain types of research is permanent physical damage and/or death. Therefore involuntary human experimentees are needed and Hardy says unsuspecting citizens are routinely used as test subjects.

Taylor, Hardy said, through microwave transmissions, was subjected to voices that told her to got to St. Vincent the night of Dec. 16, 1993. He said the voices probably pretended to be demons or Taylor, because of her religious upbringing, thought she was hearing demons and that accounts for her repeated use of the phrase "For the blood of Jesus" as a chant to ward off demons.

He said she was not threatening her son that night, but trying valiantly to protect him.

"She was displaying the traits of a mother who was bravely doing her damnedest to protect her son and ward off attackers. She was steered to do what she did."

On Sept. 28, 1994, the Los Angeles County District Attorney's Office released a report on Taylor's death that said Officers Long and Liedahl would not face criminal charges. The team of prosecutors, including O.J. Simpson prosecutor Christopher Darden, concluded the case could not be won in a court (Parker).

The coroner ruled the shooting of Sonji Taylor a "homicide." The L.A. County coroner's office, reported the *San Gabriel Valley Tribune*, was not forthcoming with the report. It was released to reporters only after an attorney intervened (Bolden). The 45-page investigative findings, prepared by Chris Darden, raised "the possibility ... that the officers are not being truthful about their actions that evening," Questions concerning the account of the shootings given by Long and Liedahl arose when it was revealed that four of the bullets that dropped Taylor were flattened, or "mushroomed," directly under her body, indicating she'd been shot repeatedly after she was prostrate. One investigator observed, "it was a bad shoot and it can't be justified" (Stein).

"If this woman posed such a danger, why was she shot in the *back*?" attorney Johnnie L. Cochran, Jr. asked. "For the district attorney's office to find that this was a justifiable shooting is outrageous" (Hubler).

Prosecutor Darden's reasons for clearing the officers depended entirely upon a legal loophole in a less than full investigation. The coroner's report acknowledged public speculation of a police cover-up. Indeed, Investigators Darden and Richard Goul wrote, "the evidence does not square with the police account." The most troubling question: "How could Taylor lunge forward at the officers and yet be shot in the back?" Darden and Goul wrote. However, they noted, the force of the bullets' impact could have turned Taylor's body around as she fell—subverting criminal prosecution of the officers." Darden claimed that the officers could not be prosecuted because, under rules of circumstantial evidence, "if a jury is presented with two rational conclusions and one points to innocence, that is the conclusion it must adopt" (Stein).

1: "Sufficient Truth": Blowback at the LAPD

"When people in the mainstream talk about the man charged with the Oklahoma City bombing—and keep in mind that was allegedly the worst act of domestic terrorism in history—they speak in much gentler terms than they do about O.J. Simpson."

—Johnny Cochran, *San Francisco Chronicle*, November 17, 1996

There are troubling contradictions, still unexplained, in the Simpson case. The *Los Angeles Times* reported: "Police detectives disregarded state law and their own departmental policy when they waited hours to summon the county coroner" (Frammolino & Weinstein).

Blood, as from a holy stigmata, materialized on a pair of Simpson's socks. AP's Linda Deutch, in her November 4, 1996 story on former police lab supervisor Gregory Matheson's testimony at the civil trial:

Matheson glossed over the socks found at the foot of Simpson's bed the day after Nicole Brown Simpson and Ronald Goldman were slashed to death.... Matheson, who is now chief forensic chemist for the Police Department, acknowledged he saw no blood on the socks when they were collected June 13, 1994. He examined them again on June 29 and still saw no blood.

It was left to defense attorney Robert Blasier to tell jurors that criminalist Collin Yamauchi studied the socks in his laboratory on Aug. 4 and found copious amounts of blood.

"On Aug. 4, is it correct that's the first time Mr. Yamauchi looked and determined blood was visible to the naked eye?" Blasier asked.

"That was the first day blood was located, yes," Matheson said.

Obviously miffed, Blasier asked Matheson: "Were you told by the plaintiffs you were not going to be asked a single question about any of the testing you did?"

The answer was blocked by an objection....

When Blasier asked about the socks, Matheson said he didn't do a close examination before writing his initial notes which said of blood: "None obvious."

"I brought them out, gave the general color description ... and there was no blood obvious on the socks," Matheson said.

In the first trial, the defense suggested the socks were pristine when taken to the laboratory, then contaminated with blood from Simpson and his slain ex-wife while they were in the laboratory.

Is Mark Fuhrman a white supremacist? The spinner of bloody tales for credulous femmes signed a book deal with Regnery Press, which bills itself as the "premier publisher of conservative books." Furhman received a $1.2 million advance from Regnery, the publisher of such Ultracon titles as *The Conservative Mind* by Russell Kirk, *God & Man at Yale* by William F. Buckley, *Goldwater: the Man Who Made a Revolution* by Lee Edwards, *Right From the Beginning* by Patrick J. Buchanan, and *Inventing the AIDS Virus* by Peter Duesburg

He has been accused at least a half-dozen times of threatening and beating suspects, particularly blacks and Hispanics. Police Watch, a non-profit citizen advocacy group in Los Angeles, has received five complaints against Fuhrman since 1988. "I work with these files every day," says Police Watch official Michael Salcido, "and I personally handled over a thousand intakes a year and I know no other officer that has five counts against him" (Noble).

Kathleen Bell's July 19, 1994 letter to Cochran is a consistent step in Fuhrman's bucolic track record:

I'm writing to you in regards to a story I saw on the news last night. I thought it ridiculous that the Simpson defense team would even suggest that their (sic) might ... be racial motivation involved in the trial against Mr. Simpson. I then glanced up at the television and was quite shocked to see that Officer Ferman (sic) was a man that I had the misfortune of meeting. You may have received a message from your answering service last night that I called to say that Mr. Ferman (sic) may be more of a racist than you could even imagine.

Between 1985 and 1986 I worked as a real estate agent in Redondo Beach for Century 21 Bob Maher Realty (now out of business). At the time, my office was located above a Marine recruiting center off of Pacific Coast Highway. On occasion I would stop in to say hello to the two Marines working there. I saw Mr. Ferman (sic) there a couple of times. I remember him distinctly because of his height and build.

While speaking to the men I learned that Mr. Ferman (sic) was a police officer in Westwood, and I don't know if he was telling the truth, but he said that he had been in a special division of the Marines. I don't know how the subject was raised, but Officer Ferman (sic) said that when he sees a "nigger" (as he called it) driving with a white woman, he would pull them over. I asked would he if he didn't have a reason, and he said that he would find one. I looked at the two Marines to see if they knew he was joking, but it became obvious to me that he was very serious.

Officer Ferman (sic) went on to say that he would like nothing more than to see all "niggers" gathered together and killed. He said something about burning them or bombing them. I was too shaken to remember the exact words he used, however, I do remember that what he said was probably the most horrible thing I had ever heard someone say. What frightened me even more was that he was a police officer.

In 1983, the volatile Mark Fuhrman was interviewed by Dr. Ira Brent in lieu of a disability claim for work-related stress. Mark Furhman confided to Brent that he "beat up" on suspects, and "blacked out," became "a wild man" (Noble). Investigative reporter Stephen Singular, in *Legacy of Deception*, found in Furhman's testimony a passage about his thoughts in the immediate aftermath of the murders: he testified that he was "'concerned with the [younger Simpson] children and the ex-husband since they [Nicole and O.J.] still had joint custody of the children.' How, I asked myself, did he know about this joint custody arrangement?" (Singular).

The planned relocation to Sandpoint in the Idaho panhandle was something of an LAPD tradition. So many officers live there, in fact, some residents claim that the LAPD runs the county (Ockenfels). Richard Butler, founder of the

Aryan Nations compound in Hayden Lake, 30 miles south of Sandpoint, told CNN: "He has to be a racist, or he'd stay in Los Angeles." A swastika loomed above Butler's shoulder. "It's hypocritical for them to say they come up here for the birds and bees and trees. If this area was all non-white, you wouldn't find a police officer within a hundred miles of here," the Nazi said.

Aryan Nations also entered the picture when an anonymous caller to the Michael Jackson talk show, aired on KABC-AM in Los Angeles, claimed to have met with "Aryan Nations types" from his past on the Colombian cocaine circuit. The caller said that since serving a stiff prison sentence, he'd straightened out his life, and today runs a local construction company.

He told Jackson he'd overheard his past Nazi cohorts "planning the murder of Nicole Simpson." Jackson, flustered, quickly ditched him, babbling "it couldn't be." But without knowing more about the story, Jackson could not have possibly known whether or not the caller was relaying the truth. Jackson, who hails from South Africa, is presumably not a psychic. He refused to delve into the caller's story, which sounded straightforward enough, if a bit unsteady with nervousness.

KABC is an affiliate of Cap Cities, a company with a long history of collaboration with the CIA—the media conglomerate, in fact, is steered by former executives of the Mary Carter Paint Co., a CIA proprietary closely aligned with the Vatican's Maltese order. In the late 1960s, the company moved drugs into the U.S., primarily heroin and LSD, and laundered the proceeds through offshore accounts (Kruger).

The call to Michael Jackson was broadcast weeks before Mark Fuhrman's famed trip to northern Idaho, the beating heart of Aryan Nations. Jackson refused to entertain the possibility that the caller he ditched in a panic may have been an important eyewitness, one who might have decimated the prosecution's case.

And the Ippolito circle is chock-a-block with enforcers capable, with an assist from infiltrators in the LAPD, of framing Simpson.

Frankie Viserto, for example. Viserto, Joey 's lead hit-man, was an original member of New York's Purple Gang, an offshoot of the Genovese Family. The Purple Gang formed in the 1970s, named after the bootleggers of Prohibition-era Detroit. A 1979 file on the gang prepared by the Florida Department of Law Enforcement notes that they operated "in Florida and may be using this state as a base of operations," and were "committing gangland murders in Florida." At the time, they ran the largest heroin smuggling operation in the country.

Viserto, a suspect in the killing of Donald Aronow, is the leader of the Purple

Gang. He is a terrorist and gun-runner. In the past, he has worked with death squads in Guatemala, traditionally a bailiwick of the CIA. A gun once found at the site of the assassination of a Guatemalan official was traced to Frankie Viserto. The BATF considers him, according to one report, a "significant criminal." Angelo Wedra, a former cellmate, told police in 1977 that Viserto claimed to have killed 15 people. "Wedra learned that Frankie especially enjoyed torturing techniques," according to the report (Burdick).

In the past, Viserto has tormented his victims with knives (Goldman was tortured). He has threatened his enemies with decapitation (Nicole was beheaded). He is known to be one of a clutch of hit-men who'd be pleased to make a revenge hit for Joey or silence a troublesome witness, ala Nicole Brown-Simpson.

For those who refrain, "who else would have killed her?" there are other possibilities.

2: "Evidence of Conspiracy"

A thoughtful examination of the case, posted on the Net by a pair of college students during the first trial, raises more nagging questions than Johnny Cochran:

> In violation of policy, evidence remained in the processing room for three days before the first piece was booked in the secure ECU (electronic-controlled unit)—seventy to eighty police personnel have keys to the processing room. The evidence remained on a table top, and could be handled by anyone with access. The reckless processing room analysis of the evidence was 50% inconclusive, but still entered by June 15—in time for the first "summit" case evaluation meeting between prosecutors, serologists and detectives while the blood samples were still unbooked and laying about the evidence processing room.

"The blood drop on Nicole's back gate wondrously appears for collection on July 3, with no photo records of its existence on June 13 or June 14," better preserved than blood collected near the bodies.

"Possibly significant EDTA (blood preservative) discovery in Nicole blood on O.J.'s sock, as Harmon begrudgingly hinted at a 'glimmer of hope' for defense in his typically biased, bonehead, pompom girl manner." (Harmon is the protégé of Judge Lowell Jenson, a central participant in the "Alameda Mafia," a circle of corrupt, right-wing public officials recruited by the Justice Department in the early 1980s by Alameda's Edwin Meese. Jenson was the second-ranking official in the Justice Department under Meese.)

"Racist cop with special animus towards black men with white women. Unexplained DNA mix on steering wheel column: other than O.J., Nicole, or Goldman.

"The suppressed 'car testimonies' of Park and Kato suggest unexplained movement of vehicle(s) *after* O.J. departed for the airport....

"While witnesses are compelled to tell the 'whole truth,' the prosecution can only argue 'sufficient truth.' In that non-intersecting domain between 'sufficient truth' and 'whole truth' lies an opportunity to establish 'sufficient confusion' in a jury, grounded not merely in speculation but also in real facts left unappropriated by a recklessly and smugly contrived theory of the case" (Larson & Wilson).

Was it smugness that led the LAPD to leak that a "bloody ski-mask" had turned up, and a "blood-stained military-style entrenching tool?" Ten days later, police stumbled on the fact that there was no ski mask, no murder weapon. In the meantime, local propagandists on far-right talk radio had a field day convincing the public that Simpson was guilty.

Liberal doses of perjury eliminated obstacles on the path to a guilty verdict. Furman wasn't the only detective to misspeak under oath. One L.A. weekly newspaper charged criminalists Dennis Fung and Tom Lange with "CRIMINAL BEHAVIOR," noting that the corporate media, the LAPD and the D.A.'s office had failed to investigate them after "Simpson's defense team showed that Fung misrepresented the facts in his testimony about the collection of evidence at the murder scene and Simpson's house. Fung also testified that he altered original documents relating to the booking of evidence. In an apparent effort to run interference for Vannatter, Lange misrepresented the facts in his testimony about the department's requirements for booking blood evidence, claiming that there was a window of 24 hours. He also testified that he took evidence collected at the scene to his house. Not only have these actions gone uninvestigated, but Fung actually received a promotion during the course of the trial" (*L.A. View*).

Convicted felon Marianne Gurchis, prepared to testify she saw four suspicious men walking away from the Nicole Simpson's townhouse, was told by police officers: "We've got the case all sewn up." She called the district attorney's office. A detective placed her on hold, said he'd get back to her: "I'm talking to a psychic right now" (Hiscock).

From the first drop of the gavel, the case was lost in constant bickering and minute analysis of the evidence by attorneys on both sides of the bench. Any mention of the Mafia or CIA was a taboo observed by both sides. Johnnie

Cochran could have effortlessly impeached the credibility of Denise Simpson by producing the photo of her beaming from the arm of her beau, the "Animal." But then any mention of the syndicate could conceivably open the door to a melée of accusations and counteraccusations, disrupting Ito's tightly-regimented courtroom.

But if the police already had the the killer in custody.

Who broke into Robert Shapiro's office, forced open a locked filing cabinet and stole confidential papers related to the case?

Why did Faye Resnick skip town?

Who broke into Resnick's apartment to appropriate documents and photographs that could link her to the Simpsons?

Who left death threats for Ron Goldman's therapist, Dr. Jennifer Ameli, on her answering machine? (Who *knew* Goldman had a therapist?) Why was her office broken into? Why were only the files on Goldman stolen (*National Examiner*)?

Who hired the car-thieving William Wasz to monitor the movements of Nicole Brown-Simpson six months before the hit?

Who stole the slander suit filed in a Los Angeles courthouse against Marcia Clark during the "Trial of the Century?" Ted Chirac, author of *The Second Gun*, an examination of the RFK assassination, related the saga of the vanishing lawsuit to Dave Manning, a board member of the Citizens for Truth About the Kennedy Assassination, in April, 1996. "Midway through the Simpson trial," Manning says, "Juan Mercado, the son of a Spanish diplomat, was washing his car. He accidentally splashed some soap and water on a car parked next to his own. The driver of the car, an upright woman, approached. Juan tried to clean if off and apologized for the accident. She kept on him about messing up the car. He tried to calm her down, but she wouldn't let it go. She got so volatile that the police were called by somebody because she was getting out of hand. Juan decided to file a complaint against this woman, Marcia Clark. He filed a slander suit. A week later, Mercado's attorney attempted to examine the file on the case at the courthouse. He discovered that no complaint, no suit, had been filed, and couldn't understand what happened to it. It disappeared" (Manning).

The revelations bubbled up in the courtroom and the tabloid press. The "respectable" news outlets were too frequently caught out napping. A point of evidence as significant as Biblical transmutations of blood on a pair of socks should have been nailed down by journalists long before Matheson's uneasy appearance in the courtroom.

And even *in* the courtroom, key points raised by the defense were suppressed by the bench: "The O.J. Simpson civil trial opened Tuesday with a flurry of rulings that significantly restrict the defense's strategy of attacking the Los Angeles Police Department as a group of inept bunglers and corrupt, racist cops who sought to frame Simpson for murder." If anything else, the first trial demonstrated that the LAPD investigators assigned to the double murders were indeed "inept bunglers." They tromped through blood on the sidewalk, took half a day to call the coroner. At least one was a "racist cop." Ineptitude and racism were the foundation of Simpson's defense argument. "This is not a case about did the LAPD commit malpractice," said Fujasaki (Simon). There is no doubt the LAPD committed malpractice. Did it extend to the framing of O.J. Simpson?

3: The "Experts"

The tabloid cover photo of O.J. Simpson sporting a pair of Bruno Magli's was validated by the Rochester Institute of Technology. According to a CIA document dated October 16, 1975, the Agency had "certain relationships" with the Rochester Institute; they were described as "special," even "particular." The College of Graphic Arts and Photography received roughly $200,000 from the CIA in grants from 1966 to 1975. The school has been adamant in maintaining its relationship with the Agency despite the periodic protests from the faculty and students. M. Richard Rose, president of Rochester Tech, was forced to resign in 1991 after acknowledging that he secretly worked for the Agency while on leave. Trustees had a secret agreement that actually gave the CIA authority over the curriculum (Mann; Glaberson).

Political researcher Paul Ruiz in Washington notes that photographers Harry Scull and E.J. Flammer, "who took 30 photographs of O.J. on the same day that Scull took his photograph, have the same lawyer and the same agent. In addition, Robert Groden says they know each other. This is important, because Flammer has insisted all along that he is '*independent*' of Scull."

In the criminal trial, the Menlo Park, California engineering firm of Failure Analysis Associates (FAA) produced a computer-animated enactment of the Brentwood killings. Roger McCarthy, chief executive officer of FAA, described the experiment as "state of the art," "sophisticated"— but he told reporters that the computer simulation was wholly based on the work of forensics experts and the choreography of *actors*. He boasted that the company exercised "complete artistic control" over the project. But there was no need for the trappings of high technology—filming the actors would have produced the same results, and not cost the "hundreds of thousands of dollars" that McCarthy's company spent on four minutes of highly impressive, if superfluous digitized animation (Armstrong).

FAA's credibility has been an issue since the company's computer simulation of the Kennedy assassination as adopted by Gerald Posner in *Case Closed*, a book that strains to remove the onus of CIA involvement but is really one more study in disinformation, a rehash of cooked evidence rejected even by the Warren Commission. The book is larded with false quotations (Scott).

McCarthy arrived at the conclusion, "the victims were tortured before they died. There was a clear indication to deliver more than death" (Armstrong).

Another vaunted expert who testified in the Simpson case was Dr. Michael Baden, formerly head of the House Select Committee on Assassination's forensics pathology panel. Baden's testimony before the committee in 1978 was grossly deceptive, according to David Lifton in *Best Evidence*, a detailed examination of the John Kennedy autopsy by military doctors. Baden's conclusion, after analyzing the panel's medical reports, held that Kennedy had been struck by two shots from behind, supporting the Warren Commission's improbable findings. Baden's supporting evidence, Lifton discovered, had been "created" to agree with the Committee's predetermined judgment that Lee Harvey Oswald murdered John Kennedy.

Dr. Weir, another expert witness for the prosecution, began his testimony insisting that his statistical DNA analysis was unimpeachable. He was proven wrong upon cross-examination, despite his professorship in genetics at North Carolina State University and 100 peer-review articles to his credit. Dr. Weir has long been an FBI consultant. In the courtroom, he never testifies for the defense. His errors consistently favor the prosecution (Gard). These were sufficient grounds to strike much of Dr. Weir's testimony from the record.

FBI Agent Roger Marx, the EDTA "expert," was accused by Agent Whitehurst, the Bureau whistle-blower, of "manipulating" evidence in the Atlanta bombing case (Ruiz).

In the end, author Joe McGinniss chose not to write his book. He prompted outrage in the courtroom early on when Ito honored the "journalist" with a front-row seat. McGinniss is the same confabulator whose *Fatal Vision* echoed the government's framing of Dr. Jeffrey MacDonald for the murder of his wife and two daughters (Constantine). The MacDonald case, too, involved drugs. As a doctor, MacDonald had treated addicts assigned to Fort Bragg employed in the importation of China White from Vietnam in the body cavities of war casualties. MacDonald himself was the target of murder. He lived to be railroaded to prison by the U.S. Army. McGinniss's account protected the identities of Army and CIA officials linked to the scandal.

The Faye Resnick book is also redolent with the politics of assassination. Michael Viner, her publisher, once resided in Washington, D.C. and worked at Georgetown University's School of Foreign Service (*Los Angeles Times,* June 3, 1996), the very epitomé of the CIA's academic presence.

The passing connections to the Kennedy killings recur, and they are not the mark of Kismet.

The Nazi-Mafia Combination that ambushed American history in November, 1963 survives to continue urging the country toward open fascist rule. Each murder along the way makes the going a little easier. Nicole Simpson and Ron Goldman were claimed by an Octopus, and the creature continues to destroy anyone threatening its avaricious grasp on power and privilege.

Sources

Alan Abrahamson & Paul Lieberman, "LAPD Detective Gets 102 Years in Crime Spree," *Los Angeles Times* (Orange County edition), September 21, 1996, p. A-13.

Anonymous, "Run for Your Life," *National Examiner,* October 18, 1995, p. 12.

George Anastasia and John Way Jennings, "Motive in Venice Bodybuilder's Slaying a Mystery," *Santa Monica Evening Outlook* (originally published by the *Philadelphia Inquirer*), March 1, 1993, p. 1A. (On Ippolito and Lorenzo arrest.)

AP Release, "Attorney Denies Cowlings Connection to Drug Arrest," *Santa Monica Evening Outlook,* March 25, 1995.

David Armstrong, "Virtual Murder: Nicole Tape Debuts," *San Francisco Examiner,* March 31, 1995.

George R. Bender, Plaintiff-Appellant, v. CenTrust Mortgage Corporation, U.S. Court of Appeals, Eleventh Circuit, No. 92-4669, May 10, 1995.

John Bennett, "House Probes Charges of CIA Tie to Drug Lord," *Memphis Commercial Appeal,* October 4, 1990.

James Bolden, "Coroner's Office Rules Shooting of Mom a Homicide," *Los Angeles Sentinel,* February 3, 1994.

Joseph Bosco, interviewed by Paul Ruiz, June 7, 1997.

Thomas Burdick & Charlene Mitchell, *Blue Thunder: How the Mafia Owned and Finally Murdered Cigarette Boat King Donald Aronow* (New York: Simon & Schuster, 1990).

Rodney Campbell, *The Luciano Project: The Secret Wartime Collaboration of the Mafia and the U.S. Navy* (New York: McGraw Hill, 1977).

John Connolly, "Cafe Nostra," *Spy,* March 1994, pp. 62–68.

Alex Constantine, *Psychic Dictatorship in the U.S.A.* (Portland: Feral House, 1995).

"Declaration of Allen Cowlings," filed at the United States District Court for the Central District of California in Los Angeles, case no. CR-92-400-DMT (Exhibit 18), September 8, 1992.

Linda Deutch, "Defense Says State is Trying to 'Burn Up' Simpson DNA Sample" (AP Story), *Boston Globe,* August 24, 1994, p. 1.

Linda Deutch, "Nicole Simpson's Life is Assailed in Court," *Philadelphia Inquirer,* October 25, 1996, p. 1.

Edward Felsenthal, "Controversy Surrounds Lawyer F. Lee Bailey," *Wall Street Journal,* March 20, 1995, p. A-1.

FEC Report, "Individual Contributors to Newt Gingrich," January 1, 1979 to FEC, period ending June 30, 1994.

Ralph Frammolino and Henry Weinstein, "Delay in Notifying Coroner Hurt Simpson Case Probe," *Los Angeles Times,* September 17, 1994, p. A-1.

Donald Freed, telephone interview. Also, Donald Freed & Raymond P. Briggs, *Killing Time: The First Full Investigation* (New York: MacMillan, 1996).

Tony Frost, "How O.J. Trapped Nicole into Life of Cocaine," *The Star,* August 30, 1994, pp. 24–29.

Nancy Gard, "Dr. Weir's Background," alt. fan.OJ newsgroup, Delphi Internet Services, June 25, 1995.

Jacqueline Ginley and Bob Porterfield, "Cowlings Visited Woman's Home After Her Arrest," *Contra Costa Times,* March 25, 1995.

William Glaberson, "Rochester Institute will Maintain Controversial Ties with the C.I.A.," *New York Times,* November 24, 1991, p. A-46.

Jan Golab, "Blue Heaven," *Los Angeles Magazine,* June, 1995, pp. 66–74. (*"Mark Fuhrman is just the latest cop to head to north Idaho,"* Ockenfels found. *"Some even say the LAPD runs the 'secret' backwoods enclave."*)

Bruce Haring, "Too Fast to Live, Too Young to Die," *Los Angeles Reader,* June 30, 1995, pp. 8. (This feature dwells at length on Charles Minor's sexual conquests, and neglects to touch upon organized crime connections. The article does, when not reveling in Minor's philandering, shed light on the famed record promoter's financial and emotional decline.)

K. Harrell, "Nicole Murder was Mafia Drug Hit," *Globe,* March 21, 1995, pp. 40–41.

J. Hiscock, "Police Ignored Four Suspects in OJ Murder Case," *Daily Telegraph,* January 26, 1995, p. A-3.

Shawn Hubler and James Bates, "Streetwise Gumshoe to the Stars," *Los Angeles Times,* September 11, 1993, p. A-1.

Shawn Hubler, "Police Won't Be Charged in 1993 Shooting; Investigation: Woman was shot seven times in the back after reportedly lunging at officers with a knife on a hospital rooftop. Questions about the case remain," *Los Angeles Times,* September 29, 1994, p. B-1.

Walter Karabian, "Just Who Is Robert Kardashian Anyway," *Armenian Reporter,* October 21, 1995.

Howard Kohn, "The Hughes-Nixon-Lansky Connection," *Rolling Stone,* May 20,1976.

Henrik Kruger, *The Great Heroin Coup: Drugs, Intelligence & International Fascism* (Boston: South End Press, 1980).

Dave LaFontaine, "Nicole's Mystery Link to Nightclub Murder," *The Star,* October 11, 1994, p. 5.

Eric Larson and Michael Wilson, "Evidence of Conspiracy," SprintLink on-line communication network, May 13, 1995.

Hillel Levin, *Grand Delusions—The Cosmic Career of John DeLorean* (New York: Viking, 1983).

Paul Lieberman, "The Gang that Couldn't Shoot Straight," *Los Angeles Times Magazine,* February 21, 1993, p. 24.

Paul Lieberman, "Restauranteur Found Guilty in Drug Case," *Los Angeles Times,* February 27, 1993, p. B-3.

Paul Lieberman, "Last Loose End Wrapped Up in ZZZZ Best Fraud Case," *Los Angeles Times,* May 5, 1994, p. A-1.

Paul Lieberman and Leslie Berger, "Police Spy Unit was Rife with Risks, Temptations," *Los Angeles Times,* July 26, 1992, p. A-1.

David S. Lifton, *Best Evidence: Disguise and Deception in the Assassination of John F. Kennedy* (New York, MacMillan, 1980).

Robert J. Lopez and Jesse Katz, "Nicole Brown Anti-Abuse Charity Beset by Problems; Embarrassments include controversial donors, felony record of fired leader. Family cites growing pains." *Los Angeles Times,* July 7, 1995, p. A-1.

Jim Mann, "CIA Tries to Get Collegians to Perform Intelligence Jobs," *Los Angeles Times,* February 26, 1993, p. A-4.

Dave Manning, executive board member of CTKA, April 24, 1996.

John Marks, *The Search for the Manchurian Candidate: The CIA and Mind Control* (New York: Times Books, 1979).

Edward Medvene, et.al., "Motion of Defendent Joseph Ippolito for Release Pending Trial," on file at the United States District Court, Central District of California, case no. CR-92-400-DMT, September 10, 1992.

Dan Moldea, *Dark Victory: Ronald Reagan, MCA and the Mob,* (New York: Penguin, 1987).

Steven Lee Myers, "Richard E. Gerstein, Dead at 68; Prosecuted Key Watergate Figure," *New York Times,* April 27, 1992, p. D-12.

"Music Executive Slain in Malibu, Woman Held," (Charles Minor case) *Los Angeles Times,* March 20, 1995, p. B-1.

Jim Newton, "Simpson Private Eye is No Stranger to Big-Name Cases," *Los Angeles Times,* July 22, 1922, p. A-1.

"Ex-Chief of CenTrust Bank is Convicted on 68 Charges," *New York Times,* November 25, 1993, p. D-9.

L.A. View, "Criminal Behavior," January 5, 1996, p. 7.

Louis Nizer, *Catspaw: The Famed Trial Attorney's Heroic Defense of a Man Unjustly Accused* (New York: Donald I. Fine, Inc., 1992), pp. 52–53.

Kenneth B. Noble, "Simpson Trial Likely to Put a Tough Detective on Trial," *New York Times,* February 21, 1995, p. A-6.

Emanuel Parker, "SONJI DANESE TAYLOR: She's Become Obsession of White Artist Since Her Death," *Los Angeles Sentinel,* April 19, 1995.

David. L. Paul, Intervener v. Resolution Trust Corporation, U.S. Court of Appeals (Miami), Eleventh Circuit, Nos. 91-5408, 91-5035.

Stephen Pizzo, Mary Fricker and Paul Muolo, *Inside Job: The Looting of America's Savings and Loans* (New York: McGraw-Hill), 1989.

D. Reyes, "Nicole Simpson Foundation Gives Shelter $10,000," *Los Angeles Times,* July 17, 1995, p. A-17.

Charles Rappleye and Ed Becker, *All American Mafioso—The Johnny Rosselli Story* (New York: Doubleday, 1991).

Paul Ruiz, Washington, D.C.-based political researcher for Citizens for Truth About the Kennedy Assassination (CTKA), interview in Los Angeles, January 4, 1997.

Mike Rothmiller and Ivan G. Goldman, *L.A.'s Secret Police: Inside the LAPD Elite Spy Network* (New York: Pocket Books, 1992). (The last chapter details the shooting of Rothmiller by an arms and drug smuggler from Orange County. Though crippled, Rothmiller had to fight for a disability pension from the LAPD.)

"Trial Journal," *San Francisco Examiner,* March 23, 1995, SFE News Service.

Peter Dale Scott, "Case Closed or Oswald Framed?" *Prevailing Winds,* No. 1, 1995, p. 52.

Stephanie Simon, "Diverse Legal Team's Task: To Prove Simpson Guilty," *Los Angeles Times,* September 9, 1996, p. A-1.

Stephanie Simon, "Judge Restricts Simpson Defense as Civil Trial Opens," *Los Angeles Times,* September, 18, 1996.

Stephen Singular, *Legacy of Deception: An Investigation of Mark Fuhrman and Racism in the L.A.P.D.* (Los Angeles: Dove Books, 1995).

Peter Sinton and Kenneth Howe, "Feds to Question S.F. Banker in Bond Probe,"

San Francisco Examiner, September 25, 1996, p. A-1.

M.L. Stein, ""Who's Telling the Truth?" *Editor & Publisher,* vol. 127: February 19, 1994, pp. 27.

Gary Thompson and Steve Kanigher, "Search for the Tiger's Treasure," *Las Vegas Sun,* December 26, 1993, p. A-1.

U.S. v. Lorenzo et. al., case no. 92-400, U.S. Criminal Court Clerk's Office, Los Angeles, California.

H. Weinstein, "L.A. Lawyer to Defend Chief of Bosnian Serbs in Trial," *Los Angeles Times,* July 10, 1996, p. A-1.

Steve Wick, *Bad Company: Drugs, Hollywood and the Cotton Club Murder* (New York: Harcourt, Brace, Javonavich, 1990).

West Legal Directory, "Howard Weitzman" profile (Los Angeles: West Publishing Co., 1995).

Steve Tinney, "Mystery Man was Stalking Nicole," *The Star,* August 9, 1994, p. 22. (Photocopies of the notebook entries illustrate the story.)

Peter Truell, *False Profits: The Inside Story of BCCI, the World's Most Corrupt Empire* (Boston: Houghton Mifflin, 1992).

UPI News Service, "DeLorean's legal team—The 'Howard and Don Show,'" *San Francisco Chronicle,* August 17, 1984.

Jaxon Van Derbeken and Terri Hardy, "Tenacity of Lead Detective Praised—Investigator Lange Given Credit for Solving String of Tough Cases," *Los Angeles Daily News,* July 8, 1994, p. 20.

Mike Walker, "I Fear I'll be Murdered," *National Enquirer,* September 6, 1994, p. 10.

ADDENDUM: THE CIA/MAFIA REDUX

EX-CON, O.J. BOND INSTANTLY AT GOLF TOURNEY
MIAMI HERALD, MAY 19, 1997

O.J. Simpson's golfing buddy in the recent charity tournament on Key Biscayne: Steve Thiele, 34, an ex-con on parole.

Thiele, once a bodyguard who ran with the Miami River Cops, now works for a courier service. He is a six-day-a-week golfer who shoots in the mid-70s. He showed up—Pings in his bag—at the Crandon Park course, hoping to meet The Juice.

"I started hitting balls and making small talk. I asked him if he needed a caddy or any type of security. He told me the way he sees me hitting, he'd like to get me on his team."

Thiele says he couldn't afford the entry fee. "He said, 'Don't worry, I'll take care of it.'"

Thiele told Simpson he had done hard time—6 ¹/₂ years—in federal prison for making a threatening phone call to a businessman who owed him money— and for beating up Ray Corona, a former bank president convicted in a marijuana smuggling case. Thiele used to be Corona's bodyguard.

Simpson invited Thiele to play with him in L.A. "He gave me his address and his phone number and told me to definitely call."

But first, Thiele says, he must get permission—from his parole officer.

From "Darkness at Sunshine State," in James Ring Adams, *The Big Fix: Inside the S&L Scandal* (New York: John Wiley & Sons, 1990), pp. 125–126:

Ray [Corona] did buy his own bank, the Sunshine State Bank in South Miami. It took two years for the FDIC to close down this bank, even after a federal indictment called it "part of a vertically integrated drug conspiracy," and Ray and his father were convicted.

As the government later proved in two protracted trials, Tony Fernendez provided funds for Ray Corona's bank ventures.... Tony Fernandez fled to the United States from Cuba in 1962 and survived for the next 14 years through low-paying odd jobs. He measured drapes, stamped circuit boards for personal computers, and, for two years, did contract work for the Central Intelligence Agency. In 1976, a friend brought him to meet a sinister figure named José Alvero-Cruz, and Tony's fortunes took a dramatic turn. Alvero Cruz was considered the largest marijuana smuggler in Miami."

From *Miami Herald* archives:

EX-BANK OFFICER ON TRIAL
DECEMBER 18, 1986

Ray L. Corona, former chairman of the now-defunct Sunshine State Bank, stood trial Wednesday for making false statements and illegally receiving nine weapons, ranging from shotguns to precision target pistols, that were shipped interstate....

SMUGGLER TELLS HOW HE INVESTED IN BANK
JUNE 3, 1987

Jose Antonia Fernandez took the witness stand in federal court Tuesday and with businesslike resolve described how former Sunshine State Bank chairman Ray Corona helped him buy 51 percent of the bank....

CORONAS
OCTOBER 22, 1987

Ray Corona, the sophisticated South Miami banker who teamed with a notorious marijuana smuggler to buy the Sunshine State Bank, was sent to prison for 20 years Wednesday.

Corona's father Rafael, 66, also was sentenced by U.S. District Judge James W. Kehoe to five years in prison and fined $10,000. He was convicted on a lesser charge in the bank purchase....

MAN IS ARRESTED IN STORE BOMBING
DECEMBER 23, 1989

Federal agents have arrested a man for allegedly bombing Classy Formal Wear and then trying to extort $80,000 with further bomb threats. Steve Thiele, of 1717 N. Bayshore Dr., was arrested by agents of the Bureau of Alcohol, Tobacco and Firearms on Thursday night and charged with bombing the store....

BODYBUILDER CONVICTED OF BEATING WITNESS
AUGUST 3, 1990

A federal jury convicted a bodybuilder with ties to Miami River Cops on Thursday of beating up banker-turned-racketeer Ray Corona in a courthouse scuffle two months ago....

FOUR RIVER COPS HAVE BEEN RELEASED FROM PRISON
AUGUST 5, 1992

At least four of the 20-plus Miami River Cops sentenced to serious prison time in the late 1980s for their roles in a huge drug corruption scandal are already out. They are: Rodolfo "Rudy" Arias, Ricardo Aleman, Luis Batista and Regino "Reggie" Capiro....

THE GOOD SOLDIER

Timothy McVeigh's Rise From "Robotic" Soldier to Mad Bomber

Sometimes the minority cannot prevail except by force; then it must determine whether the prevalence of its will is worth the price of using force.
— William F. Buckley, Jr.

The popular conception was spun by the press corps like a shallow clay urn: Timothy McVeigh, the volatile minuteman, was so bitter after failing to make the Army's "elite" Special Forces, so stuffed full of paramilitary dogma and the froth of *The Turner Diaries,* that he vented his rage on the Alfred Murrah Federal Building in Oklahoma City.

The popular conception oversimplifies. Captain Terry Guild, McVeigh's former platoon leader, told reporters that the failure to become a Green Beret left the Iraq War veteran "upset. Not angry. Just very, very disappointed."

McVeigh's sister testified at the closed grand jury hearing that he worked for a special forces unit involved in criminal activity. He reportedly trained at the School of the Americas, the CIA's academy for death squads.

As a civilian, Timothy McVeigh clung to the trappings of the military. In 1992, he joined the National Guard of Tonawanda, New York. He took a job with Burns International Security Services in Buffalo. McVeigh was assigned to the security detail at Calspan, a Pentagon contractor that conducts classified research in advanced aerospace rocketry and electronic warfare.

Al Salandra, a spokesman for Calspan, told reporters that McVeigh was "a model employee." His fellow enlistees describe him as a gun-toting, adrenal-crazed cartoon soldier. In the Army, he demonstrated a willingness to carry out orders, *any* orders. He trained on his own time while other soldiers languished in their bunks or caroused at the PX.

"He was *real* different," Todd Regier, a plumber, told the *Boston Globe.* "Kind of cold. He was almost like a *robot.*"

Within a few months, his manager planned on promoting McVeigh to the supervisory level, but he abruptly resigned.

McVeigh had "more pressing matters to tend to," the *Globe* reported. His bitterness "was becoming directed at a much larger, more *ubiquitous* enemy. "

It was in Buffalo that McVeigh's rage peaked. He complained that federal agents had implanted him with a microchip and left him with an unexplained scar on his posterior. It was painful, he winced, to sit on the chip.

It's conceivable, given the current state of the electronic mind control art, a biocybernetic Oz over the black budget rainbow, that McVeigh had been drawn into an experimental project, that the device was the real McCoy. Ironically enough, McVeigh's contention that he'd been implanted and tracked was laughed off by most sensible, media-fed folk, even as an electronics firm in Tampa, Florida—Pro-Tech Monitoring, Inc. in Tampa, Florida—introduced a satellite-tracking system, SMART (or Satellite Monitoring and Remote Tracking device) for use by the criminal justice system, a "patent-protected, space-age device that tracks and continuously monitors offenders, stalkers and provides advance warning for victims."

Jeff Camp, who worked as a guard with McVeigh in upstate New York after high school, told *Newsweek* that John Doe One was "just a very strange person. It was like he had two different personalities."

The press has long ignored the rise of mind control operations and technology, but electronic monitoring of the brain has been perfected in research laboratories more secretive than the military science units that once slipped isotopes to crippled children in their oatmeal.

The generals play it close to their armored vests, but the miniature implantable monitor was declassified long ago. Sandia National Laboratories in Albuquerque, New Mexico markets a sensor implant sealed inside a "hermetic biocompatible package" that operates on a tiny power coil, complete with a programmable sensor and telemetry circuits. Sandia's sales literature notes that the implant design "is founded on technology originally developed for weapons."

From the Pentagon's electromagnetic arsenal came Timothy McVeigh, by his own account obsessed with visions of Waco and Ruby Ridge. If McVeigh was in fact a subject of electromagnetic harassment, he marched in step with a small army of glassy-eyed felons.

No Programmed Killer's Hall-of-Fame would be complete without a bust of Dennis Sweeney, the student activist who shot Allard Lowenstein, the civil rights and anti-war activist. Lowenstein was suspected by many of working for the CIA. A Yale graduate, he marched in the Freedom Summer of 1964 in Mississippi, campaigned for Adlai Stevenson and Robert Kennedy. Yet he was a close friend of William F. Buckley, the garrulous CIA propagandist of PBS fame and Lowenstein's conservative counterpart. He qualified for the Nixon enemies list, yet associated with the bund of Plumbers occupying the White House. Lowenstein ran the National Student Association before the CIA officially took it over.

"Lowenstein," the *New Republic* reported, "for several years attempted to prove that a great conspiracy had plotted the deaths of John and Robert Kennedy and Martin Luther King Jr., and was also responsible for his own political downfall ... a force of evil that would explain his own and his movement's decline."

Sweeney, who marched with Lowenstein in Mississippi, shot his mentor seven times at Rockefeller Center. He did not flee. The assassin sat down, lit a cigarette and waited for police to arrive.

He maintained that the CIA, with Lowenstein's help, had implanted him with a telemetric brain device fifteen years earlier and made his life an unbearable torment. "Voices" were transmitted through his dental work, he said, and he attempted to silence them by filing down his false teeth. Sweeney blamed CIA controllers for his uncle's heart attack and the assassination of San Francisco mayor George Mosconé.

The murders of Mosconé and City Supervisor Harvey Milk *did* indeed have earmarks of mind control. Dan White, the "Twinkie" assassin, had been a paratrooper in the 173rd Airborne Division, in which capacity he served a tour of duty in Vietnam. He was discharged from Fort Bragg in 1967, and returned to San Francisco to join the police department. White settled in Sausolito, tooled around in a Porsche and generally lived far beyond his means. In 1972, he gave it all up and took an extended vacation since known as White's "missing year." He broke all contact with friends and family, kept no records of the trip, purchased no travel tickets, did not use a credit card. He later accounted for his mystery year by explaining that he'd worked a stint as a security guard in Alaska.

Back in San Francisco, White joined the fire department where his temper tantrums were an embarrassment to co-workers, though his work record was without blemish. In his run for the Board of Supervisors, he spoke as if he was "programmed," according to Stan Smith, a local labor leader. During Board sessions, White was known to slip into spells of silence punctuated by goose-stepping struts around the supervisors' chambers.

The murders of Moscone and Milk were accomplished with illegal hollow-point bullets. After Milk's body was cremated, the ashes were enshrined at his prior direction with bubble bath, signifying his homosexuality, and several packets of Kool-Aid. The confection was Milk's hint, specified in the will he'd revised a week before the shootings, shortly after the fall of the People's Temple (founded in San Francisco), that the murder was related to the mass CIA mind control experiment that ended with the destruction of 1,200 largely black subjects in Guyana.

"I can be killed with ease," Milk noted in a poem written the month he died. "I can be cut right down." In his revised will, he wrote: "Let the bullets that rip through my brain smash every closet door in the country."

Allegations of classified federal mind control operations have cropped up repeatedly, erupting from hidden pockets of "national security" labyrinths.

In 1984, Francis Fox of Coral Gables, Florida, the owner of a prestigious bridal shop, announced she'd been subjected to traumatic mind control experiments by CIA and military psychiatrists. She spoke to reporters for the *St. Petersburg Times* for three hours. Her story,

MILITARY CONTROLS MY MIND, WOMAN SAYS

was published on March 6, 1994. "Fox said her father was a Cuban-American," the *Times* reported. "He went into the U.S. military and was stationed in Panama, Germany and several U.S. bases, including MacDill in Tampa."

She was tormented for a year, while her father was visiting Cuba. She also was subjected to ritualized trauma by her father on instructions from the CIA to fragment her personality and "deposit the painful memory with several alter personalities."

Five months after the bombing in Oklahoma, freeway sniper Christopher Scalley claimed to take direction from "electronic appliances," as reported by the *San Francisco Chronicle* on August 19, 1995:

WHY EVIDENCE ON I-80 SNIPER LANGUISHED—
CHP WAS GIVEN SUSPECT'S LICENSE NUMBER IN JUNE

Auburn, Placer County—The California Highway Patrol received information almost two months ago leading to the man arrested Thursday in the Interstate-80 sniping spree, but an official acknowledged yesterday that the CHP did not pass it on to local investigators.

David Morillas of Loomis said his wife Carla wrote down the license number of a truck that passed them after the side rear window of their car was blown away, showering their sleeping 5-year-old son with glass in what is now thought to have been the sniper's first attack, in Citrus Heights, a Sacramento suburb, on June 27.

"We kept thinking that the CHP was checking into it," Morillas said.

He said yesterday that after his car window shattered, he saw a red Toyota pickup suddenly slow down and shift into the right lane on the roadway.

Morillas said he slowed down alongside the truck and yelled through an open window. "I was shouting at him. 'Did you see what happened to my window?' ... Finally, he said, 'I didn't see nothing.' He was kind of talking weird, mumbling. I couldn't understand him."

The tie-in between the June 27 shooting and the other fourteen sniper attacks was not made until this week, when Carla Morillas spoke to sheriff's officers. The officers discovered that the license plate number she had reported matched the tag number of their suspect, Christopher Shaw Scalley, 48, of Applegate, who was arrested Thursday.

According to arrest documents, Scalley told Placer County authorities that he had been receiving messages via radio waves and electronic appliances, and had heard voices telepathically from passing vehicles. Scalley had been arrested before for the sale of controlled substances and for driving under the influence. Scalley was booked for investigation of nine felony counts of malicious discharge of a firearm at an occupied vehicle, Placer County Sheriff Ed Bonner said.

The other six reported attacks remain under investigation.

Victims in the shootings identified Scalley from a photo lineup, sheriff's Captain Steve Reader said yesterday.

Scalley had been missing since his home was searched Tuesday. He was spotted Thursday by a television news crew in his red pickup outside a home in Carmichael, where a friend of Scalley's reportedly committed suicide Wednesday.

Placer County deputies were contacted and they arrested Scalley a short distance away.

Authorities said Thursday that they had no further information on the apparent suicide of Larry Don Shores, 58, who died from a gunshot wound to the head after visiting with Scalley at his Carmichael home Wednesday.

Shores was not considered a suspect in the sniper attacks. Authorities said they do not know if Scalley was connected to Shores' death.

There were 15 reported sniper attacks on buses, motor homes and other vehicles, mostly along a two-mile stretch of I-80 between Applegate and Clipper Gap in the Sierra Nevada foot-hills about 40 miles east of Sacramento.

Was Timothy McVeigh a Remote Mind Control Subject?

Advances in 'overhead' sensors—satellites and UAVs (Unmanned Aerospace Vehicles) included—will create opportunities not only to detect targets but to track them as they move. In [General] Fogelman's view, "this is kind of a revolution in warfare."

—General Ronald R. Fogelman, *Jane's Defense Weekly*

Presumably, research will continue to increase the effectiveness of psychological techniques for controlling human behavior. But we think it is unlikely that psychological techniques alone will be sufficient to adjust human beings to the kind of society that technology is creating.

—Unabomber's Manifesto, sec. 149

McVeigh's rage at a target "larger" and "more ubiquitous" than the Army was stoked at Calspan within a year of his Special Forces exam.

Calspan and electromagnetic mind control both have roots at the same Ivy League institution—Cornell University, Ithaca, New York. Calspan was founded in 1946 as Cornell Aeronautical Laboratory. Cornell was also the contract base of the CIA's "Human Ecology Fund," a gushing fount of financial support for classified brain experimentation at the country's leading universities.

Cornell Aeronautical was reorganized in 1972 and renamed Calspan. Six years later, the firm was acquired by Arvin Industries. Recently, Arvin-Calspan merged with Space Industries International (SII), a commercial space-flight venture based in Texas. During the Reagan-Bush era, SII expanded from a staff of 33 to over 2,700 employees.

Timothy McVeigh was assigned to the conglomerate's Advanced Technology Center in Buffalo, NY (Calspan ATC). ATC sales literature boasts a large energy shock tunnel, radar facilities and "a radio-frequency (RF) simulator facility for evaluating electronic warfare techniques."

One Calspan research lab specializes in microscopic engineering.

Calspan literature boasts that ATC employs "numerous world renowned engineers" on "the cutting edge" of science.

Human tracking and monitoring technology are well within Calspan's sphere of pursuits. The company is instrumental in REDCAP, an Air Force electronic warfare system that winds through every Department of Defense facility in the country. A Pentagon release explains that REDCAP "is used to evaluate the effectiveness of electronic-combat hardware, techniques, tactics and concepts."

The system "includes closed-loop radar and data links at RF manned data fusion and weapons control posts." REDCAP is managed by the Development Test Center's 46th Test Wing at Florida's Eglin Air Force Base.

The "ubiquitous" enemy that obsessed McVeigh in Buffalo made its presence known—possibly through a national microwave system like REDCAP—the week before the bombing in Oklahoma City. One Patriot computer newsboard claimed that a disembodied, rumbling, low-frequency hum had been heard across the country the week of the bombing. Past hums in Taos, NM, Eugene and Medford, OR, Timmons, Ontario and Bristol, UK were most definitely (despite specious official denials) attuned to the auditory pathways.

The RF hum in Eugene, Oregon in March, 1978 was so powerful that it caused headaches and nosebleeds. Nobel Prize laureate Robert O. Becker has noted that a low-frequency Naval communications line has its terminus near Eugene, Oregon. The Federal Communications Commission reported that the source of the EM signal was tiny Dixon, California (population 10,000), lying midway between Davis and Vacaville, home of the notorious prison and its Maximum Psychiatric Diagnostic Unit, designed by Brown & Root, a site of documented CIA mind control experiments on prisoners, often as a form of punishment.

The Air Force is among Calspan's leading clients, and Eglin AFB has farmed key personnel to the company. The grating irony—recalling McVeigh's contention he'd been implanted with a telemetry chip—is that the Instrumentation Technology Branch of Eglin Air Force Base is currently engaged in the tracking of mammals with subminiature telemetry devices. According to an Air Force press release, the biotelemetry chip transmits on the upper S-band (2318 to 2398 MHz), with up to 120 digital channels.

"Built onto this tiny device," the release boasts, "are programmable capabilities ranging from frequency, transmission mode, input scaling and signal conditioning. The Armament Directorate's Instrumentation Technology Branch is currently pursuing the use of subminiature telemetry to transmit data related to dolphin research."

Monitoring dolphins as they swim through the sea is an unclassified scientific pursuit. The monitoring and controlling of humans has been, for forty years, a highly classified specialty avidly studied by the CIA and military. And brain telemetering systems are but a subset of the Pentagon's "non-lethal" arsenal. The dystopian implications were explored by *Defense News* for March 20, 1995:

NAVAL RESEARCH LAB ATTEMPTS TO MELD NEURONS AND CHIPS
STUDIES MAY PRODUCE ARMY OF "ZOMBIES"

Future battles could be waged with genetically engineered organisms, such as rodents, whose minds are controlled by computer chips engineered with living brain cells.... The research, called Hippocampal Neuron Patterning, grows live neurons on computer chips.

"This technology that alters neurons could potentially be used on people to create zombie armies," Lawrence Korb, a senior fellow at the Brookings Institution, said.

The executive suites at SII and Calspan are another pocket of the military elite that jealously squanders certain advances in science and technology—the type with severe human rights implications.

The president of SII is former space shuttle pilot Joseph P. Allen, whose early accomplishments included a Fulbright scholarship to Germany (1959) and nuclear research at Brookhaven National Laboratory (1963–67), recently under investigation by the Department of Energy for conducting secret radiation experiments on human subjects. Dr. Allen was recruited by NASA in 1967. He trained at Vance Air Force Base in Oklahoma. He has also served as staff consultant to the President's Council on International Economic Policy, and was a NASA assistant administrator for legislative affairs (1975–78).

From the "mammal tracking" folk at Eglin AFB hails Richard Covey, a former astronaut who has flown four shuttle missions and taken five spacewalks, currently SII's director of business development. Covey, the fighter hawk, served two tours in Vietnam and flew 339 combat missions. An Air Force press release notes that his immediate postwar assignment was to Eglin AFB, where he was joint director for electronic warfare testing of the F-15 Eagle.

Another military scientist at Calspan, Paul Brodnicki, chaired the technical program at a closed conference on electronic warfare simulations held in February, 1994 at the US Army Research Lab in Adelphi, Maryland. Topics on the itinerary included *"off-board Radio Frequency Self-Protection."*

Calspan places much research emphasis on bioengineering and artificial intelligence. In May, 1995, Lames Llinas of the Buffalo division gave a talk at the Navy Center for Applied Research in Artificial Intelligence in Washington, D.C. While making his rounds at Calspan, perhaps Tim McVeigh picked up a company newsletter that discussed the work of Cliff Kurtzman, a graduate of UCLA and MIT's Space Systems Lab, and a "team leader" in the R&D of artificial intelligence (Calspan pioneered the field in the 1950s) and telerobotics.

Besides the Air Force and NASA, the firm is a ranking subcontractor for Sentar, Inc., an advanced science and engineering firm capable, according to company literature, of creating artificial intelligence systems. Sentar's customers include the U.S. Army Space and Strategic Defense Command, the Advanced Research Projects Agency, Rockwell International, Teledyne, Nichols Research Corp. and TRW.

All of this is to say that it is technically feasible that McVeigh had been implanted with a telemetry chip.

The "guilt by association" prize goes to retired Brigadier General Benton Partin of the USAF, who laid responsibility for the Oklahoma bombing on "*Leftists*" conducting a "psycho-political operation going on at the present time against the 'Christian Right' bogeyman." The payoff, Partin insisted darkly, was a propaganda victory for "a world commonwealth of independent states" plotting to "criminalize the patriotic support of Constitutional rights."

The press ridiculed anyone contradicting the FBI's version of events, belittled those who argued that the bombing might be a conspiracy—with the sole exception of Brig. Gen. Partin, who called a one hour press conference at the National Press Club in Washington, D.C. on June 15. The conference was attended by *over 100 reporters* representing *every* major broadcast, newspaper and wire service, independent news firm and the foreign media.

But then Brig. Gen. Partin was not exactly a disinterested party. He served 31 years in the Air Force, in the research, design, testing and management of weapons development. He was commander of the Air Force Armament Technology Laboratory. He boasted that he held authority over *all* advanced weapons concepts R&D'd by the Air Force and its high-tech contractors—which would, of course, include Calspan.

But CIA observers everywhere choked when CNN announced that a psychological trauma team, mustered by the American Psychological Association, would converge in Oklahoma City to treat survivors of the explosion and the victims' families—led by none other than Dr. Louis Jolyon West of UCLA's Neuropsychiatric Institute, the breeding ground of some of the most necrotizing Dr. Strangeloves in the mind control business. Alumni emeritus of the Institute include Dr. Ross Adey, a former NASA brain scientist with much experience collaborating with the Paperclip doctors who expatriated to the U.S. after the war.

Dr. West is a creation of the Agency's mind control fraternity. Among other totalitarian projects, he has studied the use of drugs as "adjuncts to interpersonal manipulation or assault," and employed pioneers in the field of remote electronic brain experimentation at UCLA.

West has recommended to federal officials that drugs be used to control "bothersome" segments of the population:

> This method, foreseen by Aldous Huxley, has the governing element employing drugs selectively to manipulate the governed in various ways. In fact, it may be more convenient and perhaps even more economical to keep the growing numbers of chronic drug users (especially of the hallucinogens) fairly isolated and also out of the labor market, with its millions of unemployed.
>
> To society, the communards with their hallucinogenic drugs are probably less bothersome—and less expensive—if they are living apart than if they are engaging in alternative modes of expressing their alienation, such as active, organized, vigorous political protest and dissent.

The Lost Tribes of Israel Meet Frankenstein

Ah, distinctly I remember,
it was in bleak December,
And each separate dying member
wrought a mess upon the floor.
Eagerly I wished the morrow,
for it was then that I would borrow
A pick-up truck and without sorrow,
tote the sorry carcasses of this war.
>   —Linda Thompson

If McVeigh bore a microchip, he was certainly not alone. His rambles would be tracked by remote sensors and receivers, and he would be but one of an unpolled segment of the population that has fallen under the classified federal electromagnetic mind control push. "Classified" but no mystery to victims of sadistic CIA/DoD experimentation and harassment. At present, there at least three national organizations of victims and survivors in the U.S. alone. In past mind control operations—the killings of Robert Kennedy, Allard Lowenstein and John Lennon, among others—operatives were placed in the path of the subject to program his thinking and urge him through a self-incriminating maze to the fatal act.

Afterwards, intelligence operatives (often a psychiatrist) may step forward to hypnotically deprogram the subject.

A cover-up proves the crime and raises the identities of perpetrators into

THE GOOD SOLDIER

relief. After the Oklahoma bombing, "country" lawyer Stephen Jones was handed McVeigh's case. If McVeigh was involved, Jones asked reporters, "Is he a
'Manchurian Candidate?' Is he a *patsy*?"

Stephen Jones may never publicly resolve the question. He took the case after
both of his legal predecessors were run off by death threats. Jones stepped forward to represent John Doe One. He said he had no qualms about lynch-mob
reprisals. He also claimed to have no conflicts of interest in the case. But Jones
is not the simple backwoods lawyer he affects to be.

In 1964, he was a legal assistant to Richard Nixon. Jones "stayed in touch."
He was among the "honored," he boasts, to be graced with an invitation to
Nixon's funeral in 1994.

The Nixon road to high office was paved with political assassinations. In a
1973 *Ramparts* story, political researcher Peter Dale Scott offered: "what links the
scandal of Watergate to the assassination in Dallas is the increasingly ominous
symbiosis between U.S. intelligence networks and the forces of organized crime."
The Watergate hearings suppressed critical evidence that would have opened old
wounds—did not, for example, explore the CIA backgrounds of Howard Hunt
(death squad activity and political coups in South America) or J. Gordon Liddy
(a hit-man on the White House payroll who proposed kidnapping campus radi-
cals, today the second most popular radio talk show host in the country) or neo-
Nazis entering the country from Munich (via Young Americans for Freedom, an
all American Nazi front organization), drug running, or a host of capital crimes
infinitely more serious than a routine wiretap or Nixon's Milk Fund.

The Watergate Committee also neglected to delve into Nixon's connections
to a score of CIA, FBI, Mafia and military intelligence pariahs. They and their
recruits are currently trooping along with the Nazi underground, propagandizing the militias with "New World Order" rants designed to incite "conservative"
rage with the usual ethnic and political scapegoats of organized fascism.

Congress, the Pentagon and sundry political entities still crawl with right-
wing politicians who have struck up an alliance with Nazi movements.

Time magazine reported on May 1, 1995 that George Nethercutt, "the giant-
slayer Congressman [who succeeded House Speaker Tom Foley as a Washington
State representative]," drew strength from radio shows that had callers hollering
about sightings of black helicopters and UN plots to set up a secret compound
in the state. In neighboring Idaho, Helen Chenoweth up-ended an environ-
mentalist Democratic incumbent in part by saying that the sole endangered
species on the planet was the "white Anglo-Saxon male." Ms. Chenoweth, upon
winning the election, equated environmentalism with Marxism and defended

257

Samuel Sherwood, leader of the U.S. Militia Organization, who told followers far and wide to know their legislators, because some day they might be forced to "blow their faces off."

Anne Fox, Idaho's superintendent of education, won the office with an assist from the state's 1,000 militia members. The victory was tarnished, however, when it emerged that her campaign manager and chief deputy, Terry Haws, had been charged in Alaska for giving drugs to a minor in exchange for sexual favors.

Another Patriot booster is Don Rogers, a California state senator who has shared the podium with the likes of former Klansman Louis Beam. His first political act in Sacramento was the introduction of a measure opposing the formation of a global government controlled by the United Nations.

Four leading Republican state senators backed the bill.

Larry Pratt, a Virginia state legislator, is a thumping anti-Communist. He has run with anti-insurgent movements in Guatemala and the Philippines. In 1990 he published *Armed People Victorious,* a sentimentalization of death squads, or "the people's militias." He calls for these same groups to fight the domestic "drug war."

A right-wing extremist in Colorado's state senate, Charles Duke, is running a national campaign for state legislatures to pass states' rights resolutions.

It stands to reason that Aryan Nation's leader Richard Butler, at a news conference in July 1995, enthused that the Republican Party is "waking up." Butler said he was particularly taken with California governor and frustrated presidential candidate Pete Wilson for supporting the University of California Board of Regents' decision to overturn affirmative action in admissions and hiring.

Proponents of the Beltway's "Republican Revolution," engineered by propaganda assaults to occur midway through President Clinton's first term, invited the Patriots to present their case publicly after the Oklahoma blast. Some on the Beltway have abetted the most volatile extremists linked to the Patriot movement.

In August 1995, for example, *Mother Jones* ran a feature story on the creepings of "law-and-order" Republican Phil Gramm. In his bid for the Oval Office, Gramm has scolded Clinton for overturning minimum mandatory sentencing for drug pushers. But upon arriving in Washington in 1980, he was "petitioned for help by the family of federal inmate Bill Doyle, a white, middle-class drug dealer. Doyle had served a total of fewer than seven years in jail—and less than half of his latest sentence—on three adult and eight juvenile offenses, many of which involved narcotics, guns or explosives. What did Gramm do? He lobbied long and hard to [free] Doyle. Instead of pursuing information that might have exposed the ammunition sales, Gramm had it excluded from a parole hearing."

Gramm's sudden attack of altruism was prompted by a letter that Doyle wrote to his brother Jim—a Pentagon official—pleading for aid. Jim Doyle turned to a neighbor, Mary Fae Kamm, an employee in the senator's office. The staff wrote letters of support for the accused, and went so far as to expunge Doyle's criminal files of serious felonies, including a charge of "possessing a bomb."

Doyle admits freely that he has engaged in the sale of weapons stolen from the Army by militiamen "armed with anti-tank weapons, grenades, rocket launchers, the whole show."

Gramm offered the convict taxpayer funds to start up an electronics company. Upon his release, Doyle "devoted that electronics business to helping drug dealers guard their operations against the police. Meanwhile, he opened three new drug franchises, and helped his gun-running accomplice conceal firearms from the cops."

This is the same law-and-order candidate who has set out to "remake the criminal justice system in America." He has a vision ... of slave labor. At the annual NRA convention in Phoenix earlier this year, Gramm proposed "decriminalizing prison labor" by converting "every federal prison in this country into a mini-industrial park. I want prisoners to work ten hours a day, six days a week,"

Collaborations between populist politicians and extreme-right militants (The Reichswehr) gave rise to the Third Reich. Another familiar pattern is the mingling of political vigilantés and enlisted men, and a thriving black market in armaments boosted from military bases. Shawn Helmer, a sergeant at Fort Lewis, Washington, testified that he loaded a truck with anti-tank rocket launchers and an assortment of guns looted from a local base, and drove to Florida where he planned to sell them to some of Lt. Col. Oliver North's political mercenaries. Helmer was arrested by the BATF.

Ironically, by stockpiling arms against military intrusions of government, the right wing plays into the hands of the defense establishment that markets them and invites repressive tactics. One Patriot group went so far as to hijack a TOW missile from a military convoy and attempted to blow up the Southern Poverty Law Center with it. And a month after the destruction in OKC, *Time* reported on the conviction of two firebrands from the Minnesota Patriot's Council for "planning to use a lethal biological weapon against U.S. marshals and IRS agents. Federal prosecutors are going after other members of the right-wing military group. In doing so, they hope to stop the spread of ricin, an extract of castor oil, which can *kill in minutes* if ingested, inhaled or absorbed through the skin. According to trial testimony, Patriot's Council members discussed poisoning U.S. agents by placing ricin on doorknobs."

PART II
"Hell has Victories": The Deep Politics of the Oklahoma Bombing

On April 27, 1995, the Knight-Ridder newswire announced:

WEEKS BEFORE OKLAHOMA, THREAT PUT UTILITIES ON ALERT

The U.S. Marshal's Service, a full month before the bombing, issued a warning that "Islamic terrorists" were planning to attract media attention by launching "suicide" assaults on federal buildings and installations. The memo was wired to federal courthouses nationwide. On April 23, the Carthage, Texas *Penula Richmond* published a story on Norma Smith, an employee of the courthouse across the street from the Alfred Murrah Building. Ms. Smith detailed how she arrived at work on the 19th at 7:45 AM and found a bomb squad in the parking lot between the two buildings. The spectacle was observed by other courthouse employees perplexed by the commotion.

A haunting moment of April 19, 1995 was the execution of Richard Wayne Snell in Arkansas. Among the charges filed against Snell was participation in a 1983 plot to blow up the federal office building in Oklahoma City. The *San Francisco Chronicle* reported in April 1995 that this was the very same day "on which Richard Wayne Snell, an Oklahoma native and alleged member of the white supremacist group called The Order, was executed for his part in a conspiracy to murder federal officials."

"Snell," the *Denver Post* reported, "repeatedly predicted that there would be a bombing or an explosion the day of his death."

The Militia of Montana rallied to defend the Nazi martyr, "a Patriot to be executed by The Beast." The Militia's national network of faxes and web pages were flooded with right-wing battle cries against the "liberal" justice system that had condemned the Patriot to death. From his own prison cell in Varner, Arkansas, the doomed Nazi distributed his own newsletter, *The Seekers*, the trumpet of the "war to establish righteousness."

Snell felt no remorse for the killing of a businessman and a black state trooper. Nevertheless, he had an arm-banded "spiritual adviser," the haughty Robert G. Millar, the leader of a heavily-armed apocalyptic cult near Muldrow, Oklahoma.

At a clemency board meeting, Snell quoted his hero Rudolf Hess and demanded that he either be executed or set free. He shot off a note to Governor

Tucker before his execution was ordered. "Governor Tucker," Snell wrote, "look over your shoulder. Justice is coming. I wouldn't trade places with you or any of your cronies. Hell has victories. I am at peace."

The *New York Times* conceded on May 20, 1995 that "although evidence of an earlier plot does not itself demonstrate any links between those identified as plotters then and those accused now, it does suggest that the idea of bombing this particular federal building could have been a subject of discussion among small extremist groups for more than a decade."

McVeigh once received a traffic ticket, the *Times* noted, in the Fort Smith, Arkansas area, where some co-conspirators in the original bombing plot lived. The only other known connection is his sister's subscription to the *Patriot Report,* a newsletter published in Fort Smith.

The principal prosecution witness of the 1983 conspiracy was James D. Ellison, founder of the Covenant, the Sword and the Arm of the Lord—more accurately described as a sword and arm of virtual government—a neo-Nazi sect that once thrived in northern Arkansas. In 1988, fourteen Nazis were charged with scheming to overthrow the government. One of them was Richard Butler, the guiding force of the Aryan Nations sanctuary in Hayden Lake, Idaho. Other notable *ubermenschen* put on trial were Robert E. Miles, a former Klansman and leader of the Mountain Church of Jesus Christ the Savior in Michigan, an ex-con since his school-bus burning glory days, and Louis Ray Beam, former grand dragon of the KKK and "ambassador to the Aryan Nations."

These organizations share a common set of "religious" beliefs—the "Christian Identity" strain—grounded in a mythic past of Aryan supermen with superior electrons spinning in their brains, recalling the anti-Semitic, paganistic, rune-reading, sun-worshipping cults that flourished in the early days of the Nazi Party. The movement binds many of the neo-Nazi movements in the United States.

On one hand, Identity Christians believe they are the true descendants of Adam and Abraham, that Jews conspire with the Devil to enslave the world, all explained in frothy racist diatribes sweetened with Old Glory patriotism to put the icing on the mind control. On the other, the Identity altar is littered with the occult paraphernalia of the Nazi twilight. Wesley Swift, Richard Butler's mentor, blended KKK and Nazi racism with the "lost tribe" concept and the occult. Swift often preached about Atlantis and alluded to Edgar Cayce. Identity's Pastor Arnold Murray let on that the Great Pyramid was the second revelation of God, architecturally encoded to deliver the Word to the initiated patriarchs of the Identity racial fantasy.

The most exalted is Richard Girnt Butler, a retired Lockheed engineer and a suspect in the original Oklahoma bombing plot. Butler founded Aryan Nations, an Identity church, on a 20-acre plot of Idaho panhandle, in the shadows of looming guard towers. Butler's speeches were met with Nazi salutes and culminated in cross burnings. Buildings in the Hayden Lake area were periodically bombed. Armed compounds have cropped up in Pennsylvania and Utah, with minor outposts scattered about the country. The movement has been linked to dozens of murders since 1980. Butler's Idaho HQ was disarmed in 1987 following the passage of the state's Terrorist Control Act, but it was here that Oberführer Butler played host to a vanity fair of seething neo-Nazi celebrity bombers, including Richard Snell and the Order.

One of the most sinister was Manfred Roeder, leader of the the largest and most rabid Nazi organization in Europe. American and South African benefactors subsidized his terrorist fund. In 1978 he made a junket to Brazil for a meeting with Dr. Josef Mengele and other holdovers of the Nazi regime. From Brazil he made a bee-line for the United States, where he met with Dr. William Pierce, a former assistant professor of physics at Oregon State University, leader of the rabidly right-wing National Alliance, author of *The Turner Diaries*, the blueprint for the Order's carnage. (Like many domestic leaders of fascist cadrés, Pierce entered the network through the John Birch Society, arch-conservative supporters of Brig. Gen. Partin's "Leftist International" theory of the Oklahoma bombing.)

Pierce's world-hopping German ally, Herr Roeder—then a fugitive wanted in Germany for the bombing of a Vietnamese refugee center—was an honored guest at the annual gathering the Aryan Nations compound in 1982. Like Butler, his American counterpart, Roeder was the patriarch of several neo-Nazi groups. He fed them a steady diet of Jewish conspiracy theories. All this, and he still found time to steep himself in the blood-drenched politics of the PLO.

Another crazed bomber linked to Butler's movement is Jeremy Knesal, who faces a 45-year sentence for the bombing of an NAACP office in Tacoma, Washington. Knesal's mentor at the Idaho compound was Floyd Cochran, then the Nations' resident propagandist, today a reformed fascist who lectures around the country about the evils of racism.

Under Cochran's tutelage, Knesal acquired a National Socialist perspective on religion, eugenics and "racial history."

A second bomb plot in Washington state was allegedly hatched by Darwin Michael Gray, 27, at roughly the same time the Oklahoma bombers conceived their plan. Gray is the foster brother of Kevin Harris, the Identity rebel acquitted with Randy Weaver of the murder of a deputy U.S. marshal in the shootout at Weaver's cabin in northern Idaho in 1992.

Alexi Erlanger, another familiar face at Aryan Nations gatherings, hails from Buffalo, New York, Timothy McVeigh's stomping grounds. Erlanger was Nazi to the bone, the leader of the Liberation Movement of the German Reich, a bridge to the survivors of Germany's Nazi confederacy known as the *Kameradenwerk,* or Odessa. Ladislas Farago reported in *Aftermath* that in 1973 a German-American journal called *Die Brucke* "proudly announced that Alexi Erlanger of the Buffalo chapter was heading a drive to bring two 'famous German war heroes' to the U.S.A. for a visit of our military institutions and our German community. One of the invited guests was Colonel Hans Ulrich Rudel. The other was Colonel Otto Skorzeny."

Hans Rudel, the German ace and postwar founder of an aircraft factory in Argentina, is a ramrod of the postwar Nazi "refugee" underground, a world spokesman of the neo-Nazi movement, a Mother Theresa to fugitives of the Hitler era.

Otto Skorzeny, the 6′4″ hulk of an SS commando, was trained in assassination and terrorist tactics. He was among the very first Nazi officers recruited by the budding CIA. During the war, he rescued Mussolini from his jailers and kidnapped East European politicians who refused to collaborate with invading Germans. His postwar career included the running of ratline operations for Nazis escaping via Spain and Syria. "Both the Odessa and die Spinne SS escape organizations," Christopher Simpson observes, "revolved in large part around the personality—and the myth—of Otto Skorzeny."

A member of the network that survives "Hitler's Commando" told an interviewer in 1981 that the "Nazi International" had infiltrated Texaco, Resorts International and Lockheed, among other major federally-subsidized corporations.

Tim McVeigh, the migratory hawk, lived in Kingman, Arizona, home of the Hephzibah Ranch and its Christian Identity proprietor, Jack Maxwell Oliphant, ex-convict, Mojave County militia leader, and with Butler a co-conspirator in the original plot to blow up the federal building in Oklahoma City. The ranch is 20 miles off the main road.

Oliphant has worried local lawmen since he moved to the Arizona mountains over a decade ago. From primitive training camps near Kingman and Flagstaff, the *Arizona Republic* reported on December 21, 1986 that a contingent of Patriots intermingled with the Order and Aryan Nations. The newspaper identified one Arizona Patriot as a member of Posse Comitatus, the Christian

Identity tax-protest group. (Other insidious links have been forged by this native fascist organization. In a videotape distributed by anti-abortionists, leaders of violent opposition to the clinics appear with Bryan Dale of Posse Commitatus.)

Oliphant's brigade, the Arizona Patriots, has taken refuge in the past few years in a morbid cloud of secrecy. One witness in the grand jury hearings claims that McVeigh mingled with Oliphant's mountain men. Kingman residents emphasize that local Patriots are *outsiders, clearly not from the area.* Oliphant, who shot off his right arm in 1977 while handling a shotgun, has a demonstrated penchant for ultra-violence. From the *News and Observer:*

> Kingman is a hotbed for paramilitary activity and if he mixed with militias here, he almost certainly mixed with the Arizona Patriots, said Bernell Lawrence, a former law officer who ran surveillance on the group's activities before 1992....
>
> In 1983, Oliphant bought 160 acres in the mountains from Tod Becker, a local real estate agent whose family owned the property, according to Becker.
>
> Almost immediately, men wearing military fatigues were sighted on Oliphant's land conducting desert warfare training.
>
> Oliphant founded the Arizona Patriots and made no secret of his paramilitary activities, said Lawrence, who watched the ranch first as a Mohave County sheriff's deputy, then as part of an area anti-narcotics unit and finally as a Department of Public Safety officer.
>
> The people who trained with Oliphant were typically not locals.
>
> In 1987, Oliphant and two fellow Patriots devised a plan to hold up an armored car that carried money to and from Laughlin, the cash-rich gambling town across the Colorado River in Nevada, according to statements from federal investigators at the time. One of the members of the group, who was unwilling to take part in the heist, went to the FBI and told of the plot. When agents in helicopters raided Oliphant's ranch in 1987, they also found plans to blow up the nearby Hoover Dam.
>
> Oliphant and two other Patriots pled guilty to conspiracy. Clutching a worn Bible at the hearing to enter his pleas, Oliphant acknowledged that money from the planned robbery was to be used to "build a compound for the Identity Movement" on his property, according to news accounts of the sentencing. The Identity Movement is associated with white supremacists who believe Jews are the root of evil in society, according to the FBI's case. Among the allegations against Oliphant and his co-defendants was that they intended to stop the armored car and use explosives to blow it open.
>
> Oliphant served a short prison term, then returned to his ranch and has not shown signs of restarting the Identity Movement, Becker said.

Opinions differ on whether the Patriots remain active on Oliphant's ranch today. Lawrence believes the group still trains at Hephzibah Ranch, but that in recent years the group became much more secretive.

Oliphant's desert brigade planned to pull an armored car heist and launder the proceeds in Las Vegas casinos. Two men who'd been charged in 1985 with selling Uzi submachine guns to undercover agents were also rounded up.

The Patriot Movement takes its direction from Christian Identity propagandists, strident "constitutionalists" all, most with backgrounds in military intelligence, including Mark Koernke, the Enola Gay of ultra-rightwing conspiracy theorists, Bill Cooper, Bo Gritz and Linda Thompson.

The leadership has included the likes of John Salvi, a rabid militia footsoldier from Florida accused of killing two abortion clinic staffers in Boston in December, 1994.

Francisco Duran, wrestled into submission after squeezing off a few rounds at the Clinton White House, ran with a militia in Colorado. Police found occult literature on the front seat of Duran's car, according to the *San Francisco Chronicle,* possibly originating in the cabalistic fringe of the Identity movement. The occult is often found in combination with mind control in the covert operation arm of virtual government.

In 1994, the following organizations issued alerts on the threat posed by white supremacists mixing with the Patriots: the Southern Poverty Law Center, Planned Parenthood, The Coalition for Human Dignity, the Center for Democratic Renewal, the Montana Human Rights Network and the Association of National Security Alumni, among others.

The Iran-Contra Players and the CIA's War on America

McVeigh's social circle—strutting fundamentalist Identity rebels and politically-programmed Patriots—led the press to assume that others had joined in the plot. The day after the bombing, the *New York Times* offered that right-wing militias were not believed "to have the technical expertise to engage in bombings like the one today," only to report on the very same page that a fertilizer bomb is so "cheap and easy" to construct, "anyone" can do it.

The press has speculated at length on the bombers' probable motives. That speculation has been accepted as fact, but a vengeful commemoration of the Waco and Weaver fiascos have not been confirmed as motives.

Another probable reason for the destruction in Oklahoma was offered by the Nazi Party itself.

On April 20, 1995, mailing list subscribers of the American National Socialist Worker's Party received a copy of the "Official ANSWP Statement Regarding the OKC Bombing." The statement noted that the Secret Service and much-despised BATF were investigating Gary Lauck of Lincoln, Nebraska, leader of the domestic NSDAP and the most prolific distributor of racist propaganda to neo-Nazis in Germany. With Lauck's European arrest, "U.S. officials have been doing extensive surveillance of Lauck's contemporaries in Oklahoma, Kansas, Nebraska and north Texas. These surveillance activities were being coordinated out of the OKC offices, according to our sources."

Furthermore, "the OKC office of *the ATF had plans to serve search warrants* 'by the beginning of Summer' on several well-known white supremacists."

But the warrants were never issued.

Agents investigating Aryan Nations were headquartered at the Alfred Murrah Federal Building. Evidence was stored there. The investigation may explain, as the *New York Daily News* reported on May 1, precisely why "Feds Rescue Documents, not People." Within hours of the bombing, the *News* discovered, "some rescue workers were stopped from searching for survivors while federal officials removed boxes of documents. 'You'd think they would have let their evidence and files sit at least until the last survivor was pulled out,' one angry rescue worker told the *News*.

"The worker and a firefighter said that 10 to 12 hours after the 9 AM blast on April 19, federal officials began limiting the number of rescue workers in the building to a dozen, confining them largely to the lower right side of the battered structure. Meanwhile, *40 to 50 federal agents* spent much of the night carrying boxes from the floors occupied by federal DEA and the BATF."

Was there a connection between the investigation of neo-Nazis in the southwest and the bombing? The contents of the files were not divulged, but federal agents told reporters they were "looking into the possibility that alleged bomber Timothy McVeigh and his accomplices had targeted the nine-story building in an effort to destroy DEA or ATF investigation files."

Acquaintances of McVeigh told reporters that Timothy McVeigh, like Billy Doyle, Senator Phil Gramm's Nazi cause celebré, supported himself by peddling methamphetamines. McVeigh ran his drug concession in Kingman, Arizona. Ralph McPeak, a Kingman resident and friend of McVeigh's, told the *Los Angeles Times*: "When I met him [last year], he was *wired up*. He couldn't stand still." McPeak and his estranged wife said in separate interviews that some of the same people who had frequented the house also designed and detonated explosives. Two of the acquaintances fled when a fertilizer and fuel oil bomb damaged their house. They accused "McVeigh or his associates in the *drug trade.*"

McVeigh traveled widely, always with a billfold crammed full of cash. He had no visible means of support. Drugs may explain the financing of McVeigh's whirlwind Gypsy tour around the country.

And then there were the syringes found by McVeigh and Nichols on their food trays during confinement at El Reno. Were the syringes a warning?

The *San Francisco Examiner* published a fascinating story from independent sources implicating the warden in El Reno prison:

AUG. 28, 1995

The warden of the federal prison holding the two Oklahoma City bombing suspects says the inmates are not at risk despite a report that syringes were found on their food trays.

Warden R.G. Thompson told the *Daily Oklahoman* on Monday that security at the El Reno Federal Correctional Institution is "not at all" in jeopardy. He said the controversy was "an internal personnel matter" and refused further comment.

The Muskogee *Daily Phoenix* reported that Charles Mildner, chief correctional supervisor at the prison, was suspended with pay after he ordered that only one officer be allowed to handle food trays for bombing suspects Timothy McVeigh and Terry Nichols.

Mildner's supervisors revoked the order, his attorney, David Wilson, told the newspaper.

Mildner established the policy after syringes were found on food trays going into the unit where McVeigh and Nichols are held, Wilson said.

Contraband was found again on the trays after Mildner's order was countermanded and inmates had access to the trays, Wilson said.

"What would happen if one of those two inmates were to die inside the prison?"

Even though Mildner is a member of management, he has the support of Local 171 of the American Federation of Government Employees Council of Prison Locals, whose members total more than 95 percent of the 430 rank-and-file employees at the prison. Union members planned to hold a rally in support of Mildner Monday at the El Reno city park and to picket the prison on Tuesday.

A sensitive investigation of Nazi activity and drugs was allegedly underway in Oklahoma City. If the building was destroyed, in part, to bury evidence of virtual government involvement in the distribution of drugs, it's certain that a representative from this murky milieu would step forward to float disinformation and divert attention from higher-ups.

Who should surface immediately after the bombing but a chorus of "National Security Experts" drawn from hundreds of propagandists squatting in the blinds of the corporate press.

The most strident terrorism "expert" consulted by the media was Vincent Cannistraro, the former CIA officer who ran covert ops for the NSC during the Iran-Contra debacle with its cocaine backdrop. In 1991, he told the *San Francisco Chronicle* that sinister "environmentalists" had formed "clandestine cells" plotting to create technologies to diminish, even "eliminate" *the entire human race.*

Cannistraro performed a similar service for the NSC Contragate defendants by blaming the Gander crash on Iraqi terrorists. In fact, the plane was bearing a score of intelligence agents to the U.S. when it crashed in Newfoundland. Several of them had gathered damning information on John Singlaub, North and Pentagon/CIA chicanery abroad.

In December 1990, Gene Wheaton, formerly an investigator for the Christic Institute, concluded a probe of the Arrow Air jet crash with the comment, "the official version is a cover-up, and the Canadian and U.S. government officials who are responsible have been criminally negligent or worse." On board had been over 20 crack commandos from the Special Forces, identified on the passenger log as "warrant officers." Arrow Air itself was a CIA dummy front, and bore a ton of mystery cargo when the jet and its 256 passengers crashed.

Wheaton found that Arrow had transported arms from Israel to Iran on North's behalf as part of the arms-for-hostages swap. The mid-flight explosion was a retaliatory strike by the Iranians for a swindle perpetrated by the Reagan administration's pugnacious Oliver North, Wheaton says.

Immediately after the Oklahoma bombing, the same spin doctors who muddied the water of such CIA misadventures as Jonestown and Iran-Contra hauled out the fertilizer.

Admiral Stansfield Turner, former director of the CIA, currently a director of Monsanto and a public affairs officer at the University of Maryland, suggested that it's time to "reassess the nature and extent of anti-terror measures." (As CIA director, Turner once spoke this way about the Soviet Union to scare up operating funds from Congress.) "We have to decide what to do with the FBI and other agencies [to] ward this kind of thing off in the future," said Turner, who foresaw the inevitable "trade-off between [terrorist] intrusions and our personal freedom."

Frank Keating, governor of Oklahoma, echoed Turner's sentiments. But then Keating himself is a career intelligence operative and a solid "conservative" Republican. Keating earned his B.A. in history from Georgetown University in

1966. His resumé notes that his "distinguished public service career began as an FBI agent, where he investigated New Left terrorist activities, bombings and bank robberies on the west coast." After a term as assistant district attorney in Tulsa, Keating won a seat in the state House of representatives in 1972. In 1986, President Reagan offered him the position of Assistant Secretary of the Treasury, in which capacity he supervised Interpol and the BATF. Back in Oklahoma, he served as associate attorney general and presided over the federal prison system. His wife, Cathy Keating, is a consultant to *U.S. News & World Report.*

One trail to Oklahoma bumps against Bill Clinton and the CIA-Mena drug scandal. The Agency's London Station Chief, Cord Meyer, recruited Clinton, then a Rhodes student in the UK, into the fold. The dimpled spy and and current resident of the White House has since been dragged into the muck at Mena, one of the largest aircraft refitting facilities in the country, situated just across the Oklahoma border, and may have figured in the interagency probe of regional drug operations.

As governor, Clinton failed to investigate allegations of drug running in Mena. Funds earmarked by the state legislature for an investigation of CIA activity in Arkansas disappeared under Clinton's watch.

Federal agents in Oklahoma City were not the only ones investigating drug movements in the southwest. In 1995, Gene Wheaton investigated the theft of 32 military aircraft, and was drawn to familiar territory. Wheaton was at one time an affiliate of North's. The investigator is mentioned in the disgraced NSC aide's notebooks, first as a potential ally to the contra supply effort, later as a bothersome whistle-blower. The same culprits, he said, who flew massive cocaine shipments from South America to Mena under Reagan "were running things now. It's a continuation of Iran-Contra. Everybody thinks Iran-Contra quit with Ollie North and Secord being exposed. But it's actually got bigger because the media stopped looking at it."

Some of the mud flicked at Clinton originates with Arkansan Larry Nichols, a CIA veteran of the contra guns-for-drugs network. Nichols fought under John Singlaub in Vietnam, and reported to the World Anti-Communist League official during the Nicaraguan contra war.

Singlaub is an anti-Communist of the 1950s genus, and it was during that decade, as deputy CIA station chief in South Korea, that his political pathologies found an outlet. During the Korean war he fell in with a circle of Seoul's most powerful politicians, spies and industrialists. His sole ambition in life since appears to be fund-raising to destroy Communism. In Vietnam, Singlaub organized the dreaded Phoenix Program under his Special Operations Group, a

bund of 10,000 troops unleashed in the south to conduct covert raids, assassinations of Viet Minh by the tens of thousands, psychological warfare and sabotage missions.

Ollie North was one of John Singlaub's second lieutenants.

Claire Sterling, a veteran CIA propagandist, writes that Singlaub "came to be
regarded with awe by a whole generation of military men and intelligence officers, many of whom shared his conservative views about the way things should
be in Asia. Around him grew a following that developed into *an infrastructure at
the Pentagon and CIA.*"

This infrastructure is represented in the OK bombing case by Michael Tigar,
the attorney representing Terry Nichols. In the 60s and 70s, Tigar was employed
by the law firm of Williams, Wadden & Stein. He reported to Edward Bennett
Williams, the head of the firm, a Beltway attorney long on intimate terms with
the CIA. Williams often referred to Tigar as his "most brilliant protégé."

The law firm sprang into existence to cater to the same interagency intelligence underground implicated in drug distribution, mind control and by all
appearances a U-Haul of exploding compost in Oklahoma City. A senior partner of the firm was Brendon Sullivan, the high-strung legal phenomenon who
represented Oliver North during the Congressional Iran-Contra hearings.
Williams, a Jesuit, was twice offered the post of CIA director. He refused (possibly because he was already a *de facto* CIA functionary) and by refusing shaped
history—Gerald Ford gave the job to George Bush instead. Robert Maheu, the
CIA hit man, attended Holy Cross with Williams and was a close friend. In
1958, the famed attorney paired Robert Maheu with Los Angeles mobster
Johnny Rosselli to plot against Cuban premier Fidel Castro.

The Williams' client roster has included Joseph McCarthy, Mafia don Frank
Costello, Jimmy Hoffa, Frank Sinatra, Armand Hammer and John Connally.
He was general counsel to Georgetown University, which has long maintained a
symbiotic relationship with the CIA. Junk bond magnate Michael Milken, a
client of the firm, openly wept at Williams' funeral in 1988.

Michael Tigar came to the firm after resigning his position as a Supreme
Court clerk. He represented some extremely high-powered clients for a journey-
man attorney. It was Tigar who coached Bobby Baker, the LBJ aide imprisoned
for tax fraud and influence peddling in 1967, before Senate appearances. Tigar
defended John Connally when the former Texas governor was accused of pock-
eting a bribe. Connally was acquitted. He rewarded Tigar with a prize bull. The
beast was packed off to Fidel Castro.

One San Francisco reporter suggests that Michael Tigar, with his pricey wardrobe and trademark crewcut, looks "more like a young Republican than the spell-binding firebrand he was a dozen years ago." The press has made much of his radical days at Berkeley and representation of Angela Davis, but he usually caters to the Right. One of Tigar's most controversial clients was John Demjanjuk, the accused Nazi war criminal. Tigar also represented Clayton Jackson, the California lobbyist convicted for money laundering, racketeering and offering a bribe to state senator Alan Robbins.

He agreed to counsel Terry Nichols at the request of three federal judges.

Like his mercurial attorney, Terry Nichols was turned out by the same national security bund behind the Iran-Contra swaps, Mena and the Gander bombing, not to mention a series of foreign coups, death squad outrages, drug imports and a long history of homicidal covert operations.

Terry Nichols hid a dagger under his compost-smeared cloak. Lana Padilla, his first wife, called a news conference on July 13 after visiting him in prison. She said that Nichols made frequent trips to the Philippines—so many, in fact, that the farmer from Kansas had charged $40,000 in air fares to his credit cards. Ms. Padilla also claimed that Tim McVeigh footed the bill for a 1989 trip. After his arrest, federal agents discovered that Terry Nichols had a locker full of gold and silver bullion stored in Las Vegas. Nichols, she told reporters, was given the precious metals in November, 1994, while on a junket to the Philippines, by a party unknown.

Padilla said that Nichols refused to take Mary Fay, his second wife, a mail-order bride, along when he traveled, though her family lived in Cebu—a well-known terrorist haunt in the Philippines.

Before departing for his last trip, Nichols told Lana, "I might not be coming back." He traveled with a gun, she said—and managed to pass through airport security gates. Before he left, he entrusted her with $20,000 for McVeigh in case he never returned. He did and he was noticeably on edge,

"*Those* people can *kill* you," he told Lana with a shudder, "I'm *never* going back there again." Who are the deadly mysterians who hired Nichols to perform secret missions in far-off lands? Lana Padilla suggested they were Islamic terrorists.

The U.S. has a long, sordid history of intrigue in the islands. Islamic terrorists make their home there. The investigation of the World Trade Center bombing was not as painstaking as it might have been because sandbags were repeatedly dropped in the path of FBI investigators by operatives of the CIA. One veteran FBI agent, in a *Village Voice* story that appeared on March 30, 1993, claimed that Sheikh Abdel Rahman was a core conspirator. "It was no accident that the Sheikh got a visa and that he's still in the country," one veteran FBI agent complains. "He's here under the banner of national security, the State Department, the NSA and the CIA. I haven't seen a lone-gunman theory advocated [with this vigor] since the John F. Kennedy assassination."

Jack Blum, a former investigator for the Senate Foreign Relations subcommittee, was appalled at CIA-terrorist interactions that surfaced after the bombing: "One of the big problems here is that many suspects in the World Trade Center bombing were associated with the Mujahedeen. There are components of our government that are absolutely disinterested in following that path because it leads back to people we supported in the Afghan war." "We" are a deep cover infantry of counter-insurgent drug smugglers, arms dealers, money launderers and professional liars.

There is a bridge spanning the World Trade Center and the Oklahoma City federal building. It is in the Philippines.

And it's made of gold—Japanese and Nazi gold buried in underground vaults once used to imprison and torture American prisoners of war and local insurgents. Approximately 1,000 tons of the loot was liberated by Ferdinand Marcos before his ouster. Billions of dollars worth were shipped overseas by American intelligence agents and the Mafia. Much of the horde was cabbaged away in a high-security, subterranean storage caché buried under the Zurich airport. This vault was once used to conceal European gold from Hitler's SS scavengers. Fifty years later, some of the same bullion has found its way into the campaign coffers of ultra-conservative political candidates in the U.S., according to the *Las Vegas Sun*.

But Marcos didn't recover the lion's share of the pelf. A six-month series in the *Sun* reported in 1993 that Marcos abandoned thousands of tons of gold hidden in his homeland. Gary Thompson, then the newspaper's managing editor, and journalist Steve Kanigher published photo-copies of gold certificates from Credit Suisse, deposit records from the Union Bank of Switzerland, the correspondence of Corazon Aquino and letters to Reagan administration officials documenting witness accounts that lackeys of the CIA and Army Special Forces carted off an unknown quantity of the bullion. They followed one lead after another, flying around the world for eleven months to piece together an elaborate story of political corruption and greed. The gold extraction was sanctioned by Lt. General Robert Schweitzer, President Reagan's senior military liaison to the National Security Council, and Lt. General Daniel Graham, then director of the DIA and a key consultant on the Strategic Defense Initiative. Schweitzer and retired General John Singlaub, the aforementioned veteran of the Iran-Contra affair, joined the board of Nippon Star, a Japanese conglomerate with branches in the Philippines. As they explained to two plaintive Nippon Star consultants, "the company is going out of business—the National Security Council is *taking over.*"

Among those recruited to run the intelligence front was retired Army Colonel Dan Myers, a former aide to Watergate-hit-man-*cum*-radio-celebrity G. Gordon Liddy. Eldon "Dan" Cummings, a Pentagon staffer, was named vice president.

Schwartz's ambitious aide, Oliver North, was already dabbling in the gold trade. In 1985, he attempted to sell 44 tons of Marcos bullion, worth $465 million, on the black market. He blithely suggested skimming $5 million to finance the Nicaraguan contra war, but the deal fell through when North, true to form, stiffed the Israeli middlemen on the Marcos payroll.

Tapes and documents implicating American officials in the gold transfers were withheld from the Iran-Contra committee by Major General Colin Powell, Defense Secretary Caspar Weinberger and William Odom, director of the NSA. "It wasn't so much the mention of gold that concerned them," say Thompson and Kanigher. "It was Marcos talking (on tape) about contributions to U.S. presidential campaigns and the use of the gold proceeds to fund illegal arms deals."

To extract the metal, Ray Cline, then deputy director of the CIA, organized a working group that included a chief regulator of the S&L industry. Citibank was drawn into the operation to negotiate the claims on a Philippine gold horde secreted in the Bahamas. NASA pilots drew up a plan to transport the bullion.

Bo Gritz, the Idaho militia leader who ran for president with David Duke as his running mate, also traveled to the Philippines to participate in Singlaub's gold dig. Gritz claims that he struck out—but the Special Forces veteran has been known to spin a plausible denial or two in his time.

Either Lana Padilla was right about Terry Nichols' mystery trips abroad, or she is a scholar of national security studies with an emphasis on black operations. Her reference to terrorists from the Middle East was hardly far-fetched. And General Schweitzer's crew from the NSC hired a team of attorneys to peddle gold recovered in the Philippines. Much of it was sold off to Middle Eastern terrorists. Some of them *have* indeed been linked to the World Trade Center bombing, according to the *Sun* exposé.

It is not at all unlikely that Terry Nichols should have had dealings with the rabid foreign clients of the national security sector. McVeigh had intelligence contacts as well. In McCurtain, Oklahoma a major flap erupted over a telephone call McVeigh placed a few days before the bombing. The local *Gazette* reported on July 14, 1996, "phone records indicate that on April 5, a call was made to Elohim City from a motel room registered to Timothy McVeigh." Elohim City is a "Christian" settlement near the Arkansas-Oklahoma border—and the burial sire of the venomous Richard Wayne Snell, executed for his part in the original Oklahoma City bombing plot. As it happens, two calls were placed by McVeigh to Elohim City's director of security, Andreas Carl Strassmeier. The FBI maintains that Strassmeier was a paid informant assigned to "infiltrate" the Identity Aryans at the encampment. Officially, Strassmeier was a lowly "informant," but his immediate entry into the heart of the federal intelligence underground suggests he was a functionary, a guiding light of the reactionary cult.

The Identity Nazis at Elohim City received military instruction in the use of small firearms from Strassmeier. And one witness in the case has identified him as the mysterious stranger who rode with McVeigh in the Mercury Marquis, which trailed the Ryder truck through Oklahoma City.

After the *Gazette* story appeared, Strassmeier's attorney, Kirk Lyons, a legal champion of the white supremecist cause, wrote in a newsletter that Strassmeier had fled the country, his "escape" from "death threats" conducted by Germany's "elite" counter-terrorist squad, GSG-9, via Mexico, Paris and Frankfurt. He arrived unaccosted in Berlin.

The *Gazette* detailed Strassmeier's background: "The son of [one of] Europe's most able and influential politicians, Andreas began 'visiting' the U.S. in 1988. Up to that time, the then 23-year-old German army officer served in the Panzer Grenadiers.... Srassmeier's father, Gunter, had risen to the position of Secretary of State to Berlin.... Strassmeier junior has admitted to journalists that his military assignments sometimes include *covert projects* and training... In the *London Sunday Telegraph*, Strassmeier told interviewers that he settled in the U.S. in 1989 on a 'special assignment' he was promised by the U.S. Justice Department...."

When he disembarked, posing as a tourist, Herr Strassmeier was quickly taken under the wing of Vincent Petruskie, a retired Air Force colonel and former intelligence operative for the Office of Special Investigations. The colonel set out to find empolyment for the German "tourist." Publicly, Petruskie has admitted that he sought only "odd jobs" for Strassmeier, who had his eye on a job at the DEA. Though he had no green card, the German was blessed with a Tennessee driver's license and a social security number.

"Strassmeier," the *London Telegraph* reports, "settled down and said he was acting as a middle man for an old family friend, Col. Petruskie, who he also described as 'an ex-CIA guy that my father has known since the Cold War.'"

In 1992, Strassmeier committed a traffic offense and his car was impounded by the Oklahoma highway patrol. Inside, police found a valise full of government documents. Strassmeier called in his cavalry—the State Department and the Governor's office phoned police to urge his release, as did an unnamed caller who argued that Strassmeier—his proof of citizenship notwithstanding—enjoyed the protection of diplomatic immunity.

The client list of Kirk Lyons, Strassmeier's attorney and co-sponsor in the United States, include (as do many of the arch-conservatives in McVeigh's entourage) the Identity Nazis of Elohim City, home of the original bombing plot that ended in the execution of Richard Snell and his burial in the shell-shocked hills of Arkansas.

Military-Intelligence Connections

Patriot leaders descend from the Nazi-anchored Identity movement that formed around William Potter Gale and a clutch of like-minded individuals who served under General Douglas MacArthur during the last world war—with one notable exception: Colonel William Neblett, an officer in MacArthur's entourage. In *Pentagon Politics,* published in 1953, Noblett summarized his feelings about American covert military policy:

> The power of the military must be curbed at once. To allow the professional military to control us any longer will mean the end of our republican form of government. If the Pentagon and certain politicians can keep the fear of Communistic aggression fresh in the public's mind for a few years longer, a 'Prussianized type of army' will be achieved.

The leadership of the Patriots have roots in the "Prussianized" military intelligence community. Between domestic Nazis, Patriots and the clandestine "services," there is much commingling. Members of the Wisconsin's Free Militia may drift over to the U.S. Taxpayer's Party, a "Constitutionalist" cadré run by radical right organizer Howard Phillips, a career CIA neo-conservative, and vice versa.

In 1976, a flap erupted at Camp Pendleton with the discovery that the KKK had heavily infiltrated the base. Several black Marines were assaulted by whites sporting the Klan insignia, and a cross was burned nearby. Corporal Daniel Bailey, Jr., an Exalted Cyclops, informed the local press that Marines recruited by the Klan numbered about a hundred. But the Corps managed to contain the story—until a group of black Marines beat up a congregation of white men. At the court-martial, the accused GIs testified that commanders at Camp Pendleton had ignored the flaunting of Klan regalia and assaults on blacks by KKK Marines. Pro-Nazi literature materialized on the base.

Hardline Identity Nazis mix freely with the militias. The Michigan group is friendly with the Militia of Montana, led by John Trochmann, a featured speaker at the Aryan Nations compound in Idaho in 1990.

Trochmann claims to have visited the Nazi enclave on "four or five occasions." But Loretta Ross, research director of the anti-fascist Center for Democratic Renewal in Atlanta, noted in her Congressional testimony on July 11, 1995, that Trochmann "frequently visited the Aryan Nations neo-Nazi paramilitary compound in Idaho and was a featured speaker there in 1990, although he claims to have merely spoken on morality. But according to Aryan Nations founder Richard Butler, Trochmann visited the compound many times and even helped write the group's code of conduct."

When Trochmann appeared at a post-bombing Congressional probe, the *Nation* quipped that if Senator Arlen Specter had been half as hard on the militia movement as he was on Anita Hill, his recent Judiciary Subcommittee hearing on the militias might have truly discredited the radical right. Instead, the inquiry became a soapbox for the 'patriots' rather than the critical forum that was so badly needed." Specter was provided with a letter from Aryan Nations documenting Trochmann's close relationship with the leaders of the organization, yet his gentle inquisitors in Washington neglected to ask him about it.

The Michigan Militia was thrust into the roving media spotlight by reports that Tim McVeigh had once been employed by the oratorical Mark Koernke, the leading light of the group. Koernke is a veteran of the 78th Division of the Army Reserve in Livonia, Michigan. His star in the Patriots began to rise when he traded on his self-proclaimed military intelligence background. He often refers to himself as an "intelligence analyst" and "counter-intelligence coordinator" with a "top-secret clearance."

He co-founded the Michigan Militia in April, 1994, with Reverend Norman Olsen, a Baptist preacher, abortion foe, military veteran and "intelligence specialist." The cadré has since become the largest in the country, boasting to have recruited some 12,000 footsoldiers.

The April 22, 1995 edition of the stridently anti-fascist *Germany Alert* noted that the Michigan Militia "is organized closely along the lines of the established German neo-Nazi organizations."

Koernke has boasted of commanding two "special-warfare" brigades that trained Army personnel in "foreign warfare and tactics." These claims may be exaggerated, but Koernke did in fact attend the Army's intelligence school at Fort Huachuca in Arizona. He returned to Michigan an E-5 specialist with a G-2 (security) section of a peacetime Reserve unit. Koernke's particular brand of fulmination against bastions of the looming "world order," with emphasis on the Council of Foreign Relations and the Trilaterals, smack of the dark arts of propaganda and psychological warfare, the curriculum of any self-respecting spy school.

At a militia conference in Florida, Koernke introduced himself as a "military intelligence advisor for the militias" with tentacles reaching across the country. He boasted of supplying his troops with information about "United Nations troop movements and federal government activity."

Mark from Michigan has boasted freely to friends that he was once employed as a "provocateur." For whom?

Provocateuring at the behest of an unnamed branch of government accounts for his role in a crazed scheme to blow up a local National Guard base in January, 1995. The bombing plot was conceived when some 70 recruits of the Michigan Militia Corps convened at a truck-stop near Detroit. The brigade was outraged by photographs of Russian tanks en route to Camp Grayling via railway flatcars. They interpreted the photos as proof of Russian troop movements under UN control launching an invasion on American soil.

A few days later, about 20 militia men met at a farm near Leonard, Michigan for their weekly combat training. Militia leaders laid out maps and a plan to lay siege to the camp.

"Let's go blow up those tanks and kill those bastards who put them there," one brigade leader urged.

From a summary of the planned assault on the military base:

Contact all the brigades in the state and storm Camp Grayling, killing anyone who attempts to defend the base and arresting anyone else who is left.

Photograph, for historical purposes, all foreign equipment.

Hunt down anyone involved in bringing in the foreign equipment and try them for war crimes in a revolutionary court, which denies the accused a chance for appeal. The accused would be executed as soon as possible.

Hunt down all UN forces in the U.S.

The Michigan Militia has attempted to distance itself from Timothy McVeigh. The day after the blast, Koernke's regiment faxed out messages informing the world that one of the Nichols brothers had attended a meeting, but was tossed out for circulating tax resister material. But Branch Davidian Ron Cole, a Waco survivor who knows Koernke well and has met each of the bombing suspects at Patriot rallies, insists there was a close relationship. "Tax resister material is the *kindergarten* curriculum for beginner Patriots," Cole told the *Boulder Weekly.* "The idea that they would throw him out for that is *highly unlikely.* If people in the militia movement are going to tell lies, then let's at least make them believable."

The fringe of the lunatic fringe is monopolized by Bill Cooper, a Navy veteran and commander of an Arizona militia. Cooper preaches in his shortwave broadcasts that a secret government cabal has struck an alliance with a species of hominoid-saurus reptiles from space. This "serpent cult," he says, has granted the privileged, namely conspiratorial ranks of "Jesuit-Masonry," dominion over all terrestrial Gentile non-Masons.

Echoing Brig. Gen. Partin, Cooper attributes mass murder in Oklahoma City to the fulfillment of "the hidden agenda of the Communist/Socialist Internationale."

In *Kooks,* a compendium of American extremists, author Donna Kossy writes: "Cooper was born into a military family in 1943, and upon graduating high school in 1961 (in Japan) enlisted in the Air Force. During his more than ten years in both the Air Force and the Navy, he was an exemplary member, earning medals, and steadily taking on greater responsibility. Soon after enlisting, he was graced with a secret security clearance, and outfitted with a dosimeter, worked around "REAL atomic bombs" on a daily basis. He says that he was part of the elite of the Air Force."

By definition, intelligence agents are liars. Cooper's shortwave broadcasts are feasts of capricious political fantasy, yet his protégé and worshipful booster, Indiana militia leader Linda Thompson, who spent 14 years in Army uniform, once told an audience of rapt, highly-impressionable right-wing sod-busters: "If Bill Cooper is wrong, we're *all* in trouble."

In a *Village Voice* profile of Linda Thompson, author Adam Parfrey noted that she resembles "Madge the manicurist, and that is perhaps a source of her credibility among the Patriot common folk. But similarities to the lumpen proletariat end there. According to her resumé, Thompson served in the Army between 1974 and 1978, including a stint as 'Assistant to the U.S. Army Commanding General, NATO, Allied Forces Central Europe' with a 'cosmic Top Secret/Atomal security clearance.' Thompson's military career did not end with her honorable discharge in 1978, but continued for another decade in the Army reserve."

Her computer network bulletin board asks, "What is the address of your safe house?"

"For all of those who believed the claims that I'm an 'agent provocateur,'" she argues, "notice that the ONLY information about me is what I have put out, personally, on public record (when I was arrested)." Her logic recalls Ronald Reagan's explanation to the press regarding the Iran-Contra scandal, and her political thinking is equally suggestive of Alzheimer's. Where she once flogged prolifers (or "racists wanting more white babies to adopt"), Thompson, in a recent shortwave broadcast, sniffed, "I've always been against abortion."

To critics, she argued that turnabout was fair play. Thompson claimed she pivoted to oppose abortion after viewing ghastly photos of the medical procedure. She joined with one of the anti-choice movement's most pathological proponents, Reverend Matt Trewhella, pastor of the Mercy Seat Christian Church in Milwaukee and leader of the "Missionaries of the Pre-born National." The Missionaries are among the most radical "rescue" operations in the country. Their tactics include blockades and invasions of abortion clinics, lock-and-blocks and picketing campaigns. At a recent conference of anti-abortionists, Trewhella advised his congregation: "This Christmas, I want you to do the most loving thing—buy each of your children an SKS rifle and 500 rounds of ammunition."

The comments were made at the Wisconsin state convention of the U.S. Taxpayer's Party in May, 1994. His speech was taped secretly by staffers of Planned Parenthood at the convention. Trewhella, who has signed a document advocating the slaughter of doctors and the formation of militias around the issue of abortion, insisted, "Our government wants to disarm us! What should we do? We should do what thousands of people across the nation are doing—we should be forming militias." Pastor Trewhella asked parents who teach their children to play Pin-the-Tail-on-the-Donkey. "We need to start blindfolding them, sitting them down on the living room floor and saying: 'Now put that weapon together.'"

Some of the hottest rhetoric to come out of the Thompson camp is reserved for the Anti-Defamation League, which they consider the fountainhead of all sinister conspiracies. In one of her computer network alerts she insists:

The ADL was the source of all LIES about militias, claiming militias were "racists."
The ADL provided ALL the so-called experts who testified before Congress on militias.
The ADL was the source for the lies about the Branch Davidians...

In Thompson's world, the ADL accounts for any tarnish on the reputations of the Davidians. Moreover ...

The ADL-FBI alliance is destroying our country. It has taken over our media, taken over our congress, and its terrorist backers want the omnibus counter-terrorism bill passed by the FBI. ALLIED WITH THESE TERRORISTS, THEY WILL CONTROL THE COUNTRY!

She claims to be a perennial target of the government. Within a week of the decimation of the Alfred P. Murrah building, Thompson informed her computer network, "The FBI just threatened me." Why? Because she claimed to have information that a Japanese saboteur had infiltrated the Bureau to spy on the White House. The Justice Department, she alleged, was aware of the situation and was "trying to shut down all information about it. I called the FBI to give them this information and related what information I do have, and it was an instantaneous reaction, as if I am on to what is going on."

"What if McVeigh suddenly decides to give a statement," the FBI agent rejoindered, "and says he blew up the Oklahoma building because of Linda Thompson?" (McVeigh, in fact adored Thompson.) The militia leader regarded this as a "clear threat" that the FBI intended to indict her, but the comment could be interpreted as a simple observation that her violent rhetoric had egged McVeigh on.

Like McVeigh, Thompson claims to be a victim of remote electronic harassment:

GOVERNMENT WANTS ME DEAD By The Associated Press, 5-14-95
INDIANAPOLIS – A national militia leader arrested last week ... made claims about people wanting to kill her, according to court documents.

Court records show attorney Linda Thompson told a deputy at the Marion County Prosecutor's Office that the government was trying to kill her with radio frequency weapons.

Her behavior was so alarming the deputy feared Thompson was going to shoot him or other workers in the office with the loaded .45-caliber handgun she wore in a holster, court documents stated.

Thompson was arrested Thursday and charged Friday with battery on an officer, resisting law enforcement and disorderly conduct. A pretrial court hearing was set for next Friday morning in Marion Municipal Court.

The incident Thursday began after Thompson went to the prosecutor's office and told Sheriff's Deputy Jeffrey Dunn she wanted to file battery and stalking charges against Richard Bottoms.

Bottoms is a systems analyst for *Nuvo,* a weekly newspaper in Indianapolis, who has written about Thompson's militia activities. Thompson became irate when Dunn told her that she was not providing enough details to file charges against Bottoms, according to court documents.

Thompson then began "yelling and screaming" and told Dunn that the people responsible for last month's bombing of the federal building in Oklahoma City were shooting her in the head with radio frequency weapons and already had killed six of her friends this way.

She lashes out at the FBI, derides gun control lobbyists, curses informants. But Thompson reserves her most corrosive venom for James 'Bo' Gritz. Both Bill Cooper and Gritz emerged on the radio talk show circuit in 1989, parroting public speakers of the Christic Institute at the height of the firm's La Penca lawsuit. The effect was to marginalize the group.

Gritz served four tours of duty in Vietnam. 'Bo' is a former chief of Congressional relations for the Defense Security Assistance Agency. In 1988, Col. Gritz and an associate pled guilty to shipping a quantity of plastic explosive by commercial airliner to train Afghan rebels in the Nevada desert. His counterinsurgency training of the Afghans began with his employment by the Pentagon's Intelligence Support Activity (ISA) group, a top-secret covert operations unit. The ISA was formed by General Shy Memey, then the Army's Chief of Staff, a unit so covert that even the Pentagon, CIA and White House claimed to be unaware of its existence until the unit was exposed by Gritz himself in 1982 Congressional testimony. In open hearings, Gritz let slip that his search for American POWs in Laos had support from "the Activity," a covert brigade with which Congress was completely unfamiliar. A barrage of questions followed.

Scott Barnes, a former CIA contract officer in Bakersfield, California, insists that Gritz, then working as an employee of Hughes Aircraft, claimed credit for Barnes's own attempts to document the imprisonment of American POWs in Southeast Asia. "Gritz," Thompson notes, "is a known FBI informant and has known connections to CIA" documented in her "Traitor File."

Gritz denies that he is Nazi, even a white supremacist, despite his unabashed praise of Identity:

I believe that the Identity Christian Movement will continue to grow in this nation until it is able to stand self-sufficient in spite of the government....

Basically the Zionists are taking over and we Christians are being formed into small pockets that have to go to camps twice a year to learn what's going on.... The enemy you face today is a Satanic overthrow where he would change the United States of America, a nation under God, into U.S.A. Incorporated with King George as chairman of the board, and a Zionist group that would rule over us as long as Satan might be on earth....

I am telling you that he (God) has given us all that we need. He's given us ... the Identity Christian movement.

The blue-eyed ruler of the universe also created James Nichols, brother of Terry Nichols, accused co-conspirator. The Michigan farmer often describes anyone who doesn't travel with Israel's "lost tribes" as "sheeple," a common Identity put-down.

American Patriots and many militia groups, led by hired guns of the CIA and DoD, are waging war. "Sheeple," particularly liberals, are perceived as the enemy. This same scape-goating has resulted in massive destabilization, "secret" wars and wide-open conflict in every country on earth.

The United States is rapidly becoming the terminal battleground.

Sources

Many of the principal sources are cited in the text. A number of them are listed here, as are others not cited above.

Adams, James, *Secret Armies: The Full Story of S.A.S., Delta Force and Spetsnaz,* New York: Atlantic Monthly Press, 1987.

Anonymous, "Anti-Abortion Activist Pushes Forming Militias in Wisconsin," Knight-Ridder News Service, August 18, 1994.

Anonymous, "Oklahoma City Terror Suspects Linked to Nazis?" *Germany Alert,* extra edition, April 22, 1995.

Anonymous, "Washington: Arrests in Bomb Plot," Associated Press report, July 1, 1995.

ANSWP News Service, "Official ANSWP Statement Regarding the OKC Bombing," American National Socialist Workers' Party, Inc., April 20, 1995.

Business Editors, "Pro-Tech Monitoring: Crime Fighting Surveillance Tool," *Business Wire,* May 2, 1996.

Cash, J.D., McCurtain (Oklahoma) *Daily Gazette,* July 14 1996, p. 1.

Davidson, Keay, "60s Hero from UC to Defend Nichols," *San Francisco Examiner,*

May 14, 1995.

Davis, Jayna (reporting), "OKC Blast Connected to International Terrorist?" KFOR-TV news broadcast, July 13, 1995.

Daily News staff writers, "FILES BEFORE VICTIMS—Rescuers: Feds Slowed Search," *New York Daily News,* May 1, 1995.

Dyurman, Dan, "Militia Goes Mainstream in Idaho," *Militia News from Idaho,* February 12, 1995.

Dyurman, Dan, "Rep. Helen Chenoweth: Poster Child of the Militia," *Militia News from Idaho,* June 25, 1995.

Edwards, Brad (reporter), "Did the Government Know About Bombing Before it Happened?" KFOR-TV news broadcast, August 10, 1995.

Eglin AFB Computer BBS, "Mammal Research Using Subminiature Telemetry" (on the RF tracking of dolphins by Air Force scientists utilizing monolithic chip modules and modified missile tracking equipment).

Farley, John, "The West is Wild Again—The Federal government is Faced with Localities Willing to Fight for what they Believe is Their Land," *Time* Domestic BBS, vol. 145: no. 11, March 20, 1995.

Hall, Andy, "Secret War 'Patriots' have Loose Ties to Rightists Nationwide," *Arizona Republic,* December 21, 1986.

Hamilton, Arnold, "Indictment of McVeigh, Nichols Reveals No Motive," *Dallas Morning News,* August, 11, 1995.

Janofsky, Michael, "Militia Plotted Assault on Military Base," *San Francisco Examiner,* June 25, 2995.

Jasper, William F., "OKC Bombing: Expert Analysis" (bio of Brig. Gen. Benton Partin), *The New American,* June 26, 1995.

Larson, Viola, "Identity: A 'Christian' Religion for White Racists," *Christian Research Journal,* Fall, 1992.

Laugesen, Wayne and Dyer, Joel, "Civil War: Militia Leaders Warn Government to Leave Them Alone," *Boulder Weekly,* vol. II: no. 35, April 27, 1995.

Moldea, Dan E., *Dark Victory: Ronald Reagan, MCA, and the Mob,* New York: Pengiun, 1986. (On E.B. Williams, Rosselli, etc.)

NASA public relations dept., "Joseph P. Allen (Ph.D.)" [biographical data concerning the former astronaut and Calspan president], Lyndon B. Johnson Space Center, Houston, Texas.

Sentar, Inc. company literature, from the firm's Internet BBS.

Smolowe, Jill, "Enemies of the State: America's 'patriots' have a tough list of demands: keep your hands off my land, my wallet—and my guns," *Time* Domestic BBS, vol. 145: No. 19, May 8, 1995.

Southern Poverty Law Center, "Early Warning Signs Pointed to Violence on April 19—Potential for Further Outbreaks Remains High," *Klanwatch Intelligence Report,* June, 1985.

Swaney, Mark, "Clinton/Bush: Co-Conspirators in CIA Drug Smuggling," Prevailing Winds Research: Santa Barbara, California, August 8, 1995.

Thomas, Evan, *The Man to See: Edward Bennett Williams, Ultimate Insider, Legendary Trial Lawyer,* (New York: Simon & Schuster, 1991).

Thompson, Gary and Kanigher, Steve, "The Search for the Tiger's Treasure," *Las Vegas Sun,* April–December, 1993.

Van Biema, David, "Militias, the Message from Mark Koernke," *Time* Domestic BBS, vol. 145: no. 26, June 26, 1995.

Wallace, Bill, "Militia Tied to Blast Hates Gun Control—Leaders have Said it Might Come to War," *San Francisco Chronicle,* April 22, 1995.

Weiss, Philip, "Outcasts Digging in for the Apocalypse," *Time* Domestic BBS, vol. 145: no. 18, May 1, 1995.

Woods, Jim and Riepenhoff, Jill, "Plague Vials Found in Car: Lancaster Man Charged, Got Cultures through the Mail," *Columbus Dispatch,* May 13, 1995.

Witt, Howard, "Anatomy of an OK City Conspiracy Theory," *Chicago Tribune,* May 9, 1995.

Zeskind, Leonard, "The Smell of Yesteryear: Militias and White Supremacy," *The Body Politic,* May, 1995.

CIA

Mind Control & the U.S. Postal Service

By Vincent Fontana & Alex Constantine

At a Congressional inquiry in September, 1992, an angry witness to mass murder at a Royal Oak post office charged the panel with conducting a "controlled investigation" to leave "the impression that efforts are underway to stop this tragic carnage."

He added that the investigation was not an effective response and did not lead to a cessation of violence ...

We are in need of more than political responses which produce nothing more than window dressing. Such efforts have led to:

* *Blaming the victims, declaring them to be mentally unstable.*
* *Review of a whistleblower's background, military record and prior work behavior.*
* *Hot lines to permit employees to report "unusual behavior."*
* *Blaming union officials and supervisors.*
* *The convening of a joint task force to make written pronouncements that "postal workers oppose violence."*

"Violence in the U.S. Postal Service," Congressional Hearing, Royal Oak, Michigan

The postal service has long had a cozy relationship with the intelligence "services." Former CIA employees are often granted appointments as postmasters. It's a little known fact that the system has its own built-in intelligence agency known to bug employee restrooms illegally, and the internal agency has spied on the American Postal Workers and Letter Carriers unions. The service uses its own covert intelligence network to harass whistle-blowers and sow disinformation about them.

It has also been used for human experimentation without the knowledge or consent of employees.

In 1977, after the Watergate break-in, it surfaced in the Select Intelligence Subcommittee investigation that the CIA was illegally spying and conducting field mind control experiments on unwitting subjects. The organic mysteries of the mind were decoded by CIA scientists with illegal drugs, electronic hypnosis, sleep deprivation, subliminal suggestions over controlled radio and television stations, direct microwave communication to the auditory pathways, the remote transmission of images and electronic manipulation of emotions.

There are subliminal and brainwashing techniques by which the subconscious of the individual is invaded and his thoughts or personality influenced without his consent. These influences can be smuggled in past the customs of the senses. Methods of which I am aware include ultrasonic waves. These are inaudible to the conscious sense, like the 'silent' dog–whistle. Similarly subliminal messages can be concealed in films or television programs. Of course, such means are banned, but anyone sufficiently ingenious, or some central authority seeking to indoctrinate, could succeed.

Experiments have also demonstrated that it is possible to hypnotize persons with television and radio.

Surveillance Technology, U.S. Senate Hearing

Implants—placed in the body by *human* experimenters—are another means of tracking or controlling a subject, according to the *San Francisco Examiner* (November 8, 1995):

VENTURA—He didn't want his name used. He's a California surgeon, and he's scared of repercussions.

"I'd probably be ostracized, I'd be criticized, maybe I'd even lose my license," he said. "People with credibility who put themselves forward in this field could wind up dead, in jail or out of business."

He performed the operations anyway, before witnesses and a video camera. He cut into the big toe of a woman and into the back of a man's hand. Both believed they'd been abducted by aliens. From both, he extracted small foreign objects with some unusual properties.

The object in the man was the size of a cantaloupe seed; one of the woman's two was T-shaped. The objects were encased in a thick, dark membrane. But these weren't cysts, he said. They were so tough, his scalpel couldn't cut them.

The doctor was prepared for ingrown follicles or shards of plastic. "I was as doubting as anyone else," he said. When the membranes were dried out and cut open, they revealed tiny, highly magnetic pieces of a shiny black metal. The hard membrane was composed of substances naturally occurring in the body.

The skeptics remain skeptical. "We haven't heard of anything that, without the shadow of a doubt, couldn't have been made here on Earth," said Barry Karr, director of the Center for Scientific Investigation of Claims of the Paranormal.

The hearings of the Select Committee in 1977 exposed an illegal research program that ruined lives and careers. Much of the populace did not hear of

MK-ULTRA because, with the exception of New York state, news of the hearings was blacked out across the country. The pleas of victims are still ignored and ridiculed by an indifferent press.

Subjecting private citizens to terminal experiments and remote electromagnetic harassment is not a national security issue. The SS carried out political sieges of imprisonment and human experimentation because the Jewish faith offended the dictatorship of Adolph Hitler. The Nuremberg Trials found such acts, even with the justification of war, criminal.

> Admiral Stansfield Turner, CIA director, stated in the 1977 Congressional investigation of Project MK-ULTRA, "It is abhorrent to me to think of using humans as guinea pigs." He promised Senate investigators that new procedures and guidelines would be established, and only volunteers would be used for human experimentation. He also said he would follow up and disclose all the names of private citizens who were illegally experimented on, and the Agency would pay restitution, but this was merely political rhetoric.
>
> When a lawsuit against the CIA was filed by a victim who happened to be a member of Parliament, the CIA director made a statement to one of his subordinates that he hoped that the victim would die before the case ever went to trial.
>
> Harvey M. Weinstein, M.D., *Psychiatry and the CIA: Victims of Mind Control*

The United States of America has not *openly* declared war on private citizens. But illicit human experimentation and vicious "non-lethal" radio frequency assaults have been carried out by agencies within a number of federal institutions for 50 years.

One of them is the U.S. Postal Service. When conducting behavior modification experiments on human subjects, federal agencies are required to follow procedural guidelines for protecting human rights. Behavior modification specialists are obliged to collect full written consent from their subjects. Before volunteering and signing a consent form, a subject must understand the full extent and purpose of the experiment. Research involving humans should not be detrimental to the subject's physical or mental welfare.

In the postal system, innocent victims of mind control experimentation are tortured and ultimately "tested" to death. Once an individual is targeted, mind control will follow wherever he moves, wherever he makes his occupation. Employees are often not aware that they are illegally spied upon, bugged and manipulated by a team of "controllers."

The Nuremberg code of 1947 established protocols for medical research to improve the human lot—*not destroy it.*

The University of Oklahoma in Norman, Oklahoma was known to conduct behavior modification experiments for the Central Intelligence Agency. Patrick Sherrill, 44, a mail carrier, murdered a dozen people and committed suicide. Was he a programmed killer for the intelligence community? Was he hypnotized and "psychically-driven" to grab a gun and kill his fellow employees? He was harassed by the "voices" of children. Were they really children or adults who disguised themselves with voice synthesizers to harass him? Were electronic bugs slipped in his mailbag or postal vehicle without his knowledge? Was a transmitter implanted on him surgically, enabling his antagonists to transmit radio frequencies and electronically dominate his emotions? Why did they choose him? He may have documented all of his experiences on a computer, posthumously confiscated by the FBI. There is mind control experimentation that attempts to control or kill an enemy with a computer that generates electrical impulses loaded with a post-hypnotic trigger or "trill."(See: William Nack, *Sports Illustrated*, July 9, 1995, vol. 63: no. 5.)

Several years ago in La Jolla, California, Dr. Carl Rogers addressed a symposium on the "Frontiers of Science" at the Western Behavioral Sciences Institute. Rogers acknowledged that behavioral science had developed to the point that human thought and behavior could be controlled to an unprecedented degree. "This capability is made to order for dictatorial rule," he said.

In 1989, San Diego was hit with an epidemic of murders and suicides:

John Merlin Taylor, a 52-year-old mail carrier in Escondido, CA, was described as mellow and friendly by friends and fellow employees. Taylor shot and killed his wife and two co–workers before killing himself.

William Charles Camp, 62, El Cajon, a postal worker, described as easy-going. Camp hung himself in his garage.

Donald Martin Mace, 44, a Poway letter carrier, shot himself in the lobby of the local post office—after responsibly turning in his keys.

Hector Manuel Rubio, 40, a Pacific Beach postal clerk, hung himself with a weight-lifting belt in his home.

Jay Thomas Fanum, 37, a postal clerk in Vista, perished from carbon monoxide poisoning in his own garage.

Hector Torres, age unknown, a San Diego postal clerk, plummeted to his death from the Coronado Bridge.

Was a barrage of subliminal directions to kill transmitted into their homes via television and radio frequencies? Were they driven to their deaths with strategically-planted electronic devices? Did their psychological profiles match the ones sought by a clutch of state-sponsored behavior modification specialists? Was this a "cluster of mind control experiment?" Who were the psychiatric operatives in the area?

Most of the postal workers who went berserk in the San Diego area had fatal car accidents. Were these a standard *modus operandi* in illegal mind control experiments? Were the workers intentionally discredited beforehand to provide an easy explanation of their state of depression? Did a directed-energy weapon aimed at their heads while driving cause them to lose control of their vehicles? Or did the intelligence operatives send remote control radio signals to a transmitter implanted on the targeted victim?

Dead men *do* tell tales. Several of the victims' bodies were summarily cremated—possibly to conceal tell-tale evidence of microwave damage to their internal organs. One dead postal employee had donated his body to science, but when his body was examined the coroner found internal organs badly seared by microwaves, rendering them useless. Is cremation a standard procedure in classified mind control experiments, an attempt to destroy physical evidence of murder?

The terminal use of technology, billed as "non-lethal," presents the medical profession with a challenge to study and detect forensic effects of gigahertz radiation.

Sniper James O. Huberty shot and killed 21 people at McDonald's in San Ysidro on July 18, 1984. Some of the victims were children. Did he nurse a grudge against them? Most mass murderers do not shoot children. Was Huberty tormented by children's "voices?" Mind control technicians beam microwave audiograms (digital simulations of human speech) of baleful, rage-piquing messages to the brain of the subject to mask their own voices.

The intelligence community is responsible for the killings in San Ysidro, not Huberty.

Some of the postal employees were said to have had mental problems. Did they? Or were they discredited in advance because this is a tactic used to isolate them? A personality disorder accounts for an "irrational" obsession with corruption, a strategy reminiscent of the Soviet abuse of psychiatry.

CONGRESSIONAL HEARING
USPS LABOR–MGMT RELATIONS PROBLEMS IN SAN DIEGO
EXCERPTS OF THE TESTIMONY OF RANIER THORNHILL, *DECEMBER 11, 1989*
What creates stress strong enough for my Vietnam veteran brother Donald Martin Mace to [consider] suicide in Poway as a practicable postal option? What

was the catalyst that created the abominable confusion in Escondido, or that tied the hangman's knot in El Cajon?

The FBI refuses to investigate, citing lack of authority needed from the US Attorney's office or the Justice Department....

Whatever happened to Title 18, Sections 241 and 242? After various postal employees provided written complaints citing criminal violations of same sections to the FBI and the US Attorney's office, the Justice Department declined to pursue and dropped [the case].

Here in San Diego an older male supervisor sexually harassed and selectively terminated a 20-year-old hearing-impaired woman, Kim Brooke. He is promoted and she in her quiet confused world is socially and personally destroyed. She still dreams of her past postal employment, wonders why she was scapegoated so.

I have a recent tape recording of Congressman Bates [informing] a member of his Postal Task Force group that Thornhill is "the guy that wants to kill me." Do all Congressmen have free license to defame a citizen's character without cause or due process, or is this one just trying to cover up truths he knows I have attempted to address for over five years?

Who enforces the Whistle-blower's Protection Act?

The Postal Inspection Service is utilized by local management as a personalized gestapo....

There is so much more I could tell you and prove, if you were interested and officially authorized a genuine investigation. I anticipate reprisals for my truthful testimony here, and realize beforehand that there is no help forthcoming.... If you can't help me and many others, then I intend to protect myself in the future....

I strongly assert the need for the executive branch of our government to comprehensively and immediately clean up this local postal managerial morass.

Employees testified at the September 15, 1992 congressional hearings in Royal Oak, Michigan that management and U.S. postal inspectors used "abusive tactics" and threats to silence them.

In Edmond, the local postmaster ordered employees to not discuss the mass murder there. Postal employees testified that they were harassed to stop them from talking.

Federal inspectors blamed the shootings on employee "hiring practices." Whistle-blowers are often treated to a draconian backlash. One woman employed by the mail service testified in September, 1992 that she was "a victim of physical assault and abuse":

On February 25, 1985, I blew a whistle on a postal violation of child labor law.

I notified the proper chain of command and they in turn mishandled the report. And the manager responsible was contacted at home and he [came] to the postal facility to attempt to kill me. Mr. Grell did assault me ... and he was given a letter of warning. Mr Martin was then MSC manager. I continued on with my duties that day....

I called the Postal Inspection Service and they never did anything to help me. I went to the local police and was told that since I [was] assaulted on federal property, I had to go to the U.S. Attorney.

On December 4, 1991, Honorable Judge Terry J. Hatter, Jr. found Hector Godinez and Arthur Montoya guilty of unlawful discrimination towards me as a U.S. Postal Employee.

On February 20, 1992, they sent out an open letter to all Santa Ana Division employees, attacking me publicly for having won a federal case of discrimination, and to the *L.A. Times* ... claiming I was "insubordinate."

I demand Congressional oversight of all U.S. attorneys' offices to insure that there will be, henceforth, legal prosecution [for] obstruction of justice cases and postal assaults.

The postal system is riddled with horror stories. In Minneapolis, an undercover postal inspector gave marijuana to a mail sorter grieving the death of his wife. The inspector then turned the worker over to police and had his employment terminated.

The objective is to isolate the bothersome informant, depict him as incompetent, disloyal, troublesome, mentally unbalanced or ill. The whistle-blower is forced out, frightening workmates and supporters. A psychiatric history allows postal inspectors to avoid examining legitimate allegations of corruption. The assault continues until the target is left discredited, exhausted, in poor health, financially-crippled, his career in ruins.

Psychological harassment and intimidation are carried out by hired specialists. The U.S. Postal Service and other federal agencies draw on their services.

The intelligence agencies are capable of transmitting voices and images directly to the cranium's sensory pathways. The onset of advanced radio frequency technology has given rise to a coming generation of "thought police." They are a profound threat to a democratic society. Radio frequency weapons have eased the malignant growth of fascism within the intelligence agencies. Anyone who falls into disfavor with this elite can be condemned to interminable physical and psychological torture. The victim is often murdered without a trace.

The abuse of mind-invasive technology is an unprecedented violation of privacy and freedom of thought. There are individuals presently sitting in our prisons and mental institutions who have been set up with the new thought control technology. Due process is abandoned. The victim's life hangs exclusively on the whims of the "controllers," an unprecedented violation of the individual's civil and constitutional rights.

The new "elite" death squads employ directed-energy weapons to harass and kill a designated guinea-pig. These domestic terrorists are trained in the art of persuasive coercion (CIA jargon for a harassment campaign designed to break a subject without direct physical violence).

Mind control techniques perfected by the CIA include psychological intimidation, often racial and sexual. The unsuspecting victim is treated to post-hypnotic programming, psychological conditioning, chemical harassment and biological assaults 24 hours a day. He is provoked to rage and violence at the whim of a remote handler, often to the point of killing.

Mark Hilbun, a postal worker in Dana Point, CA, killed his girlfriend and several other postal employees in a frenzy of jealous rage in 1993. Was his girlfriend, a supervisor, a behavioral modification specialist conducting classified research? Did she seduce him by sending him synthetic love with radio waves on his biological EM frequency? Did a programmer transmit repeated messages to Hilbun that she was disloyal? Was a gun placed in his hands in the grip of remotely-induced rage? Did the girlfriend play God with his life? She may have even dared him to go after her with a gun because she is "omnipotent"—she could put him to sleep with a transmitted radio frequency. If so, she found out all too quickly that she is not "God" for all her "black magic tricks."

To the intelligence community, Hilbun was a "hypno-patsy."

Bruce Clark, a postal worker in the City of Industry in California, was another. In 1995, Clark met a co–worker and shot him for no apparent reason. Was there someone in the catwalks transmitting subliminal commands to kill, images of someone he was hypnotized to fear or hate? Bruce Clark was not listening to the "voice of God," but to a mazer shotgunned to his head. A post-hypnotic "trill" may have triggered him to commit murder. Was it the clothes the victim wore? Was it something he said? Or was it in the lyrics of music playing over a controlled PA system at work? Bruce Clark was a loner. He loved cats. His friends said that Clark was not violent. He had no criminal history.

A man carrying a gun, dressed as a National Parks Service ranger, was arrested on October 6, 1995 in Yonkers, New York. He stole onto the seminary grounds where Pope John Paul II had spoken a few hours later. His name is William Wylong, a 45-year-old postal worker. He claimed he was there to "protect" the Pope.

There will be more just like him.

There is a conspiracy within the intelligence agencies to conceal field testing of highly-advanced mind control technology.

On October 2, 1995, President Clinton publicly apologized to the victims of radiation experimentation. Some victims were volunteers, some were not. The victims were not told of the debilitating effects and multi-generational consequences. It took them 40 years to collect enough evidence to elicit a simple acknowledgement and an empty apology.

The government *still* experiments on private citizens without their consent, often to death. They will continue to experiment and deny until forced to stop.

But ...

> The dangers of permitting a governmental agency to be the sole judge of the legality of its employees' actions are by this time all too painfully apparent. There is of course the danger that the Agency will quash an investigation to avoid embarrassment rather than serve legitimate governmental objectives.
>
> —1977 Senate Hearing, Project MK-ULTRA

Further Reading

Mailman Slays Fourteen, Self in Oklahoma Massacre,
   Los Angeles Times, August 24, 1986
Thrown Off Plane, Jailed in Houston,
   Los Angeles Times, August 28, 1987
Postal Employee Kills Wife, Two Co-Workers,
   Los Angeles Times, August 11, 1989
Suspect In Postal Worker Murders—Probed For Link to 'Ninja' Killing,
   New Jersey Star-Ledger, October 24, 1991
3 Killed, 8 Injured in Shooting Rampage at Post Office,
   Accused Postal Worker Charged in 1988 Murder,
   Los Angeles Times, November 15, 1991
Dana Point Postal Shooting,
   Los Angeles Times, May 18, 1993
Emotional Problems Cited in Murder of Parents,

Postal Worker Held Says He 'Just Lost It',
New Jersey Star-Ledger, November 9, 1993
Ex-Postal Worker is Charged With Slaying Four in Holdup,
Los Angeles Times, March 23, 1995
Postal Worker Held in Slaying of Supervisor,
Los Angeles Times, July 10, 1995
Postal Employee Held in Shooting of 2 Co-Workers,
Los Angeles Times, August 30, 1995
Man With Gun Arrested at Seminary,
Associated Press Wire, October 6, 1995

APPENDICES:
Auditory Perception of Radio Frequencies

Douglas Barr, a professor of electronics at the University of Colorado, has been hypnotically accessed since childhood for mind control purposes, and as an adult is a target of electromagnetic harassment. He writes:

There has been much discussion of "Microwave Hearing" phenomenon and I was intrigued by this and have done some research. It turns out that microwave hearing does indeed exist. There is a fair sized body of research available on the subject. This is one of the more complete reviews of the subject:

"Auditory Perception of Radio-Frequency Electromagnetic Fields," in: *The Journal of Acoustical Society of America,* 1982 pages 1321–1334, by Chung-Kwang Chou and Arthur W. Guy, PhD, researchers at the University of Washington.

Funded by: Office of Naval Intelligence, National Institute of Handicapped Research and the Department of Education with a special thanks to Richard M. White of the University of California, Berkeley.

INTRODUCTION
Pulsed microwaves have been heard as sound by radar operators since radar was invented during World War II ....

The earliest report we have found on the auditory perception of pulsed microwaves appeared in 1956 as an advertisement of the Airborne Instruments Lab in Proceedings of the IRE. The advertisement described observations made in 1947 on the hearing of sounds that occurred at the repetition rate of radar while the listener stood close to a horn antenna. When the observers first told their co-workers in the lab of their hearing experiences, they encountered skepticism and rather pointed questions about their mental health.

POWER LEVELS AND FREQUENCY RANGE

At very low frequency range (< 1MHz), a human-size biological object absorbs very little radio-frequency energy; however, the absorption can be appreciable at the resonant frequency near 70–80 MHz (where the long dimension of the body is approximately 0.4 wavelengths) (Durney et al. 1978). For a human head, the resonant frequency is near 600 Mhz.... Although there is universal agreement on the thermal effects of the highlevel (> 100 milliWatts/centimeter(squared)) radio-frequency electromagnetic radiation, there is considerable debate on the biological effects of low-level (< 100mWatts/cm2) electromagnetic radiation. ...

The thresholds (for hearing) of average power density of fields at the head were determined to be 0.4 and 2mW/cm2, respectively for the two transmitters. ...

In another experiment they used a 2450MHz pulse generator with pulses in the 0.5 to 32 microsecond width. The generator produced peak power of 10kW. Calculations indicated that the maximum amount of absorbed energy was 16 microJOULES/gram (They are talking microjoules per gram now instead of milliwatts per cm squared. They use microjoules when they talk of absorbed energy and milliwatts when talking about radiated wattage. The two are related of course, but the energy absorbed depends on the makeup of the human head, whereas the energy radiated is dependent on the transmission power). (ED) ...

In another experiment they used 5 to 15 microsecond pulses at 3 Ghz frequency.

DISCUSSION

The microwave-induced auditory phenomenon is an example of a microwave-biological interaction that has been WELL QUANTIFIED and WIDELY ACCEPTED (emphasis this author) as a bona fide "weak-field" effect. Although originally the hypothesis of a direct nervous system stimulation was proposed, the evidence is now strongly convincing that the hearing phenomenon is related to thermoelastically induced mechanical vibration. The same type of vibration can be produced by other means, e.g. by a laser pulse, or by activating a piezoelectric crystal in contact with the skull [implant].

The paper ends with about a page of references to other works, one of which is Frey's paper published in 1963.

So there you have it, Microwave hearing is fact, not fiction.

Douglas Barr

Case Histories of Electromagnetic Harassment

FROM *NEXUS* MAGAZINE:

EDITOR:

While reading a back issue of *Nexus* (vol. 2, no. 20), I came across a news clip entitled, "The Mysterious Taos Hum." It says that Representative Bill Richardson (D-NM) has asked the House Select Committee to investigate a noise which causes dizziness, shortness of breath, headaches, anxiety and sleeplessness, and is thought by some to be from a secret defense-related program plaguing various cities in New Mexico.

Well, I believe I know something about that sound, so here is my story.

During the years 1980–83 I was living with the daughter of the now deceased Dr. David Fraser, former head of the Department of Toxicology at the University of North Carolina, Chapel Hill. One day the daughter told me of a frightening encounter her father had with the American military. Later, when Dr. Fraser came to stay with us while on vacation in 1981, I asked him to tell me the story firsthand.

In the early 1970s, the small city of Medford, Oregon became the suicide capital of the United States overnight. (The exact dates can be found by checking national health statistics.) After Dr. Fraser was notified of this dramatic anomaly, he organized and sent a team of researchers to look for the cause. They checked the water, the air, the soil and a variety of additional possibilities, but still could find no reason for the massive increase in suicides. Then they discovered that Ultra Low Frequencies were being beamed into Medford, Oregon, from the local military base. (I never thought to ask for the name.) The researchers then went to that military base and met with its commanding officer. The commanding officer said he knew about the ULF, but his base was not responsible, and that Russians were. The ULF waves stopped the very next day.

The researchers had not only determined the military base as the source, they also determined that the ULF was coming into the homes of the populace through their television antennas, which created some sort of standing wave resonance within the structure of the home itself. Those people who did not get out of their homes became severely depressed.

As the ULF wave had now stopped, the researchers returned to the University

297

of Chapel Hill to write their report and confer with Dr. Fraser. At that time, a number of men appeared who displayed CIA credentials and said the ULF waves beamed into Medford were a "national security" matter. They went on to threaten explicitly to kill each of the researchers, including Dr. David Fraser himself, should anyone speak further about it.

As a postscript, I have often wondered how many times researchers have stumbled over the effects of secret weapons directed against the American people and have been intimidated into silence, or possibly murdered. I myself have made no public statement until now, fourteen years from the time I heard this story (and more than twenty years since the initial fact). It seems clear to me that the military-industrial complex has secretly declared war on the American people quite some time ago, and is waging a long-term psychological warfare operation, complete with fully operational, mass mind control technology.

Lastly, I don't say these things so that people will be afraid. The good news is that these cockroaches don't feel strong enough to be caught out in the light. However, should any of your readers be feeling depressed, anxious or nauseous, before calling a doctor try taking down your TV antennae.

Sincerely,
Mark M., Hollywood, CA

A letter to Alex Constantine from G.W., a victim of EM harassment living in Tucson, Arizona:

Alex:
Harlan Girard (director of the International Committee for the Convention Against Offensive Non-Lethal Weapons) has encouraged me to get in touch with you regarding my mind control ordeal.

I've had a hellish year. I began hearing "voices" last August—which promptly got me diagnosed as a paranoid schizophrenic and hospitalized three times. After the first hospitalization, it became clear that the source of this transmission was something other than my own jangled neurons, and it gradually began to dawn on me—partly because the voices themselves said it—that some facet of the government, most likely the CIA, was responsible.

I've been tortured for a solid year: sleep deprivation, electric shocks ... never once have I been let off the line. My film and video business has been stolen out from under me. I have been marginalized—both financially and emotionally.

When I have tried to obtain legal help, I've lost large sums of money, legal documents have disappeared from my files, the lawyers have mysteriously quit or been scared off the case. I now find myself destitute, unable to make any headway regaining ownership of my business.

I am saddled with enormous debts. I no longer have health insurance.

I have no idea why I've been selected for this form of torture. The only thing I can attribute it to is the breakup with my former boyfriend and business partner, David Frankel Arond. We had a film and video business—East West Films. I oversaw the office here, while for much of the last decade David did a considerable amount of work in the then Soviet Union. Among other things, we did some work for USIA [the United States Information Agency, which often fronts for the CIA overseas] both directly and via a company called Techniarts in Washington, DC that subcontracted with us. Techniarts ultimately lost its contract with USIA, and we then contracted directly with USIA on a story-by-story basis.

This may have brought me under the scrutiny of the intelligence community. The only other strange occurrence that I can think of that might have brought us under the watchful gaze of the CIA is when David was the first Westerner given an interview with Oleg Kalugin. This struck me as odd given David's lack of prominence in the media.

The events of the past year have had a devastating impact on my life. My health has suffered greatly. My hemoglobin plummeted to an alarming reading of 6.5. My thyroid is not functioning normally. The loss of my business, the lack of income and poor health has made parttime work more of a challenge than it might otherwise have been. I have no understanding about the science of ELF, microwaves and whatever—but it would seem that this must have contributed to my health problems. With no place else to turn, I have had to rely on the information supplied by concerned individuals who had looked into these goings on. Any suggestions you might have would be greatly appreciated. I live in Tucson and am hoping to connect with people in this region who have some level of understanding about the mind control experience.

Thanks,
G.W.

Correspondence

Dr. Barker (the unconventional psychiatrist in "Bleak House") surfaced in a computer discussion group for social workers in Canada on May 28, 1887. The comments are from Lynne Moss-Sharman, a subject herself in experiments conducted when she was a child, and a survivor's advocate, to a social worker specializing in childhood trauma.

May 28, 1997
From: Lynne Moss-Sharman

Jim:
Part of the healing process is taking responsibility for what one has "enacted" in the "past." Dr. Barker has engaged in a 1996–97 dialogue with Steve Smith [a victim of forced incarceration] that includes creating his own version of the Book of Revelations. At some point I think we are just dealing with out and out criminal behaviour under the guise of psychiatry and with the protection of that profession, and unless the Dr. Barkers in Canada are legally pursued there will be no moral healing. Don't forget that Dr. Ewen Cameron [a pioneer of CIA mind control experimentation] was the President of the Canadian Psychiatric Association, and Dr. Martin Orne (who was named as a torturer conducting CIA funded mind control experiments on children in the 1950s, a President of the American Psychiatric Association and more recently, Founding Member of the False Memory Syndrome Foundation) at the Presidential Hearing on Human Radiation Experiments in March 1995.

When I see things like electro-shock "Therapy" increasing 3000-fold at our regional psychiatric hospital (wipe 'em all out before it gets closed down?) in the past four years ... I do not think the torture has stopped. The public and other professions are not being informed ... I get chills thinking that Dr. Barker is still functioning as a "child/adolescent specialist" ... proclaiming himself to be the Director of The Canadian Society for Prevention to Cruelty to Children.
—Lynne

Since CIA involvement is suspected, Canadian intelligence needs to pay attention too. And government needs to address the damage caused by the secrecy that protects these institutions by walling them off from public scrutiny and supervision, so that the basic human rights of their inmates are denied. The confidentiality of Steve's records has not been in his best interests!

The 60s and 70s were a dark time in the children's treatment field, but enough people tried their best to help children that the effects of neglect and of sexual abuse and of child trauma gradually became recognized, and today we are at the threshold of being able to genuinely help traumatized people. Unfortunately that knowledge is not widely known yet.

—Jim

A letter to the author from Val Bankston, an abductee who has been repeatedly accessed by her perpetrators to the present day. Although initially believing her "controllers" to be "aliens," she has since recovered memories of human perps lurking behind hypnotically-induced screen memories of little green men.

Alex:

I remember being abducted at an unmarked clinic (by humans) where I reported for a referred mamogram. I never got the mamogram, and only remembered later that I had gone there. I had a chunk of "missing time"!

This was near the VA hospital in the San Fernando Valley. I haven't been able to find the exact spot. It made me physically ill to go around there, so I just gave up on it.

Over a period of time, I had experienced what seemed to be a number of UFO related incidents. In addition to these sightings and contacts with what appeared to be alien entities, I have flashbacks and memories of being abducted in vans and cars and taken to hospitals and drugged by doctors, set in front of TV screens and debriefed about various things that happened while "on duty" as it were. I have been tortured. I have been drugged at parties (I never eat or drink anything offered to me at a party anymore—especially orange juice) I have possessed and have been photographed wearing spy-tech devices. I have remembered using them ... I remember having had them used on ME.

I had no idea where I got my orders. I knew only that I was doing a job for a man to whom I was (am) intensely loyal. The job involved being able to operate with no memory of what I was doing, because I had to infiltrate certain groups undetected. I felt that this was my choice.

I remember also incidents of breaking and entering locations, threatening people, stealing an object from an aerospace lab, delivering articles, giving verbal encoded messages etc. My cues were either verbal or by seeing a very bright light, or encoded in the personal section of the *Recycler*. I thought these orders were coming from the UFO entities. Up until I wised up about being programmed, I used to get instructions over the phone.

Listen to this story:

I find myself approaching a doorway of a nice looking house in an upperclass · neighborhood. When I get to the door, I hand something that I can't see to a woman. She asks me to come in and join the party. I decline. I recognize this woman as my enemy, but I don't know why. My adrenaline is pumping and I know that I must go. She insists that I come in. I walk briskly away, declining curtly once again. She calls for a man in the house who joins her at the door as I am walking down the driveway to my car, which is parked up the street, out of sight. When I reach the bottom of the driveway, the woman says something that I don't understand, and I fall right down on the ground. Just like a UFO abduction experience! I look up and see the woman and the man approaching cautiously, with tense looks on their faces as though they don't know what to expect from me.

Finding myself in this condition, I remember an order to look at my hands if this ever happens. I struggle to raise my hands and look at first my left then my right hand. On my right hand is the ring, which I immediately recognize. I know that I am supposed to depress a button on the side of it. I do this. It clicks off five clicks and then delivers an electric shock to my hand. I am somewhat revived but not enough to get up and flee. I know if this happens, I must hit the button again. This time, it ticks very rapidly, many times. I get the feeling that it could be a bomb or administer a drug or something terrible like that. As I lose consciousness completely, I realize just how vulnerable I really am-following orders that could possibly kill me without knowing what in the hell I am really doing.

(I have a picture taken of myself wearing the "spy-ring." I really thought it was a watch. I can send you a copy if you like.)

My next memory was finding myself at home, in the bathroom, looking in the mirror. The ring was destroyed and in pieces (some of which were missing) on the counter beside me. I felt like hell and went to bed. I don't remember the next day or the previous day or anything else. The ring peices disappeared next time I looked.

But I have photos of myself with the ring clearly shown, taken before the event. Before it happened, I knew that I had to wear the ring at all times, and that I would be called upon to do a "job."

Love,
Val

A letter to the Freedom of Thought Foundation, an organiation of survivors, from a victim of unauthorized medical experimentation with radioactive implants.

Dear FOTF:

My name is Roland Thompson. I'm 38 and I have a radio isotopic loop implanted in my abdomen. It was placed there during a routine surgery for ulcers in 1980 while on active duty with the army.

It is apparent on x-ray and it registers on geiger counters in the range of .02-.03 millirads. At times it seems to be moved closer to the sensor of the geiger counter by my heart beat....

I've gone to several doctors and nuclear educators at my university. All of them, save one or two, are skeptical. The two individuals who have witnessed the evidence are critical to my situation; one is my personal physician who is a close friend and happens to be the coroner in my district. He is in favor of removing it, as am I, and is agreeable to video taping the operation and being present in the operating room while it is removed. I feel safer with him there and am fortunate enough to have a friend in his capacity.

The other individual is a technician in our local hospital who indulged me in a test with a geiger counter. He also has an open mind and will attest to the fact that the radiation is localized. They seem to be together on their beliefs and are convinced that i'm the genuine article. all that remains are the details of the surgery.

The physician will read the copy of the interim report on human radiation experimentation that president Clinton's advisory committee has produced. he'll also read my biography of the events leading up to the implant's discovery, contact a surgeon we both trust and I suppose we'll go from there. I would solicit advice on how to go about having the device analyzed, preserving a chain of evidence and the mechanics of involving the media in this bizarre undertaking.

Thank you,
Roland